TO DORIS MARY PARISH
1913–2000

GUS VAN SANT

GUS VAN SANT

GUS VAN SANT

GUS VAN SANT

GUS VAN SANT

GUS VAN SANT

GUS VAN SANT

GUS VAN SANT

GUS VAN SANT

GUS VAN SANT

GUS VAN SANT

GUS VAN SANT

GUS VAN SANT

GUS VAN SANT

GUS VAN SANT

GUS VAN SANT

Published by
Thunder's Mouth Press
An Imprint of Avalon Publishing Group Incorporated
161 Williams St., 16th Floor
New York, NY 10038

Gus Van Sant: An Unauthorized Biography

Library of Congress Cataloging-in-Publication Data

Parish, James Robert.
Gus Van Sant: an unauthorized biography / by James
Robert Parish.
p. cm.
ISBN 1-56025-337-1
1. Van Sant, Gus. 2. Motion picture producers and
directors—United States—Biography.
I. Title.

PN1998.3.V363P37 2001
791.43'0233'092—dc21
[B]   2001048039

9 8 7 6 5 4 3 2 1

Designed by Pauline Neuwirth, Neuwirth & Associates,
Inc.

Printed in the United States of America
Distributed by Publishers Group West

GUS VAN SANT

AN UNAUTHORIZED BIOGRAPHY

GUS VAN SANT

AN UNAUTHORIZED BIOGRAPHY

by **james robert parish**

GUS VAN SANT

AN UNAUTHORIZED BIOGRAPHY

THUNDER'S MOUTH PRESS • NEW YORK

CONTENTS

ACKNOWLEDGMENTS

SPECIAL APPRECIATION to Betty and Gus Van Sant Sr. who were so generous with their assistance and referrals.

Thanks to: Academy of Motion Picture Arts & Sciences: Margaret Herrick Library, James Alderman, Deborah Alpi, Simon Babbs, Robert Bentley, Billy Rose Theater Collection of the New York Public Library at Lincoln Center, Frank Birney, Michael Buening (Museum of Television and Radio), Sherman Burell (*Willamette Week*), Jeffrey L. Carrier, Charles Casillo, Lawrence M. Chadbourne, John Cocchi, Bobby Cramer, Ernest Cunningham, Michael Danahy, Adam Dunn, Robert Edelman, Jim Evans, Michael Faust, Bill Foster (Northwest Film Center), Alex Gildzen, Bill Givens, Garrett Glaser, Bruce Gold, Beverly Gray, Mark Harris, John Howell, Marianne Howell, Charles Hoyt, Matthew Kennedy, Dan Kimmel, Jane Klain (Museum of Television and Radio), Audrey Kupferberg, Irv Lctofsky, Frederick Levy, Andy Mangels, Lee Mattson, Doug McClelland, Jim Meyer, Eric Monder, Robert Newton, Albert L. Ortega, Paige Powell, Barry Rivadue, Jeremy Rizzi, Jerry Roberts, Jonathan Rosenthal, Brenda Scott Royce, Michael Shulman (Hulton/Archive), Arleen Schwartz, Richard A. Scott, Tom Sherohman, Anita Skinner, T. J. Skinner, André Soares, Patrick Spreng, Sam Staggs, Dot Stenning, Steve Taravella, Allan Taylor (editorial consultant and copy editor), Don Wigal, Daniel Yost, and Brian Ann Zoccola.

Special thanks to my agent, Stuart Bernstein, and to my editor, Neil Ortenberg.

INTRODUCTION

I'm not being analytical. I just create everything intuitively. If you're too analytical, what you're doing probably ends up being too specific. I think it's different to the way a lot of people work. I think the most successful painters or photographers or filmmakers or poets sift a lot of different things into one, and aren't analytical and specific and conscious of what they are actually doing. If you have a need to be conscious of what you're doing, that can get in the way of a lot of things happening at the same time, limiting the number of ways that you can express yourself in one image.

Gus Van Sant, 1993

OVER RECENT DECADES MANY distinctive independent filmmakers have made their unique mark on American cinema, including John Sayles, the Coen Brothers, Spike Lee, Jim Jarmusch, Nancy Savoca, Allison Anders, Hal Hartley, and Kevin Smith. Some indie directors like John Waters have lavished their cinematic attention on oddball types of screen characters, while others, such as Gregg Araki and Todd Haynes, have centered their movie work on homosexual themes. Gus Van Sant is reflective of all of the above but at the same time defies easy categorization.

Van Sant is one of the most singular voices to emerge from the U.S. independent film environment. A great visualist—he is a graduate of the Rhode

Island School of Design—he is at his best when spotlighting the world of the disenfranchised, such as the illegal Mexican immigrants of his *Mala Noche* or the male street hustlers of *My Own Private Idaho*. (Interestingly, such depictions are never presented in a totally grim mood, but often have recurring light-hearted tones.) Yet Gus is the same moviemaker who can turn out a huge commercial box-office success like *Good Will Hunting* for which he was Oscar-nominated in the Best Director category. He is also capable of being intellectually brazen as when he shocked the Hollywood film industry and Alfred Hitchcock purists by remaking the master's classic thriller, *Psycho*. But no matter what he chooses to direct—which includes offbeat short subjects and music videos—there is always that characteristic Van Sant point of view—offbeat, oblique, and challenging to one's perception of things.

As Oregon-based writer Katherine Dunn has observed of her friend Gus: "Van Sant has the gift of the bifurcated eye that sees his primary characters from the inside and the story from the outside. The characters speak directly to the camera in classic asides, or their jerky home movies let us see through their eyes. At other times we are high above them, seeing them small. This combination of dispassionate distance and empathic recognition produces an inextricable tangling of tragedy and comedy. His films are funny and scary at the same time. No miserable moment is untinged by the ridiculous. Every hilarity has its shadow."

As for Gus the person, he is an engaging enigma whose slightest body language may say more than any lengthy dialogue could possibly elicit from this intense person. This led one observer to describe, "Gus doesn't seem bored, but he's not excited either. He's in no hurry, yet you get the feeling you better not waste his time. It's not so much charisma, as understated power. And focus. God, what focus. . . . He does everything with his eyes and slight movements of his mouth. Maybe a shrug of the shoulders. He doesn't move his body hardly at all, a perfect way of being for someone who stands still behind a camera all day long."

Many moviemakers have a concentrated, narrow professional focus. They only want to do what they love and know best, which is to make motion pictures. Gus, on the other hand, is a remarkable Renaissance man, whose career spans not only filmmaking, but still photography, novel writing, painting, and musicianship (with several songs and a few albums to his credit).

In the American movie industry there has always been talent—in front of and behind the camera—who have led an alternative lifestyle. Most of them, to protect their careers, remained closeted to the public at large and to the picture business as well. In customary fashion, however, the often shy and reserved Van Sant did not follow the usual path. Shortly after he enjoyed his first major screen success—1989's *Drugstore Cowboy*—the media thrust a descriptive label on the Portland-based director. Largely, it was not done out of malice, but only as a simple explanation. In those years whenever his name was mentioned in the national press, it was likely to read "Gus Van Sant, the openly gay filmmaker." This did not come about because he was a political activist (he is rarely political and not an activist by nature). Rather, it occurred because he had come out of the closet in the early 1980s and saw no reason to obscure the reason why several of his movies were gay-themed. Yes, he was homosexual, he acknowledged to the press, and now let's move on to the next question. So, for several years Gus became the standard bearer of America's "queer cinema."

Because of Gus Sr.'s escalating career in the apparel industry, the Van Sant family moved several times while Gus was young. Although he spent several childhood years in Darien, Connecticut, it was not until he was a teenager and the household had relocated to Portland, Oregon, that the teenaged Gus felt a real affinity to his environment and a sense of home. Just as his uprooted childhood would play itself out in many of his films, so his attachment to Oregon's vistas and ambiance would lead to what is called his Portland trilogy: *Mala Noche, Drugstore Cowboy*, and *My Own Private Idaho*. In each of these remarkable movies Van Sant shows an affinity for fully understanding life's underbelly. His depiction of society's outcasts in these absorbing dramas is all the more extraordinary because he never lived like them in his very WASP youth. Instead, as a first-class observer, he grasped the structure of such itinerant existence and found a poignancy worth exploring artistically. Being given to intellectualization and restraint, it has not been his style to weight his on-screen depictions with romanticized trappings or, conversely, with righteous condemnation. As in all aspects of his existence, Gus Van Sant remains the interpreter, the presenter, or sometimes the doer, but never the judger of life.

Another theme of immense importance in Van Sant's oeuvre is his strong sense of family, or, as in many of his pictures, the lack thereof. Throughout his film work there is a commonality in their explication of the unconventional family unit—the so-called nuclear household. It might be a drifting band of boy hustlers or a gang of drug-addicted robbers or a quartet of South Boston pals, or a group of African-American teenagers, but they all share their lack of a traditional family life and it has marked them in ways they may never fully appreciate. It is the recurrent spotlight on such bonding groups that is a trademark of a Gus Van Sant motion picture.

In bringing his stories to the screen, he uses imagery, symbolism, colors, and sounds to convey nuances that often require several viewings before they become apparent or comprehensible. Sometimes these layer effects occur to him spontaneously or subconsciously as he is filming; other times they crop up in the juxtaposition of editing the rough footage. Says Van Sant: "I just do it. So I'm not always sure if the audience will be able to see it. It's pretty intentional, the way you cut things, the way you see things and the way you put them together, and it's there all the time . . . poetry is. But I'm not sure everybody sees it. You have to be a certain kind of viewer. I think you have to be visually oriented and you can't be too literal. It's not clear-cut. It's not messy, but it's not so specific."

As much as for the beautiful landscapes he captures on-screen, or the quirky objects that suddenly merit a close-up shot in his movie footage, Gus Van Sant is appreciated for his uncanny ability to discover and/or nurture screen talent. It was with Van Sant that such varied performers as Matt Dillon, Kelly Lynch, River Phoenix, Keanu Reeves, Nicole Kidman, Joaquin Phoenix, Casey Affleck, Matt Damon, Ben Affleck, Robin Williams—and teenaged Rob Brown of *Finding Forrester*—have shined at their best on camera. It is one of his greatest gifts as a filmmaker that Gus can seamlessly help the performer to dig into a characterization and explicate it on screen and always accomplish the feat in a nonconfrontational manner. It is his style to hire the right person for a task and then let the individual do his thing.

Gus Van Sant is also the person who developed in his formative years a strong attraction for the credo of the Beat Generation and built a lifelong fascination and friendship with that king of counterculture, William S. Burroughs Jr. It would be writer/poet/artist Burroughs—and to a lesser extent Beat poet Allen Ginsberg—who had a remarkable impact on Gus, forming and shaping his points of view on many matters. Yet, this is the same intellectually curious moviemaker who, in recent years, has become the champion of such new filmmaking talent as Harmony Korine or such unique new-generation literary voices as JT LeRoy.

And like most filmmakers Van Sant has had creative low points, as with his *Even Cowgirls Get the Blues* based on Tom Robbins's novel. The 1994 movie was a flop that might easily have ended his movie career but he rebounded with the ironic, satirical *To Die For*. Yet every time he enjoyed a filmmaking success in his post-Portland trilogy period, Gus was accused by some critics of having abandoned his status as America's maverick indie moviemaker. In their minds he had done the unforgivable—gone Hollywood. (In any other profession, going from no-budget short films to major studio megahits would be considered the great American success story.) Yet even in Van Sant's most commercial projects to date (*Good Will Hunting* and the similarly structured *Finding Forrester*) he finds ways to transform the property into his own vision, to fill the screen with Gus-type images, and to explicate the characterizations through his very special life observer's eyes.

▼

IN the texture of Van Sant's complex and intriguing life—filled with wanderlust, contradiction, and diversity—one individual holds an enormously special place in the moviemaker's mind and heart. It is actor River Phoenix who starred in Gus's *My Own Private Idaho* and became a notable friend. Van Sant had great respect for this young star's talent and for the performer's subtle instincts about life. When River died suddenly of a drug overdose on Halloween day in 1993, it was one of the worst moments in Gus's life.

Thus it is not surprising that some of the shrewdest remarks about Gus Van Sant were made by or prompted by River. On one occasion, Phoenix described his friend Van Sant as a person who has the capacity to observe a square-shaped room and immediately perceive "a fifth, black-and-white corner.... There's always from point a to point b, but Gus concentrates on the in-between." Another time, when the ever-curious River asked Gus if it bothered him when people tried to figure him out, Van Sant responded, "No, not all because I'd like to figure me out actually."

In examining the richly layered life of Gus Van Sant both as a filmmaker and an individual, it is easy to assume that this quiet, reflective man with the deep penetrating eyes, monotone voice, and immobile expression is highly cynical, pessimistic, and stuck in his groove. But just as this southern-born talent proves to be a droll raconteur, a steadfastly loyal friend, and a person who thrives on the new and unexpected, so Van Sant reveals himself to be a man of great optimism. Who else but such a person, when asked what is the happiest moment of his life, would respond with: "I always think the happiest moments are in the future."

BRIGHT BEGINNINGS

Families are interesting stuff. The dynamics of whatever kind of family you have is an orientation that you apply to the outside world. Maybe it's just the most interesting thing that I know.

Gus Van Sant, 1993

IN MID-1952 THE UNITED STATES was going through many changes. On July 2, in Palmdale, California, the F-94C Starfire, a new supersonic jet plane, made its first successful test flight. On the sixth, in Hollywood, the first TV performer-producer contract was signed by the Screen Actors Guild. July 12 saw General Dwight D. Eisenhower winning the Republican nomination for president, beating out his opponent Senator Robert A. Taft of Ohio, on the first ballot. (The Republicans also chose Richard M. Nixon, the California senator, to be Eisenhower's running mate as vice president.) On the seventeenth of the month, in Helsinki, Finland, Nationalist China withdrew from the Olympic games in protest over efforts to admit Peking to the international competition. The next day, Marilyn Monroe's latest movie, *Don't Bother to Knock,* debuted, while on July 24, Gary Cooper's Western, *High Noon,* bowed to rave reviews.

Meanwhile, in northern Kentucky, in Louisville—the bluegrass state's largest metropolis—twenty-five-year-old Gus Greene Van Sant and his wife, Betty Beasley (Seay) Van Sant, were preparing to become first-time parents. Each of the couple had grown up in the smallish town of Mayfield, Kentucky (located in southwestern Kentucky, twenty-one miles south of Paducah and sixteen miles north of the Tennessee border), about 228 miles from Louisville.

After a stint in the navy at age seventeen during World War II, Gus had matriculated at Purdue University in West Lafayette, Indiana, on a football scholarship, but left in his junior year to fill in temporarily for a salesman at the Merit Clothing Company where his father and grandfather had worked. (He never returned to the campus classrooms.) Meanwhile Betty, whose parents owned a men's clothing store in Mayfield, had attended the University of Kentucky in Lexington. The sweethearts, who were Episcopalian, married on February 12, 1950, in Mayfield at the stately home of Betty's sister. The local Methodist minister, Dr. Roy Williams, performed the marriage service for the assemblage of seventy relatives and friends.

(By this point Gus's mother Dorothy was a widow—her husband, Lewis Loving Van Sant, had died in 1946 at age forty-three. A few years thereafter Dorothy had moved to Granville, Ohio, to be near her daughter, Joanne, who resided in Westerville. The latter had joined the faculty at Otterbein College, eventually rising to the post of Vice President for Student Affairs. Dorothy Van Sant spent a few years in Granville as housemother for the local chapter of the Chi Omega Sorority House. In 1962 she moved to Westerville to live with daughter Joanne.)

Gus became a full-time traveling salesman in 1950 for Merit Clothing, which specialized in men's pants. Betty became an elementary school teacher, instructing a second-grade class. When the Van Sants moved from Mayfield to Louisville—where Gus's grandfather had once lived—they took an apartment (#I-6) at the Greentree Manor because Betty's college roommate was then residing there. On July 24, 1952, Gus Van Sant Jr. was born at the Norton Infirmary on the outskirts of Louisville. (Born a Leo, the baby shared the same birthday, if not birth year, with such future celebrities as actresses Jennifer Lopez, Lynda Carter, Anna Paquin, comedians Michael Richards and Ruth Buzzi, country singer Pam Tillis, film director Peter Yates, and athlete Kadeem Hardison.)

As a traveling salesperson, Mr. Van Sant was on the road for large chunks of time during the spring/summer and fall/winter apparel seasons, drumming up orders for the Merit Clothing Company. As such he was away from home a good of deal of time, leaving the care of their newborn son to his wife, Dorothy, and to assorted nearby relatives. When young Gus (whom the family called "Van") was hardly a year old, ambitious Gus Sr. received a new sales territory from Merit Clothing. As a result, Gus, Betty, and Van relocated to Fort Collins, Colorado, in north central Colorado, home of the state university. In his capacity as a salesman, Gus Sr. continued his seasonal traveling, covering his expansive sales territory for the firm.

In 1953, the Van Sants moved yet again—this time south to much larger Denver, Colorado, some sixty-six miles away. Hoping to stay put for a time, and having saved some money, the Van Sants bought a tract house in the University Hills area. The homes in this new development were all approximately at 1,056 square feet, some with garages, others without. The Van Sants took title to a property at 3310 South Ivy Way. To support his family, Gus covered a sizeable five-state territory for Merit Clothing, responsible for generating sales orders in Colorado, Utah, Idaho, Montana, and Wyoming. Often Van Sant would travel fifteen hundred miles in a single week of travel (always trying to be home on weekends). Each trek required loading up the car with a rack in the backseat for the eight or twelve different suit styles along with nine hundred to one thousand clothing swatches. Amazingly, as Mr. Van Sant recalled for this author, rarely were any of the myriad samples ever stolen while he was on his road trips.

Looking back to this period over four decades later, the younger Van Sant has reminisced, "One of my earliest memories is of my dad and me walking across the street in front of our house in Colorado. He had whisky in a glass with ice cubes, and I tasted it. He told me I wouldn't like it, and I didn't."

The year 1956 saw yet new changes in the Van Sant household. On June 12, Betty Van Sant gave birth at the General Rose Hospital in Denver to a daughter whom the couple named Malinda Anne. (She later gained the nickname "Sissy.") With the expansion of his family, Gus Sr. was anxious to cut back on the grueling seasonal traveling. When Merit Clothing did not make a responsive offer, Gus accepted a sales position with McGregor-Doniger, Inc. Not only was Van Sant joining a more prestigious firm—the sports clothing king of America—but his new employers required only that he trek through one state (Colorado) for his sales territory. Within less than three years, Van Sant, the forceful sales professional, was promoted to regional manager for McGregor-Doniger. The family gave up their Denver address and moved to suburban Mount Prospect (with Gus Sr. commuting by train into Denver). Their new home was at 222 South Albert Street. By now Van had begun elementary school and had joined the Cub Scouts. (Because of the family's later moves, Van lost interest in scouting and never became a Boy Scout.)

In 1961, there were two deaths in the McGregor-Doniger hierarchy. One was Harry Doniger who, along with his brother Bill, controlled the firm. The other passing was that of Oz Hand, the corporation's head of marketing and Gus Sr.'s mentor. In the firm's transition, Bill Doniger asked Van Sant to become western regional manager for McGregor. While the company's main office in that territory was in Los Angeles, the Van Sants chose to live in the San Francisco area. Betty Van Sant had a cousin who resided in pricey Atherton (twenty-eight miles south on the peninsula from San Francisco and just north of Palo Alto), located in what would become the Silicon Valley. The Van Sants lucked out. They found a seller, anxious to make a sale. They purchased a home for $56,000 at 67 Melanie Lane that had cost the owner $86,000 to build. The residence was in the foothills of town and from their house they could see the San Francisco skyline.

While pert and vivacious Betty Van Sant remained a homemaker taking care of her two young offspring, Gus oversaw the firm's eleven western states and made frequent business trips throughout the huge territory. So successful was he that after six months the firm promoted him yet again—this time to vice president of sales for the entire company. As such, he was to be based at the corporation's home office in New York City at 666 Fifth Avenue at Fifty-second Street. After a hasty family council, it was decided that Gus Sr. would immediately relocate to the East Coast, while the rest of the household would remain in Atherton until mid-1962 so that nine-year-old Van would not be pulled out of school partway through the academic year.

In June 1962, Van, who had just completed the fourth grade, and Malinda, who had been in kindergarten, had to say good-bye to their friends as Betty Van Sant moved her household across country. Fortuitously one of Gus Sr.'s business friends needed to relocate to northern California. So a deal was worked out whereby the pal would take the Van Sants' home in Atherton and the Van Sants would move to Darien, Connecticut—about forty-three miles northeast of New York City along the Connecticut coast.

By mid-1962 the Van Sants had unpacked at their new residence—this time at 50 Knollwood Lane in Darien. Located on the New England shoreline five miles north of Stamford, between Stamford and Norwalk—Darien was a bastion of the old, well-heeled part of Connecticut. One of the famous bedroom communities along the New Haven, Hartford, and Connecticut Railroad's pathway between Boston, New Haven, and New York City, Darien was a conservative stronghold, full of well-to-do, Caucasian, Protestant citizens, many of whose blue-blood family trees reached back to American colonial days. (Darien was part of the verdant turf made [in]famous in the 1940s by Laura Z. Hobson's book *Gentleman's Agreement* and the subsequent movie as being, along with New Canaan and other nearby communities, a stronghold of anti-Semitism.) While the Van Sants may have been southerners by birth, they fit in easily within the upscale community.

As for Van, now ten years old, it was not such a simple transition. This was already his sixth home address in different parts of the country since he had been born. The youngster was now participating in his third school system and the change was far harder for him than for his four-year-younger sister. He had to abandon, yet again, a set of friends made at school and his then current neighborhood.

One of the constants in all these years of continuous relocation was Betty's annual summer visit to her parents in Mayfield, Kentucky. She took Gus Jr. and Malinda with her and these treks became an important event in the children's life. The yearly stays at his grandparents was especially meaningful to Gus Jr.

With all the moving about the country (he would later term the family of his childhood as "corporate gypsies") and a frequently absent father figure, Van learned at a very early age to be self-reliant. (His mother Betty would later tell people, "Van's just always been independent.") He was also a budding nonconformist. As he has detailed, "In 1962, if you could find the remotest thing that was irreverent, it was appealing. I remember actively engaging in that kind of pursuit as a 10-year-old. If somebody said, 'You can't wear this,' you'd wear it.

[Andy] Warhol, who was 30 then, was doing the same thing. They put a banner that said 'Pop Art,' and people said, 'What's that?' and they said, 'It's our movement.' And people said, 'That's not a movement,' and they said, 'Yes it is.' It was in the air in those days. Any cause—a band or a motorcycle gang, it didn't matter. You just won if you joined whatever."

Years later, when asked to describe his formative years (in relation to the themes of his first feature film projects), Van told the *Advocate*'s Robert Hofler: "I had a family that moved around a lot in the United States, and I was always amassing a new group of friends whenever we moved. We would stay in a place for only a year or two. . . . Each city had its own group of friends. In my making a new group of friends over and over again, these themes [i.e., dispossessed family and a searching for home and an embracing of a pseudo family] became ingrained. For whatever reason, if it's just by chance, I'm drawn to these stories [in my moviemaking]." To another publication, Van Sant explained that the constant moving in his childhood to what he detailed as "all very suburban, very similar places" made it easy for him to adapt to different places, but not "necessarily to blend." Gus Jr. also noted, "I've always been the quirky 'infamous' member of the family."

On yet another occasion, in 1992, young actor River Phoenix was interviewing Gus Van Sant Jr. for a magazine piece about the filmmaker's career and their recent joint movie *My Own Private Idaho* (1991). The director allowed, regarding the film and its theme of the central character searching for his lost family and the homestead of his youth, that "I have obsessed with my family's house and where we lived when I was around six, which was in Colorado. Because I guess that's where I first lived, you know? That's my concept of home. Then we moved away, and I probably didn't like moving away. So then the house smashing in the road is like my destruction of the house that I miss. But when I painted the paintings [which sometimes featured scenes of a crashing house], I never thought, 'Oh, I missed my childhood, and now I'm showing how that childhood has been smashed in 10 million bits'—though I can interpret them that way and then be sort of surprised."

When questioned in the year 2000 about the dynamics of his family when he was a youngster, Van Sant Jr. acknowledged, "I think we were probably kind of WASPy." When the interviewer for the *San Francisco Chronicle* asked if this implied that the Van Sants were Updike-ian (in reference to Pulitzer Prize–winning novelist John Updike who often wrote about the uptight aristocratic set of New England), the new-generation Van Sant answered, "Yes, I would say. [We were] Not exactly close." The journalist prodded further, " 'Updike-ian' conjures a distance and a formality and people covering up a lot of misgivings and secrets." To this, the filmmaker responded, "It could have been like that."

When the Van Sants moved to Darien, the parents participated in forming a new local Episcopal church. It was named St. Paul's and was a spin-off of a large Episcopal church in town named St. Luke's. It would be at St. Paul's that Gus Jr. was confirmed in 1963.

Another family activity was attending the Woodway Country Club in Darien. While daughter Malinda shared her mother's affinity for tennis, Gus Jr. learned to play golf, the sport his father so enjoyed. As Gus Sr. told this author about his son: "He was never very committed to the sport, though he had promise. Fortunately, for me, he learned to play well enough so that we could enter the father/son tournaments. It has been a method of bonding that has transcended the years. We have played golf whenever we are together and can find the time or place to do so."

▼

AS his family was considered part of the affluent set, Van, like most of the scions of prosperous Darien families, attended the town's fine public school system. (He became a student at the Royle School, then moved on to Middlesex Junior High.) At home, Gus Jr., born with a creative bent, had already developed an interest in art and had begun doing paintings (following in the path of his mom who had been encouraged in the fine arts by her own mother when Betty was a child). The quiet, shy youth soon displayed a proficiency for this craft, found approval from his parents, and the avocation absorbed a good deal of his spare time. At age thirteen, the boy would win the "best-of-show" in a local art competition. Thinking back on his budding display of talent, Van Sant Jr. remembered, "The paintings were really good, but they always had a certain strangeness about them. When I was 14, there was a painting I made . . . there were three policemen done in brown, and they were just standing there. It was done with tempera and ripped paper. It was real arty and strange. My parents bought it from the art show and hung it in their dining room."

▼

IN 1966, four years after they had relocated to Connecticut, Mr. Van Sant's career in the sportswear industry—and at McGregor-Doniger, in particular—prospered even further. The family moved again, but this time they remained in not only the same state, but also within the same city. They transferred to a more prestigious home—an impressive house situated at 108 Inwood Road in Darien. At the new address, Gus Jr. gained a greater degree of privacy. He was allowed to take over the huge room over the garage, which already had a built-in bathroom. The boy transformed his new domain into his private studio/living quarters.

It was while Van was in his junior high years at the Darien public school system that the teenager got put to bed for three months with what was then termed rheumatic fever (a complication resulting from a streptococcal infection usually affecting children and which is often manifested by fever, arthritis, chorea, and heart problems). On the other hand, according to Van Sant Sr., it was more likely rheumatoid arthritis, a usually chronic disease characterized by inflammation and progressive deformity of the joints. Per the senior Van Sant, Gus Jr. matched up with eight of the ten criteria of rheumatoid arthritis.

So that their son would not fall seriously behind in his schoolwork, the Van Sants arranged with the school system for teachers not only to send over the boy's course studies, but for their boy to have private tutoring sessions at home.

▼

THE excellence of the Darien public school system was reflected by the general fineness of its instructors. According to Van Sant Jr., "When I was about twelve years old, I had some very influential teachers in my school in Connecticut. Painting was my original interest. I had a great art teacher [named Robert Levine]." As the moviemaker recounted over thirty years later in a lengthy interview with Graham Fuller, "There was a whole group of students who religiously took his art class. We all *had* to take the class, but a bunch of us worked after school because we were entertained by him and he encouraged people. He, I think, was my inspiration in the early days."

Van Sant Jr. further recollected, "I actually remember him creating paintings in class, and then, on my own, I would emulate his style of painting, which was sort of the New York advertising world illustration style, design- or magazine-oriented as opposed to fine art. There was another, famous Robert Levine who did illustrations—I remember him doing one for Aqueduct Raceway—whose style was actually quite a bit like my teacher Robert Levine's style. It was the kind of stuff that was similar to what Warhol did in the fifties, except that it was in the sixties. I remember it being acrylic mixed in with tissue paper and then paint and gold leaf. I think of it as this kind of Greenwich Village, gay thing, because my teacher was an out gay teacher in 1963, which was pretty unusual for this very WASPy area where I lived in Darien, Connecticut. So, he was an early influence. Also we were doing a lot of silk-screening, just as [Andy] Warhol was at that time, unbeknownst to me because I didn't know who Warhol was. We silk-screened posters and occasionally we would do artistic, multilayered silk-screens that were more like works of art."

As for the fact that his art teacher had an alternative lifestyle, Van Sant Jr. would assess later: "His whole kind of aesthetic was he was quite open. It was the early '60s and a lot of the boys in the school sort of had a fan club, they vied for his attention. And he was sort of promiscuous in his openness, but he also never violated the trust. It would have been pretty scandalous—the kids were 12 [to] 14 or whatever. . . . He just knew where he was, and wasn't confused by being attracted to his male students. It was just part of the whole thing. It had nothing to do with trying to get in their pants or anything like that, which is I think part of the attraction the boys had. They could be appreciated but didn't really know why. I don't think most of the kids really knew what being gay was, but sometimes he would explain it. He was a great artist, too—he was very passionate about the arts."

During these impressionable years, Van was also impacted by another instructor—his ninth-grade English instructor, David Soan: "He was a progressive writing teacher who had written this [1964] book called *Stop, Look and
Write*. It was a book of photographs, and the point was to look at a photograph
and then write about what might be happening in it. It was kind of [Marshall]
McLuhan-esque, and I think David recommended McLuhan in his class—
pretty unusual readings for fourteen-year-olds. He also showed us *Citizen Kane*
and Canadian Film Board films that were definitely influenced by McLuhan,
because they were an abstract barrage of voices and media images that didn't
necessarily make sense. I remember writing a visual piece in David's class—like
an illustrated novel, but short, ten pages or so. I still have that." For Van Sant
Jr. having a teacher such as Soan was "a major influence on me. I don't know
what would have happened had Mr. Soan not been there and he hadn't shown
that film to me. Pretty amazing stuff for a public school."

It was Soan who encouraged his teenaged charges to make 8mm movies in
class and to try out amateur filmmaking at home. Van did so with his family's
Kodak camera. In these early efforts, the boy's approach to moviemaking was
more from the point of view of a painter. Later Gus Jr. pooled his resources with
classmates John Howell and Paul Ryan and they used a Super 8 camera to
shoot an animated film that lasted, perhaps, forty seconds. As the youthful
filmmaker later described this effort: "It was called *Fun with a Blood Root*. It
was about a little flower that grows up and tickles a guy under his chin and then
he bites the flower off. And then the camera sort of widens up and it shows that
the man is also a flower."

When this fledgling film effort was completed, Gus turned over the finished
results to one of his cocreators who wanted to show it to other friends. Later,
when Van Sant asked to have it back, the friend admitted it had vanished—he
had misplaced/lost it. As Gus has recalled, "That was my first film, and within two
weeks, it was just gone." It taught him that as "a filmmaker, the first thing you
find out is that you can lose film." Putting this traumatic life experience to use,
Gus would incorporated it into his 1997 novel *Pink* as a episode told by the lead
character Spunky. (Van Sant's childhood pal John Howell would admit sheepishly
to this author that it was he who had misplaced *Fun with a Blood Root*.)

Regarding their home movie experiments, Van Sant Jr. detailed years later:
"We'd emulate guys like Norman McLaren and Robert Breer in our spare time
and then show the films in class; although I don't remember ever showing a
film myself. We'd come to Robert Levine and explain things that we'd seen over
in David's class and I remember the art teacher being jealous of the English
teacher. He claimed that they were art films and they weren't appropriate for
the English class! Anyway, between the two of them, I was influenced a lot."
Looking back on his fledgling new craft, Van said, "I never thought that I was
good at it. It was hard enough to get my sister to act in my films."

Meanwhile, for Van Sant, seeing Orson Welles's 1941 masterpiece *Citizen
Kane*, in which the young Welles both starred and directed, greatly influenced

the young man's future career choices. Like many viewers before and after him, Gus Jr. was struck by the classic movie's powerful screen images and unconventional filming techniques. But watching the flamboyant Welles on-screen in this monumental production and other movies convinced the introspective teenager that Welles was "a sort of king amongst his group; a loud, bigger-than-life character. I thought that was the way a director was." For a young man as introverted as Gus Jr., the mere thought that making moviemaking as his chosen career would mean he would have to adopt such an outgoing demeanor, presented a seemingly impossible obstacle. Thus, he put aside any serious considerations of becoming a professional moviemaker.

▼

WHEN not at home buried in his homework or creative pursuits such as painting and amateur filmmaking, Gus Jr. had his own set of pals. "When I was in junior high school we created a gang. There were only four [including Gus, John Howell, and Jim Evans] of us and we'd just seen *West Side Story* and we decided to call ourselves the Coolies. We said, 'We're in a gang,' and when the other guys said, 'Yeah?' we said, 'Yeah!' Instead of saying, 'Well, not really.' Suddenly the whole school became concerned with your gang. It was like 'There they go, they're a *gang*. They're walking down the same hallways we're walking down and they're a *gang*." We didn't even wear anything different. And the school took all four of us and separated us. And other kids wanted to join us, but since we weren't really a gang we'd say, 'You can't join.' And they'd say, 'Why not?' And we'd say, 'Because you're not cool enough. We're the Coolies.' A lot of people wanted desperately to be in our gang, so that started another gang, the Anti-Coolies. These guys didn't have the wherewithal to come up with their own name. That was the brilliant thing, that we named ourselves out of pure whim, like advertising, and they were just the *anti*-us." (The Coolies also had their own tree house. One of their pranks included purchasing a mail-order dynamite kit that they used to explode a portion of a local pond.)

▼

BY the time Gus was fifteen, he was already making the fifty-mile train excursion into New York City. He was not only attracted by Manhattan's underground art scene that he was reading so much about; he also wanted to see the experimental films being screened frequently at the Museum of Modern Art. It was from these showings that he first became intrigued with iconoclastic icon Andy Warhol. (Occasionally on a school day afternoon, Gus and his pals would take the train to nearby Stamford to hang out, sometimes visiting their teacher Mr. Levine who worked part-time in a local clothing store. There was also a brief period when Gus, Jim Evans, and two girl classmates became entrepreneurial. They rented space in an old house in town (that already contained an antique store) so they could open a small art "gallery." The venture never took off and the quartet soon abandoned the enterprise.

In past summers Gus had often visited his pal John Howell whose family had relocated to Long Island, and the boys would spend countless hours out in the water floating on the Howells' Sunfish boat, lost in adolescent thoughts about their future careers. When Gus Jr. was sixteen, he spent his summer vacation working in the mailroom of McGregor-Doniger in Manhattan. Not only did his city job give him further opportunity to make side excursions after work to more film showings, but it allowed him to explore the city's artwork, especially the offbeat sector. With his earnings accumulated from his summer job he purchased an advanced Super 8 movie camera for $500, replacing the Beaulieu 16mm equipment he had previously used. He also made another acquisition: he bought a copy of Sheldon Renan's 1967 book *An Introduction to the American Underground Film,* which discussed such genre filmmakers as Warhol, Kenneth Anger, John Cassavetes, Bruce Conner, and others. This helped to create a background in the lively arts for Van Sant, an education bolstered by his English instructor at school and by attending showings of the experiment cinema of the Kuchar brothers, Ron Rice, Taylor Mead, Jonas Mekas, Stan van der Beek, and others at the Museum of Modern Art. (As Van Sant later admitted, especially with the film work of Warhol, reading about this icon was often far more impressive than actually seeing such experimental screen work, much of which could prove to be very arty and unedifying.) And of course, for more conventional fare, he watched whatever was available on television at home, often viewing the same film over and over again.

The next summer, through his dad's business connections, Gus Jr. was hired to work at the Manhattan ad agency of Cadwell Davis Partners, working in the production department. (He was so dedicated to learning his job that often he brought work home. Van Sant Sr. recalls one time that his son stayed up the entire night working on a logo design needed at the office.) As in the past summer, after work he made it a point to go to a movie, expanding his eclectic tastes from, perhaps, a W. C. Fields comedy classic to something far more experimental. As he later evaluated, "I'm not a film-historian type, like [Martin] Scorsese, who's seen everything. I'm influenced by what I happen to stumble across."

▼

AT one point during his public high school years in Darien, Connecticut, Gus Van Sant Jr. decided he wanted to attend boarding school. His primary reason was the thought of all the freedom he might have away from direct parental supervision. "I wanted to go to prep school, but my mom wanted me to stay home. I was disappointed, though I didn't really know what the whole thing was about anyway, except what I knew from the older brothers of my friends when they came back from school. There was this one really bad kid who literally blew himself up in his laboratory. He designed a bomb he was gonna set off at the Darien Police Department. That's what prep school meant to me. I just thought, Well, you went away from your parents and you got to do what you wanted, and the reason you got in trouble was that you were doing what you wanted. Afterwards I realized prep school wasn't such a cool place."

So the preppie wanna-be remained in his upscale Connecticut town: "Darien was a racy community. The kids were as racy as the parents and the parents were, like the head of J. Walter Thompson groovy advertising, who, in 1967, was in touch with the world. These were parents who worked at the top of all the buildings in Manhattan. So their kids were products of that, whatever that is. Some of those people were making the culture, managing the Beatles, whatever was going on. The '60s happened to me in Darien. I was really young, but that might be the best way. I was working on Madison Avenue at 16 in 1969, the summer of Woodstock. My boss wore bell-bottoms and took acid on weekends. I took acid on weekends, too. I was on my way to Woodstock, but my parents wouldn't let me go because I was 16."

Gus's concerned parents had learned on the TV news that the area around Bethel, in upstate New York where the gigantic outdoor rock concert was to take place on a six-hundred-acre farm, was already a disaster area from the converging mass of 400,000 attendees. Undiscouraged, Van Sant Jr. was about to depart for the festival with a local friend, but his parents refused to let their son go. Years later Gus was still regretful: "I didn't really know that it was going to be the pivotal event of my generation. . . . It looked pretty miserable [at the time]."

But if sixteen-year-old Gus was unhappy about not participating in the mass excitement at Woodstock, he was conversely pleased with his decision about not making another major trip, one that his family was planning. The Van Sants intended to relocate to Portland, Oregon, and Gus Jr. had no desire to move yet again—especially not as he was entering his senior year of high school in Darien.

MY OWN PRIVATE PORTLAND

[Portland life] was good. The families weren't as structured as East Coast families were. There was a bigger bleed-over between the parents and the kids. It was more integrated.

Gus Van Sant, 1997

AS GUS VAN SANT JR. was completing his junior year of public high school in the spring of 1969, his goal-oriented businessman father was dealing with a delicate corporate problem at the New York City headquarters of McGregor-Doniger. By now the hardworking, high-achieving man had risen to president of the prestigious firm while Bill Doniger, the former chief executive, had moved over to be the firm's chairman of the board. Somehow the change in posts fractured the working relationship between Van Sant Sr. and Doniger. Realizing that the situation would not improve, the company president looked for a new position. This led to meetings with Warnaco, Inc., a powerful conglomerate that owned several companies in the apparel industry, including Puritan Sportswear, Hathaway, and White Stag Apparel. As a result of the negotiations, Mr. Van Sant was offered the presidency of White Stag. The only concern in accepting the lucrative offer was the need to relocate his family across country to Portland, Oregon, where the prominent clothing firm was headquartered. If Van Sant Sr. accepted the offer, he would have to be in place in Oregon by early 1970.

When Gus Jr. learned the news, he insisted that—somehow—he would remain in Darien to complete his final year of high school. While acknowledging that their artistic son was extremely self-sufficient and extremely self-willed, the parents continued to urge their nonconformist boy to join them and his sister, Malinda, in Portland.

For a time, the high school student remained adamant. He completed his junior school year, took a summer job, pursued his amateur filmmaking and his guitar strumming, and sporadically did his artwork. (By now he was finding increasingly that his painting was unfulfilling—"by the time I was 17 I had gotten to a place where it was getting kind of boring.") He continued making treks to Manhattan's Museum of Modern Art and art house cinemas to absorb the mass of experimental films and movie classics being screened. He was also expanding his cinema tastes by sampling foreign films, especially those from France and Italy.

In the process of learning more about experimental/underground cinema, Gus Jr. became attracted to the ethos of the Hippie Generation mingled with an affinity for the previous movement—the Beat Generation. As such, the teenager assiduously read the (autobiographical) works of Beat novelist and poet Jack Kerouac, including his *On the Road* (1957). He studied the poems and writings of Beat/Hippie poet Allen Ginsberg and the surreal, drug-related works of William S. Burroughs Jr., especially the latter's uniquely styled *Naked Lunch* (1959).

Like many of his peers in the freer 1960s, Gus Jr. experimented with marijuana, savoring the affects of pot, which seemed to expand his flow of thoughts and to loosen his reserved (sometimes uptight) nature. Occasionally as the decade came to a close, he tried LSD to see how the hallucinogen affected his mental processes and what it did to his inhibitions. (He would tell Kristine McKenna of the *Los Angeles Times* in December 1989: "Drugs played a big role in my life in the '60s and '70s, and I was pretty familiar with pot and LSD during that period. . . .")

Although initially he apparently kept it to himself, by this point in time the teenager had concluded that he was truly a homosexual, not just uncertain of his maturing sexuality. He documented this point in a December 1997 interview with *Venice Magazine*. In the piece he was discussing filmmakers who had influenced him, one such person being the Chilean-born stage and movie director Alexandro Jodorowsky. The latter was the auteur of the Mexican-made, Spanish-language *El Topo* (1970), an ultraviolent, eclectic religious parable with homoerotic under/overtones that had become a cult classic in the 1970s and was a favorite on the midnight movie circuit. Van Sant Jr. told *Venice*, "*El Topo* was one of the films I saw when I first came out, around '68 or '69."

But although he accepted his alternative lifestyle, the teenager seemingly did little actual experimentation at the time, whether in Darien or on his New York City excursions. In Manhattan, in particular, the gay way of life was coming wholeheartedly out of the closet, whether in the "bohemian" Greenwich Village or in the many gay bars, porno movie theaters, and men's bathhouses that were blossoming throughout the metropolis. Years later, this was confirmed by Van Sant Jr. in a June 1994 issue of *Interview* magazine. The publication was preparing an article dealing with the twenty-fifth anniversary of the Stonewall Bar riot in the Big Apple. The piece included the reminiscences of several prominent American homosexuals who recalled the effects of the mid-1969 upsurge of activists protesting—for the first time in a major, visible way—the police harassment of gays at the Stonewall Bar in Greenwich Village in late June 1969. Van Sant commented: "Stonewall is a great point in post-Eisenhower gay history, and I wasn't there. I was seventeen, a junior hippie commuting between Connecticut and Madison Avenue. I didn't know much about gay Greenwich Village except what I heard from my [school] art teacher. . . ."

▼

SOMEWHERE along the line Gus Jr. changed his mind about trekking westward with his parents. Whatever the deciding factors, seventeen-year-old Van accompanied his family to Aspen, Colorado, for a month of skiing in December 1969. (All the Van Sants were avid skiers and would spend many holiday vacations together on the slopes of Aspen or Vermont. Occasionally they skied in Europe, as in late 1968 when the Van Sants went to Austria, taking Gus Jr.'s friend John Howell along with them.)

By early 1970 the Van Sants were in Portland, Oregon—the city where it rains typically 151 days of the year, the annual rainfall averages thirty-seven inches, and the usual yearly number of freezing days is forty-five. Befitting Van Sant Sr.'s title as the president of the prominent White Stag Sportswear organization, he and his family settled into an impressive home at 9717 Southeast Cambridge Lane located adjacent to the second hole of the Waverley Country Club golf course. Ironically, Gus Sr. the avid golfer (as Gus Jr. was becoming) was not allowed to join the exclusive golf club until he had been a resident of the city for a year. The Van Sants' new residence was a stately Amish Tudor home, built in the 1930s, that boasted wide expanses of carefully manicured lawns. As in New England, Gus Jr. was given the large room over the garage as his studio apartment. The new abode also boasted a small stage in the basement rec/entertainment room.

Unlike Darien, Connecticut, where the Van Sant children had attended public school, it was decided that in Portland—a far more homogenous city as to its ethnic, cultural, and social mix—the offspring should be enrolled in a private day school. The institution of choice was the exclusive Catlin Gabel School. It was an esteemed coed facility that was the result of two turn-of-the-century schools (Catlin Hillside and Gabel Country Day) merging in 1958 and relocating to a fifty-two-acre campus on the former Honey Hollow Farm on Southwest Barnes Road. Covering prekindergarten through the twelfth grade, the school accepted a mix of paying and scholarship students to maintain ethnic diversity. The typical class contained fifteen to twenty students.

Because Gus Jr. and Malinda were starting the academic year in January 1970, Catlin Gabel, in transferring their class credits, decreed that it would be best if they each went back an academic year. Thus Van was placed in the eleventh grade and Malinda in the seventh. It was about a twenty-five-minute drive from the Van Sant home to the progressive day school and Gus Jr. was entrusted with driving his sister and himself to and from school each day.

More so than the Van Sants had anticipated, Gus Jr. and Malinda responded well to their new environment. A favorite story that Mr. Van Sant has repeated over the years, he told again to the *Seattle Times* in September 1990, while discussing the family's transfer to Portland. "The move was great . . . for Gus. One morning there was a report of black ice on the street. The school called and said that Gus and his sister didn't have to go to school. They came to me and said, 'But we like school!' In Connecticut it would've been, 'Great, let's go outside and play!'"

Among Gus Jr.'s classmates at Catlin Gabel were Carl Stevens and Eric Alan Edwards. The newcomer became especially friendly with Edwards with whom he shared a growing love of cinematography. In fact, during their senior year at school, the duo made a joint film project. Originally to be done as a silent, 8mm entry, they decided it should be shot in 16mm and in sound. Edwards handled the camera work, while Gus provided the script and direction. This early effort of Van Sant Jr. is very revealing of his sensibilities at the time, "unsettling" ones that persisted throughout the years. The narrative concerns a young brother and sister who escape the harsh city and go on a weekend excursion to the shore. The movie shows them visiting the coast, but then near the finale the girl is run over by a car. The twenty-minute entry closes with her lying in the road. The sound track is composed primarily of songs by such then avant-garde rock performers as Frank Zappa. The movie's title, *The Happy Organ*, refers to a novelty song that is never heard within the movie. A trademark of Gus Van Sant Jr.'s early films was the brief use of time-lapse photography. In this case, a sunrise was depicted as the sky goes from dark to light, with swirling clouds moving on high. (Years later, in August 1989, in reviewing the short subject for *Pacific Northwest* magazine, journalist D. K. Holm stated, "Beneath the humor and whimsy of Van Sant's work lurks a bleak, frightening vision.")

Besides his academic studies and filmmaking during his senior year at Catlin Gabel, Gus Jr., like his friend Eric Alan Edwards, was on the yearbook staff, providing photographs to illustrate the book and helping with the graphic design. Among Van Sant's shots that appear in the Class of '71's yearbook are two pages of assorted images juxtaposed so closely together that it is difficult for the casual reader to discern what the subjects actually are.

In his individual photo in the senior yearbook, Gus Jr., wearing a sports jacket and a plaid, unbuttoned-at-the-collar shirt, boasts a hairstyle that he would maintain for years, with the front locks of his dark hair swirling to the side over his right eye. If one looks quickly at the picture, with the subject's slightly bowed head and the piercing look of his solemn gaze, it reminds one of photos of the youngish Tony Perkins before the bisexual actor gained cult status as the deranged murderer of Alfred Hitchcock's classic thriller, *Psycho* (1960).

Beneath his individual photo, eighteen-year-old Gus Jr. chose stanzas from a song by Frank Zappa, the noted rock musician who had formed the Mothers of

Invention group in 1965 and whose lyrics often mixed psychedelic rock with elements of jazz and satire. The lines that young Van Sant chose to be associated with his photo are either optimistic or cynical depending on one's viewpoint—and the graduate's perspective was decidedly verging on the latter—as it told of watching rodents scurry across the floor and making up tunes about being penniless.

▼

IN 1971, for most American young men, it was a case of going to college (and getting a military service deferment) or being drafted into the army—and most likely being shipped over to Vietnam. In Gus Van Sant Jr.'s situation, because of his past bout of rheumatic fever—not to mention his still unpublicized lifestyle decision—military service was not a chief concern for him. Nor was deciding which college he wished to attend—no matter how costly the tuition might be. Charting his own course and not interested in a business career, he had one seat of higher learning in mind—the Rhode Island School of Design in Providence, founded in 1877. While he was not as passionately devoted to becoming a full-time painter as he once had been, this New England institution appealed to him because (1) it had a very high academic and creative reputation among American campuses and (2) it offered a variety of film courses. (Gus still believed that to be a professional moviemaker would require a more gregarious, uninhibited soul than he was, so he wanted the option of continuing his art studies.) Thus, with his parents' acquiescence, he applied for and was accepted by his first and only choice for higher education. Giving him confidence in his college choice was the fact that his Catlin Gabel classmate and good friend Eric Alan Edwards was also slated to attend the same campus.

In September 1971 Gus Van Sant Jr., the proud owner of a maroon 2002 model BMW, matriculated at the Rhode Island School of Design (RISD). The school is located in the College Hill section of the city along with its famed Museum of Art, which houses the state's most vital collection of fine art. RISD provides its nearly two thousand students with a choice of seventeen majors ranging from liberal arts to furniture design to interior architecture, photography, painting, and film/animation/video. (In recent years, RISD has been turning out some of America's finest new animators, including Fran Krause.)

There was another reason Gus had chosen RISD and spending four years in Providence. The Hippie Generation and the druggies (relatively innocent in comparison to later drug cultures) had made a stronghold in this historic state capital. The city was filled with whacked-out creative types for whom "higher education" had a fresh meaning. With its strong roots in the Beat and Hippie Generations' culture and personae, Gus knew he would feel at home here.

Thinking back to these fun, creative, marijuana-smoking times, Van Sant told interviewer Graham Fuller in 1993: "Yeah, the Providence Aesthetic as

Mary Clark used to call it. Mary Clark was a member of the Motels, which came out of sixties rock 'n' roll and drug influences. There was a bunch of art bands that were influenced by Martin Mull, who was a painter at RISD in the sixties and had a band called Soup. He was kind of the grandfather of my generation, though I didn't know him. A guy named Tim Duffy had a band called Snake and the Snatch and there were other bands like Iron Grandmother and Electric Driveway; they all had the same lineup, but they would change their costumes and come out and play as different bands from different eras. They were comedy-oriented, multimedia games—'painter bands' I would call them because none of the people in them were musicians, although they put together these shows which had very funny lyrics and a lot of pageantry and costume changes. Some people did performance pieces on stage, like one girl sat under a sun lamp for fifteen minutes between sets. Frank Zappa and the Mothers of Invention were probably an inspiration for all these people and I think everybody was influenced by the Velvet Underground at the time—because they were a painter band—and by the [Andy] Warhol scene."

In his first semesters at RISD, Van Sant devoted himself to required basic general education courses and others in his then chosen fields of painting and filmmaking. He continued his earlier habit of seeking out experimental, classic, and foreign films to view away from the classroom. Socially, with a bigger, more flexible, and more adult universe from which to choose his friends, he had various cliques among the art crowd with whom he associated. As he noted later, "I had moved away from the tight friends I had in high school."

If there was a chance in his hectic RISD life to be homesick it was when he wistfully missed the ambiance of the diverse counterculture groups he had encountered in Portland. As for his family, they were no longer far away. By now, the Warnaco conglomerate had transferred Mr. Van Sant from Portland back to the firm's main operations offices on Lafayette Street in Bridgeport, Connecticut, where he was promoted to Executive Vice President/Group Operations. The family relocated back to Darien, Connecticut, where they had their friends, although daughter Malinda (having been put back a year at Catlin Gabel) now found herself in junior high in the Darien public school system, a grade behind her former classmates. To celebrate their return to Connecticut, the family built an impressive house at 20 Inwood Lane. Once again, Gus Jr. was given his private domain—the big room over the family garage, which had a special sink built in to accommodate his photography work. Thus, Gus made the 137-mile "commute" for visits home.

By the time Gus Jr. entered his sophomore year at RISD in the fall of 1972 he was fairly convinced that his future was not as a full-time artist. As he explained later, "It didn't seem like painting would really be a way to support yourself. There were a lot of art students that wound up staying in Providence, or the people who went to New York City as painters and remained unemployed. It was a long road to be traveling. There was reward at the end of the long road, perhaps, but there wasn't a lot of hope. The painter students who'd come back to speak at the school, they'd reel off these statistics of how many painters were living in New York City and how many actually made it. It was pretty staggering."

Expanding on this crucial career decision, he told actor/friend River Phoenix in 1992: "I changed from painting after my first year because I thought that maybe a career in the film business was a more moneyed career than a painter's. . . . It was a safety bail-out. But, also, films were more complicated, and I'd pretty much mastered—at least in my estimation—painting. But filmmaking was a big mystery, and I thought to get anywhere in the business I'd have to work really hard and forget about painting for a while. And that's what I chose to do."

Now devoted to film in the classroom, in home (lab) assignments, Gus developed new filmgoing tastes. One was the screen work of Stanley Kubrick, the British-based American filmmaker. He impressed Van Sant not only for his innate filmmaking skills but for his ingenuity at remaining outside the bulk of film studio supervision. He was a man who, especially in his early Hollywood years, had made projects (e.g., *Killer's Kiss*, 1955; *The Killing*, 1956) that he—alone or with an associate—scripted, produced, shot, and edited. Such control gave the finished project a true stamp of individuality and displayed the moviemaker's talents to the fullest.

It had been viewing Kubrick's *A Clockwork Orange* (1971) that helped convince Van Sant that filmmaking was to be his future. In the 1990s Gus would enthuse, "*A Clockwork Orange* is the best film I ever saw. It's hard for me to defend it, though. Kubrick is really cruel at heart. . . . The whole thing about *A Clockwork Orange* is that it was a really low budget movie, like a million-and-a-half-dollar film in 1971, which was probably about the kind of film I make today. . . . He figured out how to light it and shoot it with a small crew—he just went back to something he'd done in the '50s. . . . It's a complete discipline, a filmmaker making do with what he has."

As Gus's tastes in cinema diversified, he became attracted to the work of Baltimore, Maryland–based John Waters. With such movies as *Mondo Trasho* (1969) and *Pink Flamingos* (1972), this iconoclastic talent displayed an anti-traditionalism and a gleeful sense of offensiveness that appealed to the non-conformist in Van Sant. One New Year's Eve during his RISD years, Gus, along with his boyhood friend Jim Evans, drove to Baltimore hoping to meet members of John Waters's stock company. Evans recalled for this author that long-ago night of driving around from party to party—at one of which the host had spiked the punch with acid—and then their going bowling.

By now fully aware that he would always be gay-oriented, Gus realized—this being the early 1970s—that lifestyle choice would always make him an outsider. Rather than hide from his "difference," he chose to embrace it both in his personal life and his professional career.

In this period Gus's pantheon of filmmaker idols realigned. He became less enthused by the works of once trend-setting underground moviemaker Andy Warhol and his Film Factory. (Van Sant noted later, "At RISD, everyone was into fame, that was a Warholian thing. Art was beside the point, but everyone was really a good artist.") Gus was increasingly disenchanted by Warhol's celebrity mystique as a filmmaker and an artist. This disassociation seemed ironic to one of Van Sant's RISD classmates. In a 1999 *Premiere* magazine article devoted to Gus, a former, unnamed RISD peer of Van Sant's said, "The whole way Gus sees everything that's going on but acts innocent, like he doesn't, is straight from Warhol." Another person who saw a parallel between Van Sant and Warhol (who died in 1987) was interviewer Amy Taubin. Writing of Gus in the British *Sight and Sound* magazine in January 1992, she observed, "Like Warhol, Van Sant has the charismatically absent presence of the obsessive voyeur. He also shares the slightly hunched, arm wrapped, self-protective stance of the 'pale master' and a reputation for silence, notwithstanding a gift for the gab."

▼

NOT all of Van Sant's RISD classes involved the fine arts. He had to take his share of math courses. Years later, when directing *Good Will Hunting* (1997), it gave him a frame of reference for the story, much of which was set at M.I.T. math classes and dealt with professors and students involved in higher levels of the science.

As well as intensifying his study of and interest in filmmaking and photography, Gus continued his growing enthusiasm for music, both guitar playing and song writing. At the time he did not think these avocations would be important to his career future. Rather, "I did music then for fun. That's when I was just enjoying being alive." He was turned on by any activity that gave him creative freedom. In fact, he said later, "I'd take any career if it would do that for me, it didn't matter whether it was taking pictures, writing songs, or making some written thing that you passed out among friends. I still feel that."

This music interest led Gus to gravitate to the cliques of rock enthusiasts at school. Among them was Scottish-born David Byrne and his group, the Talking Heads. "I went to their first show. At the time there was something like ten people in the band, and David Byrne sang 'Psycho Killer.' But he didn't have all the words, so they did some Velvet Underground songs too. It's weird how all these musicians go to art school." Another time, Van Sant recalled the event as: "Chris Frantz was taking one of the video courses and I remember he got his friends—David was one of them—to mime 'Mustang Sally' to a record, and they pretended they were a rock band on video. That was the first thing that I ever saw the Talking Heads do. I don't know if it was a statement, but it was like a funky art video. They wore wigs and fooled around." Regardless of the occasion he first heard the Talking Heads perform, the group's irreverence for traditions and the establishment appealed to Van Sant. It played into his growing sly sense of wit and rebellion at the upper social classes and the often shallow conventions and rules that had surrounded so much of his adolescent years.

There were other influences on Van Sant at RISD. For example, "There were two guys, Charlie Clavery and Scott Sorensen, who had a video project called *Meet the Stars*. If someone famous came to town, they would try to get into the backstage door without credentials and see how far they could get—and that was the video! Charlie would act like a newscaster, except he'd wear a wig or funny glasses, and he would try and get an unauthorized interview and sometimes he would succeed. To this day I'm influenced by them and by the Motels and the multimedia approach and the humor within their projects. You don't really see a direct kind of influence in my work; it's just that they were inspirational. Someday I'd like to make a film about them."

▼

SOCIALLY, although Gus Van Sant Jr. hung out with various circles on and off campus, he apparently was still internally a loner. This was reflected in an incident during his junior year at RISD. It was Saint Valentine's Day and twenty-one-year-old Gus had gone to a party where David Byrne and his group (then known as the Artistics) were performing. On the surface he seemed fairly relaxed and at ease, but internally he was cringing: "I remember being too nervous to dance so I pretended I was watching the band, but it felt like there was nothing to watch so I was there for no reason."

▼

FOR one of his summer breaks from RISD, Gus and his friends went on a four-week vacation to the Baja Peninsula in Mexico, south of San Diego, California. His sister, Malinda, had just turned sixteen and she kept begging her brother to let her use his BMW car during his absence. His immediate response was to say no, but he finally capitulated. While he was south-of-the-border, Gus Jr. called home and asked how his sister and his beloved car were. The parents said everything was fine. However, when he returned home he learned the truth. One day while Malinda and two of her girlfriends were out driving, she had totaled the stick-shift car. It took a lot to get the vehicle back into working shape.

Another summer he drove an MG across the country and then headed up the coast to Portland. Then one summer recess Van Sant Jr. really broke free of his pampered upper-middle-class environment (one can only imagine how his tradition-bound family regarded this hippie-like adventure!)—Gus chose to ride the rails when he was twenty. As he explained later, "It was amazing to me that kind of being loose in a day-to-day life. It's sexy in the sense that that's the whole job—to survive. When I traveled across country as a hobo I learned about survival." He also noted, "Now the trains use (flatcars), which is less protective from the elements. In my day, when they had empty (box)cars up near the front, if you were younger you could ride with the engineers or on the caboose."

▼

DURING the course of his years at RISD Van Sant made a 16mm black-and-white film short (it lasted forty seconds) entitled *Little Johnny*. That was in 1972. The next year he created another 16mm black-and-white entry entitled *1/2 of a Telephone Conversation* (it ran for two minutes). His final senior project was a 16mm color short (twenty-eight minutes). He has described it with the following: "[It] had an experimental tack, but it tried to incorporate a slick Hollywood format, like the [Jean-Luc] Godard films. Although I didn't know much about Godard, and I still don't, I've realized that that was something he was doing. His films tended to look like Hollywood films, but their stories and techniques were messed with and mixed up. I did something like that in a film called *Late Morning Start*. It was a failure, really, but it looked good and it was interesting. Its intention was to draw you into all these different stories, but not show you what happened; your attention was continually diverted. [Luis] Buñuel's *La Fantome de la Liberté* did exactly the same thing, but I did it less successfully because I didn't have the budget."

By the time of his RISD senior project, Gus was installed in a loft apartment on the fourth floor of a jewelry factory on Pine Street, which he shared with a RISD student who was a sculptor. By then Van Sant's childhood pal John Howell had already graduated from college and, with time to spare, he came to Providence. John stayed at Gus's apartment and helped Van Sant with his senior year project of *Late Morning Start*.

On May 31, 1975, Gus Van Sant graduated from RISD and received his B.F.A. degree. (He would celebrate the occasion in one of his self-penned tunes for his 1985 album *Gus Van Sant* in which he sings the text of his diploma to his own guitar accompaniment.) Always pleased by his time at RISD and what he had learned there (in and out of the classroom), Van Sant has retained close ties to the institution. In 1998, at New York City's Supper Club he would receive a RISD Award for film/animation/video.

His academic life now behind him, twenty-two-year-old Van Sant knew it was time to support himself, to satisfy his creative instincts, and to show his family that his chosen path in the arts could, and would, bring productive results.

THE GRADUATE

There was a whole 10-year period, partly in LA and partly in New York, where I was kind of directionless. and at the time there wasn't digital video. You couldn't just go make a movie.

Gus Van Sant, 2000

AT ALMOST AGE TWENTY-THREE, Gus Van San Jr. was a graduate of the prestigious Rhode Island School of Design. The question was what to do next with his life? Years later, his sister, Malinda (who attended the University of Colorado as an education major and then went into the apparel business after college), said in a rare public interview about her famous brother: "When he got out of college he could've gotten a job with a big [Hollywood movie] studio, but he said basically he wanted to be a starving artist."

Given Van Sant's individualistic, artistic nature, he inherently knew he was not cut out temperamentally to be part of a major Hollywood film studio where his independence would be sacrificed to corporate bureaucracy and movie lot politics. Instead, he could pursue experimental filmmaking, painting, and his music, living at home in Darien, Connecticut, or he could remain in Providence. But from observing what happened to past RISD graduates who stayed in Providence, he feared getting diverted from his goal of becoming a professional moviemaker.

Postponing a "final" career decision (as was possible being the scion of a well-heeled family), Gus joined fellow RISD film majors in a trip abroad. The destination was Italy and the agenda was the opportunity to observe the cream of that country's crop of current moviemakers at work on their latest projects.

While not exactly the equivalent of hands-on experience as part of, say, today's American Film Institute's apprenticeship program, it was—in the mid-1970s—a golden opportunity to savor the aesthetics of cherished cinema auteurs up close and personal.

Arriving in Rome, the group had introductions to visit the sets of many productions then in front of the cameras. They saw Federico Fellini filming *Casanova*, Lina Wertmuller as she shot *Seven Beauties*, and Tinto Brass as he completed *Salon Kitty*. One moviemaker who particularly appealed to Van Sant was fifty-three-year-old Pier Paolo Pasolini, the prolific, provocative director who had made such neorealism excursions as *Accattone* (1961), poetic entries like *Uccellacci e Uccellini* [The Hawks and the Sparrows] (1966), and such allegorical (homo)erotic entries as *Teorema* (1968). At the time the politically radical homosexual was finishing *Salò o le 120 giornate di Sodama* [Salo—The 120 Days of Sodom], an already highly controversial production based on a work by the Marquis de Sade that had been reset to World War II as sadistic Fascist rulers brutalize adolescents in the most horrific, degrading manner.

Pasolini was then on postproduction for *Salo*. One group of Van Sant's peers got to watch the genius of Italian cinema at work during a complex dubbing session. Gus, on the other hand, wangled an invitation to visit the master's home and to meet in person the illustrious artist. The American was asked by the great director what he wanted to accomplish in film. The twentysomething visitor responded he wanted "to translate literature into film." (In retrospect Van Sant said many years later, "I thought that literature could do a lot of stuff. You could do anything on the page that you wanted to do. With film, you were always trapped, you couldn't do just anything you wanted to do.")

Summarizing his sweep of the Italian filmmaking scene, Van Sant would say much later, "He [Pasolini] was very smart, but that was my impression of a lot of these guys as a 20 [*sic*]-year-old student. Italy itself was quite interesting because it was sort of like being inside a Fellini film. I could see where Fellini had gotten a lot of his material—from his own culture. The directors all had their kind of [quirks] that you would expect. We had lunch at a table with Lina Wertmuller and [actor] Giancarlo Giannini. None of us spoke Italian and sometimes we'd be interpreted through someone who did, but basically it was just being there."

If Gus or his classmates thought this whirlwind trek of culture and aesthetics would lead to a job in the Italian film industry, they were mistaken. For one thing, most of them, and Gus in particular, did not speak Italian. For another, none of them had any practical experience. And, most important, there were just too many native talents-in-the-making vying for any possible industry openings on the Rome filmmaking scene

With their visit over, the American contingent returned to the United States. (Gus went to Paris to meet his parents who were vacationing in Europe.) A few months later, on November 2, 1975, the media was filled with the news of the murder of Pier Paolo Pasolini. Allegedly he had been clubbed to death and then run over by a young man to whom the director had made sexual advances. Many others, including fellow filmmaker Bernardo Bertolucci, thought that Pasolini had been killed for political reasons.

▼

IN his teen years and in college, Gus had read several of the works of iconoclastic novelist, poet, and painter William S. Burroughs Jr. More so than such other fellow Beat Generation writers as Jack Kerouac and Allen Ginsberg, tall and lanky Burroughs fascinated Van Sant not only as a cultural icon, but also for his free-form eccentric writing style. Then, too, the bizarre life of this amazing individual grabbed the young man's attention. Like Gus, Burroughs came from a cultured, substantial family. Born in St. Louis in 1914, Burroughs graduated from Harvard University, attended medical school for a time at the University of Vienna, and although long a practicing homosexual, chose to marry in the mid-1930s. After briefly serving in the U.S. Army in 1942, he settled in New York City where he met Kerouac, Ginsberg, and others of their circle.

By 1944, the always counterculture Burroughs, who had experimented for years with mind-influencing drugs, became addicted to morphine. Although continuously gay, he divorced his first wife and moved with his common-law new wife (and her infant daughter) to Texas. There, in 1947, his son was born. After undergoing another of his attempts to break his drug habit, Burroughs, wanted by authorities for possession of illegal drugs and firearms, fled with his family to Mexico City. In September 1951 the writer accidentally shot and killed his wife. While his children were sent to live with relatives, the writer remained in Mexico until his legal case was settled and he was freed of charges.

Over subsequent years, Burroughs became increasingly eccentric and self-focused. A perpetual traveler in search of adventure, answers to life, and (brief-to longer-term) homosexual liaisons, he roamed South America and mingled with native tribes. In the interior of Peru, he hunted for the mescaline-like drug yage, which a local medicine man administered to him. Later, he made recurrent visits to Tangiers (a congenial site for gays), resided in Paris periodically, and took yet another addiction cure (which failed) in London.

Meanwhile, of all his controversial, free-form, peculiar writings, *Naked Lunch*—first published in Paris in 1959—generated the most heat. When it was published in the United States in 1962, it created a huge literary controversy and ongoing censorship litigation in different parts of the country (which were eventually settled in Burroughs's favor). By 1974, the sixty-year-old, weather-beaten, bony soul had moved from London to New York where he taught, wrote, and enjoyed being lionized by a new youth culture—the Punk Generation. He still maintained in his writing a facet that appealed mightily to the unconventional Van Sant. It was a collage technique in which he sliced up and blended into his own writings quotations from other writers, newspapers, and other printed mediums to deliberately break traditional patterns of literary form. In his daily journal, he would divide the page into three columns: one for what he was actually doing, another for his thoughts, and a third for what he was reading.

By 1975, the year *Port of Saints* was published in London and *The Book of Breeething* was distributed in the United States, William S. Burroughs Jr. was living modestly in New York City. By the latter part of that year, Van Sant was still in the Northeast, not yet having set out on his life's mission (whatever that might be). He was inspired finally to get in touch with his idol. By now Burroughs had set up residence at 222 Bowery in a converted Y.M.C.A. now used as apartments for artists. The legendary man rented the concrete space that once had been the locker room. Friends called the windowless place The Bunker, but it appealed to the paranoid author who prized privacy and safety (there were several locked doorways between the street and him).

According to Van Sant in one account: "I was in New York in 1975 and heard that he was there and that other people went to see him. So I looked him up in the telephone book and there he was." When he reached Burroughs on the phone, the elder statesman of nonconformist literature suggested that because it was approaching the Christmas season, Gus should contact him and come by after the holiday. Van Sant did just that.

Gus had a purpose in mind. Back in 1973, Burroughs's *Exterminator!* was issued. Although categorized by its publisher as a novel, it was actually a compilation of miscellaneous pieces, some of which had been published earlier in magazines. One of the collection was entitled "The Discipline of DE." In describing "DE" (Do Easy), Burroughs's exhaustive biographer Ted Morgan (*Literary Outlaw: The Life and Times of William S. Burroughs*) puts this writing about accomplishing tasks properly into the context of the man's extensive oeuvre and life changes. According to Morgan, in this piece Burroughs's "puritan WASP background came out of the closet. His thesis was that carelessness in small things would be repeated in larger ones. In small daily occurrences lay the potential for disaster. Therefore, there was a correct technique for every activity: 'Guide a dustpan lightly to the floor as if you were landing a plane.'" As Morgan analyzed, "Had he continued in this vein, Burroughs could have made a reputation for himself in the self-improvement field. What he was saying, and felt deeply, was that spilling something or breaking something was not just a moment of clumsiness but a symptom of a larger disorder. 'Who or what,' Burroughs asked, 'was this opponent that makes you spill drop and fumble slip and fall.'"

Very interestingly, Van Sant had a quite different take on "The Discipline of DE." He analyzed that it "wasn't really like any of his other stories. It wasn't as outrageous. It was a pretty matter-of-fact parody about discipline, about the art of self-control, but it was useful, too."

Finally the day of the meeting occurred. Twenty-three-year-old Gus, still very much on the surface the preppie type, traveled to the Bowery to talk with the much lionized, cantankerous Burroughs. By then, the toll of a draining life and decades of drug taking had made the man (now sixty-one) slightly stoop-shouldered. He had a pallid complexion and was already developing a wizened look. But he still had his sexual appeal and was then engaged in his latest relationship—this time with a handsome twentysomething young man from Kansas who occasionally had sex with Burroughs but functioned more as an assistant/companion/son.

Van Sant enthused about the special tête-à-tête years after the event: "Things were really happening for him then because it was the beginning of the New York punk movement and he was reading his stuff in punk clubs and becoming associated with Patti Smith and others."

During their cordial conversation, Gus explained he wished to make a screen version of "The Discipline of DE." The bespectacled, renegade man of letters certainly must have appreciated the enthusiasm of his visitor. Here was a pleasant-looking young male who championed the work (in contrast to some reviewers who had viciously dissected the overall book, *Exterminator!*), who shared an appreciation for the arts, and who was of a similar alternative lifestyle. Van Sant allowed that he had insufficient financial resources, but still hoped he could option the work to make a film short and that perhaps future earnings would make amend for the no-fee option. The host was flattered by the offer, more for the opportunity of having one of his writings picturized than from potential financial remuneration. Burroughs had already been involved in the making of film shorts years back with Anthony Balch and, from that experience, knew that the likelihood of seeing much, if any, cash from the "DE" short was highly unlikely. Nevertheless, the older man—whom Gus would describe as "hugely supportive and friendly" at the conference—graciously referred Van Sant to Burroughs's agent and the "deal" was made. It was the first real step in Gus becoming a professional filmmaker.

At their relatively brief meeting, besides exchanging pleasantries, they primarily only talked about Van Sant's adaptation proposal. Gus would not see his beloved guru in person again for another decade. Nevertheless, they would keep in touch on an occasional basis. Even as his own career was rising in the film industry during these years, respectful Van Sant remained enthusiastic about this unique mentor-of-sorts—the man who had turned out such unconventional writings, led such an antiestablishment life, and thrived on his idiosyncratic way of embracing and participating in the arts.

Discussing Burroughs in 1991, Van Sant, generally a man of few words, said, "He had specific views on everything—love, for example. He considers romance an invention of Victorian society." Gus allowed, "We tend to talk about things that interest him, poisonous snakes, alien beings, auras you can't see, guns." When asked how Burroughs affected his perspective of the world, Gus responded, "I can't say that I have a world view. I like the way Burroughs writes and the things he talks about, but I don't have the background he has. He's a meticulous student. I haven't studied."

HOLLYWOOD BOUND

It was a limited world, yet within that world there was everything, a kind of mirror to society. It had different rules. Time is different on the street. Bad things can happen. You can be set up, if people know where you are going to be at a certain time.

Gus Van Sant, 1992

BY EARLY 1976 GUS VAN SANT JR. knew he must make several life moves. At age twenty-three it was high time to be out on his own. Only then could he avoid being constantly enmeshed in an upper-class way of life bound by suffocating rules, regimens, and participants. He also appreciated that regardless of the incentives (and also being the easy way), he could never successfully or happily pursue his father's fast-track, highly goal-oriented business world. Subconsciously, at least, he must also have perceived that he could never play at the straight role and marry heterosexually to keep the general public unaware of his gayness.

Having exhausted his options at home, he finally determined to try the West Coast. After he left for college in 1971 he made several visits to Portland, and it was certainly tempting to move to Oregon and become a do-it-yourself film-maker there. Doing this would avoid being caught up in the Hollywood game he so opposed and, because of his shyness and his lack of gamesmanship skills, he intuitively feared. Nevertheless, he chose to give southern California a try to see what might transpire.

More so than in his past adventure of hitchhiking on the rails, it must have been an ordeal to take the necessary steps to bring himself to Los Angeles. He didn't have useful industry contacts, although he had a friend who negotiated a job for himself as story editor on a successful TV series. Maybe he, Gus Van Sant Jr., could make something happen for himself in California.

▼

HOLLYWOOD in the mid-1970s was well past its glory days. Just as the film industry had changed so much since its Golden Age of the 1930s and 1940s, so the "magical" town, where aspiring actors, filmmakers, screenwriters, and others gravitated, had become seedy. Celebrities no longer frequented this debilitated tourist Mecca, having long since confined themselves to the environs of Beverly Hills, Century City, and other more exclusive neighborhoods. But the sleazy characteristics that might have turned off many others appealed to Van Sant. He had had his share of gracious living in fine homes. There was something in his nature that gravitated to tougher environments where life was lived more rawly, more openly, and without that ingredient he so disliked—pretense.

Van Sant might have chosen to reside in West Hollywood, a center of West Coast gay lifestyle. But that turf was pricier than Hollywood apartments. Moreover, Boys Town, as the conclave was tagged, was filled with young, handsome, and often pretentious residents who were more thoroughly devoted to an open gay way of life than Gus most likely could or wanted to handle at the time.

Instead, the East Coaster chose to live on Grace Avenue in one of the many rundown small apartment buildings in central Hollywood, a few blocks north of the once illustrious Hollywood Boulevard. (This is the famed street that boasts the majority of the Walk of Fame with its sidewalk-embedded, star-shaped tributes to past media notables.) It was not too long before Gus discovered—and acknowledged—the obvious about this constantly busy thoroughfare. There was more to be seen on the Boulevard than the parade of gaping tourists searching for vestiges of the area's once glamorous image, and the rash of senior citizens and immigrants who lived in the area because they required inexpensive housing. For among the Hollywood Boulevard throng there was a steady flow of scruffy runaways, male hustlers, female prostitutes, derelicts, and drug addicts. These outcasts—especially the tough-acting young guys who sold their bodies to men for ready cash—appealed to the voyeur in Gus.

As Van Sant described to *Premiere* magazine's Ralph Rugoff for an October 1991 interview, "I was fascinated by this scene. It was a secret world I knew nothing about." He expanded on this revelation to *Rolling Stone*'s David Handelman: "It was like watching another life that was as removed from my life as somebody in another country and yet it was happening simultaneously in our society."

Soon Gus developed the habit of lingering over his three P.M. dinner at his favorite Hollywood Boulevard haunt—Johnnie's Steak House—where he could get a basic steak and potato dinner for around $3. He'd dawdle over his meal as he watched endlessly the parade of street people. He was particularly drawn to the often grubby male hustlers as they patrolled the streets looking for customers, for drugs, or merely a cheap way to kill a few hours till "something" happened.

"You could see all this stuff on the street—the street hustlers and everything. You'd go to a video arcade and the kids that were playing the games were the street hustlers. And you could see that their world was built around this video game. The video game to them was the same as Johnnie's to me: it was their only means of escape. Otherwise they were really oppressed humans. They had their enemies, the police, their dates and these video games. Within my world was this world, but I was shy and never talked to any of them."

The lure of this fascinating lifestyle so sparked Van Sant's interest (above and beyond the sexual allure) that he toyed with the notion of writing a story or screenplay about the subject. He began taking copious notes that, perhaps, made him feel less guilty about his voyeuristic activities at Johnnie's Steak House, the video arcades, and the other male prostitute haunts he probably sampled in the midtown Hollywood neighborhood such as the rundown hustler bars.

▼

AFTER weeks of participation in his circumspect Hollywood world, Van Sant finally took the next step to fill his days and, hopefully, to replenish his bank account. Buoyed by the optimism and resiliency of the young, he began to make the rounds looking for work. "It was great. I went to a lot of places and met a lot of people and got a lot of advice, but again, there was no work to be found." After eight months of this, he was starting to get discouraged and needed to take more direct action.

As so often occurred in Van Sant's life, what happened next seemed on the surface more like a bit of good luck generated on the spur of the moment than any part of a calculated master plan. Much as Van Sant has suggested to the media over the years that a great deal of his professional (and private) life choices are spontaneous, that assessment is tinged by his own romantic fantasy of himself being an impetuous soul.

A case in point is the career threshold act he made at this juncture. For starters, Van Sant was not a casual visitor to Tinseltown and he certainly was not without credentials. He was young and agreeable looking (two prized articles of trade in the entertainment industry), well bred, intelligent, and a graduate of an esteemed eastern college with a degree in film. While he had not attended one of the famous cinema schools like New York University or the University of Southern California, his existing range of knowledge about filmmaking, (experimental) cinema history, music, photography, and writing all combined to make him an appealing, moldable commodity—if given the chance. Furthermore, once a person got beneath Van Sant's veneer of cordiality and the seeming conventionality of this serious-looking individual with deep, penetrating eyes and a strong jaw, a wry, slightly cynical soul was displayed, one who had a unique and bright slant on life.

▼

ONE day Gus decided to phone Ken Shapiro, a man he had never met. Who and why Shapiro?

Thirty-two-year-old Shapiro was a native of South Orange, New Jersey. He made his acting debut when he was two. As a youngster he made several appearances on variety shows like *The Colgate Comedy Hour* and such dramatic anthology series as *Kraft Theatre* and *Studio One*. Once adolescence kicked in, his show business career faded. He attended Bard College in Annondale-on-Hudson (just north of New York City) where he majored in comparative religion. He went on to Columbia University's Graduate School of Comparative Religion, but left to become an elementary school teacher in Brooklyn. In the mid-1960s he bought an early type of videotape recorder and soon found himself devising taped satires of TV shows and commercials.

Inspired by his hobby, Shapiro decided to return to the world of TV. With his former Bard College roommate, Lane Sarasohn, Shapiro rented an old theater in Manhattan's East Village and, in 1967, the world's first video theater debuted. At their showcase, they presented *Channel One*, a ninety-minute composite of often outrageous and randy TV lampoons and original materials. They were shown on TV monitors placed throughout the theater to the live audience. The novelty production was a hit and was later presented on hundreds of college campuses. Shapiro and his cohorts reshot the production onto 35mm color film. The resultant movie, *The Groove Tube* (1974), grossed over $30 million on a $400,000 investment. Hailed as the latest wunderkind of the film business, Shapiro promptly relocated to Los Angeles. He signed a development deal with Paramount Pictures and, with Lorne Michaels, began preparing a new project entitled *Ma Bell*.

Utilizing the Paramount payroll and their studio facilities, Shapiro gathered together a coterie of comedy sketch writers as he and his team set out to create another hit. By mid-1975, Michaels and some of the others from the group splintered off and went east where they created a sketch comedy pilot for what became the landmark TV series *Saturday Night Live*. Rather than join them, Shapiro chose to remain in Hollywood and pursue his follow-up movie. By the fall of 1976 he was still riding fairly high in the industry and Paramount was still expecting great things from this still hot commodity.

At this juncture, Van Sant contacted the filmmaker. Gus remembers the event: "I read this interview with Chevy Chase where he mentioned this old [college] friend of his named Ken Shapiro. I knew Shapiro's movies. Someone had told me early on in my journey to Hollywood that you could contact anyone you wanted, just call them up. You could call [Alfred] Hitchcock if you wanted and bug him for a job. I realized that that's what I should start doing. I decided to call Ken Shapiro as opposed to Hitchcock because that seemed less intimidating. I showed Ken some [of my] movies; he gave me a job. . . ."

Gus Van Sant had now officially joined the Hollywood filmmaking community.

▼

FOR someone as self-reliant and self-contained as Gus Van Sant Jr. it must have been a challenge of major proportions to suddenly become part of an adult frat party—which basically is what Ken Shapiro's writing team was at the time.

With Paramount essentially footing the bill for staff and space, Shapiro enjoyed being the lion tamer supervising scripters and gag creators who were given the task of coming up with the foundation for the long sought-after follow-up project to *Groove Tube*. Now that Lorne Michaels and so many of Shapiro's circle had departed to New York to work on TV's *Saturday Night Live*, Shapiro had gathered together a new coterie. One of the group was Pat Proft, born in Columbia Heights, Minnesota. He had been an actor regular on such early 1970s TV series as *The Burns and Schreiber Comedy Hou*r and *Van Dyke and Company*. While continuing acting assignments—mostly on TV—Proft had become part of Shapiro's writing crowd. Another Minnesotan in the crew was Tom Sherohman, who attended the University of Minnesota, then became an actor, and thereafter moved back and forth between Minnesota and California seeking acting gigs. A versatile talent, he had performed in Los Angeles at the Comedy Store, taught comedy classes, and directed dinner theater. By 1975 he was in Hollywood on a full-time basis. As he recalled for this author, hardly had he stepped off the plane in Los Angeles than his friend advised him that there was a job waiting for Sherohman with Shapiro. Others at the time in Shapiro's ever-revolving team of creative associates included Archie Hahn, Jessica Ita White, and Lenny Ripps, the latter having a longer tenure with this writing group than the others.

According to Sherohman, the ambiance was extremely loose and relaxed on the Shapiro team, whether the gang worked in a conference room at Paramount Pictures in Hollywood or at Shapiro's well-appointed home on Summitridge Drive in the hilly section north of Beverly Hills. Granted, says Sherohman, "Ken could be a very sarcastic fellow" but the atmosphere was one of camaraderie. It didn't hurt matters that a lot of the time members of the group were smoking marijuana to keep their minds fertile and creative, and the ambiance convivial.

When Gus came aboard the Shapiro bandwagon, he was entrusted to take notes of the daily script conferences and keep matters organized for this comedic think tank. For one as subtly methodical as Van Sant, this job did not present any problem. He found, for a time, that being part of a studio bureaucracy had its perks. "I was just completely absorbing the whole lore of Hollywood. The Paramount lot had a huge history, and you could just wander around and see remnants all over the place, of all the previous periods." As time progressed, however, the newcomer became a bit more jaded about his work for Shapiro: "He would have comedy writers come in day and night and come up with ideas and play off each other. It was really fascinating. I was the guy who rolled the joints. That's basically what I did . . . and I was paid by Paramount."

At the time, Shapiro's gang was still busily trying to work the kinks out of their *Ma Bell* project, detailing the life of an eighteen-year-old who tampers with the phone system (to get free calls) and an assortment of so-called phone freaks. As Van Sant would recall, "It was a pretty exciting project. Ken was a very countercultural sort of person who smoked joints during the day as he wrote, scheming on his next film project for Paramount. At the time, it seemed like the kids were taking over the studios. As Ken's assistant, I thought it was going to be Easy Street for me from then on, which it wasn't."

Soon after the novelty of the job wore off, Van Sant began to get frustrated—not so much at the relatively easy position, but at his own nature. As he explained about working with Ken and his squad, "There were 800 funny things happening a day and I would say one thing." It seemed his idiosyncratic sense of humor just did not jibe with the freewheeling group. For example, there was a sketch he wrote about cars that spontaneously exploded. He proudly presented it to the team, but it was poorly received. The Shapiro groupies said, "Well, why does the car blow up?" Deflated, Gus kept trying to explain to them: "It was really just to see things blow up. That was where the humor was."

It was during this period that Gus had the opportunity to upgrade his living conditions. (By now Van Sant was sharing an apartment on North Argyle Avenue in Hollywood with his longtime chum John Howell who had come to Los Angeles thinking he too might break into the film industry.) Only eight years older than Van Sant, Shapiro invited Gus to take up residence in the pool house at the Beverly Hills digs. Van Sant, wanting to save money for his own possible future movie projects, accepted the offer. He moved into the pool house, which meant that instead of having to commute to work, which often occurred in the evenings, he could take the little tram from his apartment to the main house higher up on the hill. (At one point while Van Sant was living in the pool house, childhood pal Jim Evans came out to Los Angeles and stayed with Gus at Shapiro's estate.)

As the months passed, Van Sant became more attuned to the politics of the studio system, but was still amazed that the talented Shapiro, who had a proven track record with *The Groove Tube*, couldn't get another project off the ground at Paramount. When studio executives seemed stalled on *Ma Bell,* Shapiro et al. began working on concepts for *Groove Tube II*, among others. But still the studio never gave Shapiro a go-ahead on any of his submissions.

As time wore on, Shapiro finally realized that, for whatever reasons, Paramount was never going to make one of his projects. He and his writing team—which now consisted of Tom Sherohman, Arthur Sellers, and others—embarked on a madcap trip on Shapiro's double-decker English bus/office, during which they came up with a new comedy script, *Modern Problems*. That project finally got green-lighted at Twentieth Century-Fox Films and Shapiro was back in the filmmaking business.

But the turnaround in Shapiro's fortunes did not benefit Van Sant. By now, Shapiro had decided to move to Brentwood and that was the end of Gus's upper-scale living situation. Then, as the crew was assembled for *Modern Problems* (which eventually was to star Chevy Chase and be released in 1981 after surviving the politics of several changeovers in regimes at Fox), there was no general assistant's spot on the team for Van Sant. Shapiro's wife had been given that berth and there were too many producers involved with the picture for Ken to give all his friends work on the picture.

Nonetheless, the years with Shapiro had not been a waste. The employment, which was not always full-time, left Van Sant with opportunities to continue drafting his own scripts as well as to mingle further with and observe the different strata of the Hollywood scene. Working with Shapiro had another effect. Witnessing how a studio could beat down an individualistic creative artist taught Gus a lesson about what happened to a talent who did not or could not play the Hollywood game properly. Understandably Shapiro was bitter about his ill treatment at Paramount and by the long process of enduring corporate intrigue as management changed repeatedly at Fox and further stalled *Modern Problems*. It was Shapiro who sternly warned Van Sant about the Hollywood studio system: "If I were you, I would just get out of it, because it can't work."

It was solid professional advice that Gus Van Sant took to heart.

THE PLAYER

I was working in an environment with all these comedians so I had this very incorrect view that I was one of them. I made the wrong type of attempt. Instead of playing against Hollywood, I was playing into it.

Gus Van Sant, 1997

DURING THE LATER 1970S WHILE Van Sant worked for Ken Shapiro, Gus did not abandon his research to become better prepared to be a filmmaker. Besides viewing as many movies as possible he felt he should study the scripts of famous pictures. He spent his spare time at the public library reading screenplays—they ranged from 1941's *Citizen Kane* to 1975's *Jaws*. One that continued to make a real impact on him was Stanley Kubrick's *A Clockwork Orange*. Discussing this 1971 landmark entry by his director icon, Gus explained, "It had a completely different format. The descriptions ran down one side in a single-word column that read like a poem, but it came out the exact same number of pages as a traditional screenplay. I thought, 'This is wild; you can do anything you want! It doesn't matter, because the movie is what counts." It was another breakthrough for the emerging craftsman.

Also in the late 1970s Gus had a few assignments as production assistant on feature films. He hated the menial work, but it was ready cash. One of the movies was *Skateboard* (1977), which did much of its location work out in the High Desert. Van Sant's boyhood chum John Howell was also employed on the low-budget production. Howell recalled for this author the time that Gus was charged with driving a recreation vehicle full of needed materials up a winding mountain road and the Winnebago somehow charged into the landscape. Van

Sant was so frustrated about the mishap that he was determined to avoid if at all possible such production assistant work in the future.

▼

FOR a few years now, one of Van Sant's ambitions was to make a screen rendition of William S. Burroughs Jr.'s short piece, "The Discipline of DE." He finally decided to do it now.

To fund his screen project, Van Sant relied on the income he was making as Shapiro's assistant. He also used the money he earned while on a trip to Portland, Oregon, where he worked as sound man for Penny Allen's locally filmed feature *Property* (1978) for which Van Sant's pal Eric Alan Edwards was the cinematographer. To cut down on expenses, Gus shot *Discipline* in 16mm black-and-white and sound. He relied on his growing network of contacts among film actors and technicians for advice and resources. His mentor Ken Shapiro provided the short subject's narration, and others of the Shapiro writer crowd participated: Tom Sherohman played the guest who visits the colonel, while Michael L. McManus was hired as Two-Gun McGee.

Cast in the lead was actor Frank Birney, a graduate of the American Academy of Dramatic Arts, whose career including working for the Army Security Agency in Europe. He had done theater with Tom Sherohman in Minneapolis and then had come to Los Angeles with a sketch revue entitled *Cheeks*. While breaking into the Los Angeles scene he was sharing an apartment with Sherohman in the 600 block of North Orange Drive, south of midtown Hollywood and just below Melrose Boulevard. Birney and Gus had become acquainted at one of Tom's many parties for the Minneapolis/Shapiro group at the Orange Drive apartment. Performer David Worden, also staying at Sherohman's digs at the time, was assigned to play the student in *Discipline*.

Within the nine-minute *The Discipline of DE*, the colonel, finding he has too much spare time, constructs his own version of the calendar. He divides the year into ten months of twenty-six days each. Before long the colonel has become an avid disciple of "DE" (i.e., doing easy) and presents for the viewer's edification several examples of how to accomplish daily tasks in a simple, relaxed manner. For example, it might be learning to guide the dustpan to the floor as if you're landing a plane, or the most expedient way to clean the bathroom sink toothbrush glass, or how to push your chair back from the table and stand up without hitting the table with one's legs. As the colonel espouses, "He who has learned to do nothing with his whole mind and body will have everything done for him."

The concluding sequence of the film short is set in a small western saloon where the colonel—now Wyatt Earp—advises a young gunslinger how to outshoot his opponent: "It's not the first shot that counts. It's the first shot that hits." (The western barroom scene was lensed at Tom Bergin's Irish Pub on South Fairfax Avenue in the Miracle Mile area of Los Angeles. The locale was another of Gus's favorite eating places and he persuaded the owner to allow him to film there.)

Today, in reminiscing about the making of *Discipline* with Van Sant behind the handheld camera, Frank Birney lights up with enthusiasm about the "fabulous" experience in making this short subject. Of Van Sant, he says, "He just knew what he was about, what he wanted, and how to get it from the actors."

In assessing *The Discipline of DE,* it is easy to see the variety of influences of the 1960s underground cinema that had so impressed Gus in previous years. In the context of Van Sant's later work, this short subject reveals repeatedly the filmmaker's delight in his own sense of what is truly absurd in our daily lives. Often accused by others of being far too serious, here Gus exposes his brand of offbeat humor, in which he obviously looks at the world through different eyes than most of us. If one appreciates that his view is tinted by a dislike of social hypocrisy, excessive regimen, and pointless decorum, then his approach to Burroughs's serious presentation of DE makes more sense. What results on-screen is not a philosophical discourse about the effects of the smallest action on one's life, but more the flavor of a 1940s Pete Smith or Robert Benchley comedic how-to short subject. *Discipline*, with its Zenlike attitude toward minimal effort in life, seems to reflect, as several have noted, the filmmaker's own approach to working.

Also of interest in Van Sant's brief celluloid essay is his delight in close-up shots of objects, such as focusing on a coffee cup, or a toothpaste-smeared toothbrush glass. (This fascination with minutiae would crop up again in close-ups of ordinary, everyday objects in his 1989 *Drugstore Cowboy*.) Sometimes the focus of Van Sant's handheld camera was on the male anatomy. One sequence in which the off-screen narrator is enthusiastically reciting his Doing Easy spiel, the subject under discussion is how to best open and close a zipper. Gus might have used any visual representation to illustrate the situation, but he depicted a young man zipping and unzipping his fly, with the camera closely focused on the DE student's crotch. Another of Van Sant's filmic techniques that would reappear later (particularly in 1991's *My Own Private Idaho*) is the use of on-screen title cards to progress the narrative flow from one episode to another.

If nothing else, *The Discipline of DE* was a marvelous learning experience for Van Sant to practice his evolving theories of story approach, film composition, direction, and editing. It also proved that he was capable of making a professional, albeit, short film. The concluding shootout sequence in the bar was the one that gave him most concern: "It was a traditional scene. A guy comes through the door and pulls his gun. I do remember sitting in that bar for a long time the night before, really concerned. It was technical, you know. It was hard. I drew a storyboard, about 10 shots. I was still new. I was afraid I wasn't going to get it right."

As would prove true with his later work, Gus fussed a great deal with *The Discipline of DE* in postproduction. He tinkered with the editing and inserted relatively simplistic special effects. Once "finally" done with the project, he was confident enough in the results to submit it to film festivals. To his delight, it was shown at the New York Film Festival in 1978 to a positive reception. Van Sant was even more excited when, through Ken Shapiro's connection with the *Saturday Night Live* crew and Gus's association with William S. Burroughs Jr., the short was almost aired on network television on an episode of *Saturday Night Live*, one in which Burroughs was scheduled to participate. Said Van Sant years later, "I thought I'd hit the big time. But they decided it was too long."

▼

THE *Discipline of DE* was a good professional starting point for Van Sant and it gave him a fresh sample to demonstrate his filmmaking capabilities. The short would be screened frequently over the years at film festivals, Van Sant retrospectives, and art house showings. Today, *The Discipline of DE* is available commercially for home viewing as part of the VHS tape *Since Stonewall,* an independent short film compilation promoted as "Ten great short films from the '70s, '80s, and early '90s, reflecting the feelings, fears, humor, artistry, and changing realities of gay America." (What seemingly qualifies *The Discipline of DE* for its homosexual thematic ties to this prerecorded tape collection is the lifestyle of Van Sant and that of the late William S. Burroughs Jr.)

▼

DURING Van Sant's stint with Ken Shapiro, Gus also contributed to a stage show. This work came about through the Minnesota contingent of Shapiro's writing team. Actors/comedians/writers Pat Proft and Tom Sherohman, who had performed together over the years, wanted a new showcase for themselves. As such they, along with Leonard Ripps (another of the Shapiro conclave), actor/writer Steve Stucker, and Brian Ann Zoccola (an actress who had studied at the Royal Academy of Dramatic Arts, had played off-Broadway, and been in revues and dinner theater on the road and in Los Angeles) put together a skit revue entitled *Rabies!* Directed by Sherohman and produced by Irv Letofsky (the husband of Zoccola), the film and video sequences for the sketch show were created by Gus.

At the time, the Kentucky Fried Players, a sketch group (of which both Proft and Stucker had been members) had been performing successfully in a seventy-seat theater in Century City, California, not far from the Hillcrest Country Club. The Players had made a deal to do *The Kentucky Fried Movie* (1977) and the theater space was sitting vacant. Letofsky subleased the building for *Rabies!*

Van Sant created some satirical commercial skits for *Rabies!* including "Psycho Shampoo." It satirized the famous shower scene of Alfred Hitchcock's movie *Psycho* (1960).

As Brian Zoccola recalled for this author, the show rehearsed for three to four weeks. While many of the live sketches would change both before and after the comedy opened, the film/video skits remained frozen. Zoccola describes the Van Sant of that period as a very quiet fellow. Regarding his method of directing, she remembers him as not the type to give direct feedback to the actors, but always allowed them to explore the acting possibilities themselves. She recollects, "A rare person. He'd see something unique and it was always a surprise. . . . The mirror he holds up is a fresh view."

Renaming the 'theater at 10303 West Pico Boulevard' Our Lady of Laughter, the troupe opened *Rabies!* on Wednesday, January 5, 1977, with two performances every Friday and Saturday evening. In the who's who section of the playbill for *Rabies!* Gus listed himself as a native of Portland, Oregon. The production received pleasant but mild reviews and lasted through March of that year. Gus's "Psycho Shampoo" bit survives as a bonus item on the DVD version of Van Sant's *Psycho* (1998).

▼

ALL through this period Gus was coming up with ideas for short subjects. One of these was *Fly Flame* about a "middle-aged white man's relationship with a house fly." Frank Birney starred in this one-minute entry, which was shot at Gus's apartment, the DeMille Manor on North Argyle Avenue above Franklin, where from his place the filmmaker had a bird's-eye view of Hollywood.

Meanwhile, in the many months since he had arrived in Los Angeles, Gus had never abandoned his absorption with Hollywood's gay underbelly. He began drafting different scripts that would revolve around the male street hustlers, their attitudes, and their ways of life. While he was trying to make his words and his vision jell, he happened upon—either for the first time or possibly anew—John Rechy's *City of Night*, the 1963 novel that dealt in poetic but brash terms with the world of male hustlers in New York City and Los Angeles. (Re)reading the novel, Van Sant decided—at least for the time being—that Rechy had told his tale so well that he should put aside his screenplays on hustlers. For a time Gus entertained the idea of optioning *City of Night* as a screen vehicle but didn't have the necessary funds to follow through on the notion.

▼

TAKING very much to heart Ken Shapiro's advice to mistrust studio bureaucracy, Gus Van Sant was determined to make a full-length independent movie that would *not* be tied to the whims of a major film lot. With his male hustler story line put aside, he turned to something to reflect some of his observations as a newcomer to Hollywood and what he had observed over the recent years.

At first he envisioned his narrative as a sort of Peter Pan in Tinseltown. Somewhere along the line it changed to a utilization of Lewis Carroll's *Alice in Wonderland*—with dashes of Voltaire's *Candide*—and the script emerged as *Alice in Hollywood*. It was a tongue-in-cheek, comic tale of an aspiring actress fresh out of college who grapples with the grubby world of talent agents, smut films, and talent agents. Unable to find backing for his economy production—which was to be shot in 16mm black and white, and sound—Gus allowed his father to come to the rescue with most of the picture's $20,000 budget.

In casting the lead, Van Sant turned to suggestions from character actor Frank Birney who had been in *The Discipline of DE*. It was he who introduced Gus to actress Anita Skinner. Born and raised in Kankakee, Illinois, she had studied theater at Illinois University at Champagne and Webster College (in St. Louis), had a scholarship to Julliard courtesy of John Houseman, and was a graduate of their four-year drama program. After a season (1975–76) at the Tyrone Guthrie Theater, she went to New York where she did stage and TV work. She earned a role (as Melanie Mayron's roommate) in Claudia Weill's well-received movie *Girlfriends* (1978) and was nominated for a Golden Globe Award for her screen performance.

Signed for the lead in *Alice in Hollywood*, Anita learned that one segment of the movie was a satire of the pornography filmmaking world and that she had a nude sequence in which her character makes love to a porno star named "Big Jim Jones." She agreed to do the scene *if* her actor-husband, T. J. Skinner, could play the part. Born and raised in Minnesota, T. J. had graduated from the Neighborhood Playhouse School of the Theater in New York, served in combat in Vietnam, and then began acting and directing in stage, radio, and television in Minneapolis, New York City, and Los Angeles. During the filming of *Alice*, T. J. would assist Van Sant in many capacities on the project besides acting.

Other roles in the project were filled by friend Tom Sherohman, actress Brian Ann Zoccola (who had been in *Rabies!*), Frank Birney, and an assortment of talent who answered casting calls or were referred by word-of-mouth. It was a long process—because of financial constraints—in getting the production ready for the shoot, which began in late October 1979.

As would happen on later (major) Van Sant film projects, much of what transpired on the set of *Alice in Hollywood* was inspirational at the moment, with Van Sant giving his cast a good deal of acting freedom. Adding to the impromptu nature of this nonunion project, Gus took advantage of real-life situations and incorporated them into his movie. For example, one day they came across a fender-bender traffic accident on Hollywood Boulevard—the locale for many of the movie's scenes. Van Sant whipped into action, got his camera ready, put his key actors in place, and yelled "action!" Poof—the unstaged, uncostly scene was now part of the narrative. Another time Gus read that the premiere for Bette Midler's movie *The Rose* (1979) was set for a Century City cinema. With cast and crew brought to the site, Van Sant filmed such celebrities as Peter Falk, Raquel Welch, Sally Kellerman, Milton Berle, and Hugh Hefner as they paraded down the red carpet and into the theater. After the notables had gone inside and before the crowd dispersed, Van Sant shot scenes of *his* film's leading man (Mark Pixler) walking down the carpet and waving to cast members, including Anita Skinner, who had jammed in front of the actual spectators.

For the scenes within the Cinema Motel (rooms $6–$8 nightly), Van Sant used his own apartment located in midtown Hollywood not far from Franklin Avenue and Gower Street. Even Gus's beloved Johnnie's Steak House on the Boulevard made it into the film as the site of several restaurant scenes (although for the interior of the eatery the more upscale Masquers Club allowed the crew to shoot there). The TV Western (*The Roughnecks*) within the movie was lensed in Griffith Park, not far from the famed Griffith Observatory. If any locale was the "star" of the production, it was Hollywood Boulevard and its characters parading along the busy street.

As T. J. Skinner recalled for this author about Van Sant: "The kid was absolutely fearless with his technique." Skinner still remembers the time during the making of *Alice* that he wheeled the filmmaker down Hollywood Boulevard in a "borrowed" hospital wheelchair used as a dolly for the shot Gus wanted. Says Skinner: "Can you picture Gus sitting in a wheelchair, holding the camera for a terrific dolly shot? With the actors doing a walking scene. Amazing!"

The bare bones of the *Alice in Hollywood* plot concerns fledgling actress Alice, coming to Tinseltown from Phoenix, Arizona. Her efforts to gain auditions leads nowhere. She is befriended by a sarcastic legless Vietnam veteran (Sam Diego) who begs change on Hollywood Boulevard. While treating herself to lunch one day at a landmark Hollywood restaurant, Alice chats with the customer at the next table. He turns out to be hunky but jaded TV star Roy Brown (Mark Pixler). He discourages her about any chance of success in the industry, and his prognostication proves to be true—for the time being. Out of desperation she appears in a porno movie with Big Jim Jones (T. J. Skinner) as her co-lead. Later, she wangles an audition with a lecherous filmmaker (Nigel Bullard) who miraculously chooses her to play opposite Roy Brown in a new TV movie. In the process of gaining stardom, she forgets the simple folk on the Boulevard who knew her before she became famous.

Since every penny of Van Sant's budget went into the production costs of this nonunion vehicle, the cast agreed to work for free, hoping that the finished film would be sold for distribution and that industry exposure would result in possible future income. In typical indie style of the day, expenses were minimized whenever possible. For example, from his apparel industry contacts, Gus Van Sant Sr. (the film's financier) provided Anita Skinner's changes of wardrobe. Makeup was generally handled by the actors. Typically, the cast's dressing room was the backseat of someone's car or a deserted stairwell of a nearby building. Costly city permits for shooting were ignored.

What really motivated the cast and technicians on their daily (and evening) grind to complete the movie project was, as Anita Skinner says, the dedication of Van Sant to the film and the "charisma of his passion." She recalls that whenever they had conference meetings at his rundown Hollywood apartment, she was struck by the barrenness of the place where he lived alone. In his bedroom there was a little cot where he slept and the rest of the room was brimful with his editing table and stacks of film reels and other moviemaking equipment. It was obvious to Anita and T. J. that Gus was totally committed to guiding his ambitious project to completion. This dedication inspired the couple and other participants in the production to do their utmost to fulfill their unpaid chores. Brian Ann Zoccola, seen as the casting director in *Alice,* today still has vivid memories of how quiet a person Gus was at the time, but who was "one of those people when I first met him I liked him." She recalls how relaxed he made it for the actors on the improvised set. Occasionally when the *Alice* group had time to kick back, they would smoke pot, or if money was "plentiful," Gus would treat them to dinner at Johnnie's Steak House.

By Thanksgiving, the film had wrapped. (Van Sant had run out of money to do any additional lensing.) Along the way many scenes in the "final" screenplay had been dropped and others added. That was nothing unusual for many filmmakers, but it would become a trademark of Van Sant as the years went on. In his methodology, nothing was ever "final"—even at the time of the first screenings.

On Monday, November 26, 1979, Gus invited the cast and crew to his apartment for a showing of the *Alice in Wonderland* footage. The screening started at about six P.M. and lasted until around three A.M. the next morning. Exhausted but pleased with the results, the invitees left. Then began the editing process, which dragged on for several months as Gus continually tinkered with the film and took time out for working for a paycheck to keep him going in Hollywood.

As time wore on Van Sant finished—temporarily, in his viewpoint—with the postproduction work on the picture. Through Ken Shapiro, then at Twentieth Century-Fox making *Modern Problems*, Gus was able to show his footage to an assemblage of industry people on the lot, but nothing developed from this networking. Van Sant tried to enter the film in both the Los Angeles and the Atlanta Film Festivals but was turned down. "So I felt like it didn't have a market at all. It was supposed to be a feature-length film, and I didn't think it really held up at an hour and a half, so I cut it down to forty-five minutes. It was a kind of ridiculous comedy, which is a dangerous area to work in. Even the big-budget films that attempt the ridiculous comedy genre fail. I was trying something too difficult, although I didn't know it at the time."

As 1980 wore on he worked further with *Alice* but regardless of what he did to the project nothing came together. He tried his now customary technique of swapping scenes around to change the narrative flow, but the featurette remained seemingly unsalvageable.

When he had commenced the project, Van Sant had envisioned that "it was a comment on Hollywood friendships; the way I guess I'd learned to know them. How people climb up a certain ladder and have business relationships instead of personal ones. It had that side to it, but it wasn't really stressed. The other side was this absurd comedy that was supposed to be a take-off of *Alice in Wonderland*." As time moved on, he concluded that the problem with *Alice* was that "I made the wrong type of attempt." His picture was too derivative of typical Hollywood fare; it lacked sufficient individuality.

Eventually, perfectionist Gus would trim down the forty-five-minute *Alice* to a twenty-nine-minute entry and transfer it to VHS. He then gave Anita and T. J. Skinner a copy of the featurette. Viewing that heavily edited footage today, the narrative is understandably choppy; by today's standards the indie-filmmaking style of *Alice* is largely unsophisticated. The haphazard production values of the film go without saying. Nevertheless, there are many pure Van Sant trademarks within the truncated *Alice*.

For example, despite the catch-as-catch-can nature of the narrative and the naïveté of the remaining story line, several of the performances stand out. Anita Skinner is quite natural and persuasive in many of her scenes as the rags-to-riches screen heroine, and Sam Diego as the handicapped Vietnam vet gives a solid performance along the lines of a restrained Jerry Stiller. If the characters of the unsavory porno filmmaker and the tyrannical TV director are clichés, they are nevertheless colorful. So are the Boulevard folk seen strolling along the street. The weak link in the acting is that of Mark Pixler as the TV star. He lacks the charisma and the physical presence to make the role work on any real level.

In Alice's porno sex scene within the film there is a humorous take on the usual grinding and panting of the coleads. She lies immobile on the floor and her on-camera sex partner (T. J. Skinner) pumps away on top of her. The camera focuses largely on their faces, which gives the sequence a peculiar but intriguing intimacy. Alice's other on-screen sexual coupling is with the randy TV director. Rather than show the activity in full view, the scene is broken up into flashes of light in the darkened bedroom as the twosome go through their motions, with most of the dialogue spoken in the dark or with the camera away from their supposedly naked bodies. (This foreshadows the famous still-shot montage of the ménage à trois in *My Own Private Idaho*.) Again intrigued with lensing close-ups of inanimate objects, Van Sant includes a zoom shot of the previously discussed vibrator that lies on the floor near the bed the next morning.

And within the abbreviated *Alice*, Van Sant plays with the flow of the chronology. For example, in the midst of Alice's restaurant luncheon, the story line jumps back and ahead as her career efforts falter and then succeed. There is an extended sequence of the cowboy star posing for a still camera as it grabs various facets of his face (none of which are very attractive). Later there is a parallel photo shoot of Alice as she becomes attuned to the lens and makes it her friend.

Interestingly, and not so unexpectedly, in the surviving footage of Hollywood Boulevard street life the camera pans through the crowd of passersby and remains focused on a hustler type (bare-shirted, wearing walking shorts and a cowboy hat) as he meanders down the street shaking his booty. Within this film, which originally started as a study of male Hollywood street hustlers, that is all that survives of that theme in the "director's cut."

Years later in discussing this abortive, much-referenced, but never publicly shown production, Gus Van Sant would sum up: *"Alice in Hollywood* had been a really big disappointment; that just crushed me. But maybe it was good that the first one wasn't successful—I probably learned from that." He also hastened to remind the interviewer: "I never got my money back from that."

HOME AGAIN

The subjects of my films have sort of . . .
they were about gay characters. They
were what brought me out of the closet.
. . . Yeah, the films brought me out. That's
what my interest was. These gay characters and gay stories. And I was gay. My
private life became my public life.

Gus Van Sant, 1998

DURING THE EXTENDED postproduction phase of *Alice in Hollywood* in 1980, Gus Van Sant grew more discouraged about the prospects of his unfinished film. Whenever his finances grew perilously low he took tem-porary jobs to keep himself going. When he had "spare" time he went to movies and continued his scriptwriting chores. In 1993 he told interviewer Graham Fuller about one of them: *"Mister Popular,* originally called *The Projectionist,* was a story about a high school kid who influences his fellow students by sub-liminally introducing advertising images through audio-visual techniques. He gets the student body under his control and becomes the most popular kid in the school. I wrote it while I was living in Hollywood as the next project that I was going to do after *Alice."*

▼

ONE might have thought that Van Sant, now in his late twenties and on his own in Hollywood, would have put some of his reserve behind him and experi-mented in the active homosexual social/sex life available in Los Angeles. This was the pre-AIDS era, before sexual coupling became so potentially dangerous. As gay rights accelerated in the 1970s, many gays in all walks of life had come out of the closet, especially in the City of Brotherly Love, which, like New York City and San Francisco, was a gathering place for those with an alternative lifestyle. By this point, L.A. police harassment/entrapment had lessened considerably, making many gays far less paranoid about socializing openly at gay gathering spots. The bar/club scene was thriving in upscale West Hollywood and on a lesser level in proletarian Hollywood. (Gus's various apartments in midtown Hollywood were not far from such blue-collar gay hustler bars as The Spotlight, My House, and The Gaslight.) And whether on Hollywood Boulevard or Selma Avenue in central Hollywood or along Santa Monica Boulevard from Hollywood to the fringes of West Hollywood, any hour of the day or night, there was a constant procession of young, hunky street hustlers available for whatever the paying customer had in mind. For those inclined to the outdoors, there was the gay section of nearby Venice Beach where the sandy expanses were packed with attractive homosexual men.

In discussing this transitional period of his life, the film director told Robert Hofler (the *Advocate*): "I wasn't really out in the 1970s. At the time I lived in Los Angeles. From the stories that friends of mine who were into the club scene there told me, it sounded incredibly wild and crazy—lively, late, exciting." When asked by Hofler if the enticing tales about gay clubs didn't intrigue him sufficiently to venture forth, Gus responded, "No, it really wasn't a life that I was connected with. . . . I was just doing my films. I was locked in my own film world. And I was writing scripts."

So for the time being, apparently, Van Sant, focused and concerned about the course of his professional future, kept his emotions and sexual urges largely repressed. He evidently continued to sublimate his needs and interests into being a heavy-duty observer of male hustlers/street people as they navigated their defined world of particular Hollywood streets and gathering spots (such as video arcades and open-air fast-food stands). He seemingly contented himself with living voyeuristically through his scripts, his in-progress *Alice in Hollywood*, his other film shorts of the period, his photography, and his music writing/playing.

When Van Sant was asked by the *Advocate*'s Hofler when he did finally unlock himself from the sexual closet, the moviemaker responded, "Probably when I was around 30. I was a late bloomer."

▼

IF Van Sant was passionate about his filmmaking, about being loyal to his widening circle of friends, he also remained faithful to his movie director idol Stanley Kubrick. When the master's latest picture, *The Shining*, an adaptation of Stephen King's thriller starring Jack Nicholson, opened at Mann's Chinese Theatre on Hollywood Boulevard in late May 1980, Gus walked down to the famed cinema from his nearby apartment for the nine A.M. showing. He repeated this routine for a week. He hoped Kubrick's latest offering would inspire and instruct him, even though he didn't think it was "such a good movie."

▼

AS 1980 wore on Gus was at a low emotional ebb: "I got really fed up with L.A. I was writing screenplays on spec that weren't selling. I was getting editing jobs when I could. I was mostly working as a temporary secretary." It was not the way Van Sant had pictured his future as he approached the age of thirty.

It was at this juncture that Gus Van Sant Sr. stepped into the situation. Not that the Van Sants had ever been out of the picture. It had long been weighing heavily on the father that for so much of his children's maturation—especially his older child's—he had been on the road for business or heavily focused on his corporate rise in the business world. As the years went by, he regretted that new career opportunities had forced his family to relocate so many times and that his children had been pulled out of so many schools and had to go through the process of making new friends so often. On the other hand, as he says today, if he had not chosen that life path, the Van Sants would not have set up house in Portland, Oregon, which proved to be such a meaningful chapter in Gus Jr.'s life.

Whatever the family thought or assumed of Gus Jr.'s lifestyle, it was difficult for the parents, especially Gus Sr., to conceal their concern of when and how their son was going to settle down in life. More so for the business world–oriented father than the genteel, artistic Betty Van Sant, it was hard to envision that their son's hoped-for moviemaking career would beat the odds of likely anonymity and financial insecurity. The Van Sants had showed their faith in their offspring when they helped to finance the $20,000 for *Alice in Hollywood*, but so far that investment had not paid dividends—either financially or professionally—for their son.

By now, Gus Sr. had left Warnaco and had spent a few years as Group Vice President at Consolidated Foods Corp. Eager for fresh challenges, he had inaugurated a new business venture. He took over a women's sportswear firm called Paula Saker & Co., which had an office at 530 Seventh Avenue in New York City and its computer/warehousing in Secaucus, New Jersey, directly west of midtown Manhattan. Gus Sr. kept his son abreast of the new project—now called G. G. Van Sant & Co. One day, after sensing how at loose ends his boy was in Hollywood, he made a request to his son for "one year of his time." He wanted Gus Jr. to return to the East to spend twelve months working with his father at this new bare-bones enterprise.

Years later, Gus Jr. would say offhandedly, "When my father offered me a job working in his warehouse in New Jersey I realized that made about as much sense as working as a temporary secretary in L.A." (According to Gus Sr.: "the idea was to have someone there in whom you could place total trust. . . . There were two people in the warehouse, plus additional help, when needed. Gus was in charge of that.")

Yet, at the time, it must have been a terribly discouraging ordeal for the budding filmmaker to admit this (temporary) defeat and, essentially, go crawling home at the age of twenty-eight. But with *Alice in Hollywood* in limbo (and the

$20,000 and toil it had cost preying on his mind), he had few current prospects in Tinseltown. Then, too, there was the disillusioning example of observing his talented mentor/past employer Ken Shapiro fighting a lopsided (and losing) battle with studio bureaucracy to keep his unique viewpoint and career alive within the cannibalistic movie capital. All in all, it was a bad time for Gus Jr. From a mixture of respect for his parents and a strong sense of frustration and despair, he finally agreed to come back to Darien, Connecticut.

His Hollywood friends bid Gus good-bye, many of them probably wondering if one day they too would be hightailing it back home. Among the well-wishers were Anita and T. J. Skinner. Today, jumping back in time two decades, Anita can still recall T. J. and her waving farewell to Gus as he drove out of town in his jam-packed old BMW. Anita says it must have taken a lot of courage for Van Sant to return to the home nest.

▼

ARRIVING back in New England, the once independent Gus Van Sant Jr. had to slip back into his role of dutiful son. Living in his parents' spacious home—even with his own quarters above the family garage—it must have been difficult to maintain his independence as an adult. Add to this situation Gus Jr.'s alternative lifestyle and the fact that his world of creative arts was so distant from that of the world of women's apparel and entrepreneurship.

True to his word, Gus Jr. began working at the clothing warehouse in Secaucus, New Jersey (about fifty-five miles and a little over an hour's commute each way from Darien). As a general assistant to his father, he did his best to be productive during the day. But says Gus Sr. today, he can still visualize looking over at wherever his son might be in the middle of some task and he would observe Gus Jr. stopping to make notations to himself in a notebook.

While Gus had surrendered himself in physical form to the business world, in spirit he was still a practicing screenwriter/filmmaker. Like any good scenarist he was always writing new scripts or refining works-in-progress. One of his current projects was *Corporate Vampire:* "It was about a corporation that had a very exclusive higher echelon of presidents and vice presidents that was all vampires and a man who is promoted and initiated into their group. It's a *Rosemary's Baby* kind of thing." Another item was *Fizzle*, the tale of a once honor student who stumbles into becoming the town fool. (Other topics explored in his scenarios over these years involved "country clubs, commuters, and debutantes.")

Indubitably Van Sant Sr. must have hoped that somehow Gus Jr. would become more pliable to entering the business world—one where the father could truly help his son with advice, networking connections, and productive support. That, however, was not to be. As the senior Van Sant has recalled, "I asked him to help me out for a year and he did. It was 364½ days and I'm sure Gus didn't like a day of it."

Unbeknownst to his parents, Gus Jr. had gotten in touch with Frankie Cadwell at the prestigious Cadwell Davis ad agency in New York City where he had worked one summer more than a decade before. With his talent, he lucked out. He was hired as assistant production manager at the salary of $44,000 a year. The fact that he had an honest-to-goodness "real" job pleased the Van Sants very much.

At the ad firm Gus was soon assigned to such accounts as NoSalt and Pretty Feet 'n' Hands, not exactly items to truly inspire the creative, individualistic artist. In typical low-key fashion, he later described his agency tasks: "I was a junior producer. I did the technical work of booking mixing stages, that sort of thing. It wasn't really that important, what I was doing. I organized the company's slide show and stuff like that."

▼

BUT with his aptitude and creative flair he did well in the position—at least as far as his employer was concerned. On the employee's part, it was all part of a bare-bones master plan: "The idea was to spend money on getting to work and lunch and save everything else." As he phrased the career strategy, it was "a long-shot bet on my future." Later, he acknowledged about this monastic, close-to-the-vest phase of his adult years: "I wasn't living any kind of life."

When not working or writing screenplays or doing photography, Gus kept his filmmaking skills intact by executing film shorts that he envisioned as a visual diary. Perhaps, one day they could be spliced together to make a long chronology of his life. Among the autobiographical 16mm shorts he made during the early 1980s in Connecticut was *My Friend*, a three-minute entry in color in which he discusses a sexual attraction to a good friend. Narrated in a deadpan funny style, it still has a daunting side, as the viewer is told: "I'm falling in love with a guy. So that's frightening, isn't it? It's frightening to me?" Another entry, *Where Did She Go?*, also in color, is a three-minute short inspired by the death of Gus's paternal grandmother Dorothy Green Van Sant who, on her deathbed in Westerville, Ohio, gave her beloved grandson marketing advice: "Buy IBM." In addition, Gus made *Nightmare Typhoon* (aka *Hello, It's Me*), a seven-minute, black-and-white mix of fun and peril as an anonymous telephoner plagues Van Sant with spooky persistence.

As if these off-work creative activities were not enough, Gus Jr. made time to expand on his musicianship. He took several of his self-composed numbers and recorded them, with him playing the guitar, providing the vocal, and blending in occasional percussion, and an array of sound effects ranging from the sound of rain and thunder to a plane taking off. Most of the songs captured at home in 1982 and 1983 would be issued by Pop Secret Records (Portland, Oregon) in late 1997 on an album (29:58 minutes long) entitled *18 Songs About Golf*. As the title indicates, all the cuts are related to golf (his father's passion and Gus Jr.'s interest). Divided into two groupings ("The Front 9" and "The Back 9"), the numbers (reflecting the influence of his association with the Talking Heads at the Rhode Island School of Design back in Providence) deal with aspects of life using golf terminology and analogies.

In between long guitar riffs, Gus sings—in an okay but vocally limited range—of "the course of love." In "Ladies Day" he records of the first time he ever heard a woman yell "fuck you" on the green. His persona comes most alive in the enthusiastic "The Elvis of Golf Courses." In "My Caddy Sings," about a businessman with his vocalizing golf bag carrier, there are moments when the descriptions almost reflect moments from the life of Sr. and Jr. Van Sant. One gets the impression listening to the rather short cuts that, as a youth, Van Sant may have had the usual aspirations of being a rock star, but that as he reached his thirties, he was having more modest expectations from his musical interests. Yet, the fact that he chose to express himself in song and verse, record it, and allow the numbers to be issued later, says a good deal about the conflicting worlds of the private and public Gus Van Sant Jr. On the one hand, he was the shy, somewhat outwardly repressed individual. while on the other, there beats within him a multitalented artist determined not to let his retiring nature get the better of him. It is as if the conviviality traits of his southern stock and the conservative taciturnity of his New England years were still warring within.

By the time *18 Songs About Golf* was released for public consumption, Van Sant had become a well-known entity. Thus, this modest album was reviewed. Matt Ashare (*Boston Phoenix*) wrote an appraisal under the headline: "Gus Van Sant; Incredibly Strange Music." He weighed, "The rough-around-the-edges lo-fi aesthetic of *18 Songs* places Van Sant the musician roughly a decade ahead of the items, since bedroom four-tracking didn't come into vogue till the early '90s. But his ties to a musical past are also apparent—his deadpan, out-of-tune vocals, for example, are very Lou Reed (think of Lou doing some of his sillier genre excursions, like the Velvets' 'Lonesome Cowboy Bill'). And the simple, rather goofy premise brings to mind another Reed disciple, Jonathan Richman."

▼

GIVEN his upbringing and his personality, it was not surprising that twenty-something Gus Jr. kept many things from his family. For example, an Oregon friend (filmmaker Penny Allen) had once given him a copy of a small book, *Mala Noche,* written by Walt Curtis (the street poet of Portland) and published in 1977 by a small press. It was a passionate—sometimes lyrical, sometimes graphic—autobiographical account of Curtis's sexual infatuation with the young Mexican boys (undocumented aliens) existing on Portland's skid row, in particular Curtis's lust/love for one of them, a teenager named Johnny. Gus Jr. was fascinated by the honesty and ardor of the text, but did not feel comfortable leaving it in open view in his home quarters: "It was the kind of thing that I remember keeping hidden under my bed because it was real explicit sexually and it just seemed like a dirty book."

Rereading the book over the months did several things for the restless Van Sant. It made him think again of his (so far) abortive film scripts on street hustlers in Hollywood and how he had long wanted to picturize this world so unfamiliar to most people, whether straight or gay. It rekindled his longtime attraction to the ambiance of Portland, which was in many ways so very different from life in Darien, Connecticut, or even Los Angeles. Finally, it prompted Gus into making the decision to return to Oregon and somehow follow through on the idea that had been brewing within him.

Somehow he would film *Mala Noche*. And unlike *Alice in Hollywood* he would in some way make sure that this production got well beyond the editing room.

THE GREAT NORTHWEST

Things were cheaper in Portland. I had friends who were filmmakers up there who had equipment. At the time the TV news was still being shot on film, so it was easy to get extra stock if you knew somebody.

Gus Van Sant, 1997

ALWAYS ONE TO HOLD HIS own council, in late 1983 Gus Van Sant sprung the last-minute news on his family that he was quitting Cadwell Davis Partners. He told them he was moving back to Portland where he intended to adapt a book (*Mala Noche*) to the screen. His parents begged him to remain in the East and to keep his Cadwell Davis job. But Gus Jr. was determined. He had "spent as much time as I could stand" at the Manhattan firm.

The day approached for Gus Jr. to leave for the West Coast. His aged 1972 BMW 2002 was stuffed with his "essentials." Gus Sr. and his wife Betty looked at the overloaded maroon vehicle and then glanced at one another in dismay. They quickly offered their elder child Gus Sr.'s gray BMW 528 car that sat in the garage. Before Gus Jr. drove off, the father, always the astute businessman and certainly remembering the fate of *Alice in Hollywood*, reminded his son once again, "Whatever you do, don't put your own money into the film."

▼

FOUNDED in 1845, Portland is Oregon's largest city. (The area was once the home to Native American tribes who were dispossessed by the settlers.) An industrial port city in northwest Oregon, it is located on the Willamette River near its convergence with the Columbia River. A supply depot for gold rush participants of the 1860s and 1870s, Portland later became noted as a lumber port. During World War I, and more so during World War II, there was a huge influx of blue-collar workers coming to the city to work on Swan Island, the center of shipbuilding and repair.

From the 1970s onward, the City of Roses, as Portland is also known, began dramatically to diversify its industries because many local natural resources (including timber and salmon) had been ill-used and were in danger of depletion. As a result manufacturing and (high) technology became increasingly important to the city, which continued to attract a diversified ethnic and socio-economic population.

At the time that Van Sant returned to Portland in late 1983, the city was embarking on a redevelopment program to revamp the riverfront, downtown square, and neglected areas in the city's southeast, north, and northeast sections. But in the early 1980s there were still pockets of the inner city that were more seedy than colorful and that remained full of transients, derelicts, and street hustlers. Portland was famed for its deeply rooted mix of hippie and pioneer cultures, its microbrewed beers (supposedly there are more breweries in Portland than in any city in Germany), and its NBA basketball team, the Trail Blazers. The city would also become famous as the world headquarters of Nike footgear.

In addition, Portland boasted a strong regional cultural community that encompassed novelists, poets, painters, and moviemakers. In the latter category were Penny Allen (*Property*, which Van Sant had worked on, and *Paydirt*) and Don Gronquist (*Unhinged*). Said Van Sant: "There was a group of filmmakers . . . who all had offices in this one downtown building. Included in the contingent was well-known animator Will Vinton who won an Academy Award for best animated short in 1974—he devised Claymation. I think that was the biggest deal that had ever happened in Portland, when Will won that award."

Summarizing his move to Oregon, Gus stated, "There was a small film community there with one or two cameras floating around and some aspiring filmmakers who I could probably get to help me out. So I moved there to make the movie [*Mala Noche*]."

When Van Sant arrived anew in Portland, it was not as a high school student living in his parents' home nor as a visitor seeing friends while on a summer vacation from the Rhode Island School of Design, nor as a freelancer handling sound for *Property*. He was thirty-one years old, he had come to this metropolis to stay, and he intended—somehow—to make a full-length feature film of *Mala Noche*.

This time when he showed up in town there was a sense that Gus was now his own person, no longer living in the shadows of his family or encumbered by his postcollegiate floundering. He seemed emancipated, both in knowing what he wanted to do with his life professionally and also fully aware of how he would do it. For reasons best known to him, he also had adopted a seemingly new attitude toward his sexuality. No longer was he closeted to himself or to others or sublimating his sexual urges in an overdrive of work. (That had been his path in Hollywood in the late 1970s. Several of his heterosexual pals from the Ken Shapiro/Minneapolis clique told this author that the question of Gus's sexuality back then was never discussed, let alone thought about, nor was it any sort of issue with the group. As they agreed, it just did not occur to them that sexual activity played a significant role in Van Sant's life at that time.)

Now Gus made no bones about being gay. Apparently it was a liberating situation that not only permitted him to be his true self socially but also allowed him to deal with his professional ambitions more effectively.

▼

ONE of Gus's friends from earlier times in Portland was William "Tiger" Warren, the son of an entrepreneur noted for cofounding in 1943 the Cascade Corporation, a major manufacturer of hydraulic attachments for lift trucks. When the firm went public in 1965 it had worldwide sales of over $234 million. While the older son, Robert Jr., followed his father into the corporate hierarchy of Cascade, gregarious, macho Tiger wanted more adventure. He was involved in financing the Hollywood-made *Skateboard* in 1977 (on which Gus had been a production assistant), then later helped to make the Portland-lensed *Rockaday Richie and the Queen of the Hop*, as well as the locally filmed *Unhinged* directed by Don Gronquist. In 1981, Tiger, about the same age as Gus, had begun the Macheezmo Mouse restaurant, which featured low-fat dishes to attract health-conscious customers (including aging baby boomers). Begun on a $5,000 investment, the venture was already quite successful and on its way to becoming a chain and a multimillion-dollar business. For a spell when Gus came to Portland this go-round he stayed in the converted carriage house apartment on the plush estate of Tiger's first wife located in the woody area of Dunthorpe, a suburban area of Portland about seven miles from the downtown area.

A reporter from the local *Willamette Week* visited Gus's abode in May 1984 and described it thusly: "Downstairs is the garage which is used to house horses and wagons. Upstairs is an apartment that was at one time the original Riverdale schoolhouse. (In the apartment was a school bell left over from prior times. There was also a squirrel who lived in the wall.) The roof slopes upward like a steeple. Scattered on the floor are cameras, editing equipment, musical instruments and Van Sant's oil painting. A skylight beams down on the work table." (The Gus Van Sant Jr. of this period was clean shaven and dressed in modest preppie fashion, often consisting of knit shirt, sports jacket, and slacks.)

Once settled in, Gus began networking among Portland filmmakers. As he told *Daily Variety*'s Paul Duran in 1996 of his moviemaking peers: "It was very close-knit and supportive. I remember hanging around all day with the same group, in offices, cafés, long lunches—talking about what we were going to make. There was one guy who was going to make a horror movie, another who was going to make a romance. Everybody had an angle, and so I guess my angle was that I was going to make a gay movie, which was totally weird at the time."

Keeping in mind his father's advice, Gus sought backing for his feature film. He kept hoping not to tap into his savings from his recent ad agency drudgery. But financing for his unconventional, gay-themed film was not forthcoming. While promoting his project and enduring the arduous networking—not always easy for the reserved Van Sant—he accepted any kind of work that would cover his bills. When he couldn't snare film editing jobs, he was industrious enough to do paintings (mostly landscapes with floating objects in the foreground: cows in one, sombreros in another), which he sold to nearby restaurants, hotels, and individuals. For a time he taught a film production class at the Oregon Art Institute and became friendly there with Bill Foster, who was later the director of the Northwest Film Center—where retrospectives of Van Sant's films would be screened over the years. Occasionally then, and more so in the late 1980s, Van Sant "did some really low-budget commercials, with $800 to $2,000 budgets."

Once into his Portland regimen, Van Sant continued making short subjects. In this era before video camcorders and digital cameras, making (Super) 8- or 16mm films was hardly an inexpensive process. But these few-minutes-long entries were within his budget if he scrimped in other ways. In 1984 one of his entries was *Nightmare Typhoon*. In his film miniatures he often appeared as a wry, deadpan narrator who introduced the footage that followed. (His appearances were not narcissistic-driven, but practical—it saved the bother/cost of adding additional actors to the projects.)

Naturally likeable and appreciated for his honesty and loyalty, Gus soon developed a coterie of local film industry friends, which led, eventually, to a showing of his short movies at Portland's Northwest Film Study Center. Kristi Turnquist (*Willamette Week*) reviewed the "retrospective." She noted that other area filmmakers (e.g., Penny Allen, Don Gronquist) had sought to approximate Hollywood-style production values, but Gus did not seem to want to bother. "In his autobiographical films, he's the star, he often holds the camera, he writes, directs, produces, and edits. His work also has a consistently idiosyncratic, personal style—a refreshing break from the stereotypical 'Northwest film' which has been criticized for dwelling on people and their relationship to their environment rather than their relationships to other people."

While others were already taking Gus's filmmaking seriously, he kept a perspective on his career achievements to date. He humorously told one local publication that he was thinking of editing footage from his short subjects into a weekly show to be aired on Portland cable access, sort of a soap opera vérité: "I'm thinking of calling it 'The Puddles of Portland,'" he grinned. On the subject of the newcomer's sense of humor, local cinematographer Eric Alan Edwards, a Catlin Gabel school classmate and a longtime friend of Van Sant said, "Gus has an odd sense of humor that smacks of cynicism, but he's an

enormously positive person. . . . Gus comes by his non-conformism very naturally. It's like the Tom Waits' quote, 'They all come from good facilities, they just
developed ways about themselves that weren't right.'"

Now that he was truly an emancipated adult, Van Sant apparently felt more
equipped to indulge in sexual liaisons and further explore sexual relationships
within the gay world. He told actor/friend River Phoenix in a 1992 interview
about a threshold affair that occurred in 1984: "It wasn't my first sexual relationship. It was the first one that was really like . . . See, I worked all those
other years, so I had to catch up."

As 1984 wore on and funding for *Mala Noche* had not materialized, Gus refused to be discouraged. As he informed one Portland journalist at the time:
"Success is only a phone call away, I always says. There's time. After all, William
Burroughs wasn't a success until he was 55." Besides, he added with perhaps a
bit of bravado, "The money's not a problem." What was the crucial issue now
was to find the teenager to play Johnny, the Mexican boy with whom the Walt
Curtis lead character becomes obsessed. "I could start setting things up tomor-
row if I found him today. It's sort of like looking for Scarlett O'Hara for *Gone
With the Wind.*"

When asked by a journalist to list his filmmaker heroes, Van Sant responded
with Stanley Kubrick and David Lynch (*Eraserhead, The Elephant Man*). He
elaborated: "Lynch is like Samuel Beckett. He doesn't need much, just a chair,
a man and another chair. That's something that attracts me quite a bit." He also
noted that it was Kubrick who predicted, "In the future, film will be really
cheap and everyone will be doing it and these heavy budgets will be a thing of
the past." And to demonstrate that his interest went beyond the film industry,
Gus played for the reporter a tape of songs he had written and performed.

▼

BACK in 1977 Gus had gone from Hollywood to Portland to work on Penny
Allen's locally made feature *Property*. The star of sorts of this production was
thirtysomething Walt Curtis, a local in-your-face poet, painter, book scout, and
preserver of the history of Oregon literature. This passionate, outspoken, and at
times eccentric man was called by many the "Unofficial Poet Lauriat of
Portland." As Van Sant would recall *Property*, which dealt with local counterculture society: "In the first scene that I remember working on, Walt was trying
to paint a watercolor but was constantly interrupted by a telephone sitting next
to him on the kitchen table. . . . Walt was pulled out of his real life by acting in
Penny's film. I think she had him talked into playing the lead, until he saw it
was way too much distracting work. . . . As Penny's film progressed, Walt became less a center-of-the-action character in *Property* and more one of the ensemble."

Almost from the start, Van Sant was curious about this bushy-haired, balding
individual whom Gus has described as "a kind of whacked-out Northwest version

of Woody Allen." Van Sant went to Penny to learn more about this unusual person. She handed Gus a copy of the small book *Mala Noche* and suggested he read it. Just as had been the case with John Rechy's *City of Night*, the film potential of Curtis's tale immediately struck Van Sant. As he explained later, "I pursued the project because of its precise yet wino blurry inside knowledge of life on the streets of a depressed Portland neighborhood, which every summer would turn into what Walt called 'Little Mexico.' Walt's writing was completely stripped down to the barest visual elements. Black and white observations about the Mexican's outlaw plight. Of trying to earn a decent living in America by working on farms picking fruit and vegetables."

As Van Sant saw it, in Curtis's book "there are strict observations of America's relationship to its southern neighbor. Exploitation being the central theme in overview of both the illegal migrant's existence in the city of Portland and in Walt's fascination and relations with Pepper and Johnny. A privileged American, Walt in a position of power, runs a grocery. He works the cash register and counts the money. He can hand out sandwiches for free, or charge full price. Privileged in their youth, the boys play games in the street with the police, laughing at getting caught, risking their lives. They can hand out their friendship, or remain elusive."

One can see how such narrative themes would intrigue Van Sant who had observed parallel types of street life in the "wilds" of Hollywood and who had sought to capture the special world of runaways/male prostitutes in his screenplay drafts. Then too, as moviemaker Penny Allen observed of Gus: "He's drawn to the underculture, probably because things are expressed there that were not part of his upbringing." She further elucidated, "It's not the bland emotionless façade that the corporate world represents to him."

It was not until a few years later, after Van Sant had failed in Hollywood with *Alice in Hollywood* and had licked his wounds back home in Connecticut, that he became impassioned by the desire to make *Mala Noche*. For one thing, "I thought *Mala Noche* was the kind of story that Hollywood wouldn't ever make and it was my new philosophy that my next project *should* be something they wouldn't ever make. That way you could keep it pure, simply in terms of the subject matter."

Then, too, always attuned to trends within the film industry, Van Sant was aware of the financial success of the groundbreaking foreign film *Taxi Zum Klo* [Taxi to the Toilet] (1981). This innovative autobiographical movie by director Frank Ripploh told of gay life in West Germany as it detailed the adventures of a randy schoolteacher. While sexually explicit, the ninety-eight-minute picture was also humorous, charming, and captivating.

As Gus observed, "*Taxi Zum Klo* was making a lot of money and it was so out there, and very straight audiences were going." As such, "I remember that being a cue that I could maybe film Walt's story and get my money back. When you're making a film you always wonder whether or not it will break even." And what appealed to Van Sant about *Mala Noche* was that its themes extended beyond its obvious initial audience. "It was unrequited gay love for sure. But I thought that if it was a good movie, it would relate to anybody—not solely to a gay audience."

Another of Van Sant's film marketing assumptions about *Mala Noche* was that "at gay film festivals there wasn't any product. Just seven-year-old Swedish and Dutch movies that just had one character that was gay. I thought that if *Mala Noche* just didn't work at all, if it didn't come off and was just a total disaster, it would still have this one small niche which would be at gay film festivals."

With all of the above in mind, Van Sant negotiated with Walt Curtis and acquired the screen rights to adapt *Mala Noche* for the screen at a reported cost of $500. Not a lot of money in film industry terms, but enough for Gus at the time to know that he was damn serious about making this gay love story happen on camera.

MAKING *MALA NOCHE*

I didn't really have a career to jeopardize when I made *Mala Noche*. I just thought it would be something interesting to see. . . . I think a lot of people were wondering what I was doing. I just sort of went ahead with it. I think it worked out.

Gus Van Sant, 1990

THROUGH THE PORTLAND CIRCLE of film-makers Gus Van Sant met journalist Daniel Yost. His brother Jack had helped Penny Allen raise $125,000 for *Paydirt*, her 1979 follow-up film shot locally (as had been *Property*, on which Gus had been the sound man). After his own initial efforts to find funding for *Mala Noche* brought no immediate tangible results, Van Sant turned to Jack Yost to ferret out potential backers for *Mala Noche*. Jack was only somewhat interested in the project because he thought the film's gay lifestyle subject matter—let alone that it was to be shot in black and white and 16mm—gave the movie limited audience potential. (On the final credits of *Mala Noche*, Jack would be listed as one of the production associates.)

As 1984 wore on, Van Sant grew impatient of waiting for show business angels to materialize. His anxiety led him to do just what his dad had advised against—he used his own savings to finance most of the $25,000 budget for *Mala Noche*. More precisely, as Van Sant Sr. candidly told the *Seattle Times* in 1990 about his son's savings: "every last penny went into the movie." And Gus Jr.'s sister, Malinda, living in Seattle in 1990, told the same journalist about the family's re-action when her brother announced that he was actually going to film *Mala Noche*: "Honestly I think we all thought he was a little crazy. But I don't think he had any self-doubt, because he has a vision, and to him it's going to work out."

By September 1984, with feedback from author Walt Curtis, Gus had written three screenplay drafts of *Mala Noche*. Van Sant's largest concern in the adaptation process was to keep the spirit of Curtis's original work, with the dynamics of its interwoven themes: gay lust, Latin-American machismo, exploitation of minorities, the changing power between participants in a one-sided emotional relationship, class structure, and contrasting cultures. As Van Sant has explained, "It's hard sometimes to stay true and not get lost. In the case of *Mala Noche*, Walt Curtis was around and he showed us some things that we could do that he remembered doing, that weren't in the book."

Neither ferreting out the funds nor translating the story into cinema terms proved to be the most difficult element in the preproduction process. The toughest hurdle was finding the right two people to play the Mexican youths. While there were numerous Hispanic (Americans) in the Seattle area—including migrant farmworkers and illegal aliens who wanted to get far away geographically from the Mexican/U.S. border—the typical Latin-American machismo (male pride) prevented most potential contenders from participating in this homosexually oriented film. Eventually, through casting calls and word-of-mouth, local amateur boxer Ray Monge agreed to tackle the role of Pepper.

With limited options, Van Sant finally selected Doug Cooeyate, a Pueblo Indian, to portray Johnny, the street teenager after whom the lead character lusts. Cooeyate was a Beaverton High School junior who played guitar with a heavy metal group called Raging Darkness. As Cooeyate informed a Portland publication at the time, it was his mother who suggested he audition for *Mala Noche*. "She saw it mentioned in the paper and said 'Do it!' I wandered into the Civic Theater and suddenly there was this skinny guy waving a Polaroid [taking test shots of auditioners]. It was Gus." Doug insisted to the media that the controversial angles of the story line did not trouble him. "It's human stuff, and the message is positive in the end. Besides, this guy, Gus, is a pro, right? He knows what he's doing . . . doesn't he?"

With these two key parts cast, Van Sant concentrated on finding the lead performer. At one point he considered using forty-two-year-old Walt Curtis to play himself on-screen, but then chose to go with a performer closer to Walt's age at the time he fell in love with the real-life Johnny. Moreover, Van Sant recalled all too well from working on *Property* with Curtis that neither the latter's heart nor his talents lay with acting. Fortunately, Portland/Seattle had a wide circle of professional actors who worked primarily in local theater. Van Sant spotted stage actor Tim Streeter working in a production of Sam Shepard's *Curse of the Starving Class*. Facially Tim resembled Richard Hatch (*The Streets of San Francisco*, *Battlestar Galactica*) but was more expressive in body movement and with a five o'clock shadow on his face could look a bit seedy (as the part required). Tim accepted the focal role.

As for locations to re-create the skid row ambiance of Walt Curtis's book, Portland's inner city had not yet been revamped from the way it was in the early 1970s when Curtis's narrative took place. Gus chose Portland's Burnside area, which had rundown hotels, wino groceries, and filthy back streets. In selecting his grimy locales, Van Sant refused to heed advice that such depressing settings might turn off filmgoers: "I wanted to make the movie I wanted to see, not the one that I thought would please other people."

With the bulk of his budget going for film stock, equipment, actors (who received token payments), and the upcoming postproduction fees, Gus had to work on the cheap. There were no Hollywood studio perks such as cast limousines, portable dressing-room trailers, or equipment trucks. Everything that Van Sant required for this very personal project was carted about in a rundown Volkswagen van. He had a crew of three, which included Portland cinematographer John Campbell (then a news cameraman for the local television station KPTV). In turn, they had to rely on half-broken lighting equipment. As for sound engineer Pat Baum, he carried a tape recorder on a strap.

Unlike Van Sant's later, major productions, there was virtually no rehearsal period for *Mala Noche*. (By then poet/author Walt Curtis had already instructed Tim Streeter on the mannerisms he should use in playing Walt, coached Gus on the psychology of the Hispanic street culture, and gave "pep talks" to actors Doug Cooeyate and Ray Monge who were playing, respectively, Johnny and Pepper. Otherwise, Walt was not directly involved in the physical production of the movie, except for a momentary cameo.)

As the film's star Streeter has described the experience: "We didn't really rehearse. A lot of the supporting 'actors' are actually living their lives on-camera, and they weren't always aware that they were being filmed. At times we'd joke, 'Is he shooting now?' 'Does he have film in the camera?'" Gus's theory in making this picture was: "The first take is often the liveliest." He wanted the film to have a documentary-like tone in which a rolling camera was "no big deal. When you've got a crew of just three people, it's a lot easier to work that way." Not that he was unprepared for each day's shooting. He detailed: "*Mala Noche* was storyboarded and we stuck to the storyboards; I figured out what we were doing before I shot it."

For four weeks in the fall of 1984, Gus, along with his small crew and cast, shot their drama. (The film's full title is *Mala Noche, or Bad Night*.) The apartment where the on-screen Walt lives was filmed at The Lawn, the Portland building where Walt Curtis had resided when the actual story occurred. A mock bodega was constructed to represent Demetri's Grocery where Curtis had once worked part-time. Whenever they had to move to a new location, Van Sant would pile the equipment and small cast/crew into his dilapidated van and off they would go. Frequently, to feed his squad, Gus took them to a local Mexican restaurant, trading meals for paintings he presented the eatery.

Sometimes they filmed in the evening to capture the city's special look—especially that of Old Town and Southwest Sixth Avenue in the heart of Skid Row where not even the dark or the gleam of rain could glamorize the settings. In shooting these nighttime sequences, and even in the daytime scenes lensed in the grubby convenience-store set, the squalid bargain-rate hotel, or the lead character's tiny, seamy apartment, Gus gave an Ingmar Bergman look to the lights and shadows of the vista being captured in black and white. This effort was helped by cameraman John Campbell, who was an aficionado of the Swedish moviemaker and spent countless hours as a college student in art house cinema watching Bergman screen classics.

(Some time later, in analyzing the visual influences on *Mala Noche* with its expressive close-ups, unusual camera angles, and tightly compacted visual frame, Van Sant allowed that the style was "probably a combination of things. It was black and white and Orson Welles's cinematography [e.g., 1958's *Touch of Evil*] and David Lynch's *Eraserhead* were very influential. David Lynch had a certain lighting style—pretty minimal, but also very expressionistic—which I adopted when we were lighting interiors. He used spotlights and so I got a bunch of spotlights. Stanley Kubrick's black-and-white films were another influence.")

Novelist, journalist, and Van Sant friend Katherine Dunn visited the *Mala Noche* "set" and recorded that Gus always seemed to know exactly what he was doing but maintained a loose atmosphere, taking suggestions as well as cues from the actors and the particular situations of the set itself. From her vantage point, Gus displayed an openness that earned respect from his performers. (Others in the cast included bits by Don Chambers, a colorful figure in Portland's inner city, as well as Doug Cooyeate's sibling Matt playing Johnny's boxcar companion in the film's opening sequence.)

One of the more challenging sequences to lens was the sexual coupling of the characters played by Walt Curtis and Pepper. For starters, Ray Monge as the Mexican teen was reluctant to shoot even a simulated homosexual love scene on camera. Then, too, Van Sant, as in his later features, was never one to exploit the act of physical passion on-screen by lingering on it or even showing it too completely—even in simulated movie terms. (This seems, at first blush, to be contrary to such a dedicated life observer—some might say "voyeur"—as Van Sant apparently was at the time. Yet this particular aesthetic was just another aspect of his complex nature.)

To accommodate his actor's feelings, as well as the censorship standards of the times for even independent mainstream films (in contrast to out-and-out porno entries), and Van Sant's own philosophy of such on-camera action, Gus shot the *Mala Noche* male-to-male sexual interaction in dark shadows. He shifted from the Walt Curtis character (who is seen removing all his clothes and revealing brief frontal nudity to the camera) to that of Pepper lying on the sleeping bag on the floor. As the clumsy "love"-making proceeds, the shots are deliberately choppy intercuts that fabricate the illusion of sex taking place. Yet so much transpires in shadow or is focused on the participants' faces that little nudity or sex play is actually seen within the interlude.

Years later, in talking with the *Advocate*'s Robert Hofler, Van Sant had this to say about *Mala Noche*'s one final-cut sequence of on-camera fornication (between the Curtis character and Pepper) where the Curtis character is the bottom partner of the duo and Pepper is the top. "A lot of directors don't have graphic sex scenes. Before 1960 there were none. The reason for that, besides morality, is that it's a subjective situation. Since the audience isn't having sex while they're watching the scene, they're removed all of a sudden from what's going on. You can be part of certain dramatic situations, but when it involves sex it has to be presented through a character you're identifying with closely enough so that you're involved in the sex scene itself. It's difficult. My movies have had really good sex scenes, though. My first one, *Mala Noche* [1985], had a terrific sex scene."

(For some viewers, however, Van Sant's terminology seems inappropriate for this *Mala Noche* sequence. While the footage in question may have been an expressionistic, artistic depiction of the gay sex act—dictated by the times, by one of the two actors' reluctance when doing the scene, by censorship standards, and by Van Sant's own beliefs—it is strange semantics to call that particular interlude a "terrific sex scene." Interesting? Yes. Aesthetically appropriate? Yes. But "terrific" as in hot-and-steamy simulated sex? Hardly.)

In the same conversation, Van Sant continued, "It wasn't hard-core, but it was relatively graphic. . . . It was sort of a *Death in Venice* [scene], but with contact. It was all about this one thing, so the sex scene is a centerpiece. It was written with this in mind, so it was easier to get across to the audience. A lot of times sex scenes become a bumping and grinding activity, and then it's not particularly sexy."

Another concern while filming *Mala Noche* was the sound. This aspect of the production was also done on the cheap with a minimum of equipment and hardly the latest available technology. Thus, there was the challenge, in particular, of shooting the outdoor sequences and having enough silence in the vicinity to allow the actors' dialogue to come across clearly. Postproduction dubbing (looping) seemed the obvious answer to clean up this problem. But there was another hurdle involved. Doug Cooeyate, who played Johnny, a character with a fleeting ability to converse in English, did not actually speak Spanish sufficiently well enough to handle several of his lengthy interchanges in Spanish with his street friends. (Most of Johnny's conversations with the Walt character are physical gestures or a few words of broken, hesitant English.) To resolve the predicament, Van Sant had these speeches dubbed in later by another person. (Since there are on-screen subtitles for much of the Spanish dialogue spoken by the Johnny and Pepper characters, and many of these particular moments are in medium or longer shots and often in nighttime scenes or in semishadows, this dubbing is not that obvious to the viewer on a first-time seen basis.)

Also, as would become a trademark in the next several Van Sant productions, there is the use of home movies (with a few shots in color) interspersed in the middle of the film and within the closing credits. When asked what inspired this device, Gus told the journalist: "*Paris, Texas* [the 1984 film by Wim Wenders] used home movies and I think I had seen it just before I began *Mala Noche*. There was a passage in *Mala Noche*, the novel, where the boys take photographs, but I had them making movies instead; it worked much better." Thus in *Mala Noche* (as in his next project, *Drugstore Cowboy*), Van Sant turned over the movie camera to his actors. He asked them to stay in character and shoot home movies of each other. He then included this footage of the lead cast mugging for a shaky camera in the final cut.

Almost before he realized it, principal photography on *Mala Noche* ended and it was time to start the arduous postproduction phase of assembling the footage into a cohesive narrative flow.

▼

IN the now-edited *Mala Noche*, as the opening credits unroll, there are montages of down-and-out characters and rundown storefronts in the marginalized part of Portland's inner city. The narrative begins with the legend—as does the book original—"If you f**k with the bull, you get the horn." This gritty chronicle tells of Walt, a Caucasian around thirty who is the cashier/manager of a small convenience/liquor store in Portland's grubby Skid Row district. He is openly and happily gay and doesn't seem overly depressed working in the midst of transients, winos, and migrant workers.

This happy-go-lucky character (always in need of a shave, generally bleary-eyed, and, when on the streets, always wearing a dirty, ragamuffin raincoat) is immediately attracted to a newcomer to the store. The latter is a sixteen-year-old Mexican. Johnny is a newcomer to the city, an illegal alien who has wandered into the shop out of boredom and hunger. He has just reached Oregon after hitching up north. (Johnny's stowaway arrival forms the film's opening scene as he watches the landscape of the Northwest mountains pass by from his railroad boxcar perch.)

It develops that Walt, who spends his off-work hours drinking in grimy bars with his equally lonesome male and female acquaintances of various ages, is more than just attracted to the youth. As he informs his pal Sarah, "I'm in love with this boy. I don't care even if it jeopardizes working at the store. I have to show him I'm gay for him." His woman friend offers to invite Walt and Johnny over for a home-cooked meal and the encouraged man rushes off in search of his inamorato. He comes across the youth enthusiastically playing games in a video arcade surrounded by other runaways/street people/young hustlers.

At dinner at Sarah's, which includes Johnny's friend Roberto (nicknamed Pepper), horny Walt is wide-eyed with lust for Johnny. By now Walt is enveloped in his latest romantic fantasies, which seem to be his chief priority. As the evening proceeds he discovers that Johnny has no use for "putos" (homosexuals), especially if they have no ready cash. Over time it proves that what the street-savvy but immature Johnny (who insists that he is straight) will accept from his admirer is occasional nonsexual attention (when it suits his mood), the chance to drive Walt's ramshackled car, the offer of free food at the convenience store, and someone to keep under his power.

Despite being rebuffed by the manipulative Johnny (who is almost always in the company of the nonchalant, observant Pepper), Walt continues his one-way pursuit. He even follows the object of lust to his grimy hotel where the hefty female desk clerk refuses to allow the nonguest to go upstairs. (Later, the impassioned Walt envisions going to Johnny's room at midnight and prostrating himself at the boy's feet to show him how much this gringo adores him. But reality is far different. One night he climbs the building's fire escape to Johnny's room only to knock on the wrong window and then encounter the same angry female hotel clerk who again chases off the embarrassed man.)

Walt thrives on this unrequited love. Another night, not having enough money to pay for Johnny's services, the store clerk invites the more pliable, hunkier Pepper back to his place. In the course of the evening they have sex, with the Mexican boy taking the dominant role. The next morning Walt discovers that money is missing from his wallet. He assumes that during the night Pepper helped himself to $10 from his host's wallet. Angry and amused, he reflects on having been worked over physically and literally by his guest. As Walt saunters down the Portland streets to work waving cheerfully to neighborhood characters, he wonders how many of them know of his treatment at the hands of the callous Pepper.

Later on, Johnny disappears, leaving Pepper to his own devices. Walt attempts to befriend the morose teen, especially when he becomes ill with a fever. But even once they are roommates of sorts, Pepper continues to degrade the pliable, often passive Walt.

Thereafter, one night while Walt is at work, the police are summoned to the building by a disgruntled downstairs neighbor. Pepper, with his stolen gun in hand, thinks the law has arrived to send him back to Mexico. He attempts to flee and is shot in a confrontation with the cops. Walt arrives in time to cradle the dead boy in his arms.

Time passes. One day Walt spots Johnny on the mean streets. He learns that his object of desire had been captured during a police sweep of illegal aliens and had been shipped back across the border to Mexico. The boy had promptly swum back to the U.S. side of the river and headed back to Portland. Now he is more tolerant of Walt's attention, that is, until he learns that his friend Pepper is dead. Blaming Walt for his pal's demise, he angrily rushes from Walt's room, carves "puto" into the man's door, and takes off.

Not accepting this rejection, Walt continues to cruise the streets looking for the Mexican boy. He glimpses Johnny hanging around a street corner and good-naturedly, as if nothing bad had transpired between them, optimistically cajoles, "Come down to the store . . . and talk to me, all right?" The film ends ambiguously with a shot of Walt driving his car down the Portland street.

The movie's dialogue, much of it extracted from Walt Curtis's book original, is filled with musings on cultural and class distinctions, mostly spoken by the frequently bigoted and aggrieved lead character who often expresses biased remarks as he rambles aloud about his "ignorant Mexican teenager." For example, as Walt meanders to work after his night with Pepper, he thinks in voice-over: "Every street Mexican on Sixth will think he can stick it in me, but they never were too smart to begin with, or they wouldn't be here." Another time, after Walt has foolishly let the reckless Johnny wildly drive his car, the store clerk says, "The boy's insane like all Mexicans about driving fast and crazy." Further on, Walt complains aloud regarding the unsophisticated Pepper: "His sexual desires are very stereotypical and mine aren't."

At yet another moment, Walt has a more sympathetic perspective about his young prey: "A gringo like me has an easy life, a privileged life. I see someone attractive like Johnny doesn't mean I should be able to have him because he's hungry, on the street, desperate." There are even times when love-struck Walt is perceptive about the contradictory nature of his dependency on these young men: "F**k it. Do I need them that badly? Of course, I do." Or there is the moment of revelation in the midst of his obsession: "Johnny will never, never go anywhere alone with me; I find that sad and absurd."

Perhaps the most famous dialogue line in *Mala Noche* occurs when Walt, ever playing the munificent mentor, allows the untutored Pepper to drive his car. Despite step-by-step directions, Pepper is unable to navigate a roadway curve and lands the vehicle in a ditch. The exasperated Walt yells, "You drive like you f**k!" (The intertwining themes of cars, the open highways, and relationships will play a recurrent theme in Van Sant's films).

▼

AFTER the dubbing of *Mala Noche* was completed, the "final" cut could be achieved. This was painstakingly reached by Gus only after much tinkering and rearranging of the order of scenes (another standard Van Sant process). The next step was adding in music, an unobtrusive score credited to Creighton Lindsay. The track also contained several songs ranging from "Gracias a la Vida," "Balderama," "Hasta la Victoria," and "Guaguaanco" to "Now Is the Hour" and "Sgt. Pepper's Lonely Hearts Club Band." The song "Morir por tú Amor" by Ron Swager (English version) was sung by Van Sant on the sound track to his own guitar accompaniment.

Now "all" that remained was getting *Mala Noche* seen by potential movie distributors. Little did the optimistic Van Sant realize that his real work had actually just begun.

DOING THE ROUNDS

[Mala Noche] finally broke even this year. It only cost $25,000 and it's taken almost ten years to make its money back.

Gus Van Sant, 1993

IN THE HOLLYWOOD STUDIO SYSTEM where feature films are usually targeted for a particular theatrical release season even before production begins, postproduction (especially editing) is on a defined schedule once principal photography wraps. On the other hand, with an independent film such as *Mala Noche*, in which the director/backer is also editing the project, it becomes more a matter of it being finished when its maker can do so. For such a meticulous person as Gus Van Sant—one who happens to enjoy the process of sifting through footage, shifting the scene order, etc.—it was not a quick cycle. Although one part of the filmmaker surely must have wanted to shop the movie to film festivals and distributors, another part of him certainly did not want to let go of his "baby." For once he began screening the "finished" *Mala Noche* he would receive industry feedback about it. And having endured the bitter, negative experience of *Alice in Hollywood*, he must have had (subconscious) thoughts that the longer he tinkered with his new movie, the longer before he would know whether the film community voted it thumbs-up or -down. And if the response was not good, it would be another crushing defeat, despite his self-sustaining self-confidence in a project once he had committed himself to it.

Then, too, the film editing process dragged on because Van Sant, having invested all his financial resources into *Mala Noche,* needed to take on other work (editing, teaching, painting, etc.) to sustain himself from month to month. Also, being a Renaissance man of sorts, he had other things going on in his professional life. He was still very much involved in his music. Through his Portland friend Tim Kerr, who owned TK Records on Southwest Front Street, Gus arranged a musical reunion with his idol William S. Burroughs Jr. The concept was to have the maven of the Beat Generation read four selections (with his voice electronically manipulated for effects), while Van Sant and others provided musical accompaniment. (One of those providing guitar backup was Doug Cooeyate—the Johnny character of *Mala Noche.*) The short album was entitled *The Elvis of Letters* and contained a quartet of cuts: "Burroughs Break," "Word Is Virus," "Millions of Images," and "The Hipster Be-bop Junkie." "The Hipster Be-bop Junkie" came out on a seven-inch red vinyl single on Dutch East Records abroad and in the United States on the Single Only label.

Also in 1984–85, Van Sant recorded more musical numbers for another solo album, which would be distributed finally in 1997 by Dan Frazier's Pop Secret label. (As Frazier told the *Oregonian*, Gus had phoned him and inquired if he wanted to release the songs. When Frazier was asked by the publication to describe the album, he said, "Musically, it's hard to characterize. It's all over the place.")

The twelve cuts (lasting 28.22 minutes) include such Gus compositions (which he plays on guitar and other percussion instruments and to which he sings his own lyrics) as "Momma Can't Walk," in which the parent not only can't amble, but is dead, "Golf Committee," and "Stranger." In the realm of vocals and guitar playing his modest musical talents were on par with his earlier vocal sessions at home in Darien, Connecticut, in 1983. The topics of his "new" songs ranged all over the spectrum, from talk/singing his Rhode Island School of Design diploma ("RISD"), to a number about the type of woman (!) he liked ("My Kind of Girl"), to another entry ("Elvis") about the king of rock 'n' roll.

Perhaps the most intriguing of these tracks is "Independent Wealth." In this number Gus reminds his "stone face daddy" that the singer's creditors are waiting. He points out that his parent owes it to his offspring to help out . . . or else. One can only wonder how autobiographical this selection is. As on his earlier album (*18 Songs About Golf*), Gus provided the cover artwork—one of his broad-stroke landscape paintings.

▼

IN the mid-1980s before the advent of such useful indie film showcases as the Independent Film Channel and the Sundance Channel or the wide use of home video rentals, the smartest route for an independent moviemaker to build industry word-of-mouth was to get his production entered at the many film festivals around the world. Hoping to start momentum for *Mala Noche*, Van Sant had a local showing in Portland in November 1985 as a warm-up to the movie being screened elsewhere. Although the Sundance Film Festival rejected Van

Sant's production for its January 1986 showcase, it was accepted by the Gay Film Festival and had the first of four screenings there on January 9, 1986, at the Eighth Street Playhouse in Manhattan's Greenwich Village. Many of Gus's friends came to the showing, including his Darien, Connecticut, school chum John Howell and the latter's wife, Marianne. After the screening, the entire group adjourned to a nearby restaurant for a celebratory dinner.

Elliott Stein (*Village Voice*) reviewed *Mala Noche* at the time, observing, "[T]hings do not end well for anyone, but this melancholy tale, buoyed by Van Sant's authentic cinematic intelligence, is far from a downer." Stein noted further, "This gritty 16 mm film looks good but never fussily prearranged—it all just seems to be happening, falling into place before a camera." Stein rated the film's star (Tim Streeter) "superb" and detailed, "It's a lovely performance at the heart of a moving and memorable first film."

Mala Noche next played at the Berlin Film Festival, the same year as the British-made, gay-themed *My Beautiful Laundrette* made such a stir at the competition. *Mala Noche* debuted at the city's Aterlier Theater on February 24, 1986. The trade paper *Weekly Variety* judged that it "seems to be aiming for the same audience as *Stranger than Paradise* [1984] via its offhand humor, studied yet vaguely realistic dialog and throwaway acting. The Jim Jarmusch film was much more successful, but this debut by Gus Van Sant shows lots of promise and is basically a likeable effort." The industry journal projected, "Shot in very high contrast black and white, with lots of oppressive shadows, pic looks good on the big screen, but will probably suffer when transferred to video."

Mala Noche was unspooled at the Edinburgh Film Festival shortly thereafter and also played a special engagement in London and thereafter was presented at film festivals in Vancouver, San Francisco, Boston, and Key West. It again played in Oregon on May 28, 1986, at the Eleventh Annual Seattle International Film Festival. While receiving endorsements and honors at all these venues, no American distributor stepped forward to make a deal to release this unusual gay feature. It was screen product not easy to categorize. While it was dramatically sound and humorous, it had an overt homosexual love story (which concerned distributors about the possible reaction of mainstream audiences). On the other hand, *Mala Noche* was certainly not pornographic (which might have occasioned some distribution interest in other quarters). As such, Van Sant's film languished except for more (gay) film festival showings and minor theatrical distribution in Germany and a few other European countries.

When *Mala Noche* had brief screenings in London, Mark Finch of the (British) *Monthly Film Bulletin* described it as "giddy collection of scratchy urban snapshots which—despite the [production] synopsis—owes less to the choreographed delinquency of films like Paul Morrissey's *40 Deuce* and *Mixed Blood* and more to literary antecedents. . . . Specifically, *Mala Noche* is poised between two historically discrete genres of gay fiction: the ineradicable nihilism of John Rechy's *City of the* [sic] *Night*, and the confessional style of recent story collections, to soft eroticism of the yuppie gay press with titles like *Flesh, Meat and Cum.*" Finch emphasized, "But to call *Mala Noche* a 'raw and raunchy' gay film (as the press notes do) is misleading and even spurious. What is fascinating is how the film orders itself around a uniquely gay point of view."

Stubbornly convinced that he had a movie product that people would come to see if only they had an opportunity to do so, Gus continued to tread the festival circuit (which often cost him registration and other fees, not to mention lost personal income from editing and other paycheck assignments).Then *Mala Noche* was accepted to play at the Los Angeles Gay and Lesbian Film/ Video Festival in 1987. It was the break that Van Sant had long been looking for, as some members of the Los Angeles Film Critics Association caught the feature there and were impressed. Within the LAFCA, it was nominated and won in the category Best Experimental Independent Film, a prize usually bestowed on a new artist for a meritorious movie that has not been well exposed to date.)

The Los Angeles Film Critics Association winners were announced on December 19, 1987, and the awards were presented on January 21, 1988, at the Westwood Marquis Hotel in Los Angeles. Gus almost did not attend: "I'd won a lot of awards. When they called I just said, 'Thanks. Can I have a friend pick it up?'" But Van Sant soon realized exactly what he had won and from whom. (This was the same esteemed group that had years before given this particular award to such experimental filmmakers as Jonas Mekas and the Kuchar brothers—all models for Van Sant in his early years.) Thus, Van Sant had a change of heart and came to Hollywood—the town that held such bittersweet memories for him because of *Alice in Hollywood*—to collect his prize.

While the Los Angeles Film Critics' prize that Gus claimed was not in the Best Picture category (that went to John Boorman's *Hope and Glory*), it was nevertheless a prestigious victory. And thanks to the attention drawn to *Mala Noche* by this victory, the feature was later booked into the Angelika Film Center in New York City for midnight showings in May 1988. While this was not a lucrative screen booking, it did prompt several major publications to finally review the over-three-year-old feature.

V. A. Musetto (*New York Post*) pointed out that the semidocumentary style of *Mala Noche* was reminiscent of *Streetwise*, the 1984 portrait of teenage vagrants in Seattle. The reviewer then weighed, "Van Sant makes no overt attempt to judge these people or their subculture, but you come away with a sympathetic feeling toward them. You may be put off by the gutter language and sex, but it is crucial to the atmospheric slice of street life that Van Sant and his cast of non-professionals—taken from the slums of Portland—so vividly create. You're not likely to soon forget them or their predaceous way of life. What better recommendation is there?"

Vincent Canby (*New York Times*) enthused, "It's a measure of the talent of Gus Van Sant that his *Mala Noche* . . . remains as steadfastly, honestly grim as the Portland, Ore., skid row where most of it takes place. . . ." Canby further cheered that it is "a very well-made movie, terse and to the point, nicely photographed by

John Campbell and written and directed by Mr. Van Sant with sardonic humor." He also pointed out that Tim Streeter "gives an exceptionally intelligent performance as Walt . . ."

It was not until December of 1989 that *Mala Noche* had a major review in the *Los Angeles Times*. Then, Peter Rainer judged: "The ardor in this film isn't only in its love story; it's also in Van Sant's experimental, poetic use of the medium. Maybe that's why the doomed, unrequited romantic passion at its core nevertheless seems weirdly, vibrantly hopeful. Van Sant can't pretend true nihilism because he's too enraptured by the possibilities of his new-found art." Rainer concluded: "There's something primitive yet deeply sophisticated and modern about Van Sant's approach: He recognizes the emptiness of the pop landscape but also understands how that emptiness validates people's lives."

Hal Hinson (*Washington Post*) assessed the "raw and authentically personal" *Mala Noche* in mid-1990: "Partly the film is fueled by Van Sant's romanticism of losers; it's fascinated by the poetic allure of poor beautiful boys riding the rail into the promised land and ending up dead, crumpled on the pavement in the middle of a street, thousands of miles from home." He perceived, "It's Van Sant's conception of Walt, and the diffident self-awareness in Streeter's performance, that holds these feelings in balance and saves the movie from soft-headedness. It lets us see how Walt inflates his infatuation with Johnny for dramatic effect. He's obsessed, yet still he's playacting, hyping his own emotions because that's how he feeds his romantic conception of himself. Nowhere is Walt's place of choice; for Johnny and Pepper, it's a prison they carry with them. And Van Sant navigates the distinctions between these two worlds with intelligence and invigorating style. This is a knockout debut."

In the midst of all this positive response (but scant commercial availability or financial returns on *Mala Noche*), there was one person who, for a time, grew increasingly disenchanted with the film's growing reputation. Ironically it was the author of the original story of *Mala Noche*. As Curtis writes in the expanded edition of the story published in 1997 as *Mala Noche and Other "Illegal" Adventures*: "About 10 years ago as there began an orgy of applause for Van Sant's career, my feeble little ego began to freak out. Gus was being written up everywhere. . . . Had he stolen, expropriated, finagled, finessed, ripped off my 'street poet' persona? I anguished. . . . It was a bit unnerving to see a territory of human suffering and existential angst that I, as a writer, had taken years to cultivate . . . suddenly be splashed all over *Interview*, *Newsweek*, the *New York Times*, the *New Yorker*, and the *Village Voice*."

Getting to the crux of his displeasure, the often-described-as-misogynistic Curtis delineated, "Gus was still nice to me, but he was getting all the attention from our *Mala Noche* project. Whose fault was that? He invited me to movie premieres, we talked on the phone. We were 'friends,' but—My ego was bruised knowing it took a film maker . . . to publicize and make famous . . . my little novella. . . . I realize film is a 'hot' medium, and books are a 'cool' one. But

I'm the 'street poet,' who lived the life and put the words down on paper. . . . I'm the real STREET POET! Not Van Sant. Don't you get it?"

But there was a happy coda to Curtis's accelerating discomfort with Van Sant. Curtis reports, "At the [1991] premiere of *My Own Private Idaho* at the Baghdad Theater in Portland, I realized how much I had misjudged Van Sant. To help Outside-In, the street clinic, Van Sant came up with the idea to make the opening a fund-raiser. Twenty thousand dollars was earned for the 'street youth' transition program. . . . I went up to Gus and hugged him. 'You have great heart (soul). I wasn't sure in the past.' "

Thus by June 1993, when a fresh 35mm print of *Mala Noche* was shown at the San Francisco Gay Film Festival at the city's famed Castro Theatre, both Van Sant and Walt Curtis were present for the occasion. Curtis would recall, "The film looked ravishingly beautiful 'blown-up'—yet retained its Skid Row bitter-sweetness. . . . It seems I've waited forever for the film to reach a larger audience. I realized then how deserving of praise this particular film is."

Later, Curtis asked Gus to write a foreword for the 1997 book edition of *Mala Noche*. The filmmaker penned, "Walt Curtis is one of our very rare and dignified poetic powers, and I am fascinated by the extremes of the story of *Mala Noche* every time I read it. The film that was made from this story is only a mirror, and a hazy mirror at that. When you read from *Mala Noche*, you are drinking at the source. It is as if you are experiencing the thing as it is happening and living there yourself."

▼

ALTHOUGH *Mala Noche* has yet to be made available on VHS tape or DVD disc for home viewing, the movie continues to be presented at film festivals and retrospectives and has been shown on a few specialty movie cable channels. As such, its reputation remains alive and grows, along with Van Sant's standing within the motion picture industry. The picture continues to be (re)assessed as a landmark in the history of American independent filmmaking. For example, in *Independent Visions* (1994) by Donald Lyons, the author praises the film: "*Mala Noche* is, to an amazing and beautiful degree, a movie shot in black, a black out of which will emerge a face, a boot, a pumpkin, a coffee cup, an ashtray—little pieces of life fighting to be seen against an enveloping darkness. This is a Portland of the lost and the losing." Lyons points out that "*Mala Noche* is full of cars and rain and cigarette smoke. These cigarettes—tobacco and pot—symbolizes Van Sant's overall attitude to pleasures, obsessions, addictions; to him they are simply inflections of character, modes of coping, ways of living. What interests the director more than the substance is the spirit: his heroes have an openness and a sometimes paradoxical innocence of spirit that, while leaving them defenseless before life's sucker punches, yet awards them small decisions along the way."

As to the *Mala Noche* cast, Lyons finds lead actor Tim Streeter the perfect "incarnation of the Van Sant hero, a hero haunted but hip, driven but cool." Lyons observes, "It is also a tribute to Van Sant to have coaxed realistic and honest portrayals of the Mexican youths out of Doug Cooeyate and Ray Monge; they become not merely objects but feeling subjects."

▼

AS noted, one of the most satisfying aspects to *Mala Noche* is Tim Streeter's performance as the lovelorn, bestubbled store clerk. He encapsulates a giddy sense of reckless abandon as the Caucasian enthralled with finding the perfect (fantasy) Mexican (-American) young man to love and possess. His perform-ance—perhaps thanks to Gus's nurturing—is flawless and should have sparked a bright film and TV career (which somehow never happened). One can only wonder how much of the passive, voyeuristic Walt, constantly observing the coveted street teens, is a reflection/recreation of Van Sant's past experience as the ongoing observer and nonparticipant in the Hollywood street scene of the late 1970s.

Much within *Mala Noche* is pure Van Sant. The unsentimental, sometimes cynically humorous approach to the homosexual love story could have floun-dered in another's hands and become a soppy, sentimental gay romance. Conversely, there is a characteristic discreet handling of the sex scenes, as would be true in such later films as *My Own Private Idaho*. Also there is no proselytizing or apologizing for the alternative lifestyle, making *Mala Noche* re-markably objective in its presentation of its gay themes.

As would be true in several later Van Sant movies, *Mala Noche* abounds in dysfunctional characters who form a strange nuclear family with unspoken rules that guide their interrelationships. The homeless Mexican youths have created a street community that sometimes includes the parental figure of Walt. It is the latter who offers the youngsters financial help, understanding, and tending. There is also the characters' fascinations with cars. (Walt cruises the mean streets in search of his beloved or relaxes in one as he monitors the Mexican street hustlers. Johnny and Pepper show their delight in driving their benefac-tor's vehicle.) In addition, there are the treks by the Mexican youths from south of the border to Portland in search of a better life—to some place they can call home. (This foreshadows the search of the lead character in *My Own Private Idaho*, forever seeking his childhood home, his lost youth, and his mother.)

In the cinematography of *Mala Noche*—capturing the grim inner city and the striking Portland skyline accented by shadowy patches and sparkling facets glis-tening in the rain—John Campbell achieves Van Sant's goal of a quasi-documentary look. The camera work bolsters the validity of the gritty tale and reflects the script's impartial depiction of hustlers, whores, winos, and derelicts who, in true Van Sant style, are never judged or glamorized within the produc-tion. Other Van Sant visual touches are the uniquely framed scenes with their distinctive camera angles. Then there is Van Sant's typically very mobile camera, which makes his movie really move. Also to be noted are the many close-ups of objects to punctuate story points, a mark of Gus's moviemaking. (A particularly effective one is the wine bottle rolling in the gutter during the opening credits.) Another soon-to-be-familiar Gus technique is his use here of a kaleidoscopic effect as the Walt character is vomiting over a toilet bowl.

Also to be acknowledged is the additional camerawork of Van Sant's longtime friend Eric Alan Edwards. The latter provided the time-lapse photography for the swirling clouds on the Portland landscape. This "gimmick" would be repeated in Van Sant's upcoming features, by which time Edwards was promoted to co-cinematographer. Finally, not to be overlooked is the previously mentioned home movies utilized at the film's end. Another of Van Sant's characteristic touches, these shots provide insight into the characters and the actors who play them.

While its small budget limited the scope and sources of music available for use within *Mala Noche*, Gus's choices are a sign of his music background and his innate sense of selecting numbers that make their own points in harmony or counterbalance to what is transpiring on the screen at the moment.

Above all, following the moviemaking tradition set by Alfred Hitchcock, Van Sant performs a low-key (what else from this reserved filmmaker?) cameo in *Mala Noche*, herein as a tenant in a shadowy apartment building where Walt is seeking Pepper.

10

SELECTED SHORT SUBJECTS

When I was poor I tried desperately to sell out to anybody. Before *Drugstore Cowboy*, I was working as a temporary secretary. I was doing commercials, public service announcements, and things like that in Portland on a $500 budget, making $100 for myself. In a good week I'd make $25. I was selling off my books to make the rent.

Gus Van Sant, 2001

BY 1985, WHILE *MALA NOCHE* was in the protracted editing stage, Gus Van Sant was scrounging for money to keep going. He taught a time-lapse photography class in Portland, took editing assignments for commercials, and did whatever else that might bring in a few dollars. There were times when he was hard-pressed to pay the rent. (During the mid-1980s he moved to a very basic apartment over a Xerox store in a far less elegant part of the city, where his rent was under $300 a month. In this haven he stored his film equipment and footage with things strewn everywhere. Sometimes there were even derelict drunks on the landing to the apartment's front door, they having learned that the compassionate tenant wouldn't chase them away to walk the bleak streets all night long.)

When asked by the press if his affluent father helped out with his overhead, Gus acknowledged, "I didn't live off of him, but sometimes if I was in a jam he'd help me out." As with everything, that was a price to pay for the parental assistance that continued sporadically throughout the remainder of the 1980s: Van Sant recalls the recurrent dialogue between his dad and him: "He kept saying find a job. I kept saying, I have to perfect my craft. I can't give up now. I've spent 38 years trying to do this. I'd be an idiot to give up and he'd say, well maybe you'll never be able to do it. I wasn't facing the fact that maybe I was lousy at my job and wouldn't be able to make movies. That maybe I should jump into retail. He wanted me to go into the fashion business, to take over his business. I just kept saying I've gone way too far."

In between editing *Mala Noche* and struggling for financial survival, Gus tried to network from Portland to get the finalized *Mala Noche* seen by the movie industry and to make contacts within the international film festival community to have his picture screened. Also, Van Sant remained creatively busy. This activity included not only his paintings (which he sometimes sold to pay bills), still photography, and music recording, but his ongoing array of short-subject films.

One of his mid-1980s brief entries was entitled *Switzerland*. It featured a teen male calling himself Mike Schweizer who says on camera that his dad is a farmer in Switzerland. Actually the youth's name is Michael Parker and at the time he was living in Portland youth shelters, hanging out in a bowling alley, accepting the kindness of strangers, and involved in some substance abuse. (Parker would tell *Rolling Stone* magazine in 1991: "I thought if I told Gus how things really were, he wouldn't want anything to do with me.") Michael was one of a number of marginalized individuals who increasingly formed part of Gus's expanded social circle in Portland during the 1980s, mixed in with various groups about town, from the social set to the filmmaker's contingent, and to the gay set. For a time, Parker lived at Van Sant's downtown apartment, paying for his own food and board.

In another of his movie shorts, *My New Friend* (1987), the rise and fall of a friendship is encapsulated within three minutes. In the flow of short blackout sequences the new pal is shown standing in a downtown Portland park. As the scenes progress it becomes quickly clear to everyone (except Van Sant the protagonist) that this latest acquaintance is not trustworthy. The short concludes with Van Sant waiting by a telephone for a call (from his friend) that never comes.

One of the most unique of Van Sant's experimental black-and-white 16mm short subjects of this fertile period is 1987's *Ken Death Gets Out of Jail*. It "stars" twenty-two-year-old Kenneth Murray Mieske whom Gus had known in Portland for a few years through mutual acquaintances. The short depicts Mieske crouching by a busy roadway, discussing in stream-of-consciousness fashion a wide range of topics from his recent incarceration to his undeserved reputation (i.e., bad rap) as a poor lover. Although he seems to be answering questions spontaneously as the offscreen director asks them, the dialogue actually had been scripted ahead of time.

What would give *Ken Death Gets Out of Jail* its special cachet was what happened to Kenneth Mieske in the months *subsequent* to his rambling appearance in this film and what would become public of his sad and unsavory past. The revelations were prompted by events that happened early in the morning on November 13, 1988. In those wee hours, an Ethiopian national (a student named Mulugeta Seraw) had been viciously pummeled to death with kicks and punches as well as repeated blows from a baseball bat while the victim had been standing on the corner of Portland's Southeast Thirty-first Avenue and Pine Street talking to two other dark-skinned friends. Soon thereafter, Ken and two other Portland men (both under twenty-one years old) were arrested and charged with the alleged murder.

The media described the homicide of Seraw (who died of a fractured skull) as a racial act by skinheads (wearing steel-toed boots and military-style jackets, and sporting shaved heads). When news of the slaying circulated around town, the outcry from Portlanders over the atrocity led to over fifteen hundred locals taking to the streets in protest. (The eventual well-publicized criminal trial gave new awareness around the country to skinheads and the latter's then not-well-known connections to the Neo-Nazi movement. Eventually, Seraw's family filed a lawsuit against a California-based white supremacist named Tom Metzger who headed the White Aryan Resistance. Although Metzger had not been directly involved in the student's killing, it was contended that his preaching of racial hatred had motivated the attackers.)

During the investigation of the accused, it developed that Ken Mieske had been known to Portland pals for the last four years as Ken Death. One of the places at which he lived, situated at Northeast Twenty-eighth Avenue and Couch Street, was dubbed "Death House" because it was filled with memorabilia and images of death. The inquiry made known that Mieske had been abandoned at an early age by his natural mother, then was adopted by a friend of his parent, and later lived on the streets of Seattle. Eventually he found a "family" of his own in a fringe element of Portland's (underground) artistic community. The press pointed out that this loosely knit group on the outer strata of the creative cliques ironically contained many minorities.

One of those who had known Mieske from the early 1980s onward was Chris Monlux, a former disc jockey and law enforcer who had just opened the Boulevard Café on Southwest Barbur Boulevard in Portland. Around 1983, according to the account printed in the local *Willamette Week*, Mieske had drifted into Portland and had worked periodically at Monlux's café. Sometimes Ken stayed at Monlux's home. Described by the publication as living an alternate lifestyle, Monlux stated, nonetheless, that sex was not a key part of his relationship with Ken: "It was more like I was his uncle, surrogate parent or foster parent."

By 1984 Monlux had sold the Boulevard Café and had entered the music business full-time with partner Mike Quinn with a label called Monique Presents. (It was detailed that Mieske had introduced "death metal" acts to Monlux, whose company was already bringing interracial and third world musical groups to Portland for performance and recordings.) In February 1984 Ken was reportedly convicted of attempted possession of cocaine and sentenced to two years' probation. In November of the next year, he and a pal were arrested for alleged theft of packages of meat from a store. In 1986, Mieske, through a series of mutual acquaintances, won a small role in a music video (to Paul Simon's song "Boy in the Bubble") being shot in Portland.

In late 1986 Ken's parole was revoked and he was sentenced to the Oregon State Correctional Institution in Salem. By January of 1987 he was transferred to the state prison at Pendleton where he served the remaining eight months of his court-ordered jail time. According to statements made by Mieske's girl-friend, it was during this period that the prisoner was recruited into the white supremacist movement. Once released from incarceration in late 1987 Mieske moved into the home of his girlfriend's parents. It was during this period (when he made *Ken Death Gets Out of Jail* for Van Sant) that he supposedly teamed up with racist skinheads and helped to launch Portland's East Side White Pride group. Also with his free time, Ken became the lead vocalist of a new band called Machine, which reportedly performed a hate-ridden (i.e., racist and anti-gay) act onstage. (In fact, two nights before the killing in question in November 1988, Machine performed at a Pine Street club.)

Once on the outside Mieske had remained in touch with his longtime friend Monlux who, according to the *Willamette Week*, was, in turn, an ongoing ac-quaintance of Gus Van Sant. (Monlux is listed in the end credits of *Mala Noche* as one of the production associates and he has a bit walk-on part in the film.) In Jim Redden's article ("The Faces of Death") for the *Willamette Week*, published after Ken was arrested on the murder allegations, the reporter points out that in the short subject *Ken Death Gets Out of Jail*, apparently unnoticed by Van Sant, Ken is wearing a black leather jacket that boasts the double-lightning-bolt in-signia of the Aryan Brotherhood. (At his trial, Mieske was sentenced to a lengthy prison term. Transferred to a New Mexico penitentiary in 1995, Ken is not eligible for parole until the year 2022.)

While *Ken Death Gets Out of Jail* featured Van Sant's most "notorious" lead performer to that time, it was *Five Ways to Kill Yourself*, a three-minute black-and-white entry from 1987 that, along with his *My New Friend*, won for Gus the Teddy Award in the Best Short Film category at the Berlin International Film Festival in 1987.

▼

AS 1987 progressed, *Mala Noche* continued to be shown at film festivals, but that did not create the big cultural news regarding Van Sant in Portland that November. It was the announcement of an upcoming event on the twenty-third of the month at the Media Project located at 716 Southwest Sixteenth Avenue. D. K. Holm (*Willamette Week*) enthused, "With his sophisticated visual style, emotional range and deadpan wit, 34-year-old independent Portland filmmaker Gus Van Sant is a major artist by any standards, local or national. If it's not al-ready obvious (and it might not be, because his quirky films, despite some in-ternational recognition, are seldom shown in these parts), this should be clear in the forthcoming Gus Van Sant Retrospective. . . ." Thirteen items from the Van Sant canon were to be screened.

Holm continued, "Good, thoughtful retrospectives are rare here. Occasionally, two or three works from a regional filmmaker's oeuvre may be programmed one evening, but opportunities to assess an artist's output—to monitor the changes in creative focus, observe the growth of confidence and style and appreciate the maturing of a personal vision—are slim indeed."

The program for the well-received evening included many of Gus's short subjects, including *The Happy Organ* (1971) made by Van Sant and cinematographer Eric Alan Edwards while they were at Catlin Gabel School. Of *My New Friend*, Holm judged, "The simple style—and his simpleton's manner of talking—are hilarious." Another brief entry was Gus's 1975 Rhode Island School of Design project, *Late Morning Start*. In the program notes for the evening the filmmaker wrote that the picture is "a failed experiment . . . but interesting even so." As to the excerpt shown from the full-length *Mala Noche*, newsman Holm judged, "Though his work has a zestful crackle and a pleasingly topnotch look— never has Portland been grayer than in some of the black-and-white shorts or more moody and hard-boiled than in *Mala Noche*."

▼

AS Van Sant continued his still unsuccessful efforts to make *Mala Noche* and his filmmaking career "happen" in a major way, he did what had become second nature to the multitalented man. He fostered his creative activities in yet another arena. He and three other dark-haired individuals formed a band called Destroy All Blondes. It consisted of Pat Baum (his soundman on *Mala Noche*) on drums, Bruce McKay on bass, with Mary Saltveit on guitar and Gus on lead guitar and vocals. They made their debut on Tuesday, October 27, 1987, at the Satyricon Club located at 125 Northwest Sixth Avenue. In a more expansive mood than usual, Van Sant indicated to the press: "We're still trying to figure out what kind of music it is. Some people are telling me it's art rock. Someone else said it sounds like Anthony Perkins meets the Velvet Underground. There was one song that everyone definitely liked, so maybe we'll make it longer."

Gus would continue off and on with the Destroy All Blondes group for about one and a half years. One of his chief aims with the activity, besides his love of music, was to prove to himself that he could overcome his shyness at appearing before an audience and that he could function suitably in such a situation. In that regard, the experiment was a success. The band performed infrequently, and when it did it drew a crowd of largely students and young artists. One of their 1988 appearances was at a benefit for *Forbidden City*, a film then under development by the Pander brothers, two Portland illustrators who boasted a large, fashion-conscious following. One of those who caught a performance of Destroy All Blondes was Jim Redden of the *Willamette News*. He cited Gus's nasal monotone, which he said "bears an eerie resemblance to the voice of Lou

Reed, the Velvet Underground's former guitarist and vocalist, perhaps best known for his song 'Walk on the Wild Side.'"

▼

ANOTHER aspect of Gus's growing mystique as a many-sided creative artist was due to his paintings. As one Portland journalist of the day described the works: "In contrast with his films, many of Van Sant's paintings have a light, surrealistic quality. . . . Inanimate objects occasionally float about pastoral landscapes, connected to the scenery only by the shadows they cast." By this point in the later 1980s, several of Van Sant's pieces were already owned by Portland's leading art collectors, including Arlene Schnitzer (founder of the former Fountain Gallery).

▼

BY the late 1980s, Gus had been a full-time Portland resident for several years and was accepted now as a "native." With his many-layered personality and multidimensional talents he was a well-known figure about town. As his movie short subjects began to win awards, his *Mala Noche* continued to be screened at film festivals, and his work in the art and music fields brought him to the notice of local audiences, more people wanted to know greater details about their increasingly well-known native who was not too proud to take temp jobs when the situation warranted. The fact that he was gay did not seem, at least on the surface, to affect the growing esteem in which this unpretentious, self-contained man was held in Portland.

In the first blush of enthusiasm once *Mala Noche* had been completed, edited, and begun to be self-promoted by Van Sant (he sent video copies of the movie to one and all), he was asked what he wanted to do next professionally in the cinema world. "Get *Mala Noche* distributed in the United States," he might have said, but instead waxed about such dream screen projects as picturizing William S. Burroughs Jr.'s *Naked Lunch* or turning the 1968 book *The Electric Kool-Aid Acid Test* by Tom Wolfe into a movie. He also admitted he had one of his own scripts to consider as a potential vehicle to direct. It was entitled *Code of the West* and was an updated version of William Shakespeare's Falstaff plays, with Van Sant's version set in Portland.

▼

BY the time Gus had won the prize for Best Independent/Experimental Film from the Los Angeles Film Critics Association in December 1987, he had already snared talent representation in Los Angeles. When Gus called the agent with the news, the fledgling moviemaker asked, "Think it'll be any help?" The immediate response was, "Are you kidding!" The creative rep continued, "All we have to do is take off the word 'Experimental' and you've just won the prize for Best Independent Film."

True to his agent's prediction, the good reviews that *Mala Noche* had been generating at film festivals began to take on genuine importance. Now that he was legitimatized by his award from a prestigious critics' association, Gus was valuable in the eyes of the Hollywood establishment. In 1988 Van Sant began the much-maligned but essential process of "taking meetings" with studio executives and other potential movie backers. This career step meant quick in-and-out trips to Los Angeles (a city he didn't appreciate because of his past experiences there) and discussions with studio corporate "suits" (with whom, as the total individualist that he was, he had nothing in common) to discuss potential projects. It was an industry game he was not comfortable with, but one he was counseled was necessary if he wished to make a new picture.

By now Gus, growing even more ambitious with his career plans, had several pet projects he wanted to translate to the screen. Thus, he had plenty to discuss with the film-lot executives. One vehicle was called *Satan's Sandbox,* a prison tale about a psychotic killer, a transvestite, and a young gang-rape victim in which all the lead characters die. Another was entitled *Drugstore Cowboy,* a dark comedy about thieving junkies. The third was a tale of two teenage male prostitutes and was called *My Own Private Idaho.* When the generally conservative studio executives heard the titles and Van Sant's brief but enthusiastic pitches, their unproductive responses were, "Gee, Gus, they sound really literary. But we can't do films like *that.*"

11

ROPING *DRUGSTORE COWBOY*

Directors shouldn't be obliged to take a moral position on their subject matter because then they're dictating to the audience—and unless you're making a political film you shouldn't be doing that. People should be allowed to make up their own minds. My position on drugs [in *Drugstore Cowboy*] comes through if somebody is really looking for it, and though my position is admittedly highly ambiguous, it was never my intention to make a pro-drug film.

Gus Van Sant, 1989

LATER IN HIS CAREER Gus Van Sant would be repeatedly asked why within his first completed feature films (e.g., *Mala Noche*), he turned so frequently to sordid subject matter. After acknowledging one time that such topics are "certainly very much apart from my own upbringing," he said, "I think it's that . . . [these films] had settings that were unfamiliar enough to me that they seemed like fairytale land. Perhaps a need to tell a certain type of story that was set in a place that I didn't know anything about; adventure in a place that I didn't know anything about; adventure could be had because it's a land far away. . . ." Concerning these first movies he explained further that each was "close to each other but far away from the public, from the viewers, in the sense that *Star Wars* or pirate adventures are far away from them. It's a storyteller's technique to remove you from everyday life into a new area, so parables can be had." On another occasion, Van Sant said about the nonmainstream ambiance of his early films: "This world is something I've found and can understand, and as a low-budget film maker, it's also attractive because it's accessible."

On the same topic, a Portland publication once quizzed Eric Alan Edwards, Van Sant's longtime Oregon friend and frequent cinematographer, as to why Van Sant was drawn to life's disenfranchised on- (and off-) camera. After establishing that "Van Sant has long sought out people who live on the fringe of society—the disenfranchised who have no role in the American dream," Edwards observed, "It's too facile to say he's just a rich kid attracted to sleaze. If I wanted to put it in psychological terms, I'd say that children are attracted to things their parents are not. If you're from an upper-middle-class family, you have to find those things out for yourself. There's a certain strength of character you get from that."

Nick Wechsler, who produced Van Sant's *Drugstore Cowboy,* would say on the subject: "Gus goes against whatever the societal edicts are at the time. But I don't think that's particularly indicative of just him. The hip, bohemian artistic group of people in any decade of American society are always driven to anti-heroes who experiment with drugs and sex. That's not unusual. The unusual thing is getting movies made about those subjects."

▼

JACK Yost, who had been involved in raising some of the financial backing for *Mala Noche,* had an older brother, Daniel. The latter had first met Gus Van Sant in the late 1970s through their mutual Portland friend, cinematographer Eric Alan Edwards. Dan Yost had become a news journalist writing for the Sunday section of the *Oregonian* and other publications.

On one occasion in the 1970s Dan Yost interviewed and came to know book writer Thomas E. Gaddis, and even took a writing class from him. Gaddis had authored the 1955 biography *Birdman of Alcatraz: The Story of Robert E. Stroud.* The popular book—later made into a feature film with Burt Lancaster—dealt with one of the more amazing prisoners in the annals of American penology: a two-time killer who, during fifty-four years behind bars, became a noted ornithologist and author. Through that book and his work with incarcerated individuals, Gaddis gained a reputation as a man sympathetic to prisoners. One day a manuscript came in the mail from an imprisoned man named James Fogle, asking Gaddis's advice on the writing. Later, Gaddis turned Fogle's "submission" over to Dan Yost knowing that Yost was interested in the book world and screenwriting and perhaps there might be something in the story Yost could work on with Fogle.

As for Jim Fogle, he had spent a good deal of his life in jail. Born in Wisconsin in the 1940s, at the age of twelve he was already full of wanderlust. After running away from home (Olympia, Washington) several times, he landed at the Green Hill School for Boys near Chehalis, Washington. When he was sixteen, Fogle joined the army on a falsified baptismal record. While in the service he somehow went on the run again, this time in a stolen car. The police caught up with him, and the U.S. Army promptly removed him from active duty, sending him to a federal reformatory in Oklahoma. Over the next several years Fogle was constantly in trouble with the law. (The longest time he was outside of jail was a six-month period when he worked as a machinist fixing oil drilling rigs in Wyoming.) Then it was back to the highways, with more charges of burglary, forgery, and parole violations. By now, Fogle had spent time at San Quentin in Marin County, California, the Multnomah County Jail in Portland, and the federal penitentiary at McNeil Island near Tacoma, Washington.

It was while behind bars in 1961 that another prisoner told Jim Fogle about the idea of robbing prescription drugs from the pharmacy departments of drugstores. When Fogle was next released from prison, the apt student robbed a drugstore in Van Nuys, California, stealing an assortment of prescription drugs including Dexedrine, morphine, Percodan, Preludin, and Dilaudid. Always on the run from law enforcers and high on drugs, the only time Fogle broke his dependency habit was when he was in prison. During one of his periods behind bars—around the late 1960s—Jim began typing out stories on a typewriter. As he would recall to Kit Boss (*Seattle Times*): "One day I told my old cell partner, 'Hell, I can write a better book than this.' It wasn't as easy as I thought. I kept readin' and tryin' and studyin' other people. But I'm a little lazy, you know? If I can't get on the right trip it's hard to keep goin'."

In 1979 Fogle was living on the outside. On his birthday that year, he and his associate robbed a pharmacy near Elcho, Wisconsin (the town where Fogle was born). In the melee that followed his crime partner was shot in the stomach (and died the next day in the hospital), while Jim received twenty years for first-degree robbery. (Fogle began serving that term concurrently with his Washington State Penitentiary prison sentence for other robberies.)

▼

IN the mid-1970s Dan Yost got to know Fogle (through occasional visits to the prisoner and via correspondence). Yost became particularly intrigued with Jim's manuscript entitled *Satan's Sandbox*, the one set in San Quentin Prison and involving a love triangle among inmates. Yost appreciated that there was a good story there but the property was not in proper shape to show others. As Dan Yost modestly recalled to this author, he (Yost) primarily cleaned up the bad grammar and poor spelling. Enthusiastic about the manuscript and Fogle's innate talents, Dan peddled *Satan's Sandbox* to literary agents, some thirty publishers, and several movie studios, but with no success. Later, around 1974, Yost adapted the property into a screenplay. According to Yost it was not a difficult task because the manuscript was already almost a screenplay with "very rich dialogue" and "succinct prose." (Thereafter, after taking a screenwriting class, Yost wrote a new draft of the scenario more closely following the traditional screenplay format and style.)

Still unable to sell *Satan's Sandbox*, Yost kept it on his shelf for years, along with other efforts that Jim Fogle had periodically sent him. Meanwhile, in 1980, by which time Fogle had become inmate #215788 at the Washington State Penitentiary, Jim tried writing his autobiography. But after some six hundred to seven hundred pages Fogle threw it out, deciding the narrative made his life seem pointless. It was nowhere as interesting, he reasoned, as an unpublished book he'd written a few years earlier that still sat on Yost's shelf. That one, entitled *Drugstore Cowboy*, was based on his experiences as a drugstore rustler, although its lead character, Bob Hughes, was modeled after other thieves he had run with over the years. In the narrative, the protagonist, Bob, decides to go straight, while in real life Fogle only broke the drug habit when forced to on the inside. (The imprisoned Fogle became a member of a substance abuse support group while incarcerated at Walla Walla prison.)

In the early to mid-1980s Dan Yost, who was now writing screenplays himself—and had aspirations of becoming a filmmaker (which he would do with such entries as *Love & Sex, Etc.*, [1996], and *Actress*, [1999])—kept in touch with Gus Van Sant, often encountering him at Portland parties, especially at the home of Eric Alan Edwards. After Van Sant's *Mala Noche* began making the rounds of film festivals and gaining a positive reputation for Gus, it was bandied about that Gus's career would soon be on the fast track.

Yost asked Gus if he might be interested in any of Jim Fogle's writings as possible vehicles to direct. Gus read the cleaned-up manuscripts to Fogle's *Satan's Sandbox* and *Drugstore Cowboy* (but not Yost's screenplay of *Satan's Sandbox*). Initially, Van Sant was more intrigued with *Satan's Sandbox*. As Gus has recalled: "It was a prison triangle involving an effeminate black transvestite, Ivy, who ran a beauty parlor in prison, and two other inmates, Mike, and Ivy's former lover, Zitner, who was a real guy. . . . Mike, who was about eighteen and had been thrown into prison for causing a traffic accident where two women were killed, falls in love with Ivy and they have this torrid semi-gay love affair, to the amusement of Zitner. It was a comment on sexuality in prison, which had different rules from sexuality outside of prison."

Gus told Dan Yost that he liked both *Satan's Sandbox* and *Drugstore Cowboy* and that he wanted to mention the former to industry contacts and to write a (new) screenplay for each. In about a month's period Gus had written the two screenplays. As Van Sant began talking up the two projects to industry contacts, the plot line of *Satan's Sandbox* proved to be too far out there for any Hollywood studio to deal with at the time.

As for *Drugstore Cowboy*, with its tale of a druggie gang on the loose, the timing also seemed to be off. This was not the 1960s and 1970s—the age of flower children and hippie power—when such Hollywood studio film fare as *The Trip*, *Beyond the Valley of the Dolls*, and *Panic in Needle Park* freely discussed or, in some cases, even advocated the use of drugs. Now it was the period of the Ronald Reagan presidency, and First Lady Nancy Reagan had inaugurated a high-profile "Just say no" antidrug program in the United States. This led most of the studio suits to reject *Drugstore Cowboy* as an unfeasible topic to produce. As Van Sant explained, "There were a lot of people in Hollywood saying this is an immoral film that promotes drug use."

Van Sant tried to persuade the studios that, in his opinion, not all addicts are dirty and scabrous (which the executives assumed would turn off potential filmgoers from seeing a film about druggies). As Gus reasoned, "It can look clean, depending on your situation. The junkies that I know have gone into certain depths that are real dramatic, they show scars and marks and wear heavy makeup to hide it. Our characters at times look like that, but from their point of view they try to take care of themselves, and that exists, there are addicts who take care of themselves." No one on the film lots, however, responded favorably to his theories.

Along the way—around August 1987—a deal was made between Yost (acting on behalf of himself and Fogle) and Van Sant and signed over a meal at a Nibblers coffee shop in Los Angeles. Yost/Fogle would receive $20,000 ($12,000 to go to Fogle, $8,000 to go to Yost) for their contributions to the *Drugstore Cowboy* project, and Fogle would be credited as the author of the book original. In addition, Yost, for his work over the years in reshaping the prisoner's manuscript, would receive coscreenplay credit.

Discouraged but persistent, Gus continued to tout the *Drugstore Cowboy* script. So did Van Sant's agent at the influential William Morris Agency who kept reminding film executives of his client's recent award from the Los Angles Film Critics Association for Best Independent Film. While none of the big studios would commit to *Drugstore Cowboy*, the script eventually perked the interest of producers Nick Wechsler and Karen Murphy who made small independent pictures. At first Murphy didn't see the dark humor in *Drugstore Cowboy*, that is, until she met Gus Van Sant. Then she came to understand his offbeat sense of absurdity and how it had positively impacted the *Drugstore Cowboy* screenplay with a clever boisterousness that arises from the insights into the peculiarities of the junkie subculture.

Among their many submissions in mid-1988, Wechsler and Murphy took the project to Avenue Pictures, a fledgling U.S. distribution company with headquarters at 12100 Wilshire Boulevard in Los Angeles. There, it came to the attention of executive Laurie Parker. She had previously worked with such indie filmmakers as Spike Lee (*She's Gotta Have It*) and Jim Jarmusch (*Down by Law*)—both of whom Van Sant had been compared to—and liked the submitted property. Parker termed the *Drugstore Cowboy* script "very funny and just very humane."

In turn, Laurie Parker talked up the project to Cary Brokaw, head of Avenue Pictures, who agreed with her recommendation to consider the project for production. As Brokaw said later: "I saw this film as raw and real and not romanticized. The screenplay delivered vivid characters and shows a world a lot of people have never seen. Its precedents are things like *The Hustler*, *Midnight Cowboy*, and *Dog Day Afternoon*." (On another occasion Brokaw would expound, "We thought that previous films about drugs, conventional antidrug films, if you will, were too simplistic and one-dimensional and failed to fully explore the power and desperation of this world.")

A deal was struck whereby Avenue Pictures would make *Drugstore Cowboy* in the fall of 1988. When Van Sant heard the news that the picture had a go-ahead he was "in shock."

▼

BEFORE *Drugstore Cowboy* could be cast, it went through the usual quick rewrites, making the drama less bleak without sacrificing the spirit of the original manuscript. In creating the tone of the screenplay, Gus kept to a particular guideline: "Not being a drug addict myself I was making it for myself and for the public as a way of experiencing the life of a drug addict."

As Gus analyzed the film's perspective, "The events in the story line take place from the junkies' point of view, and it's hard to show both the outside and the inside, so we didn't attempt to. From their point of view everything is going real well." Expanding further on this, he said *Drugstore Cowboy* is "a vision from a junkie's mind. So the design and spirit of the film are a little removed from reality, a junkie fantasy where everything works out. But there is also the downside, when the junk wears out."

The screenplay was reshaped to properly depict the characters' rosy high when they are on drugs and to portray their harsh reality when they are sober. Gus's advantage was that the narrative's discussion of the junkie's life rang true because it was created by someone who had led that kind of life. But to be sure he didn't miss any aspect of the subject matter, Gus also turned to Jim Carroll, the former substance abuser who had written the critically acclaimed *Basketball Diaries*, the classic 1978 memoir of coming of age in the New York drug culture of the late 1960s. (This classic book would finally be turned into a film in 1995, costarring Leonardo DiCaprio and Mark Wahlberg.) Van Sant found Carroll's input very useful. Said the moviemaker: "He had gone through the plotting and intricate planning, the thinking of things throughout the night that never wind up being done, the fantasies and projects that our characters are involved with." Yet another influence on *Drugstore Cowboy* were the writings of Gus's literary hero, William S. Burroughs Jr., in particular Burroughs's *Junkie* (1953). Then there were the striking photo books (*Tulsa* and *Teenage Lust*) of photographer Larry Clark, which graphically revealed the world of druggies.

As the "final" screenplay was crafted, *Drugstore Cowboy* emerged as a sort of drug addict's *Bonnie and Clyde*. (It was definitely an antidote to *St. Elmo's Fire* and *Less Than Zero,* which were 1980s brat pack movies about rich druggies.) *Drugstore Cowboy* was a dark comedy about a band of junkies who rob pharmacies to feed their habits. But these drug addicts are not unprincipled individuals. In their own strange way, especially regarding the two lead figures (Bob and Dianne), these junkies are highly moral, with their own rules as to what is right and wrong within their world. (They are also superstitious creatures, having an entire catalogue of what causes good or bad luck.)

As in his past screen work, Van Sant remained nonjudgmental of his characters. In converting the dark first draft of *Drugstore Cowboy* into the final black comedy that works on both allegorical and realistic levels, it was Gus's goal not to create any false moves in the plot line. He didn't want the characters to do anything noticeably inconsistent with their natures just to appease the conventions of Hollywood. But in one particular area, Gus yielded to those in charge. It had to do with the film's finale, where the gunshot-wounded Bob is being taken to the hospital by ambulance. As executive producer Cary Brokaw stated about the smoothing out of the screenplay for eventual filmgoer consumption: "The contradictions are still there and still intriguing. Gus just found a way to allow today's audience to root for Bob's survival without resorting to a happy ending in the Hollywood style."

In refining the scenario, Van Sant also avoided preaching a hypocritical anti-drug message within the picture. This restraint later led Paul Andrews (*Seattle Times*) to decide about *Drugstore Cowboy*: "What makes the film unique: [it] blends absurdist humor with a near documentarian realism. He tells the truth about drugs. They have a certain fascination. They open up your consciousness. They're fun. They carry the danger of any addiction, but do not turn everyone's brain to fried eggs. They're like fast food, except that fast food takes longer to kill you and is legal."

As Gus joked later in 1989: "It's probably true that the movie will make a junkie want to go out and take drugs, but this isn't a political statement about drugs. I guess I do expect some sort of backlash."

12

FILMMAKING—
GUS VAN SANT STYLE

I was having a complete blast doing
this film. It was my first big movie. . . .
For me it was unbelievable, sort of like
a moment in life where as long as no
one's asking, you're going to go ahead
and keep shooting until someone says
you're not supposed to be doing this.

Gus Van Sant, 1999

UNDER THE AEGIS OF Avenue Pictures' chairman Cary
Brokaw, Gus Van Sant kept revising the *Drugstore Cowboy* script in the late
summer of 1988—to punch up the redemption of the lead character, Bob
Hughes. At the same time, the casting process began in haste in Los Angeles
and New York, as it had been decided to shoot the film in Portland that
October, hopefully before potential deep winter weather set into Oregon.
During part of August 1988 Van Sant was in New York City on the casting mis-
sion and stayed at the Gramercy Park Hotel.

After the fact, Van Sant would say that his ideal first choice to play Bob
Hughes in *Drugstore Cowboy* was screen veteran Jack Nicholson, the star of
such diverse fare as *Easy Rider*, *Chinatown*, *One Flew over the Cuckoo's Nest*,
The Shining, and *Prizzi's Honor*. "I'm sure Jack would have played it more dia-
bolical." However, (1) the budget could not afford the Oscar winner, (2)
Nicholson was always booked well in advance for screen projects, and (3) at
age fifty-one, Jack was too mature by nearly two decades for the key assignment. It was a part thirty-eight-year-old Mickey Rourke (*The Pope of Greenwich
Village*, *9½ Weeks*, *Angel Heart*) could have tackled, but his career was still in
partial high gear, which made him out of reach to the *Drugstore Cowboy* production. Brat packer Charlie Sheen (*Platoon*, *Wall Street*, *Young Guns*) might

have stretched into the part, but there again his career was still too hot, which meant he had a full lineup of commitments. Then too, on camera he tended to be flip and soft, or callous and one-note, none of which would have helped the Bob Hughes characterization to carry the film.

Instead, Van Sant chose twenty-five-year-old screen veteran Matt Dillon who had been acting in movies since 1979's *Over the Edge*. The handsome talent from New Rochelle, New York, had become a teenage heartthrob and reached his professional peak—so it seemed—with Francis Ford Coppola's drama *The Outsiders* in 1983 and Garry Marshall's nostalgic romantic comedy *The Flamingo Kid* the following year. Thereafter, Dillon's career had stumbled badly with such box-office misfires as *Target* with Gene Hackman, the Australian-filmed *Rebel*, the interracial story *Native Son*, *The Big Town* with Diane Lane, and *Kansas*, a real bomb with Andrew McCarthy. Dillon was in need of a solid comeback vehicle. What mostly likely appealed to Gus about the handsome actor was his ability to combine street toughness with vulnerability.

Negotiations went forward, but Dillon had "concerns" regarding the role. One of them was the time period of *Drugstore Cowboy*, which at that point was going to be present day. Dillon suggested that the era should be pushed back to the more "innocent" period of 1971. That was before the era when dirty hypodermic needles used for drug taking caused AIDS or before the popularity of crack and other heavy-duty drugs made substance abuse such a bad scene. Van Sant had the wisdom to see the virtue in this alteration and hastily made the necessary changes to the script (most of which had to do with topical references and to costumes, vehicles, and settings). That accomplished, the negotiations continued and Dillon was signed for the key assignment. Desperate for a screen hit to jump-start his flagging career, the actor accepted half his usual salary for *Drugstore Cowboy*.

Even with the casting of Matt Dillon, Gus had operated in the casting meetings in a rather unorthodox way. Unlike most film directors, he always took black-and-white (later in his career he switched to color) shots of candidates with whom he met, using an old Polaroid camera to take four-by-five-inch pictures. As he would describe in *108 Portraits* (1992), a volume of photos he shot over the years: "The faces in this book were originally Polaroids used to cast the movies I have made. Beginning with my film *Mala Noche*, I took the pictures of the lead actors, so that when planning details of the shoot I could stare at the pictures and imagine the characters coming to life, and how they might visually relate to one another. As my films grew larger and when I started to get more money to make them, I used the Polaroids of the faces to do the initial casting." Then, having collected the shots of the sixty or more actors he has met to discuss the current project, the next step in Gus's routine follows: "[I] sort of display them on the wall or use them almost like playing cards to figure out your cast. Play eight guys down and see, like, if they're working together. Like, take one out and put one in like solitaire or something. I can do that endlessly. I can sit there and mix and match for days and days."

This process has led the filmmaker to muse, "As I look closely at the pictures, I am reminded about the power a single person carries around with them. Everyone is different, and yet they all look somehow the same. They all embody huge potentials for success or failure, for nervousness or calm, for sainthood or deviltry, and have individually their proportionate share of both. They remind me of the moment the picture was taken, and how that moment is linked to their past, their present, and their future."

▼

FOR the role of tough, randy Dianne, Bob Hughes's feisty drug-dependent wife, Van Sant could have gone in the direction of an established actress such as Mare Winningham (*Nobody's Fool, Who Is Julia?, Made in Heaven*). Another possibility for that part had been Patti D'Arbanville (*Modern Problems, Real Genius, Fresh Horses*). She was the still-youthful-looking thirtysomething talent who had been discovered by Andy Warhol and cast in *Flesh* (1968) in a lesbian love scene. And if the budget could have afforded it there were such potentials as Jamie Lee Curtis (*Trading Places, A Fish Called Wanda, Dominick and Eugene*).

The actress, however, who really craved the role was Kelly Lynch. Minnesota-born Lynch had an intriguing background, one that would make her naturally sympathetic to the screen part of Dianne. In 1980, the twenty-one-year-old beauty suffered two shattered legs as the result of a serious auto accident. During eight months in the hospital, she became addicted to the painkiller Demerol and her weight tumbled from 125 to 85 pounds After making a dramatic recovery she established herself as a model famed for her long legs and light-colored hair. She made her first film, *Portfolio,* in 1983. More recently, she had played bimbo-type roles in *Bright Lights, Big City* with Michael J. Fox, *Cocktail* with Tom Cruise, and *Road House* with Patrick Swayze. Now a single mother with a three-year-old daughter, she was desperate to break out of bad movie parts that had led one film critic to describe her as a "grade C Kim Basinger."

As Lynch later said of trying out for *Drugstore Cowboy,* "I went after this like you can't imagine. I had been pigeonholed as always being the beautiful girl, and I was tired of that." Before her audition with Van Sant, she did not sleep the night before. She arrived at the crucial casting meeting with dirty hair and a T-shirt that sported a likeness of Donald Duck making an obscene gesture and saying "Quack Off, Jack." Gus, the master of clever understatements, would say thereafter of Kelly's audition: "I was impressed. I thought she was a kind of cowgirl."

Another of the key roles was that of Rick, the second-in-command of Bob Hughes's drug-stealing quartet. The part of the lifelong minor league criminal went to Minnesota-born James LeGros. With his stocky frame, compact build, and dirty blond hair, he was certainly no competition for Brad Pitt, but he had a knack for alternately looking vapid, tough, gentle, and aware. What also must have appealed to Van Sant about this surfer dude was that he shared with Gus a dislike for Hollywood and the film industry power games.

To play the young, needy Nadine, Van Sant considered, among others, former porno star turned actress, twenty-year-old Traci Lord. Instead, Gus went with virtual newcomer Heather Graham. The eighteen-year-old actress (a profession of which her FBI father and schoolteacher mother were quite leery) had had to drop out of the 1989 sleeper *Heathers* because her parents thought the film had too much salty language. Thus far she had only played small roles, such as in the TV movie *Student Exchange*, an uncredited bit in the Arnold Schwarzenegger–Danny DeVito comedy *Twins*, and a part in the vapid youth film *License to Drive*. Now of an age to make her own professional choices, she wanted the role of amateur grifter Nadine. With her fresh-faced beauty Graham could look the part of the novice in the film story's drug group, a mixed-up young woman who badly needed to be wanted.

In the movie business, like any industry, established participants are used to receiving recommendations from fellow workers. One that came Gus's way was the tip to use Rodney Harvey for the supporting role of David, a neighborhood druggie/small-time dealer who has a major impact on the Bob Hughes character. At the time, Allan Mindel, one of the founders of the modeling firm Click and of its film division, Flick, represented such performers as Kelly Lynch, Uma Thurman, and David Duchovny. It was Mindel who proposed the twenty-one-year-old Philadelphian for the *Drugstore Cowboy* acting assignment.

Harvey was extremely handsome—in the Peter Gallagher and Jason Gedrick mold. A once tough Philadelphia neighborhood kid, Rodney had been discovered walking along a New York street by filmmaker Paul Morrissey. Five-foot six-inch Harvey made his screen bow in Morrissey's *Delivery Boys* in 1984 and since then had appeared with favorable results in, among other entries, *Five Corners*, *Salsa*, and *Spike of Bensonhurst*. Rumored to be bisexual, Harvey insisted he was straight. A client/protégé of Mindel, Rodney had been having a lengthy but troubled relationship with actress Lisa Marie who once had been a model with Mindel's agency. (She had met Harvey on a photo shoot for Bruce Weber, another acquaintance of Van Sant's. In fact, Weber is acknowledged in the "thanks to" category in the end credits of *Drugstore Cowboy*.)

Either undetected or ignored in the haste to cast Rodney Harvey in the David role, the actor had a serious drug problem that was already threatening to sidetrack his promising screen career. Harvey's substance abuse reached a critical level during *Drugstore Cowboy* preproduction. According to Mindel in a lengthy December 1998 *Premiere* magazine article that tracked the rise and fall of Harvey, "I called Gus [Van Sant] because Rodney had gone out on a binge, and I said, 'I'm taking Rodney off the movie.'"

Quickly needing a replacement, Van Sant turned to another five-foot six-inch actor who also happened to be twenty-one. It was Ohio-born (and Los Angeles–raised) Max Perlich. The quirky young performer with the squinty eyes and hyper look had made his screen bow in 1986's *Ferris Bueller's Day Off* and since then had been in such screen excursions as *Can't Buy Me Love*, *Vibes*, and *Plain Clothes*. Perlich got the role described in the final shooting script of September 30, 1988, as "a long-haired hippy about twenty-one years old."

Then there was the part of Dianne's fed-up, sarcastic sister. That abbreviated role went to Amanda Plummer (*The World According to Garp*, *Hotel New Hampshire*, *Made in Heaven*), the thirty-one-year-old daughter of actors Christopher Plummer and Tammy Grimes.

Another key acting assignment was the part of Tom, the old druggie who had years earlier introduced Bob Hughes to the world of substance abuse. Van Sant needed no suggestions for casting this role. He thought it belonged to William S. Burroughs Jr., the man he had venerated for so many years and who had already allowed Gus to film his short story (*The Discipline of DE*) and who worked with Van Sant on a joint collaboration for the CD album (*The Elvis of Letters*). Burroughs's well-publicized history as a drug user and writer of druggie topics made this elder spokesman of the Hippie Generation a natural to take on the part.

Van Sant has related about winning over Burroughs's participation for *Drugstore Cowboy*: "He was very interested in the screenplay. He didn't want to play the character Tom the way he was originally written in the screenplay, which was as this sort of pathetic loser. He wanted the character to have some more pride. So he came up with the idea of making Tom be a junkie priest. He pretty much created the stuff in his scenes on his own." Given a relatively free hand with the part and the restriction of shooting his scenes entirely within a day or two, Burroughs came aboard Gus's new movie. As Van Sant has said of his mentor, "He was always very game for these 'projects' as he called them. Life to him was a 'project.'"

Performers were quickly hired to fill other featured roles: James Remar (*Cruising*, *48 Hours*, *The Cotton Club*) as the pursuing Portland police officer; Grace Zabriskie (*Norma Rae*, *An Officer and a Gentleman*, *The Big Easy*) as Bob Hughes's suspicious mother; and Beah Richards (*Take a Giant Step*, *Mahogany*, *The Big Shots*) as the African-American drug counselor. Ray Monge and Doug Cooyeate—both from *Mala Noche*—were given modest assignments in the new project, as was Michael Parker, the latter being one of Van Sant's young friends from Portland. (Others considered for possible roles in *Drugstore Cowboy* included actor Kevin Dillon, Matt's younger brother; Flea, the guitarist from the group the Red Hot Chili Peppers; and actor Anthony Kiedis.)

As the October 1988 shooting date approached, there were yet more changes to the script that had been in the director's words "workshopped a lot. . . . We smoothed out a lot of the rough edges. It evolved into more of a story of Bob Hughes's personal strength than it was initially."

Drugstore Cowboy was now ready to start production.

▼

FULLY aware how much his performance in and the success of *Drugstore Cowboy* itself meant to his own career, Matt Dillon put a lot of research into his pivotal screen role. To get into the proper mode to play Bob Hughes, he visited the story's author, James Fogle, in Washington State Prison to size up the man and get a better feel for the convict's prior way of life. (Fogle repeatedly insisted to Dillon and the others that Bob Hughes in the fiction was not he, but a fellow journeyman criminal with whom he used to work.) Dillon also went to drug addicts' hangouts in New York City to gain flavor; he attended Narcotics Anonymous meetings to observe how recovering substance abusers acted and reacted there. He also relied on his own experiences. As he told *Rolling Stone* magazine: "I had a friend who served time for robbing a taxi driver. Another friend died of an overdose. Hey, look where it got them."

The on-site researching had a cumulative affect on the usually glib Dillon: "After going through a lot of dope neighborhoods you get depressed. I came home one day and started crying. You get to the point where you start questioning, 'Am I an addict?' even though you don't use drugs. I started finding all those personality traits—like fear, you know. I talked to other people who've played addicts. They all went through it, that obsessive junkie behavior.'"

From all this field research Matt developed a workable take on his character: "There are certain gestures almost every junkie does. With their eyes, with their hands, with their wrists and downwards, always with the arms out. It's like he's saying, 'Like give me something, man—like I want something.'"

By the time *Drugstore Cowboy* was ready to start filming, Dillon, who had worked closely with Van Sant in the preparatory stages, now felt much better equipped to tackle the demanding role: "So many times in films, the drug addict is portrayed as a guy who is miserable getting high. Those films get it wrong. When Bob is high, that's when he thinks everything is great. I felt obligated to be honest about that. We didn't want to batter people over the head with sermons. We tried to be true to the characters and figured that if we succeeded, the morals would fall in place."

▼

VAN Sant had insisted upon using Portland, Oregon, for the filming and it had been an uphill battle with Avenue Pictures, who wanted to shoot the picture nearer to Los Angeles. Gus felt he had to accommodate the story line, which in James Fogle's original novel was set in the picturesque Pacific Northwest. It also allowed Gus Van Sant to use familiar surroundings, to have known "hometown" technicians and friends at hand to advise, support, and perhaps help out on the project in some capacity. Then, too, he could stay at his own digs during the filming. In addition, the location shoot for *Drugstore Cowboy* infused the local economy, which certainly gave Van Sant bonus points with Oregonians. (Gus also used actors from the region for small on-camera roles, such as Eric Hull who played the druggist in the film's opening heist scene.)

With his artist's eye, color and decor are key elements in setting the right tone for any of his movies. For *Drugstore Cowboy*, Gus and production designer David Brisbin agreed to use tones of green to set the film's motif. While many in the industry consider a green color theme in pictures as unflattering and thus taboo, for Van Sant this "don't break the rules" dictum makes the concept all the more appealing. (As Van Sant phrased it on the director's commentary of the 1999 DVD version of *Drugstore Cowboy*: "Because we [Van Sant and David Brisbin] didn't like it, we thought we wanted to go for it.") Thus, for *Drugstore Cowboy*, which was being shot in color even though Gus felt that black and white would have better suited the story's ambiance, green became the "black" on the palette of the production design. It resulted in emphasizing the natural greenery of the Oregon locale, the lime-green vehicles (for police cars), the Kelly-green clothing, with the period (to represent 1971) furniture ranging in shades from forest green to chartreuse. Many of the interiors have walls painted a tint of green.

Brisbin would say of his working relationship with Gus on *Drugstore Cowboy*: "The things that Gus has affection for are sometimes surprising and that will make a big difference in the production. I come from an approach of design, Gus comes from an approach of collecting, and these are two conflicting attitudes of how you create the image." But the production designer acknowledged that with Van Sant "picking pieces out of what I have carefully designed and put together, we've come up with something I think is very true to the atmosphere of the script."

As to the seventies outfits for the cast, costume designer Beatrice Aruna Pasztor (who would become a staple of the Van Sant filmmaking team) refused to use the cliché of T-shirts and levis for the druggie gang principals. Instead, for example, she garbed Matt Dillon's character in V-neck sweaters, mohair sweaters, velour shirts, and (plaid) slacks.

Cinematographer Robert D. Yeoman (*Hero, Rented Lips, Johnny Be Good*) had a particular work method in starting a new picture shoot. It had to do with *The Conformist*, the 1971 feature by Italian filmmaker Bernardo Bertolucci: "On every movie I work on, I like to sit down with the director beforehand and look at that film because it's very inspirational. Everyone should see *The Conformist*. To me it's kind of a Bible of filmmaking. We also looked at [Martin Scorsese's] *Taxi Driver*, as Gus felt that it contained certain visual parallels to *Drugstore Cowboy*. Another film was *Fat City* by John Huston. I've admired Conrad Hall's photography in that film for a long time. Using these and other films as a reference, Gus, David Brisbin (the production designer), and I were able to discuss the visual elements that would constitute the look of *Drugstore Cowboy*." This was particularly important in *Drugstore Cowboy* because the use of green as the film's color theme meant there needed to be high-contrast lighting created for the setups of scenes.

Once the shoot got under way, Yeoman proved to be of tremendous assistance to the relatively new feature filmmaker in other areas as well: "Gus was used to the ease of 16 mm. He planned some camera moves, such as inside a car, that may have worked in 16 mm but in 35 mm would have been next to impossible. He proved to be very flexible, however, and soon adapted to the limitations of the larger format." And it was Yeoman who also suggested following Robby Müller's (*Paris, Texas*; *Down by Law*, *Barfly*) European cinemagraphic style of giving more consideration to camera placement than coverage in a given scene. Fortunately, the dry October weather and overcast skies allowed Yeoman to shoot the outdoor scenes in natural light from any direction without interference from distracting sun rays.

Meanwhile, Van Sant's biggest concern—which he joked about to some but was deadly serious about to himself and his confidants—was how he would adjust to shooting a relatively big-budget film (just under $7 million—compared to $25,000 for *Mala Noche*) with a crew of sixty or seventy constantly on hand. With such a sizeable squad and the cost of each wasted moment cutting into the budget, Gus had the difficult task of adjusting to a production in which he was not virtually one third to one half of the full crew. And if he had to learn to think quickly on his feet, as obstacles or new ideas made the planned (storyboarded) shot unfeasible or less inviting, he also had to adjust to the inevitable process of accepting that there were times when he had to stand back, drink coffee, and kibitz with others while the technical crew worked out a given problem. (As the director phrased it, "I'm just caught in the middle of this traveling circus sort of thing which . . . goes at its own pace.") Thus, making *Drugstore Cowboy* taught Van Sant the virtue of creative flexibility on the set: "So you go with the flow and you make it [i.e., the production] the thing it sort of wants to become on its own and you help it in that direction."

Van Sant, as always, played his emotions close to the vest and camouflaged his concerns from the actors so as not to cloud their creativity. Nevertheless, several of the cast during the making of *Drugstore Cowboy* had ample opportunity to make observations about their director who had little previous experience working with professional film actors. Said Matt Dillon: "He's got a real voyeuristic side to him; he's tricky that way, you know? He's always got this look on his face like there's some private little joke in the back of his mind." Heather Graham noted, "You never know what he's thinking or what he thinks of anything you're doing." She also pointed out, "He doesn't really tell you all the time, 'I want you to do this, I want you to do that.' He just kinda lets you figure it out and let you do it over and over again till you figure it yourself." Grace Zabriskie commented, "I think maybe he has a little of a first-time director's fear of saying, 'I didn't like that approach, could we try it again.' When he liked it, I knew it." James LeGros recalled, "Gus was forever taking pause and looking around the set and saying, 'Who are all these people?'"

Kelly Lynch, who seemed totally relaxed during the tough shoot, informed *GQ* magazine that Gus was a director who "gently guides you toward a getter performance, doesn't shove anything down anyone's throat. Usually, the bigger the budget, the more black-and-white the film is—it all becomes so obvious and right there. What this pictures does is very subtle and so rare in big-budget films. It's not making any big statements; it's saying, 'This is the way it is.'" To *Venice* magazine, Kelly Lynch would assess that she and Dillon "thought it was a very funny movie. A lot of people thought it was sad and so down, but our characters aren't; there's such ambiguity. Our characters feel high and whatever that goofy feeling is that junkies drift on for a while until the house of cards blows away."

A production worry for Van Sant and his staff was to insure that in the outdoor location work the period flavor was maintained. For example, despite posted notices that all vehicles manufactured after 1971 be removed from particular northwest Portland thoroughfares, there were some close calls with drivers who had not heeded the requests.

As was becoming a trademark of Van Sant's films, at one point in the production of *Drugstore Cowboy* he turned a Super 8mm camera over to the principal actors so they could take home movies of each other to be integrated into the feature. Gus's primary instruction to the performers was to "stay in character." Thereafter, he incorporated the footage—largely rough takes of the actors and even Van Sant mugging and making silly faces for the shaky camera—into the final cut.

Then there was the production day when Dillon did the sequence in which his character first shoots up. "If you'd shown me a needle six months before, I would have been put off by it. But when it came time for that scene, I just tied up and popped the needle [using distilled water]. But jeez, I could feel the tension on the set while I was doing it."

▼

AS the relatively fast six-week production schedule moved on, it came time for Burroughs to make his appearance on the set for his compacted sequences. With Van Sant's approval the elder man and James Grauerholz (Burroughs's much younger, longtime close friend) had revamped his role. Gus said later: "Burroughs contributed all of his own dialogue with a few exceptions which I'm proud of because he gets to say things I wrote. . . . [H]e wanted to just shoot for a day, so we limited it to one day, even though there are a lot of scenes. It was sort of a hard day, but we did it."

Burroughs's scenes were largely played with Matt Dillon's character and occur in the final portion of *Drugstore Cowboy*, primarily at the St. Francis Hotel, a depressing establishment in Portland. Said Dillon, who by then had gained great confidence in his tricky characterization: "It was a tough couple of days the Burroughs stuff. It's not like we're really conversing. We are vaguely conversing. I never thought of it the whole time we were shooting, but now I see it as being more surreal than anything else. My character is struggling with his life, and Burroughs is a kind of ghost, cleansing me and redeeming me."

For Van Sant, who had so long idolized Burroughs, it was an enormous thrill to have this icon on his film set and to direct him. Even more exciting was to know that this writer was speaking some of Van Sant's own dialogue on camera. The brief experience of working with "one of my heroes" was a high point in the filmmaker's life. (In subsequent years, Van Sant and Burroughs became closer friends.)

▼

AS the filming proceeded, expectations that *Drugstore Cowboy* was turning into a special movie became increasingly clearer to the cast if not always to the higher-up executives on the project. Said Kelly Lynch: "We knew we had caught a wave. . . . We were going with it. You could feel it every day."

Finally, some six weeks after they began, principal photography on *Drugstore Cowboy* wrapped. The last scene shots were at an old brick apartment building on a corner on Stark Street, off Burnside, near downtown Portland, and a fill-in scene of Bob Hughes and his cohorts emptying out a load of drug goodies from a drugstore pharmacy.

Then, with what seemed like lightning speed to Gus Van Sant, the cast and crew took off. What the day before had been a busy production office was now empty and deserted. Having wondered how he would deal with a big cast and crew on *Drugstore Cowboy*, Van Sant suddenly found himself missing them— they had become his family and life these past months.

Now "I'm left here with nothing but an editing room and some film, but all the people are gone."

13 THE HATS PAY OFF

What attracted me to . . . [*Drugstore Cowboy*] was the gritty quality of the writing—that seems to be a word often applied to my work—and the strong point of view, like in *Mala Noche*. It's seen from the eyes of the writer, a con man: the fast-moving and frenetic life of petty crime and drug-taking. The principals are two couples, a gang of four, one couple in their mid-twenties, the other a few years younger, but the thread is superstition and hats.

Gus Van Sant, 1988

REPEATEDLY, OVER THE years, Gus Van Sant has been asked if the humor within his playful *Drugstore Cowboy* came from the original manuscript by the incarcerated James Fogle. "A lot," he has said. "It depends on how you read the novel, but I thought all the humor was in there. We didn't punch it up or anything, we didn't make it funnier or try to make it heavier, we kept true to the comedy in it."

What sets up and allows much of the natural comedy is the special world created within *Drugstore Cowboy*. While the story line is set in the pre-"Say No to Drugs" era of 1971, the characters exist in their own special "reality." There is no mention of the Vietnam War, the Kent State massacre, flower power, President Richard M. Nixon, or other issues of the day. This druggie gang has nothing to do with that matter-of-fact world. Instead, they are focused—through their leader Bob Hughes—on drugstores and how these tantalizing emporiums can satisfy their junkie needs. Within this frame of reference, their only contacts with the "real" or "other" world is the variety of drugstores and the bothersome police.

In the ongoing hazy swirl that makes up the lives of Bob and his crew, they are not ruled by society's usual conventions. Rather, they are controlled, as Hughes says in one of his monologues, by "the dark forces that lie hidden beneath the surface, the ones that some people call superstitions. Howling banshees, black cats, hats on beds, dogs, the evil eye." In Bob's drug-induced existence, his lunatic logic seems to make perfect sense and is a "reasonable" guide for living.

It is hats that provide a key theme throughout *Drugstore Cowboy*. They symbolize Bob Hughes's commandments regarding superstitions. As Van Sant has offered, "Like many people in this milieu who live by their wits, Bob . . . has intuitive feelings about when to move ahead with his inspired criminal acts, and when to lay low. Mirrors are important. You should never look at the back side of a mirror because you'll be looking at your inner self, a side you've never seen before. Not just black cats are bad—all cats are. Talking about dogs is really bad. There are also good signs to look for, as if whoever manages such things is telling you, 'Get out there and get it, kid. It's there for the taking, and it's free this week.' But the king of the omens is hats. . . . Beware—the owner of a hat may have the evil eye, so if anyone puts a hat on a bed, it's trouble. I think it comes from Eastern cultures, related to hair, heads, evil spirits living in a hat. If they put their hat near where you sleep—watch out."

The harrowing story of *Drugstore Cowboy* concerns Bob Hughes and his followers in 1971 Portland, Oregon. There they practice their craft—robbing drugstores and hospital pharmacies to satisfy their druggie cravings (*not* to score drugs to sell for profit). The quartet is composed of street-smart but extremely superstitious Bob, his randy wife, Dianne, as well as another couple, the impressionable and goofy Rick and the young, insecure Nadine.

While enjoying the fruits of their latest haul, the group is visited by a junkie acquaintance, David, who lives nearby. Bob, who thinks himself superior to everyone, treats David contemptuously. Later the gang's house is ransacked by law enforcers led by narcotics officer Gentry, the latter determined to bust Bob and his team once and for all. When Bob and Dianne visit his mother to get his remaining clothes, all he can think of is stealing drug money from her purse. Later, Bob concocts an intricate plan that causes one of Gentry's fellow officers to be shotgun-wounded by a neighbor. This leads Gentry and his men to beat up Hughes. Deciding their luck has turned sour, the four addicts leave town.

One evening their latest drugstore raid nets the gang a very strong drug (Dilaudid). Later, while Bob, Dianne, and Rick are unsuccessfully breaking into a hospital pharmacy, Nadine overdoses. When the others return to the motel, she is dead, having earlier mischievously set a hat on her bed. After narrowly missing being caught by police who have converged at the motel for a convention, Nadine is buried in the countryside. Bob is now convinced that her death is a final omen—that he should abandon drugs.

Back in Portland alone (Dianne cannot imagine a life without drugs and has gone off with Rick), Bob joins a rehabilitation program and finds work in a machinery shop. At his rundown hotel, he encounters Tom, a former priest and longtime drug addict, who initiated Hughes into substance abuse. Later, Dianne visits Bob, foolishly leaving him a stash of drugs and telling him that she is now working for and living with Rick. After Hughes gives the unwanted drugs to a receptive Tom, David and a masked helper break into Bob's room. When he insists he has no drug stash, David (who has never forgiven Hughes for stopping him from strong-arming a crying teenager) beats him up and then shoots him. As the ambulance takes Bob to the hospital, he refuses to tell law enforcer Gentry who shot him.

▼

AS the postproduction phase of *Drugstore Cowboy* began, Van Sant grafted onto the film several of his special touches. Some of them were of second-unit nature, such as having his cinematographer friend Eric Alan Edwards shoot footage of the swirling Portland skyline using time-lapse photography. This "gimmick" became central to Gus as he expanded his concept of showing a junkie's reverie by having spinning objects twirl onto and off the screen, often against the backdrop of swirling clouds. One such sequence occurs after the picture's opening heist as Bob shoots up in the backseat of the getaway car. During his reverie drug paraphernalia (especially a spoon) are recurrent themes along with floating/bouncing items (such childhood image as toy planes, fig-ures, cows, and chickens to reflect Bob's blissful childlike nature). Another time—just after burying Nadine, Bob has another vision—this time assorted hats pass in front of his eyes, emblems of the bad luck he and the others have suffered because Nadine placed a hat on her bed. These hallucinatory mo-ments—most of them afterthoughts to the final shooting script—appealed to Van Sant's artistic nature. He also believed they would make filmgoers feel that they too were experiencing aspects of a drug high.

As to the creation of these special effects, Van Sant explained, "They were just little models that we rented or bought. We made them spin and shot them against a white wall and then double-exposed them like they would have done in the thirties. It was pretty simple. We didn't have very much money for special effects, so we did them on our own. One word for those scenes would be expositionary."

It was not until this postproduction phase that Gus inserted another of his familiar effects, the close-ups of inanimate objects (e.g., shots of coffee cups, light bulbs, lit cigarettes) that often punctuate or end a scene within *Drugstore Cowboy*. He did this in a two-day period where there was no longer a large, costly crew on the payroll and he could handle the tasks with just one or two others. As he has related, "We chose specific places in the film where those close-ups would appear and then we got props and actually shot them in the editing room. That light bulb [shown in close-up in the film] was from the edit-ing table lamp! . . .

"A lot of people think it works well in the film because a drug addict might focus on something that small, a light bulb or a match or something like that, and just stare at it, which is true, actually. Maybe we were cueing off a sort of aesthetic that was working its way into the script from the book. It was a stylistic device that I'd been playing with since I started photographing objects in the sixties. I remember buying bellows for my camera so that I could shoot things extremely close up."

During the next months, as with *Mala Noche*, Gus labored intensively over the editing process. He rearranged scenes, shortened some, deleted others. He sometimes showed the assembled footage to Portland friends (and the reaction was not always enthusiastic). As time progressed, and Avenue Pictures had ongoing concerns whether the latest cut was still too graphic for the censors and/or the public, several editors worked on the project. More tense months went by in 1989 as *Drugstore Cowboy* was constantly reshaped. (In the process, a few goofs crept into or remained in the feature film. For example, in the opening sequence of *Drugstore Cowboy* as Bob Hughes struts down the Portland street toward the drugstore he is about to rob, the film crew and equipment are accidentally reflected in the drugstore plate glass window. During the break-in at the hospital pharmacy Hughes's black gloves that he has been wearing magically disappear in a scene shot change as he is prying open the metal lock of the drug drawers.)

In the postproduction cycle, the rather abbreviated role of Dianne's sister—played by Amanda Plummer—was deleted. An opening sequence of Bob musing over writing a guidebook to drugstore robberies was dropped. The screenplay section in which Hughes envisions himself being shut up behind bars as he and his crew are about to rob a drugstore became part of a later montage at the motel—where paranoid Hughes is sure the law will discover Nadine's corpse hidden in the ceiling crawlspace. (This leads to dream moments of Bob visualizing himself being handcuffed, suffering the verdict as a gavel bangs on a judge's bench, and being shut behind clanging bars.)

During the actual filming of *Drugstore Cowboy* some of the swear words in the final shooting script were removed; others were cut now in postproduction. A brief sequence in which Dianne visits a doctor's office and pilfers drugs from the examination room cabinets was snipped out. The home movies taken by the cast as they goof about a railroad terminal yard where a forlorn dog with bandaged ears is wandering about were now interwoven into the opening and closing credits, with snippets used elsewhere in the film to accent the characters.

This home movie gimmick footage, more so than in *Mala Noche*, provides introductions and personality traits of the on-screen figures. As Van Sant has explained, "I thought they were Bunuel, Daliesque. They were images we put in as abstract expressionism, as things the character was feeling or thinking at the time. They were just an abstraction of the visuals and went into his [Bob Hughes's] thoughts. . . . [We] used it as a memory thing, a memory of the past for Bob as he's in the ambulance on the way to the hospital."

Elliott Goldenthal, whose first credit as a film composer was another drug-themed picture (1979's *Cocaine Cowboys* with Jack Palance and Andy Warhol), provided the score for *Drugstore Cowboy*. With Gus's approval Goldenthal created a very adept score that utilized unusual musical sounds (e.g., chimes and bells sounding during one drug-induced sequence) to heighten the unreality of the bizarre, emotional roller-coaster existence of the druggie quartet.

In the choice of music (including many 1970s hits) for *Drugstore Cowboy* the musically oriented Van Sant worked closely with Goldenthal. The picture opens and closes with a rendition of "For All We Know" by Abbey Lincoln, in a rendition that Van Sant had heard the artist perform on a late-night talk show and oozed the intimacy needed to set the right atmosphere on screen. The picture's other most discussed song track was Desmond Dekker & the Aces singing "The Israelites" as Hughes and his team trek from one Oregon city to another hoping to elude the law and find a new haven to begin their next drugstore robbery spree. Other songs utilized included Bobby Goldsboro's "Little Things" as well as Rony Erickson & Jack Johnson's rendition of "I Am."

▼

FINALLY scheduled for limited release in October 1989—Avenue Pictures was unsure of how the movie would be received—*Drugstore Cowboy* was entered in the Toronto International Film Festival being held that September. At the festival press conference for the movie, Gus Van Sant was asked how he expected the public to react to a drug-themed picture in this strongly antidrug era. The director told the assemblage: "Well, it's . . . all ready to go out to the public. The MPAA [Motion Picture Association of America] which is in Washington and Jack Valenti [its president] rated it 'R.' We thought we would have some problem with the depictions of drug use, mostly the needles and things."

Gus allowed, "I think there will be a lot of people who won't see it at all, who might boycott it or speak about it in a bad way, so I'm expecting that kind of thing. But I'm not expecting any problems really. Negative publicity could help, depending on who it's coming from—actually I was thinking about that [in a joking tone] somebody you would want to oppose this film—send them a copy of the film, that sort of thing."

The actual Toronto screenings went extremely well. Influential newspaper and TV reviewer Roger Ebert was one of the most enthusiastic viewers in the audience. Costar Kelly Lynch would recall, "I remember Roger Ebert almost knocking me down at the Toronto Film Festival, just like a schoolboy, going, 'Oh my god, it's such a great movie! And you're so good, I knew people like that, you don't know what you've captured!'"

But as the October 1989 limited release date approached, Cary Brokaw, chairman of Avenue Pictures, rightly was concerned about the temper of the country and its potential reaction to *Drugstore Cowboy*. With understatement he acknowledged that making the $6 million to $7 million film under the pressure of America's then current antidrug campaign "was kind of daunting." Yet he stressed, "We wanted to do something bold, to work in a genre of which there were few or no recent examples."

Nevertheless, Avenue decided *not* to be daring in its promotional campaign. Bingham Ray, executive vice president of marketing/distribution for Avenue, acknowledged to the trade press: "During the rough-cut stage we thought the ratings board might give us an X for graphic depiction of drug paraphernalia and drug abuse. We were planning a strategy on how to use that." Now that it had the more marketable R rating (which meant a larger audience age-range than an X-rated film could potentially see the picture), Ray explained, "We are concentrating on the strength of the picture—the relationship of Bob and Diane. We wanted an accessible (advertising) image that doesn't violate what the film is about. It's a movie about people." What was developed for the poster artwork deliberately played down the movie's drug theme. It depicted coleads Matt Dillon and Kelly Lynch in a benign embrace that avoided suggestion of the picture's dark and at times bleak ambiance.

After its lengthy maturation, the 100-minute *Drugstore Cowboy* (different earlier cuts ranged from 90 to 108 minutes) debuted on October 6, 1989, at New York City's Carnegie Hall Cinema and five days later at the Nuart Theatre in Los Angeles. (These were *not* prestigious showcase sites to open a new film.) Stephen Holden (*New York Times*) enthused, "It offers a cool-eyed vision of young addicts adrift during the twilight of the counterculture. Both in its delineation of character and in its evocation of an era when drug taking still carried an aura of hipness, the film rings deeply true." The *Times* critic endorsed *Drugstore Cowboy*: "The film takes us so deeply into this shabby, transient world that we feel its texture—both its scary thrills and its bleak, fatalistic uncertainty."

As to Van Sant, Holden decided that *Drugstore Cowboy* "fulfills the promise suggested by his grainy low-budget 1987 film *Mala Noche* . . . As in *Mala Noche*, Mr. Van Sant . . . neither glamorizes nor sharply censures his characters." Regarding the film's performances, Holden judged, "the only false note is struck by the writer William S. Burroughs . . . [T]he cadaverous Mr. Burroughs gives one of his standard performances, raving in a feverish monotone. His appearance slightly throws off the mood of a film that is otherwise a very impressive look into a dark subject."

Sheila Benson (*Los Angeles Times*) rated *Drugstore Cowboy* "an electrifying movie." She went on to say, "The wonder is that a movie this alert, this razor-funny and this compulsively watchable can be made about it [i.e., drugs] without betraying its blitzed-out characters." Benson also noted, "But when it wants to be, *Drugstore Cowboy* is laconically comic, humor that comes from a mix of precise language and the slow-mo reaction time of people moving under drugs."

J. Hoberman (*Village Voice*) ranked *Drugstore Cowboy* a "tough, funny film made with considerable verve and no small amount of guts." *New York Post*'s Jami Bernard offered, "It is as accurate a portrayal as any of the peculiarly insulated life and concerns of the addict." Hal Hinson (*Washington Post*) also had a positive report: "This is a drug movie made from the inside out, by people who understand the life. . . . Van Sant gives his material shape and an invigorating, syncopated style. It keeps coming at you in surprising, dazzling ways. It jazzes you."

One of those to find fault with *Drugstore Cowboy* was D. K. Holm of Portland's *Willamette Week*. In reviewing this hometown production, he noted sequences such as when Bob Hughes shoots up his drugs and animated figures prance across the screen. "And to the extent that Van Sant gets some of the tone of the winkling carousel of tuning out, the scenes are effective. We know what he *means*. But in a city with a filmmaker such as Jim Blashfield—a master of crisp and clear, swirling, multilevel images—audiences have higher standards for animation." Holm hastily acknowledged, "Everything else is top notch."

Another who was not entirely satisfied with the new release was Terry Kelleher (*Newsday*): "The difficulty with *Drugstore Cowboy* is that the characters stubbornly refuse to do the expected thing. Their behavior can seem illogical, unmotivated, implausible and therefore unacceptable. It fails to jibe with what we know about drug addiction. Or what we *think* we know." Then, too, David Denby (*New York*) chided, "Here and there Van Sant tries for hallucinatory imagery—little black animals and the like flying through the air upside down. But lyric bliss is not his thing. He's best at the funny-sinister everyday life of young dopers, the frozen stupidity and sneaky smarts, the rhythm of frenzied activity and bombed-out catatonia."

But such qualified responses paled next to the hosannas from the likes of Roger Ebert (*Chicago Sun-Times*): "Like all truly great movies, *Drugstore Cowboy* is a joyous piece of work. I believe the subject of a film does not determine whether it makes us feel happy or sad. I am inutterably depressed after seeing stupid comedies that insult my intelligence, but I felt exhilarated after seeing *Drugstore Cowboy*, because every person connected with this project is working at top form. It's a high-wire act of daring, in which this unlikely subject matter becomes the occasion for a film about sad people we come to care very deeply about." In short, said the enraptured Ebert, "This is one of the best movies of the year."

Steve Vineberg (*Film Quarterly*) congratulated Gus for "creating a leapfrogging rhythm out of odd slanted angles and quick cuts, and a skewed vision of the world out of his unpredictable, often magical focus on unexpected objects (or ordinary objects seen in extraordinary ways.)." Vineberg approved that "[w]hen Bob boils water for tea in a little tin pot in his room, Van Sant's camera practically dives into the bubbles[;] . . . when Bob switches on a light, Van Sant gets in close enough that we can read the wattage on the bulb. And there are free-form sequences where the implements of Bob's lifestyle—capsules, spoons, matches—as well as tiny trees and at one point a blue gun float by like the uprooted bits of Dorothy's farm during the cyclone in *The Wizard of Oz*. . . . Van Sant has a gift for this kind of lopsided allusiveness and home-grown collage surrealism. He also has a gift for conveying outsiders' perspectives."

Capping his critical endorsement, David Ansen (*Newsweek*) praised, "The emergence of the 36-year-old Van Sant, who lives in Portland, is the most heartening news from the American 'independent' cinema since Steven (*sex, lies and videotape*) Soderbergh." Ansen concluded, "Van Sant has an unforced lyrical touch and a feel for low life that's free of both condescension and macho romanticizing. Every minute of *Drugstore Cowboy* is vital and alive, even when its junkie protagonist seems barely to be breathing."

As positive word-of-mouth spread about this unusual American production among reviewers and audiences alike, perhaps the most meaningful response to *Drugstore Cowboy* for Gus Van Sant came from James Fogle. The incarcerated man had to view his story on a prison VCR. According to Gus: "he said he thought it was 'real good'—those are his words, he uses 'real good' a lot." (In the months that followed, Fogle gathered together a packet of clips about *Drugstore Cowboy* that he kept under his cell bed. But despite the success of the film he still had his prison routine to follow. In the early 1990s he would be paroled from prison, but then ended up back behind bars. By the turn of the new millennium he was a free man again, but not in good health.)

In the wake of its favorable release, *Drugstore Cowboy* garnered several awards, including 1989 New York Film Critics (Best Screenplay), 1989 Los Angeles Film Critics Association (Best Screenplay), 1989 Pen Literary Award (Best Screenplay Adaptation), 1990 National Society of Film Critics (Best Director, Best Film, and Best Screenplay), 1990 Independent Spirits Awards (Best Cinematography, Best Male Lead, Best Screenplay, and Best Supporting Male), and 1990 Berlin International Film Festival (C.I.C.A.E. Award—Forum of New Cinema). Commercially, this surprise hit grossed $4.73 million at the domestic box office alone. When *Drugstore Cowboy* was released on home video in 1990 it became one of the five best-selling entries of that summer.

All in all it was quite an achievement for the independently made feature film.

▼

OVER the years since its initial release, *Drugstore Cowboy* has retained its lustrous image, even in the face of a grittier later film (the British-made *Trainspotting*, the 1996 feature directed by Danny Boyle and starring Ewan McGregor that examined the drug underground culture in Edinburgh, Scotland). For many *Drugstore Cowboy* is a demystification of the glamorized outlaw as presented in Warren Beatty's *Bonnie and Clyde*. For Gus the essence of his new film was, "We took a difficult subject and weathered the audience through it. . . . We just took a cold look at a difficult subject . . . that's the strength of the film, I think, the risks that I take."

A few years ago when the Edinburgh University Film Society in Scotland showed *Drugstore Cowboy* as part of its season, Alistair Harkness wrote in the program notes: "*Drugstore Cowboy* marked the rebirth of the American indie and, by transferring the setting from the 'bright lights, big city' scenario to the grainy, rain-soaked atmosphere of Portland, Oregon, circa 1971, Van Sant has created a film which has become as much a document. He presents a reflection on the burnout of the early seventies and the inevitable consequences of sixties hedonism, as applicable to the post Reagan fall out amidst which the film was made."

But *Drugstore Cowboy* also has a special relevance within the canon of Gus Van Sant's work. It marks his transition from small-time indie filmmaker to one who could work successfully on a much larger budget for a Hollywood-based independent movie production firm. The success of the picture elevated Van Sant into the public awareness, far more so than the extremely limited release of *Mala Noche* had allowed.

The technical sophistication of *Drugstore Cowboy* boasts a complement of professional qualities—ranging from the color cinematography to the proficient music score and its unique production design. Within these technical trappings, the "old" Gus Van Sant still shines through with his attraction to non-mainstream characters living a marginalized, transient existence. As in *Mala Noche* the narrative is presented with humor rather than somber neorealism. The fantasy moments (e.g., Walt's dream of a midnight rendezvous at the fleabag hotel with his Mexican street hustler) that had adorned *Mala Noche* are greatly expanded upon in *Drugstore Cowboy*. But this time, they are dealing with screen characters constantly on a drug high or a paranoid, chemically induced stupor. Thus, the cinematic flights of imaginations are even more appropriate to the on-screen figures and their way of life.

In *Mala Noche*, Van Sant had shown store clerk Walt creating briefly a family of sorts with two Mexican street boys. In *Drugstore Cowboy*, the nuclear family unit is more fully developed but even more bizarre. In many ways the essentially decent Bob Hughes and the unregenerated Dianne, who are married, are blue-collar-type parents who provide for the less tutored junkie thief Rick and the true novice, Nadine. (It cannot be coincidence that Nadine's name is an anagram of Dianne, another example of the film's suggestion that Nadine is the offspring of her female role model.) Throughout the movie, like any middle-class parents, Bob and Dianne teach their "children," showing them the ropes of daily life, setting out rules to live by, and doling out rewards or punishments for the way the two young crooks follow their elders' directions. In the end, the two younger ones flee the nest: Nadine in death; Rick to follow in his mentor's profession. The twisted take here is that Dianne, deserted by her spouse, goes off with her "son" to be part of his gang and to be his old lady. It is a Freudian subtext that is another example of the complexities often found in Van Sant's characters who, on the surface, seem rather simplistic.

Drugstore Cowboy also manifests Van Sant's continued fascination with the Portland skyline and the byways of the economically diverse city. Then, too, there is the director's attraction to cars, not only as a means of convenient travel, but also as transportation to search for a change of living quarters (i.e., a new homestead). This focus on vehicles leads to another wonderful, classic dialogue line in *Drugstore Cowboy* in which Dianne complains to her sexually indifferent or drug-induced impotent spouse: "You won't fuck me and I have to drive." (At another point in *Drugstore Cowboy* Dianne comments about her spouse: "Bob's like a rabbit. In and out in no time with no fuss.")

Like Walt of *Mala Noche*, Bob Hughes fully indulges his every whim in his self-centered life. But in *Drugstore Cowboy*—perhaps more a result of production company pressure to have the antihero be redeemed by the finale—Hughes comes to a far greater understanding of his addictions, albeit guided by his superstitions (i.e., "You gotta know how to read the signs"). Nevertheless, Van Sant, who thrived on antiestablishment behavior and rebellion against authority, could never have his ex-druggie Bob end on a truly positive note just for the sake of box office.

As Van Sant suggests on-screen and in commentary over the years, Bob's fate in the narrative is not that rosy. With his critical injuries he may well expire en route to the hospital. On the other hand, if he should survive, he is in an interesting situation. As he points out in the closing monologue: "The chicken shit cops were giving me an escort to the fattest pharmacy in town." So it may be that Hughes, who said earlier to his drug counselor (Beah Richards), "I like drugs. I like the lifestyle. But it didn't pay off," may be returning to the world of addiction. The ambiguous ending to *Drugstore Cowboy* foreshadows a similar fate of the lead character in the later *My Own Private Idaho,* who is also last seen inside a vehicle.

Another element within *Drugstore Cowboy,* and one that would increasingly intrigue Van Sant the filmmaker, is the use of the visual signs he places within the film telling of upcoming events. Beyond the color choice of using green, which ties together themes within this movie, there is the moment in *Drugstore Cowboy* where Bob is at the motel office requesting an extension of his room rental, so he can decide how to dispose of Nadine's body. As he talks to the motel clerk, Hughes stands in front of a seascape suggesting that he is in "deep water." Later at the St. Francis Hotel in Portland, as Hughes takes the drug supply Dianne has dumped on him to Tom the priest, Bob walks along the seedy corridor and is seen with the big red EXIT directional sign framed over his head. It clues the reader that Hughes is on his way out.

As in the subsequent *My Own Private Idaho* where Gus allows his actor/protégé/friend River Phoenix to rewrite one of his key sequences in the film (i.e., the campfire love admission speech to Keanu Reeves), so in *Drugstore Cowboy,* Van Sant's mentor, William S. Burroughs Jr., is given full reign to readjust his characterization and to revamp his dialogue. As such the director allows his Beat Generation hero to proselytize in his own unique cadence: "Narcotics have been systematically scapegoated and demonized. The idea that anyone can use drugs and escape a horrible fate is anathema to these idiots."

And finally, and most important, as in *Mala Noche* and the later *My Own Private Idaho,* Van Sant remains deliberately nonjudgmental about his characters in *Drugstore Cowboy* and refuses to romanticize their hazardous lives.

Undoubtedly, Gus must have wished over the years, and especially now, that people in his own life would offer him the same courtesies.

14

PORTLAND LIFE

When I got the first check [for the $150,000 fee for *Drugstore Cowboy*], I took a picture of it . . . and before that happened I remember calling my Dad and saying I really think this is it, that I've got a way to make money. And until I made those checks he had no confidence.

Gus Van Sant, 1995

AS THE INDEPENDENTLY made *Drugstore Cowboy* proved to be a solid critical and relatively commercial success, the accomplishment had a great impact on both the professional and personal life of Gus Van Sant. Its effects would permeate his coming years in many overt and subtle ways. As Van Sant told southern California journalist Jerry Roberts in 1995, *Drugstore Cowboy* "sort of made it easy for five years."

There is nothing that the Hollywood film community likes better than a winner, and Gus was one. With a packet of good-to-rave reviews, awards bestowed by film critics associations and festivals, and a modestly budgeted feature (by industry standards) that had done decently at the box office, he was the bright new American indie filmmaker—the proverbial flavor of the month—that Hollywood intended to woo into its establishment fold. Gus experienced the same sort of attention from the studio executives that a few years earlier had been bestowed on the likes of David Cronenberg, Martha Coolidge, Emilio Andolino, the Coen Brothers, Spike Lee, Kathryn Bigelow, and Jim Jarmusch. (Interestingly, at the time—perhaps due to the intense months of concern about the fate of the prerelease *Drugstore Cowboy* while it underwent an assortment of editing hands and executive decisions—Gus did not yet perceive of himself as a successful filmmaker: "Whereas with *Mala Noche* it seemed I achieved less than I had aimed for. And with *Drugstore* it seemed less. I don't know if it was. Just judging from my expectations.")

Using Gus's agent at the William Morris Agency as the official intermediary (as etiquette demanded), Hollywood courted Van Sant. It was a bittersweet victory for Gus who, nearly a decade earlier, had left the film capital after the failure of his feature(ette) *Alice in Hollywood*. Even more recently when he had tried to interest a distributor in *Mala Noche* there had been no takers in the southern California movie community. The same was true even a scant two years before when he had tried to interest film companies in the now-acclaimed *Drugstore Cowboy*.

But in typical Hollywood fashion the projects offered Gus by the studios were variations of what he had already done: druggie stories, criminal capers, or, in a different but unappealing (to him) genre, vapid suspense pieces. Van Sant explained the process thusly: "They'll come to you and say they have a project they think you'll be interested in, and then they'll say something like, 'It's a little more commercial, though.' Right then the alarm goes off and you think, 'This is the wrong way to go.' That's my decision, whether I want it more or less commercial."

Among the screen properties Van Sant turned down were *Sleeping with the Enemy* (Joseph Rubin eventually directed this 1991 release) and the *Cape Fear* remake with Robert De Niro attached (Martin Scorsese ultimately helmed this 1991 entry). Another vehicle suggested to Gus was *Mad Dog and Glory* to be executive produced by Martin Scorsese. Van Sant has recalled, "The budget was huge. They were very aggressive in pursuing me. I was really flattered, but I just couldn't do it." Why did he turn down this offer? "Because of the script. I thought something was needed in the end. And it's really scary if you don't believe every bit of the way in the script." (John McNaughton eventually directed the 1993 *Mad Dog and Glory*.)

There was another request for Gus's filmmaking services, this time from the Burbank studio home of Mickey Mouse and Donald Duck. But again Van Sant declined because it violated his principle (what he has called his "cardinal rule") that he must have a solid working script before he will do a movie: "There was a really good project I wanted to do called *Day After Day*. It was at Disney. They told me the story, and I thought, 'This is fantastic. I'm going to do it.' They sent me the script. And my inclination was to say, 'This came from a novel. Where's the novel?' After hemming and hawing they gave me the novella, and the author's name had been whited out on every page. For whatever reason. I guess they didn't want me to know where it came from. Maybe they didn't want me to contact the author. I found that the novel was better."

Van Sant also had meetings with executives at Universal Pictures. Not quite sure what might entice this offbeat newcomer who seemed to be rising to the "important" directors' rank, they suggested that perhaps Gus might like to remake something from the Universal movie library. He was shown a list of likely candidates. Nothing appealed to Van Sant's defined tastes, but in a moment of amused cynicism he suggested redoing Alfred Hitchcock's *Psycho*. If the suits at the meeting thought this thirty-seven-year-old "upstart" was joking about remaking such a beloved classic, he carried his impulsive idea once step further to show that he was indeed serious. He said that not only did he wish to redo *Psycho*—which was obvious heresy to any Hitchcock devotee—but he wanted it to be a scene-by-scene remake of that landmark 1960 cinema thriller. From the shocked looks he received from the Universal representatives, they obviously thought anybody who had such a notion was possibly more deranged than *Psycho's* lead character, Norman Bates.

Van Sant also mentioned to Universal and to other studio management teams that a pet project was a script he had written entitled *My Own Private Idaho*. When he explained that the story dealt with two male hustlers and one of the duo's search for his lost childhood, the conversation quickly shifted to more mainstream, less controversial screen subjects. Even Avenue Pictures, which had nurtured *Drugstore Cowboy* to box-office approval, was not interested in *My Own Private Idaho*, even when Gus restructured the budget to be $1.5 million, far less than *Drugstore*.

Meanwhile, with his newfound acclaim, Gus started receiving a flow of submissions in the mail, some directly sent to him, others via his Los Angeles agent: "I got scripts about drug addicts, people on the fringe of society, offbeat people. If I had gotten a script I liked, I would have gone for it, but I didn't. I'm not really searching for projects about the seamier side of life, even if it does look that way. After *Mala Noche* and *Drugstore Cowboy*, it was logical for producers to send me scripts about horse handicappers, con men, and people who live in trailers."

▼

IF in the heady months following the opening of *Drugstore Cowboy*, Van Sant could not find a satisfactory (major) studio project to do, he had the knowledge that for the first time in years he was financially stable, at least for the time being. (Gus claimed that previously he had not earned more than $10,000 a year as a filmmaker—all of which had caused him to lead a modest lifestyle.) The *Drugstore Cowboy* salary and his industry/filmgoer recognition also meant that he no longer had doubts whether or not he was truly a "professional" filmmaker. As he explained to Maggi White of Portland's *Downtowner*, "I've wanted to do film all my life but I used to have to pay for it myself. It keeps getting more intense, this process of doing film. Now I can continue at thirty-seven years old. I finally got what I want." Or, as he said at another time, "Well, the goal was really just to get paid for it, just to make a living and be able to do it full time."

And, most of all, Van Sant had finally demonstrated to his father that, after all these years of floundering (at least in other people's eyes), he had proven himself in his chosen profession. No longer would he have to hear about, or worse yet, consider the possibility to "get serious and go into the clothing business." His family had to admit that Gus Jr. was a legitimate, full-time movie-maker. Said Gus Van Sant Sr. in the fall of 1990 about his son: "He's extremely focused and dedicated to his art—it's nice to see him get some recognition af-ter all these years." He admitted that as recently as two years before he had been advising his offspring to get into retail during the Christmas rush. But, the parent acknowledged, he was glad his son hadn't listened to him: "Fathers never know what they're talking about anyway." (By now Gus Sr., who would close his G. G. Van Sant & Co. in 1991, had taken on the position of business manager for his offspring, a post he actively pursues to this day. The senior Van Sant is also managing director of corporate markets for Polo Ralph Lauren's ap-parel and lifestyle accessories.)

With this approbation for *Drugstore Cowboy*, Van Sant looked to his next project—whatever it actually would turn out to be—with enthusiasm and con-fidence. As he told the Oregon's *Statesman Journal* in November 1989, "I feel really optimistic about it. I know I can make a better film."

▼

ALTHOUGH Gus's name was not yet a household name, he was becoming ex-tremely well known. The degree of fame he had achieved as a filmmaker had not yet placed him in the stratum of a major celebrity who would be recognized and perhaps bothered by the public anywhere in the United States. But his ac-tivities were certainly more noted now, especially on his home turf of Portland, Oregon.

For some who knew him, the increasing degree of professional success Van Sant was experiencing was a surprise. As Gus's friend Bill Foster, director of the Northwest Film Center, discussed with the local paper, the *Willamette Week*: "There are a lot of Portlanders who have made movies or who are doing docu-mentaries, but Gus is unique in terms of his trajectory." This led the article's author, reporter Jim Redden, to point out to his readers, "Oddly, within the spectrum of Portland filmmakers, Van Sant seemed one of the least likely to land such a deal. In the past, his films have been among the least commercial produced in Portland. Most of them deal unflinchingly with such disturbing themes as drugs, death, poverty and failed sexual encounters. Although many successful Hollywood films have also tackled such topics, Van Sant's work is different: There are no good guys or bad guys in Van Sant's films—just people struggling in quiet futility with the hands they've been dealt."

Others, like novelist and Van Sant friend Katherine Dunn, recorded, "Gus is one of those people who's extremely loyal to those who have helped him in the past. He still has in this town flocks of people he considers indebted to for life because they once gave him a cup of coffee." His loyalties also extended to in-stitutions of learning he had attended. For example, in the spring of 1990 he would give the commencement address at the Catlin Gabel School that he had attended twenty years earlier. It meant that he had to fly back and forth to

Portland from Seattle where the Seattle Film Festival was hosting a Gus Van Sant retrospective of his screen work. But he willingly did it for Catlin Gabel. In his lecture to the graduating class he suggested, "Parents want you to get out and make money so they know they succeeded in raising you." In his summation he told them, "Just lie. When your parents ask you what you're going to do [with your life professionally], make something up."

▼

SO far, the mounting success had not yet noticeably changed Gus Van Sant's lifestyle. For starters, he was not interested in "going Hollywood" and becoming part of that scene. (Gus Jr. much preferred working in the Northwest: "I like shooting here because it's where I live and it's accessible.") As Gus Van Sant Sr. described for the press, "He'll go to Hollywood only if he has to, and when he has to. Gus can live very simply and has no materialistic desires, although he'll spend anything on the latest modern equipment for his filming."

As the moviemaker further explained on one of his quick trips to southern California: "I'm going to stay in Portland because there's much less stress there. I'm pretty naïve when it comes to business, and working as a filmmaker in L.A., you really have the sense of being in the heart of the lion's den. I don't know if I'm ready for this town yet. I feel lucky to have gotten such good reviews but it didn't make me feel like wow, 'I'm great.' I still feel like wow, 'Maybe I'm not so great.'" Another time he amplified further on this key topic: "There's a point where an independent filmmaker gets absorbed by a studio, and then the work changes, not always for the better. This [Portland] is my home. Nobody bothers me. I don't keep up with industry talk or trends. I just go ahead with the films as I see them." Further on the subject of Portland (where, according to Gus, "everything's tame and sort of friendly") he stated, "People in the Northwest tend to be more eccentric than people elsewhere. This place is full of folks who disdain the things that you might go to Los Angeles for: a big house, a lot of money, ego."

▼

NEWFOUND fame or not, Gus Jr. still tooled around the City of Roses (population: 437,000) in unostentatious style, driving the 1982 BMW his father had given him years ago. His dress code of the time was basic jeans, shirt, and, if it was raining, a yellow slicker, or if cold, a parka with a fake fur collar, or a windbreaker or navy-style pea jacket. His appearance during this period was frequently unshaven and rumpled-looking—a far cry from the preppie look of his growing-up years. He unpretentiously mingled with the locals and spent time perusing the city's new and used bookstores such as Powell's City of Books. He liked eating breakfast at the Pancake House, and, if he was forced to conduct an interview at, say, a trendy downtown Portland espresso bar, he would slink furtively and shyly into the establishment's shadows.

Also, Gus was still living in his same inexpensive downtown apartment. It was situated on a quasi-seedy street filled with vacant storefronts. (This was before further urban redevelopment changed portions of Portland's inner city.) Located on the top floor of a two-story retail building that had seen better days, it was one of two boxy but roomy upper-level units. Climbing up the flight of stairs one might have to navigate around empty wine bottles left by assorted transients who might, on occasion, be found sleeping in the doorway to the apartment.

The living room/work area of Van Sant's apartment was typically cluttered with masses of paper, but not messy. The walls of his home office/studio were usually covered with film posters, newspaper clippings, letters, and postcards. Scattered among the wall "decorations" were photos of Dennis Hopper, Matt Dillon, Andy Warhol, William S. Burroughs Jr., and, at the time, cast members from *Drugstore Cowboy*. (The production clap slates from both *Mala Noche* and *Drugstore Cowboy* were each framed in glass and hung on adjoining walls.) A stack of scripts was typically piled on one of the room's bookcases. Also to be found in Gus's workspace would be his acoustic guitar (frequently out of its case), and his cat, Junior (who had "starred" in the 1987 Van Sant diary short, *Junior*), could be seen frequently lazing about the room.

▼

WHEN Gus had lived in Hollywood in the second half of the 1970s, his life had been absorbed in breaking into the filmmaking world and his social life was largely wrapped around his core of friends from work situations (such as the Ken Shapiro/Minnesota crowd). Whatever his sexual preferences might have been at that time, he shared it with few people in the Los Angeles set. By the time he moved to Portland on a full-time basis in 1983 he was thirty-one, and had seemingly come to terms with being openly homosexual. Although out of the closet on the Portland scene, he apparently didn't go about town or within the film community advertising his alternative lifestyle. Yet, anyone with perception who had seen *Mala Noche* would have realized that the filmmaker of this evocative mood piece had to be well-acquainted with, or was part of, the gay culture. Then, too, in promoting *Mala Noche* to the film festivals, Gus Van Sant sought out, or was sought by, the gay festivals to screen his picture and participate in forums on gay cinema and gay filmmakers. This had also led to the director giving interviews to gay publications and to appearing on such TV fare as a Portland public access talk show alongside of an African-American transvestite.

In Portland he had various sets of friends in which he mingled, but which did not overlap much, or at all, with one another. As in his everyday life, his gay friends and acquaintances came from assorted social levels, parts of towns, and cultural backgrounds. Although seemingly reserved, shy, and self-contained, apparently—as would become clearer during the coming months when he made his next feature film—Gus was attracted to the rougher, less "civilized" segment of the gay lifestyle. While he might hang out with more affluent gays in a tight circle who took trips together to Mexico and elsewhere, he was equally or more drawn to street types. This would have led him, most likely, to those bar and club establishments that catered to the hustler trade and to associating at some level with those older men who were attracted to street-savvy male prostitutes.

This hustler attraction was not new to Van Sant, who had been magnetized by the street life of Hollywood back in the 1970s; the fascination had led him to drafting screenplays focusing on that subculture. And Portland, especially before the urban redevelopment and before the onslaught of the AIDS epidemic of the mid- to late 1980s, was a frequent destination for runaways, male hustlers, and such. In 1985's *Mala Noche* this is explored to some extent, but the film really focuses entirely on Hispanic street boys, as had its book original by Walt Curtis. The starring figure in Gus's 1987 short subject *Ken Death Gets Out of Jail* was one of these street types—one with a criminal record—that magnetized Van Sant's interest on assorted planes.

It was not, however, until some months after *Drugstore Cowboy* went into release and made Van Sant a rising commodity in the world of American pop culture, that a national magazine (*Newsweek*) in profiling Gus referenced him as openly gay. In a later interview (October 31, 1991) with *Rolling Stone*, Van Sant would claim that this was the first occasion the fact had been so baldly stated to his parents.

The word *openly* has to be taken in context. Over the decades, in the Hollywood film establishment, there had been several "openly" gay or bisexual movie directors at the film studios, just as their been a number of "openly" gay or bisexual film actors and stars at the major studios. But generally, such openness ran to being an established fact among the individual's circle of friends or favored coworkers and to be something understood or suspected by the outer circle of acquaintances, film lot employees, and studio executives. This was especially true during Hollywood's Golden Age before the fall of the studio system in the 1950s and 1960s. Those "openly" gay or bisexual directors included George Cukor (*A Bill of Divorcement*, *The Women*, *A Star Is Born*), Edmund Goulding (*Grand Hotel*, *Dark Victory*, *The Razor's Edge*), Mitchell Leisen (*Hold Back the Dawn*, *Frenchman's Creek*, *Captain Carey U.S.A.*), and James Whale (*Frankenstein*, *Showboat*, *The Road Back*).

In the more permissive America of the 1960s, filmmaker, painter, and pop culture faddist Andy Warhol left little doubt via his films or in person that his sexual inclinations were toward men. By the 1980s moviemakers who focused largely on homoerotic themes were no longer relegated to the "underground" porn circuit, but their work was an accepted part of the indie film movement. (A lot of this "coming out" trend was due to the militant gay activism of the 1970s and thereafter.)

But just as gay and lesbian filmmakers and actors in the early 1980s, like those in other walks of life, had reached a point where they felt coming out—at least within the movie industry—would not end their professional careers, the AIDS virus epidemic broke out around the world. With the public hysteria about contracting the deadly disease, anyone who was HIV positive or had AIDS did their best to conceal it for fear of severe ostracism from the rest of the world just when they needed friends or work the most. And because for a time AIDS victims were so frequently gay male individuals, it created yet another reason for most straight and gay AIDS victims to closet their terminal ailment. In the process, there was a rise of antigay and antilesbian backlash across America. As such, a good many gays returned to the closet or feared coming out at all.

Now here, as the 1990s were getting under way, Gus Van Sant the film-maker was being "outed" to the world as "openly gay." This was essentially a first for a mainstream Hollywood filmmaker: to have the public at large—let alone the film community—fully aware of (not just suspect) his lifestyle. To Gus's good luck, *Drugstore Cowboy* had been a hit so his "openly" gay status did not especially bother, at least on the surface, many in the Hollywood studio system. These executives were more concerned about whether this helmer of unusual movie topics could turn a profit at the box office, and were hopeful they could snare him into making something *they* considered commercial. The filmgoing public at large who had attended Van Sant's earlier features (*Mala Noche*, *Drugstore Cowboy*) were not going to stop seeing his new movies—as his full-length film work to date had already explored the gay and/or drug cultures. Thus, they wouldn't be shocked if the "openly gay" director helmed a topic similar to his earlier works. Van Sant's core audience of moviegoers were generally broad-minded picture enthusiasts who thrived on trend-breaking, unconventional work by indie directors or others who responded to the particular non-mainstream lifestyles Gus was exploring on camera.

What was not so widely circulated at the time of Gus's mainstream "outing" was that he currently had a long-term boyfriend in Portland. He was a young Dutchman from Rotterdam named D-J Haanraadts. They had been together to one degree or another for several months by the time of *Drugstore Cowboy* and on that film he received credit as second assistant editor. The media, out of concern for being politically correct, respecting Van Sant's privacy, or from the interviewer's lack of knowledge or interest in the relationship, seldom asked about Gus's significant other. Nonetheless, Gus talked briefly about D-J to *Monk* magazine in 1995. In describing Haanraadts, Van Sant detailed, "Well, he's also extremely adventurous. When he's my age he's not going to be any different. But in that way we're a good pair. Because one guy can do one thing. Like he's really bad with money. When he has it he blows it because he's Dutch and he expects he'll get it in the mail."

Gus's attitude about his lifestyle choices and what was or was not important to keep away from the media or from his business and social circles was, as with most elements about Van Sant, not based on a typical set of priorities. They hardly were what one might have anticipated given his cultural, academic, and

social background, or even his Beat/Hippie Generation interests, or, for that
matter, given his years living in the world of free-spirited creative artists. As
with everything—including his moviemaking choices—Gus Van Sant had his
own unique way of looking at the world.

Above all, this approach also applied to his gayness. When asked about the
subject by *Rolling Stone*'s David Handelman, Van Sant responded, "I haven't
really personally felt any discrimination, but I'm not really that, you know,
spotable as a gay male. Your sexuality is a private thing—and as far as culture
goes, I don't think of a gay culture separate from mass culture. I just look at it
as human culture. I mean, it's obvious that there's all kinds of stuff oriented toward heterosexual culture, because that's the majority, but it's also oriented toward white culture, because that's the majority. It's not surprising, and it doesn't
bother me.

"Inside certain other cultures, artistic ones, a lot of friends of mine that are
straight feel left out, because the major composers and artists of this century
are all gay. They feel inferior, to the point where they wish they were gay. So—
it just depends on what group you want to join."

THE ROAD TO *IDAHO*

I've got an idea for a film, and I'm trying to make something good. I'm not
really trying to figure out what the market wants.

Gus Van Sant, 1990

AS GUS VAN SANT moved into the 1990s things suddenly became very busy for him. If committing to a film project originated by a
Hollywood studio required him to be really energized before he could obligate
himself to such a major career task, there were other types of filmmaking that
paid well and demanded only a fraction of his time. With his deep interest in
contemporary music, his great sense of visuals, and an intriguingly unique way
at observing life, Van Sant was a natural to direct music videos.

Gus began working in this short-form film arena in 1990. He directed
"Tarbelly and Featherfoot," a single from Victoria Williams's album *Swing the
Statue* on the Mammoth label. Also that year, he helmed the music video to
David Bowie's "Fame '90," a single from the rock star's *Changebowie* album. It
allowed the moviemaker wonderful quick opportunities to exercise his imagination and bring a fresh viewpoint to the music video idiom that MTV had made
so popular with the young generation. (In the next few years Gus would direct
music videos of Tommy Conwell's "I'm Seventeen," Tracy Chapman's "Bang,
Bang, Bang," and Elton John's "The Last Song.") Perhaps working on the increasingly high-profile videos helped to sublimate the loss Van Sant felt over
the disbanding of his band Destroy All Blondes. The dissolution of the group,

which Gus's writer friend Katherine Dunn described as "deadpan punk," occurred as the result of the other members moving out of the Portland area.

If Gus the musician was inactive, he was making further forays into another creative area, his paintings. Several of his works now hung in the imposing Heathman Hotel in downtown Portland at 1001 Southwest Broadway at Salmon. Some of these pictures (such as "Tops," an oil painting on paper) would be excellently reproduced on note card packets sponsored by the Heathman Collection. Over subsequent years there would be several showings of Van Sant's artwork, especially at the Elizabeth Leach Gallery at 207 Southwest Pine Street in Portland.

While all this was happening, Gus agreed in principle to collaborate on a screenplay for Universal Pictures with director Paul Bartel. The latter was a multitalented filmmaker (*Death Race 2000, Eating Raoul, Lust in the Dust*) who had most recently received story credit for 1989's *Scenes from the Class Struggle in Beverly Hills*. Like so many others on the Hollywood movie scene, Bartel had worked for a time at Roger Corman's film factory in the 1960s and 1970s and had even made on-camera appearances in such Corman releases as *Grand Theft Auto* (1976) and *Piranha* (1978). (Reportedly during Van Sant's mid-to-late-1970s tenure in Hollywood he had briefly done a bit of production assistant/crew work for Corman's movie plant, but nothing that earned him screen credit.) With Bartel's unusual choices in filmmaking subjects, he was well suited to work in tandem with Van Sant on a screenplay.

Bartel's project, which Gus was joining but for which no final deal memos had yet been signed, was a "fictional biography" of filmmaker/artist/life observer Andy Warhol, who had died in 1987. (With Van Sant's interest in the world of underground/experimental cinema in high school and college, Warhol as a subject seemed a reasonable topic for Gus to be interested in tackling.) In a trade press article of April 1990 the two director/scenarists insisted their film-to-be would be nothing like Chuck Workman's recently released full-length documentary *Superstar: The Life and Times of Andy Warhol*. Nor would it be based entirely—if at all—on Victor Bockris's recent book *The Life and Death of Andy Warhol* (1989). The two filmmakers announced, "It will be speculative in parts, and nonchronological, and have certain elements of fantasy." At the time Bartel and Van Sant were considering such actors as John Malkovich, Willem Dafoe, and John Hurt to play the title role. Paul Heller was to produce the project while Gus was to direct. Although he was a rising name director, Gus did not yet have that much clout and had to sign away his right to the final editorial cut.

As weeks passed less and less was heard about Van Sant's participation in the Warhol project. After several months it became clear that Gus was no longer associated with it. A few years later, Van Sant admitted to Virginia Campbell of *Movieline* magazine that "I kind of bailed out on the movie we were doing" on Warhol. Other more intriguing opportunities had materialized for the Portland moviemaker.

Interestingly, in Gus's 1999 *Movieline* magazine conversation there was a lot of (wistful) enthusiasm for the Warhol vehicle that he had left: "There was a script called *Art Wars* . . . the pop artists challenged the abstract expressionists. They showed up and said, 'We're the new cool thing and we're not afraid of you,' and they started taking their space in the galleries. It wasn't even that pop artists were trying to take over. It was the '60s themselves, the climate of change that needed to happen. I tried to put that in the screenplay. The pop artists were funny and irreverent—that was the tone of the '60s."

While Paul Bartel's 1990 project on Warhol faded at Universal Pictures, his curiosity about Warhol did not. In 1996 Bartel was an actor in the movie *Basquiat*, a screen biography of the nineteen-year-old graffiti writer (played by Jeffrey Wright) who took the New York art world by storm only to die in 1988 at age twenty-eight. Playing the on-camera Andy Warhol—who discovered the talented street artist—was David Bowie.

Van Sant's interest in Warhol reemerged briefly in the early 1990s when he thought a screen biography on Andy might be a good one for River Phoenix. Gus later reconceived the notion as a gargantuan twenty-four-hour miniseries: "It would be a really big deal, an epic like *Berlin-Alexanderplatz* [the 960-minute, 1980 West German TV miniseries directed by Rainer Werner Fassbinder] and a tribute to Warhol's movies like *Empire*. You'd need that much time to do it all, beginning with the Abstract Expressionists in the '50s, when Warhol came to New York from art school."

▼

IN the midst of Van Sant's increase of professional activities on many fronts he became a home owner. Using funds accumulated from *Drugstore Cowboy*, the music videos, and other creative endeavors (all of which had put him in a much higher tax bracket), the purchase made sense. The impressive and spacious piece of real estate was located at 1883 Southwest Vista Avenue in affluent Portland Heights. The Tudor-style house was known as the James W. Cook residence. It had been completed in 1908 by the pioneer salmon canner with refinements made in 1912. Built in the bungalow/craftsman style, the three-story abode had 4,591 square feet of living space, with a 1,924-square-foot unfinished basement. In 1987 the interiors and garden had been totally renovated by the current owner. In the process the Povey stained glass windows, the mahogany wainscoting, moldings, carved capitals, and many built-in glass-front cabinets were retained. The home boasted six bedrooms (three of which had fireplaces), three full and one half bath, a double garage, and a complete apartment on the lower floor for a housekeeper or nanny. Situated on a upper elevation street that overlooked the city, there were impressive vistas of Mount Hood, Mount Saint Helens, the Willamette River, and downtown Portland. Van Sant purchased his new residence in August 1990 at a price of $635,000.

While Gus Van Sant Jr. was now a member of Portland's quietly moneyed landed gentry, he had not suddenly become aristocratic and snobbish. For all the time he would live in his fancy new digs over the next years, he would not devote much energy to the realm of interior decoration. Rather, he carried over his old habits of filling available living space with his equipment, film scripts, books, paintings, music instruments, and other possessions. Apparently, it was just not in Gus's nature at this point in life to wish to impress others with high-toned, decorated living quarters. In fact, for the time being he kept his inner city loft apartment above the closed-down photocopying shop. He would maintain this no-frills rental for the next several months until the tattered building was marked for demolition.

▼

IN 1990, as Van Sant was briefly involved, and then not, with the Andy Warhol screen biography, he was still getting lucrative offers to direct features chosen by the major studios and scripted by others. As Gus admitted modestly to the *New York Times*: "They'd pay you, you know, like a million dollars, and they were going to be $20 or $30 million films, and they kept asking over and over again. I would have done one of them, but there was always something wrong. They weren't clicking for me." (Meanwhile, Van Sant's friends were telling him, "You should really make a horror film—those sell," and others kept advising him, "Why make films about ugly people? Make happy, feel-good films.")

Then Van Sant thought he had found the perfect screen property. It was *Even Cowgirls Get the Blues,* the 1976 best-seller by Tom Robbins, the iconoclastic writer who lived in Washington in La Conner, on the Puget Sound north of Seattle. The spring 1990 deal made with Michael Medavoy, chairman of TriStar Pictures, called for Gus to not only adapt and direct the Robbins vehicle, but to produce it (although it was allowed that the day-to-day producing tasks would most likely be relegated to someone else). In usual trade paper hype, both Robbins and Van Sant stated how pleased they were to find someone like Medavoy who really understood the book. (Medavoy had first become interested in Gus adapting/directing *Even Cowgirls Get the Blues* when the executive had been at Orion Pictures about a year before.)

As if this were not enough to keep Van Sant extremely busy, there was a brief flurry in this same period when Gus and veteran screenwriter and occasional actor/director Buck Henry (*The Graduate; Catch-22; What's Up, Doc?*) were touted as going to collaborate on the screenplay of Tom Wolfe's *Kandy-Kolored Tangerine-Flake Streamline Baby*, the colorful 1965 novel about a hot rod. It was a trend-breaking book in its time, made famous by its Ph.D. author writing on a low-brow topic in upscale language. Author Kurt Vonnegut once described the tome as an "excellent book by a genius who will do anything to get attention."

The Wolfe project, however, was not to be. As Buck Henry has detailed, "Gus and I talked about it for a couple of days and then we had a meeting at a studio, at the end of which I thought, 'I can't face the possible opprobrium of not just one, but two major authors.'" Henry concluded his reminiscences of this unrealized screen production with "I think a screenwriter does take into consideration what hangs over the project—its provenance is very important."

As spring 1990 progressed toward summer Van Sant's professional priorities shifted yet again. While trying to tame the wild plot line and prose of *Even Cowgirls Get the Blues* into a viable screenplay, Gus was preparing a project he had first thought about in the mid-1970s when he was living in Hollywood and observing the street hustler culture. At the time he had started several different screenplays on the topic, but remained convinced that the subject matter had been far better treated in John Rechy's novel, *City of Night*. (Gus would have liked to option that popular book for filming, but knew he could not afford the asking price.) While Van Sant "officially" put aside his hustler scenarios, he kept returning to them over subsequent years.

At the time he chose to make the screen version of Walt Curtis's *Mala Noche* in late 1984 it was because he still was not satisfied with his own, long-marinating screen drafts about the lives of male prostitutes. Then something happened as he completed the Portland shoot on *Mala Noche*: "I passed a police tape on the way to filming. I found out that this kid had been killed by some other street kids who wanted him to work for them. . . . The incident brought back this script about street hustlers that I'd been working on in 1978, and I rewrote most of it between 1985 and 1989."

In the long process of revamping his hustler story set in Portland (which at one time or another was called *In a Blue Funk* and *Minions of the Moon*), Van Sant remained intrigued with an earlier idea. That had been sparked by watching filmmaker Orson Welles's *Chimes at Midnight*, a 1966 Spanish-Swiss production in which Welles adapted parts of several Shakespearean plays (including *The Tragedy of King Richard the Second; The History of Henry the Fourth*, Parts I and II; *The Life of Henry V*; and *The Merry Wives of Windsor*) into one narrative and in which Orson played the rascally Falstaff. This cinematic achievement—despite the artistic problems engendered by a lack of proper budget—had so inspired Gus that one of his early screenplay drafts about male prostitutes involved adapting segments of Shakespeare's Prince Hal tales into his contemporary account of hustlers, although he carefully avoided being influenced by the visual images that Welles had utilized in *Chimes at Midnight*.

As time wore on, the screenplay based on the Prince Hal variation ranged from being part of the full story to becoming the entire project. (This thematic expansion occurred when Van Sant's agent showed Gus's property to executives at Twentieth Century-Fox and someone at the studio was very partial to the Bard.) While Gus was uncertain about the use of the Shakespearean idiom for average filmgoers, he eventually concluded (or compromised) that the

Shakespearean/*Chimes at Midnight* influence should only encompass a portion of his totally revised scenario.

Then Van Sant decided to graft the Shakespeare-inspired plot thrust onto other similar thematic ideas he had been developing over time. One of these separate narratives, then a twenty-five-page short story, was called *My Own Private Idaho.* It focused on characters called Ray and Little George: "Ray [Monge] was the guy who played Pepper in *Mala Noche* and Little George was his cousin. They were real people but the characters that I was writing were like Mike and Scott [of another of Van Sant's screen stories]. They were two Latino characters on the streets of Portland. Ray was eighteen, a street hustler, and Little George was a thirteen-year-old homeless kid with a dog. They were on the road in search of their parents, or some relative, to a town in Spain that had the same last name as Ray's character. I don't think I had a town name in my story; I was trying to figure out what that was going to be. Ray was going to randomly look up somebody with his last name and assume that he was related, and the people in the town were going to think that they were American relatives. Then they were going to live in Spain until Ray fell in love with a girl and went off on their honeymoon, leaving little George behind with this dog. That's where that part of Scott and Mike's story came from in the film."

Meanwhile, Van Sant had been working on another male prostitute script entitled *Boys of Storytown,* which contained the above-mentioned Mike and Scott characters. This story arc dealt with the duo living on the streets. The Mike character suffered from narcolepsy—a disorder in which the individual suffers from frequent, uncontrollable attacks of deep sleep. (Gus later said that this medical malady concept came from his teen years when he had read *Silas Marner,* the 1861 British classic by George Eliot.)

According to Van Sant's 1993 interview with Graham Fuller, in this plot line "Scott has just come to town and runs into this German guy, Hans, who Mike had lived with for a while. In the [final] movie he doesn't, but in one of these early scripts, he lived with Hans for half the film and they had this funny domestic relationship. Then Mike leaves Hans and goes back on the street and there's a character named Bob. . . . I don't remember what happened after that. It could have just been a half-written thing."

Eventually, Van Sant grafted together elements from all these scripts, including the Prince Hal one. Of this amalgamated scenario, its creator would say proudly, "The non-Shakespeare parts in *Idaho* are the most creative part of any script I've done."

▼

IN reconstructing the long maturation from the later 1970s onward of what became *My Own Private Idaho,* Van Sant has said, "I had basically finished the *Idaho* script eight months before *Drugstore* came out [in October 1989], but I hadn't had many meetings about it. When *Drugstore* started to get press, people in the industry started to talk about it. . . . So I was this hot new filmmaker among this group of hot new filmmakers trying to get attention from the people who back films. Every time I met them, I told them I was going to do *My Own Private Idaho* and that it would only cost a million dollars. They would be very supportive and would want to read it, but after they read it they didn't really want to finance it."

Regarding the wearisome process of finding an interested producer, Van Sant detailed,

"They always had me send the script. They don't say, 'We're not touching that.' They say, 'Let's look at the script.' I send it to them, and then they say, 'It's not anything we can do.' Which may mean, 'We're not touching that,' when they finally read the script. But there's no particular homophobia. It's more like homophobia based on their perception of the public's homophobia. If they think they can make money on it, they're gonna do it."

As Gus explained further, "It wasn't just the gay content; it was a lot of things. It was partly the way the script was written, which originally had lots of different-sized lettering, unlike a normal script. It was also short—about eighty pages—and the Shakespeare threw them. Basically everything. I think the very first sentence says Mike [the lead character] is getting a blow-job in a motel room. Then he's out on the road and he passes out, and the script talks about the house crashing into the road. It was very disjointed for the [script] readers in Hollywood." Van Sant reasoned about those who read his daring script: "I didn't care. I wanted them to be scared. The smart ones could read through, could get past the first blow job and see what was going on."

Perplexing the Hollywood establishment with his proposed screen projects was nothing new to iconoclastic Van Sant. While it may seem a minor matter to most people outside the industry, the format and look of his scripts—which the establishment at the studios found so repugnant—was just another quirk of individuality that this very independent filmmaker refused to relinquish at the time. As Gus later detailed with full antiestablishment glee: "The typeface of the original screenplays [i.e., *My Own Private Idaho* and *Even Cowgirls Get the Blues*] is a sort of patchwork I arrived at with my Apple computer. They were submitted this way and worked on by all departments in this form. The films of *Idaho* and *Cowgirls* began with unusual screenplays and everything that happened after that was a direct result of the way that they looked when people first read them. They are unconventional enough to have turned off a lot of people in the 'business' simply because those people were in the 'business' of conformity, as is most of Hollywood. I am not. To me this is extremely significant."

▼

BEFORE *Drugstore Cowboy* established Van Sant in the bigger leagues of current American moviemakers, he had been thinking in terms of shooting *My Own Private Idaho* in 16mm, using unknowns—anything to keep its budget down and allow him to get his favorite property into actual production. But there were several people besides Gus's agent who were working to get the funding to package this project, which was so meaningful to Van Sant. One of them was Laurie Parker.

Parker had been the production executive at Avenue Pictures who had been one of the first there to spot the merits of *Drugstore Cowboy* when it was submitted. She had worked closely with Gus during the making of the film. Now fully convinced of his talents, she was among those who sought out financing for *My Own Private Idaho*. The promise of the needed funds materialized. An outside investor was willing to put up $2 million for the male prostitute tale, so the screenplay redrafting on *Even Cowgirls Get the Blues* was put on hold.

It finally looked as if *My Own Private Idaho* would, after all these years, become a reality.

16

ENTER RIVER PHOENIX

Maybe it's a mistake to make [My Own] Private Idaho at this particular point in my career, but everything always feels like maybe it's a mistake. I have this project ready to go, so I don't care if it's right or wrong—I'm just gonna do it.

Gus Van Sant, 1991

IN THE LENGTHY GENESIS of writing *My Own Private Idaho*, part of Gus Van Sant's research on street prostitution had been to read such books as John Rechy's well-researched *City of Night* (1963) and watch such graphic and stark documentaries as the Oscar-nominated *Sleepless in Seattle* (1984). An even more important part was Gus's studying these teens and young adults for hire on the streets. Ever the quiet spectator, during Van Sant's years in Los Angeles in the later 1970s, he had observed the hustlers on Hollywood Boulevard. He had watched them as they went on the prowl, relaxed in seedy coffee shops and video arcades, or walked the streets aimlessly (passing the hours between tricks, drug boosts, or crash-outs at a friend's pad or pay-by-the-day hotel/motel room rented by their customers).

Earlier, in 1969, Gus had surveyed a similar scene in Oregon. As he has recalled: "And I moved to Portland as a teenager. I grew up in the suburbs. Then I discovered 'Camp,' where the boys cruise around. That certainly isn't the suburbs. That's for sure." Later, in 1983, the filmmaker returned from the East Coast to make his home again in Portland. By now, in his early thirties, Gus had come out of the gay closet both to himself and others. As such, he observed the local gay scene—in all its strata—in a less passive way. When Van Sant shot *Mala Noche* in late 1984, he saw the street hustling scene in that part of town up close in all its seamy aspects. While editing *Mala Noche*, he met blue-eyed Michael Parker, an acquaintance of Gus's pal Chris Monlux. Parker, sixteen and homeless, had spent the last few years as a street hustler, doing what needed to be done to survive.

As Parker told John Glatt for *Lost in Hollywood: The Fast Times and Short Life of River Phoenix* (1995): "My time on the street was really a search for acceptance. My father left when I was very young and I was looking for acceptance. And I was going to get that any way that I could, even if it was a dirty old man that wanted my body. It wasn't a gay thing. It wasn't a straight thing. It was a search."

It was Parker, Gus has said regarding the evolution of *My Own Private Idaho*, "who became the sort of guide to the character of Mike in the film." (Parker told John Glatt for his River Phoenix biography that when he met Van Sant, "I was still streeting. I wasn't a street person but I still hung out on the street. I knew what was going on. I guess Gus was attracted to that and wanted to know more." The young man also informed Glatt about Van Sant, "He's very voyeuristic when it comes to that kind of thing."

It was observing and learning from Parker that led to having the Mike character be narcoleptic. While Parker did not suffer from that affliction, the filmmaker has explained, "he smoked a lot of pot, and as a sort of defense mechanism, he would say he had forgotten something. You know, if you said, 'Why weren't you here when you said you'd be here?' or whatever, he'd say, 'Well, I don't remember that.' So it seemed like he had narcolepsy." And for Van Sant, as his screenplay developed, he saw that this ailment could serve several purposes in the plot line: "It's a metaphor for the profound effect Mike's emotional life has on his physical life, and also for his helplessness on the street. Plus, it was a nice way to [segue] from one scene to the next [as Mike passes out and later revives], a time-traveling sort of gimmick."

Another person who provided information on the ways of street hustlers was Don Chambers. Van Sant had known him for some years. (In *Mala Noche*, Chambers is one of the unseen faces around the barroom table as the Walt character introduces Pepper to his drinking buddies.) Chambers had lived for years in Portland near the bus station where transients and homeless people used to camp out until the late 1970s. As Van Sant recalled for journalist Dale Reynolds: "The kids would work the streets for money and they'd live in the camps. Chambers used to tell me depression-era stories of the camps, and I adapted them to today. I wanted the Shakespearean connection mainly because it is so timeless."

An additional individual who provided source material for the project was Robert Lee Pitchlynn, a former rock promoter in Portland who, during an adverse financial period in the past, had been forced to live on the streets. As times "improved" for Bob he took over an old house on Missouri Street, a then very downscale part of town. Knowing the perils of being homeless, he had made his house a refuge for street kids. (Mike Parker was one of those who had lived there for a time.)

It was Chambers, in fact, who unknowingly had helped Gus in the melding together of the story ideas and scripts that eventually became *My Own Private Idaho*: "One night I was watching Orson Welles' *Chimes at Midnight*, and thought that the *Henry IV* plays were really a street story and I knew this fat guy, named Bob, who had always reminded me of Falstaff and who was crazy about hustler boys. It was then that I decided to combine the two stories."

Over time, Van Sant heard a great many accounts of sordid life experiences from Mike Parker and other such young men Parker knew or mutual friends introduced to Gus. (Another person who provided research information along the way was young Scott Patrick Green, who by 1990 would be working as Van Sant's general assistant.) In the process, Van Sant's fictional portrait of the street scene grew more detailed and confident.

As for the basis of Scott, the rich kid in *My Own Private Idaho* who goes slumming in the underbelly of Portland and Seattle, Van Sant acknowledges, "Well, he's probably me. I can use my own background as an example for Scott's background . . . Scott comes from a wealthy family and his family is mayor because Prince Hal [in the Shakespearean dramas based on history] came from royalty, and that was the closet thing I could find to royalty in Portland. I think the film might have suffered a little bit from that because there is a difference between being a king and being the mayor's son. The reason Scott's like he is, is because of the Shakespeare, and the reason the Shakespeare is in the film is to transcend time, to show that those things have always happened, everywhere. That's why Mike and Scott end up with the boys in the piazza in Rome, which is just like the street scene in Portland."

Just as Gus's past feature films had not moralized about the lifestyles of the male prostitutes (of *Mala Noche*) and druggie thieves (of *Drugstore Cowboy*), so with *My Own Private Idaho* he chose to treat his subject matter nonjudgmentally, in fact, with compassion. As the filmmaker would explain, "That's one of the points of the movie. There are very bad parts of the street scene, but I didn't have Mike go through any horror stories. Any street hustler who's sold his body for money can tell you scary stories; we're just not showing that side of it. The energy of the finished screenplay is from Mike's point of view, it's not an objective point of view. That's got a lot to do with the strength of my movies setting this mood which enables people to get further into the characters. It's not rational."

On the other hand, Van Sant did not want to go in the opposite direction by glamorizing this marginalized side of life. He reasoned, "I don't think I've romanticized this world, nor do I find it in need of romanticization because it's not depressing to me. These characters live in a world with highs and lows just like any world, and the beauty of their world is the same as the beauty of any world—just the beauty of life. Nor are these characters any lonelier than anyone else—I think people are all pretty lonely. I can only speak from a man's point of view—maybe it's different for girls—but men, by nature, are lonely." (Another time, when the filmmaker talked on this topic, Gus said, "You know, everybody has the same capabilities of tragedy and comedy and romance and loneliness within their beings. I don't' see street hustlers as any less worthy of being romanticized than anyone else.")

Knowing that by portraying male prostitutes in his movie he would have to show them at some point in time on-screen at work with customers, Van Sant developed a point of view to handle the situation. It was geared to avoid rejection by potential backers of the movie or, later in the process, by the film industry's censorship board. It was a concept formulated on good business sense and a lesson learned from *Drugstore Cowboy*. In short, he wanted to avoid narrowing the range of possible filmgoers coming to see a movie because its topic (here male sex acts; in *Drugstore Cowboy* it was the druggies' lifestyle) was too edgy. This led Gus to decide, "I want to portray them in ways that aren't lurid. The sex in *Idaho* is never that important. It's sort of something that they do—routine. And as long as you got the idea that they are routine sexual objects, it isn't really about sex."

This concept tied in with another of Van Sant's theories about presenting sex on camera. He reasoned, "Just to do it from the point of view of the partners involved in having sex. That's the way to get around it. And if you can get there and make the camera not a voyeur but a participant you can sometimes get away with a little more. But it's still a problem because of our own perceptions of sex. I mean, I'm embarrassed by certain things. Being 'bad' is part of it, although it doesn't have to be that way, and I think other cultures know that. But our culture's pretty uptight."

Bound into his approach for depicting the sexual act in *My Own Private Idaho*, Van Sant appreciated that showing physical coupling—whether between straights or gays—"should be more positive." He assessed, "You know, men are embarrassed by sex because they don't understand it. They can come to grips with death and use it as an icon. And they can use love as an icon, or sex even, but the actual involvement of that intimate moment—the sexual moment—is somehow embarrassing because maybe we don't understand what it is."

Thus, for Van Sant: "In my films I just try to be aware that people don't understand it. And I just try and walk in that direction and say, 'Well, this is this.'" Yet, despite the filmmaker's confidence (and glibness) on the topic, when it would come time to direct the sex scenes in *My Own Private Idaho*, he would find "it was tough to do."

Although many who later saw or heard about *My Own Private Idaho* would miss the point, that is, just because the picture dealt with male prostitutes did not necessarily make this a story of two lead characters who are gay *and* are selling their bodies for money. The rebellious Scott character, who has turned to the streets to embarrass his status-conscious family and is biding his time until he inherits money, claims not to be gay in the story line and has a heterosexual relationship later in the plot. As for Mike, his central need is for someone to comfort and care for him. Emotionally damaged as a child, he is seeking shelter in and from life. It is a matter of indifference whether he finds this with a man or woman.

Understanding that the male hustler subculture covered a broad spectrum of types drawn into the lifestyle for many reasons, Gus also appreciated another point that helped to shape the character portraits in *My Own Private Idaho*. It was "the paradox of people having sex with someone of the same sex yet refusing the label that this gave them."

▼

AS Van Sant reached a final screenplay of *My Own Private Idaho,* it certainly must have pleased him to see so many divergent story ideas and influences come together into what was, for him, a workable screenplay.

He had long been happy with the title of *My Own Private Idaho* he had chosen for this screenplay. That had derived from a song lyric sung by the rock group B-52, as well as trips Van Sant had made to Idaho in the early 1980s. It seemed suitable for the now-evolved theme of the movie in which Idaho is really a state of mind. "It's like home," Van Sant has said, "a place of refuge or comfort."

The splicing in of the Shakespearean characters, themes, and language (as adapted/updated by Van Sant) was now a key part and, for Gus, a very valid aspect of the screenplay. He felt it enhanced his original story of a young man seeking his family and eventually going to a foreign country to find them. Van Sant must have felt thankful that his watching of Orson Welles's movie *Chimes at Midnight* had led him to contemplate how the Prince Hal and Falstaff characters could play a role in his screen work. He wondered, "What would it be like in modern times, a fallen aristocrat and street robbers? And what if Hal and Falstaff had more than just a friendship, but a sexual relationship and love?"

As for incorporating the Shakespearean-style text into his screenplay, the filmmaker insisted, "I don't see the Shakespearean passages as disrupting the story of Scott and Mike—rather, they make the point that what happens to these two people has been happening to people for centuries. I find it comforting that the same stories repeat themselves over and over, and I wanted to underscore the timelessness of the story Scott and Mike are enmeshed in."

Countering another objection he had received from a potential producer, Gus stated, "I don't think the Shakespearean dialogue will go over people's heads either, because you don't have to know the classics to understand how this dialogue fictions in the film. People who hang out a lot together often develop a kind of private language and that was another thing I was trying to show by having them fall into Shakespearean tongue—I wanted to underscore the sense of camaraderie these people share and to show how separated they are from 'normal' society. I've altered Shakespeare's verse pretty playfully and some people who know Shakespeare might find delight in the way it's been altered, but there will probably be others who'll object to what I've done."

Besides Shakespeare, there had been other literary examples that had sparked this screen work, which "uses life experiences in a metaphorical way."

Van Sant has acknowledged, "Some parts are influenced by Beckett . . . in the style of the road adventures." (Of Beckett's importance, Van Sant has said: "You emulate people at different times and build a foundation for your identity by learning from others. I relate to Beckett's world view. Samuel Beckett's work is about nothingness, and a lot of that rubs off in *Idaho*.") Regarding other literary guides for the creation process of *Idaho*, Van Sant has pointed out, "The visit to the brother was influenced by Sam Shepard, the playwright who wrote *Buried Child*. It's mixed together into its own thing, with references that came from all over the place. *Idaho* is not literal. I haven't had those experiences. They come from the imagination which is sometimes more truthful than a documentary."

As to the geography for the story line, the plot always had the primary setting as Portland. So far as choosing the lead character's destination in the final story line—which at one time was Mexico—it was a more complicated sifting-out process. Per Van Sant: "I considered Greece, Spain, lots of other places. The characters have to go overseas to search for the mother of one of them. . . . He finally choose Italy as the needed site: "I wanted a timeless quality to the story, a sense that gangs like this have existed forever. That's one reason for the Shakespeare references and the medieval costumes in the robbery scene. Rome has the wonderful homoeroticism of the Renaissance in the art of Leonardo da Vinci and Michelangelo, and its male prostitution tradition goes back to B.C. . . . My characters go to Rome and see gangs that are like themselves. It's like they go all the way over there and meet themselves, only they don't speak the same language."

▼

AS Van Sant prepped *My Own Private Idaho* in 1989, he was still of the mind to use a cast of (relative) unknowns. For the main role of the narcoleptic Mike, Gus had settled upon his acquaintance and former Portland street person Michael Parker. The latter had already appeared on screen for Gus, playing a bit part in the closing section of *Drugstore Cowboy* as the crying youth being badgered by Max Perlich. This assignment was set in the director's mind when, during a Los Angeles trek, Van Sant was participating in prefilming promotion for the project that was to appear in a mid-1990 issue of *Interview* magazine. The shoot was set for the Shangri-La Motel in Santa Monica. Well-known photographer Bruce Weber was doing the session. According to Van Sant: "It was like a publicity stunt. I had bussed Mike down from Portland specifically for the picture, thinking that Bruce would probably like the way he looked. So there's this picture of the two of us in front of this mirror, and Mike's hair is wet and he has no shirt on, and it says that he is going to star in *My Own Private Idaho*."

To play the part of Scott, the mayor's son, Gus decided to go with someone who had a little more heat attached to his name. Rodney Harvey came under consideration. He was the handsome young actor from Philadelphia who had been suddenly yanked from the cast of *Drugstore Cowboy* by his agent, Allan

Mindel, because Rodney was sidetracked by a serious bout of drug usage. Since then, the charismatic Harvey had been cast in the Fox-TV series *The Outsiders*, based on the 1983 Francis Ford Coppola feature that had starred Patrick Swayze and Tom Cruise. In the small-screen rendition, Rodney was cast as Sodapop Curtis, the character played by Rob Lowe in the film original. The series debuted in late March 1990 and despite the game cast, which included David Arquette and Billy Bob Thornton, it never made a sufficient dent in the audience ratings. By that summer, the Fox network was airing reruns of the series, which it had already canceled. That left Harvey available to pursue—with the guidance of Mindel—the role of Scott in Van Sant's forthcoming feature. (Allan Mindel would be coexecutive producer, along with Gus, on *My Own Private Idaho*).

While all this was transpiring in late 1989 and early 1990, *Drugstore Cowboy* was receiving good word-of-mouth within the film industry. It gave Van Sant newfound status within the movie business. Gus and/or his advisers had the notion that if they could attach bigger names for the two male leads, they could somehow find the additional financing to pay for the higher-priced talent.

Van Sant has recalled, "After the awards frenzy on *Drugstore Cowboy*, it was obvious this would get made. So, on my own, I sent scripts to the people I wanted most. I didn't think they would go for it, but at last I was in a position where I could send a script to a star I'd never met with a good chance that he'd read it. I was just thinking, if this was a made-in-heaven project, who would I want? And then I got them?"

In this process, the names of two very hot young performers kept rushing into Van Sant's mind. They were nineteen-year-old, clean-cut River Phoenix (*Stand by Me, Running on Empty, Indiana Jones and the Last Crusade*) and twenty-five-year-old Keanu Reeves (*River's Edge, Bill & Ted's Excellent Adventure, Dangerous Liaisons*), who had just filmed together the black comedy *I Love You to Death* (1990) and had become good friends. Like much of the filmgoing world, Van Sant regarded the wholesome-looking, quietly sexy Phoenix as a budding great actor, one who had already received a Best Supporting Actor Oscar nomination for his remarkable performance in 1988's *Running on Empty*. He seemed to have the dramatic intensity necessary for the role of Mike Waters.

What attracted Van Sant in particular to the exotically attractive dude named Reeves was his performance in 1989's *Bill & Ted's Excellent Adventure*. Gus thought it qualified him for uttering the potentially stilted Shakespearean-style dialogue that the character of Scott Favors uses within a portion of *My Own Private Idaho*. As Gus reasoned of Reeves's smash-hit *Bill & Ted* entry: "They had their eloquent way of speaking—a false eloquence, their own valleyspeak. So I thought of it as characters who are speaking in their own secret language when they're together—it's their way of having fun." For Van Sant, this equated to the formalized dialogue à la the Bard that Scott uses in the midportion of the movie. Buoyed by that thought, the director concluded, "I figured that when we got to the set, we'd find out if it was ridiculous or if it was working."

Although Van Sant might have seemed wrapped up in his own little world, he was well aware that his on-the-cutting-edge drama was not exactly the typical box-office project that a rising young star (and his handlers) would consider viable. Gus could easily envision Phoenix and Reeves's agents/managers studying the *My Own Private Idaho* screenplay, which opened with the Mike Waters character having oral sex-for-pay with a fat, unattractive older man in a seedy hotel: "As soon as they read that they're thinking of their client, picturing him giving head, and that prompted them not to get it. The idea of young guys having sex with older guys for money—it's like off the scale of life."

Having submitted the script to the agents of both Phoenix and Reeves, Van Sant grew impatient when he had no constructive response. He thought back to a lesson he had learned about show business in the 1970s when he called author/poet William S. Burroughs Jr. and filmmaker Ken Shapiro directly to ask about a project, or a job, he had in mind. Not only had he gotten to talk directly to these two individuals, but he had achieved his objectives on each occasion.

As Van Sant has recalled, "Right about then there was a mix-up between River Phoenix's agent and my producer, Laurie Parker, as to exactly what *My Own Private Idaho* was going to be, because there was another script, called *Revolver*, that somebody was offering River with my name attached. The agent didn't know why the producer of *My Own Private Idaho* didn't know about *Revolver*. She assumed that *My Own Private Idaho* was some sort of trick and she wouldn't let us speak to River. But somehow we found him and I talked to him about the project. Then I had a meeting with Keanu Reeves, who said he was looking for a low-budget film. I told him that it would be done up in Portland and that it would be a small thing, and he thought it was cool."

Keanu recalled his get-togethers with Gus on *My Own Private Idaho* thusly: "I don't know, man, Gus Van Sant gave me a call. . . . We went out a couple of times. He's a solid dude, you know. I expressed my interest. I read the script. I thought it was an amazing script. Just in terms of narrative, man, there's cows, *bang! bang! bang!*, porno shops, salmon swimming, blow jobs, money-exchanging and then I bust out in Idaho, *smash!* And then Shakespeare. It's *Henry IV* and I'm, like, doin' voice-overs on camera. Like soliloquies. I have all these soliloquies. I just walk into the camera.

Reeves was sufficiently intrigued with Van Sant's project and the potential of working again with River (whom he revered as an excellent actor) that he volunteered to visit Phoenix and hopefully convince him to take on the role of Mike Waters in *My Own Private Idaho*. Keanu drove his 1974 Norton Commando motorcycle from Canada to Micanopy, Florida, near Gainesville where River was then living. The two young stars discussed Gus's film, both as to its acting challenges and the potential hazards of playing male hustlers (gay or not) in a mainstream feature. Given the homophobic temperament in AIDS-plagued America at the time, playing in *My Own Private Idaho* could easily destroy—as their handlers feared—their professional path to major stardom.

It didn't take long for Phoenix to see the film's potential for a star dramatic turn, and, even more important, its potential of elevating him from the status of teen heartthrob to legitimate major movie star. He and Reeves agreed that if each would do the part, the other would, too—otherwise each would say no.

A few weeks thereafter, an enthusiastic Van Sant flew to Florida to meet with River Phoenix. Before the filmmaker arrived, Phoenix had screened a print of *Drugstore Cowboy* and was impressed by the performances Gus had drawn from his cast, especially Matt Dillon. River and Gus had had long phone discussions concerning the possibility of his taking on the complex, daring role. Phoenix still wasn't sure if he should accept the chancy part. Gus told the actor (twenty years Van Sant's junior) about Mike Parker, the young man who had inspired the role. In fact, Van Sant had made VHS tapes of Mike talking about his street life and these were given to River to help him see the depth of the assignment.

According to John Glatt in his River Phoenix biography, when Gus flew back to Oregon, Phoenix was still not convinced about accepting the assignment. While he liked Van Sant as a person and a director—and they shared a mutual interest in being band musicians—the rising star was now concerned about another wrinkle in the equation; Phoenix sensed that the director had a "crush on and was pursuing him."

Van Sant's own take on this pivotal meeting with Phoenix is outlined in his 1993 conversation with interviewer Graham Fuller: "I then went and spent half a day with River in Florida because he was having a hard time making up his mind. Suddenly there was this buzz about the film because all the producers in Hollywood who were trying to cast River and Keanu in their movies were getting the word that they were going to be in *My Own Private Idaho* and they wouldn't have the time to be in other movies. All these people were coming up to me and congratulating me, even though River and Keanu hadn't committed yet."

Phoenix and Reeves wavered for weeks. Finally, as Phoenix stated, "We were driving in a car on Santa Monica Boulevard, and were talking really fast about the whole idea. We were excited. It could have been like a bad dream—a dream that never follows through because no one commits, but we just forced ourselves into it." Finally the two talents said yes. (Later, Van Sant analyzed that River and Keanu may have accepted the parts ultimately because "they probably felt the risk. If there's no risk at all, it's not that much fun.")

Bringing the stars aboard meant the delicate reshuffling of Mike Parker and Rodney Harvey out of their lead assignments. As Gus phrased it: "That knocked the original choices, Mike and Rodney, into second-string. They were still in the film, but as different characters. We couldn't turn down the opportunity to work with these bigger names."

But the hiring of River Phoenix carried a downside with it. He was already committed to another feature, *Dogfight* (1991), to be directed by Nancy Savoca in Seattle, Washington. That meant that *My Own Private Idaho* could not start shooting until late in 1990. During this delay period, the original investor for the movie evaporated and the project's producer Laurie Parker had to search for a new backer. However, with Phoenix and Reeves attached to the project, it was not the epic struggle of before. Parker made a deal with Fine Line Features, a division of New Line Cinema. The picture was now budgeted at $2.5 million.

It was mid-1990 and *My Own Private Idaho* was a go!

17

PORTLAND AND IDAHO

In some parts of society, this [male hustlers] is everyday life, and you don't see it in other movies. In *Streetwise* [Martin Bell's 1984 documentary on Seattle's homeless teenagers], they showed these kids on the street, and these cars coming by, picking up girls. But they *never* showed it happening with the boys. It was this gritty documentary, but they didn't show the male prostitution. And that's the reason that I wanted to do this film: because it's always left out! People don't like to think about it. [*My Own Private*] *Idaho* shows you they are people not to be ignored, in the same way that *Drugstore Cowboy* shows you that heroin addicts are people, too.

Gus Van Sant, 1991

WAITING FOR RIVER PHOENIX to fulfill his prior obligation to complete the movie *Dogfight* in mid-1990 and for Keanu Reeves to shoot the very physically demanding action entry *Point Break* with Patrick Swayze was both an inconvenience and a blessing. The postponement of starting *My Own Private Idaho* allowed the two young stars plenty of time to research their daring screen roles as male prostitutes in Van Sant's upcoming project.

Of the two *My Own Private Idaho* coleads, Phoenix was the more cerebral performer. As always, he found it necessary to research a part deeply in order to find his character's center and to develop the needed character motivation. In April 1990, while River was shooting exteriors for *Dogfight* in San Francisco, Van Sant's young friend Mike Parker came down from Portland to meet with the actor. For Parker, it must have initially been an awkward encounter. Not only was River set to play variations of Mike's life on camera, but Phoenix was performing a part once "promised" to Parker. But River—who had already studied the videotaped interviews Van Sant had made with Parker—was very empathetic to his ex-street person tutor as they talked extensively about the dimensions of the off- and on-screen Mike Waters.

Parker later told John Glatt for *The Fast Times and Short Life of River Phoenix* that Phoenix had already had an involvement of sorts with a male member of the *Dogfight* cast to prepare for his *Idaho* role. As to whether Parker thought that the rising young screen star had any homosexual inclinations, Parker said, "I think maybe he had feelings that way. Everybody has a level of curiosity. River struck me as real curious. Maybe not because he was gay but because he wanted to understand. I can see him doing something like that, getting into it, figuring the role out and coming to see it from every point of view. River wanted to become Mike Waters."

Phoenix also gained insight into the world of the mean streets from Matt Ebert, who was working on *Dogfight* as a production assistant. Later, River would take Ebert with him to the *Idaho* shoot as his assistant. (Ebert would tell *Esquire* magazine in 1994 that Phoenix was already using drugs in this period, stating, "River started with heroin out of malaise.")

As River completed *Dogfight* he linked up with *Idaho* coplayer Keanu Reeves so they could explore street life. (Van Sant had already assigned the duo to read John Rechy's *City of Night*, the novel about male hustling in Los Angeles.) Reeves has recalled the pair making a field expedition while both were in Los Angeles: During their L.A. research excursion, they got caught in potentially dangerous turf: "We'd accidentally wandered into the no man's land between two street gangs. They thought we were invading their territory. It was terrifying—and there was no way we could tell them we were actors, they'd have cut us to pieces. We pretended we were ordinary guys—and then ran like hell!"

June 1990 found River in Portland to dig even deeper into the lifestyle of his *My Own Private Idaho* character. In these weeks as the social rapport between Van Sant and Phoenix developed, so did the strong professional bonds between the director and the much younger star. River and Keanu (when he was in town) were taken on tours of Portland's underbelly by Gus, and Gus introduced the two and others of the *Idaho* acting contingent to members of this subculture. Reportedly, the latter were not made aware of exactly what the actors were researching in Portland.

One of the supposedly uninformed was Robert Lee "Bob" Pitchlynn, the springboard for the Bob Pigeon character in *My Own Private Idaho*. Pitchlynn told John Glatt for his River Phoenix book: "Gus showed up one night at my house saying he had a birthday present for me. He had River with him and I was mad because he had brought somebody over without asking me first. We were sitting on the porch talking for about an hour before I even realized that he was River Phoenix." Bob also remembered, "Gus had already talked to me about doing the movie which had something to do with me as a character. I just didn't realize how much so. We were tutoring River and Keanu and they were picking up characterization from us. We never ever got paid for it." (In actuality, Pitchlynn played a small role in *My Own Private Idaho*, cast as Walt. He had also had bits in *Mala Noche* and *Drugstore Cowboy*.)

River and Keanu frequently returned to Bob Pitchlynn's domain where sometimes the two actors—both avid musicians—would play guitar and absorb the flavor of the post-Hippie street folk who hung around Pitchlynn's place. Sometimes the young stars would be joined by Michael Balzac (aka Flea) of the popular rock group the Red Hot Chili Peppers who had been cast by now to play Budd, the counterpart of Pitchlynn's younger friend, Conrad "Bud" Montgomery. (Bud was taking care of Bob Pitchlynn who was suffering from emphysema.)

During the summer of 1990 Phoenix, Reeves, and sometimes fellow *Idaho* cast member Rodney Harvey (now demoted to the lesser role of Gary, a street hustler) explored the Old Town district of Portland. These outings included visits to the bar City Nightclub (a gay spot mentioned in the script of *Idaho*). Frequently their tour guides were Mike Parker and Gus's affable assistant, Scott Patrick Green (who had been a partial basis for the Scott Favor character). In recalling these researching treks, Phoenix told Lance Loud (*American Film*), "I spent quite a few hours on the street in Portland between eight and four in the morning."

Under the tutelage of the street hustlers, Phoenix, Reeves, and Harvey learned how to spot potential clients cruising in cars along the byways and alleys of Portland's then tawdry Old Town district and what to say after strangers pulled over to make a deal for sex. According to Phoenix, "The next step would be to just open the door and get in. That's when we'd tell them to fuck off." River especially remembered one would-be "john" who, after being rejected by the movie stars-in-disguise, kept circling the block and yelling, "But I'm so lonely!"

Green recalled to Glatt for his River Phoenix study that sometimes the ever-curious River would talk to these johns "saying what he would and what he wouldn't do. But after we agreed to the deal I'd say, 'I'm sorry. We can't do this.' And we'd jump out of the car leaving these guys wondering what the hell was going on."

Phoenix, Reeves, and the others were encouraged by their director to get as deeply as possible into the souls of their characters, just as Van Sant had instructed Matt Dillon to do in *Drugstore Cowboy*. (Later, there would be unsubstantiated rumors that the filmmaker had actually encouraged the two movie leads to go out and have gay sex experiences so they would better understand the makeup of their characters.) When Reeves was asked once how he'd prepared for his *Idaho* role he shot back testily to the reporter, "I didn't have to suck d**k, if that's what you mean!" And that was the end of the interview.

Phoenix's chief coach was Mike Parker. The latter says in *The Fast Times and Short Life of River Phoenix*: "I showed River how to market himself on the street. You have to look real innocent and display. In my experiences there are two kinds of hustlers, the ones that are rowdy and look like they haven't taken a bath in a week and the glamorous ones, who don't have hair out of place. River took the underdog, grunge-type look, which is a definite pickup on the street." In Mike's estimation of Phoenix's method acting preparations: "I think he pulled out all the stops to get into his role for *Idaho*. He found it so challenging that it took over his whole being. Maybe he just went a little too far."

▼

BY September 1990 the cast for *My Own Private Idaho* was finalized—or so it was thought.

At one point it had been touted in film industry trade papers that British actor Daniel Day-Lewis (*My Beautiful Laundrette, A Room with a View*), who had won an Oscar for 1989's *My Left Foot,* would be part of *My Own Private Idaho*, cast in, most likely, the Bob Pigeon role. That hiring did not materialize. Next, raspy-voiced veteran actor Lionel Stander—best known for playing Max the chauffeur to Stefanie Powers and Robert Wagner in the TV series *Hart to Hart* (1979–84)—was hired to join *Idaho*. The eighty-two-year-old performer was to be Bob Pigeon. But by late October when rehearsals for the picture had ended, Stander had come and gone from the production. Upset by losing the acting role, Lionel was further humiliated when he learned that someone on the *Idaho* production staff had reportedly stated that Stander was discharged because of his failure to make prior disclosure of alleged physical infirmities (e.g., hearing loss, inability to bend). (Stander would die in November 1994.)

The next to inherit the role of raucous Bob Pigeon was filmmaker William Richert (*Winter Kill, The American Success Company*). He had directed River Phoenix in *A Night in the Life of Jimmy Reardon* (1988) and River thought he would be just right for the key role. Before long both Phoenix and Keanu Reeves were touting the virtues of Richert to Gus. The problem was that Richert was not interested in the part; he was involved with an attractive young woman at the time and felt that taking the unflattering role of the chicken hawk Bob Pigeon would hurt that budding real-life relationship. Nevertheless, Phoenix was determined to have William in the part and Van Sant was so confident in his charismatic young star's intuitions that he was pliable to most requests from River. Thus it was not difficult for Phoenix to engineer a meeting between Gus Van Sant and Richert. The latter finally acceded to Phoenix's many entreaties and signed on for the film.

Others who joined the cast included James Russo (*Beverly Hills Cop, The Cotton Club, We're No Angels*), hired to play River's on-camera brother. Grace Zabriskie, who had played Matt Dillon's mother in *Drugstore Cowboy*, returned to the Van Sant troupe, this time as a wealthy Portlander with a craving for young men. Then there was Udo Kier. Kier, a German-born actor, had started in the cinema playing handsome young men. By the mid-1970s, he was starring in two Andy Warhol–produced features: *Blood for Dracula* and *Flesh for Franken-stein*. By 1990, when he joined the cast of *My Own Private Idaho*, the forty-six-year-old performer had that decadent, quasi-obsessed look that made him just right to play the European Hans, the traveling autoparts sales executive who has a thirst for male hustlers.

Others given small acting assignments in *Idaho* included Eric Hull (from *Drugstore Cowboy*—as the mayor's aide), Phoenix's assistant Matt Ebert (as one of the porno magazine cover boys), Mickey Cottrell (*Idaho*'s publicity person— as an eccentric john), Wade Evans (a pal of the director—as another of the colorful hustler clients), Tiger Warren (Gus's longtime Portland friend—playing himself), Tom Peterson (a Portland appliance dealer famed for his wacky TV commercials and a good-luck charm to Gus movies—as the police chief), and Conrad "Bud" Montgomery (the real-life companion/helper of Portland's Bob Pitchlynn—as one of the rock promoters robbed in the park). Oregon film director Don Gronquist also had a walk-on bit, as did Ray Monge (*Mala Noche*). Van Sant even cast himself in a silent cameo—as the ponytailed Idaho hotel bellboy.

By this juncture, Gus had already moved into his expansive new home on 1883 Southwest Vista Avenue in Portland. (The back door of the manse boasted a sign that read BACKDOOR GUESTS ARE BEST.) During the preproduction period when Phoenix was frequently in Portland he had often stayed there in order to go over his characterization with Van Sant. Also, at Gus's there was plenty of space for him to jam on his guitar and hang loose.

Describing a visit to Van Sant's new digs sometime in this period, journalist Lance Loud reported for *American Film* that inside the imposing edifice, it was "more like an avant-garde frat house, decorated with only the barest necessities mixed with quirky earmarks of personal humor and style. In the foyer, one of Van Sant's own oil paintings, a pastel still-life of UFO-like sombreros hovering over a desert, is dwarfed by a sculpture that looks like an orange dumpster spewing a picnic table and benches out of its top. In the large kitchen, featuring two restaurant-quality stoves (he doesn't cook), stacks of head shots compete for table space with the salt and pepper shakers. In the otherwise cavernously empty living room, one moth-eaten couch is accompanied only by a broken-down hi-fi perched precariously on a folding chair, its needle still resting in the groove of *The Velvet Underground—Live*. Downstairs, amid the disarray of discarded musical instruments, a script for Van Sant's next film, *Even Cowgirls Get the Blues*, with the words *rough draft* on the blue cover, lies casually on the carpet."

▼

AS scene and line rehearsals began in late October/early November 1990 for the new movie, Reeves was recuperating from his tough shoot on *Point Break*. Many participants there noticed how deeply Phoenix had already submerged himself into his demanding role, looking akin to a real street kid complete with secondhand clothes, greasy hair, and a general unkempt look. Because of his ever-probing nature and total immersion into the character he was far more into his part than his older costar, Keanu Reeves. Gossip about how far River was burrowing into his characterization surfaced in the press, including a blind item that suggested he was "shacking up with drug-using streetfolk."

During this period, River chose to make Gus's home his headquarters once again, rather than stay, as initially planned, at Portland's Mallory Hotel. It was not long after he was ensconced at Van Sant's that others of the cast (Reeves, Rodney Harvey, Michael Parker, Flea, and actor Shaun Jordan) chose to camp out at their director's spacious house. It quickly turned into a crash-pad dormitory with futons, musical instruments (including guitars of all kinds and drum machines), and personal possessions spread out everywhere.

The energetic guys took to having late night rock 'n' roll jam sessions at the house that reportedly turned into full-fledged partying with the guest list including their girlfriends and buddies. Allegedly the clamorous fun times frequently and/or incessantly pushed on into the wee hours of the morning. These shindigs were generally held in the basement of Gus's home where his production company was based as well as Van Sant's Steenbeck editing deck and other filmmaking equipment. A maid came by the house frequently to keep the mounting disorder in check.

Wild rumors circulated then and for a long time thereafter about the supposed drug use by several of the *Idaho* acting clique. (When asked about this by the media Reeves would insist that drugs were "not really" part of the scene: "We smoked a little weed once in a while, sipped some red wine." In late 2000 Scott Patrick Green would tell Oriana Green for *Just Out* magazine, "All the stories you've heard are wildly exaggerated. If some of those stories were true it would've been even more fun.")

Years after the fact, in the December 1998 issue of *Premiere* magazine, Jane Goldsmith, Van Sant's script supervisor on *My Own Private Idaho* (as she had been on *Drugstore Cowboy*), described her attempts back in the fall of 1990 to lecture the *Idaho* squad about their excessive substance abuse: "I was getting down on them because of them using heroin, and they didn't appreciate that from me. River [Phoenix] would argue with me, but everyone else was just like, 'Shut up.' Or they would just nod out." Another source cited for the same *Premiere* piece described that, at the time, Harvey had reported back to him "all about that little shebang [in Portland]. About how those guys hit it like nobody's business. Seven in the morning, pulling needles from their arms. He [i.e., Harvey] said they'd walk from the house to the set after shooting heroin all night."

William Richert's estimation of the situation among the *Idaho* actors was, "These kids couldn't take care of each other. They went to a place that was loaded with junkies. And they're actors exploring characters. It's like scientists that take their own drugs. On a certain level, what they were doing was part of the game. They went into their roles as deeply as they could go."

As news circulated about the purported wild drug times going on at and off the *My Own Private Idaho* set the unconfirmed stories spiraled into urban legends within the film industry and resonated with segments of the general public hungry for juicy dirt. By Thanksgiving 1990 these extravagant tales had reached a new high. Purportedly, while a crew member from the *Idaho* team was in Los Angeles for the November holiday, he reported back to the Portland squad that "the word is that the film has been halted because we're all drug users, Gus doesn't know how to direct and the actors are having sex and prostituting themselves." In actuality, as *Idaho*'s produce Laurie Parker would later inform the media, when this alleged report of crazy times on Gus's new film was supposedly happening, the company was actually feasting on a turkey Thanksgiving dinner that was "like *Father Knows Best*."

Both in late 1990 and often over subsequent years, the question would be asked where Gus Van Sant was while all these allegedly excessive goings-on were transpiring at his Portland home and supposedly on the set. (In actuality, it was not long after the director permitted the *Idaho* troupe to take over his house for the duration that he found the general turmoil so disruptive to his concentration on the movie that he retreated to his old apartment in the inner city to gain a bit of solitude.) As to why the director didn't become concerned about the "situation" at his place—if there truly was one—script supervisor Goldsmith has offered, "Gus is a very enigmatic character. Gus doesn't judge. He's more of a voyeur. He wouldn't participate—but he would never lecture. He would never tell anyone else how to live their life. That's just how he is."

When Van Sant was directly queried about the suspected reckless behavior on the *Idaho* shoot, he responded, "I was encouraging people to understand the life, not live it. I don't know anything about shooting up in my house. I wasn't party to it if it happened." There was also the topic of why the cast had chosen to live communally at Gus's. It had given rise to overheated speculation that maybe orgies were going on at Gus's home. (None of this conjecture was ever substantiated.) Van Sant's answer on this subject was, "Living together in a house is not so unusual for the type of people I know who are trying to make films. . . . In college, everyone made films in the houses they lived in. It wasn't foreign to me. It might be foreign to the way one would think a Hollywood film would be made . . . but then again, I have a big house."

▼

IN assembling his crew for *My Own Private Idaho*, Van Sant utilized several individuals from his past movies. David Brisbin (*Drugstore Cowboy*) returned as production designer. In choosing the color palette for this feature, Brisbin noted that he and the decision makers referenced particular painters to gain a certain look. Brisbin explained, "We turned to [Vincent] Van Gogh and [Jan] Vermeer. A palette emerged that was primarily reds and yellows. Contemporary remnants of the Shakespearean appear in the design, costumes and of course the Falstaff beer that everyone drinks." (Another scheme used for thematic reasons was salmon, reflected, for example, in the color of the zipper jacket worn by Mike Waters as well as the tint of the bedroom walls in the home of Grace Zabriskie's character.) Van Sant and the others also studied such films as Werner Herzog's *Stroszek* and *Herz aus Glas* [Heart of Glass] and Stanley Kubrick's *A Clockwork Orange* as reference points to help establish a visual mood for *Idaho*.

One of the key sets in *My Own Private Idaho* was the derelict fleabag Portland hotel where Bob Pigeon and his bunch have rooms at one point in the narrative. (Five dilapidated buildings in the Portland area were used to represent the one structure.) Per Brisbin: "This hotel is meant to be a once-grand and fabulous place remodeled in the '60s, using really terrifying colors—ugly browns and horrible oranges—and coffee shop spaceship light bulbs, with just a bit of the Shakespearean effect pasted over the top. If you think of the design aesthetic Denny's Meets Shakespeare you get a pretty vibrating mix."

Then there was the question of using Portland's Washington Park, in particular, a section that had been a popular gay pickup spot. Located there was a landmark statue of two Native Americans, one of whom was pointing into the distance. The figures were called *Coming of the White Man*. Van Sant found that so amusing that he knew he had to use the locale somewhere in *My Own Private Idaho*. But it was soon decided there was too much greenery around the actual statue, so Gus's staff got inventive. They found a platformed elk statue in a downtown locale. Then a crew member, covered with patina-tone makeup, sat astride the animal, and a placard was affixed to the base of the elk statue that read THE COMING OF THE WHITE MAN. The setting was featured in the *Idaho* sequence in which Mike Waters awakens from a narcoleptic episode to find that he is back in Portland and that Scott Favor is watching over him.

Also back on the film team were cinematographers John Campbell (*Mala Noche*) and Van Sant's longtime friend Eric Alan Edwards (who had done time-lapse photography for *Mala Noche* and *Drugstore Cowboy*). It was an unusual concept to have two cinematographers on one, normal-size picture, but then *My Own Private Idaho* was not a typical film. Said Edwards at the time: "Everybody in the crew has had to accept that we're doing this film a bit differently from the traditional way." He described working with Van Sant as a process of "unlearning" and that "jump cuts here are a plot device." He also pointed out, "It was like being asked to be out [of] control, when your whole job in the world is being in control of things. But Gus knows that if we put the polish into this film that normal professionals would, that he wouldn't have the freedom he thinks he needs for the actors and for himself." He added, "I work with him the same today as we did on our first film, twenty years ago: free, loose, spontaneous. Improvisation can be as important in camera work as it is in acting." Co-cinematographer John Campbell observed, "Gus speaks in an actor's language. He's careful not to overdirect."

As she had been on *Drugstore Cowboy*, Beatrix Aruna Pasztor was the costume designer for *My Own Private Idaho*. She was required to devise interesting but realistic outfits for the street people characters, the bizarre clientele of the hustlers, and the scenes in which upscale individuals appear. Missy Stewart, set dresser on *Drugstore Cowboy*, was set decorator on *My Own Private Idaho*. Film editor Curtiss Clayton, one of those involved with *Drugstore* Cowboy, was hired to do the same on the new production.

▼

STARTING his third feature film (leaving his *Alice in Hollywood* to one side), the now experienced Van Sant was much more self-assured about the film-making process. As he explained, "Confidence, sure, but I also know by now what's going to work and what isn't. I already have a sense of the technical things that might go wrong. So I have more freedom. As far as pulling perform-ances goes, I try and build the character with the actor, suggesting things to him before we even start shooting. I never really say, 'This character has to reach the innermost depths,' because it's suggested in the script already, and we've already talked all about it. Every actor knows how far he wants to go, or I want him to go. So I leave it up to him. . . . I don't really react."

Unlike past projects where he utilized storyboards (i.e., the drawings or photographs showing the progressions of set-up shots within a film sequence) mostly to guide his scene-by-scene progress, this time Van Sant allowed himself to be freer and more spontaneous. Thus he used the *Idaho* storyboards (exe-cuted by Arnold Pander who, along with his older brother, Jacob, were local fashion-conscious artists with filmmaking interests) as points of reference only. In doing so, all the subconscious thoughts on the project Gus had accumulated to date came to the surface. Van Sant reasoned, "To storyboard this one would have been really imposing. In order to do that, you always have to know that when a character walks into a room, he has to turn right, walk to the window and then go out the door, right? But then the actor can't run into the room, run around in a circle three times and jump out the window, 'cause that's not on the storyboard."

He further said, "I was really just making it up as I went along. I rehearse that day, and I make up the shot then. Of course, the whole time I'm working on a film, I'm on location, and I'm thinking. Things are always suggesting them-selves. But they're never set in stone until right after the rehearsal. And then I just tell Eric (Portland-based cinematographer Eric Alan Edwards), 'This is the shot.' I never make up the next shot until after the first one."

According to Van Sant the picture was "shot without any shot list. . . . On *Idaho* we didn't decide in which order we were going to shoot. We always shot the 'first' thing, whatever I decided it should be, and then I'd choose the second shot. We'd usually start wide and then go closer, because it's easier to light that way."

As to the interaction between cast and filmmaker, Gus noted, "I talk about setting a lot. I talk about characters I knew who are like the characters in the screenplay." The director cited *Idaho* examples. "Keanu would come up with things on his own, specific things as to why Scott would turn his back on his friend, and the responsibility he has to his father, and what it's like to have that responsibility, to have a parent who gives you a lot—and then takes it away." Gus further noted, "River was totally different. He has this kind of Mozart quality of just burying himself completely in research. He does it through a sort of osmosis; everything you give him feeds into this plant that's growing out of the information he's got. He tape-records things, and talks to people; he has his own sources. It's more tactile: River will create something out of mixed media —films, writings, records, people talking, this whole wild thing. With Keanu, you give him a book, he'll read the book. River might read part of the book, and if he's interested he'll read the whole book. Keanu will read what you give him like you were giving him instructions: he follows them."

Working with William Richert on *Idaho* presented the potential problem of one filmmaker taking direction from another as well as the fact that Richert had recently directed Phoenix in a picture. But said Van Sant: "Bill's an effusive, loud character who likes to tell stories. I thought he'd be River's mentor, and I was worried that maybe Bill would just take over. . . . But he was my greatest supporter, and he was totally reliant taking direction from me. He's a director who hasn't acted for a long time, and he could see things from my point of view."

On the shoot, Van Sant typically wore jeans, a shirt, a (tattered) sweater, Converse high-tops, and a green hat with its bill turned to the back. Frequently he sported a few days' growth of facial hair. He had his own unique protocol for interacting with cast and crew. According to the *New York Times*' Thomas J. Meyer who visited the *My Own Private Idaho* location: "On a film set, Van Sant sits with a veil of hushed concentration that separates him from everything around him. He'll break the silence only occasionally to approach an actor after a take and mumble, 'That was a good one,' or maybe, 'Let's do one more.' Actors develop a sort of secret, mute communication system with him, but they can still be caught off guard. 'He's a subliminal director,' says River Phoenix, who compares working on a Van Sant picture to being guided by a hidden remote control."

In fact, on the set self-contained Van Sant would speak so quietly that often an assistant had to repeat his boss's spoken cues into a megaphone so everyone could hear. For reporter Meyer, Gus emerged "a portrait of detached, quiet authority." Cinematographer Eric Alan Edwards told the visiting journalist about Van Sant both on and off the set: "He's always thinking and focused and concentrated. But he has a sort of a strange sense of surreality about him."

Producer Laurie Parker had her own take on Van Sant the moviemaker: "Gus is extremely reticent sometimes to articulate fully what he wants. He's much more than words. He can show you with art or music." For example, when it came time to explain to the appropriate technicians about a special effect he needed to have occur within the narrative, he did a sketch showing a farmhouse falling on an open road, and then told staff members, "Do this."

During the course of the shoot, which began November 1, 1990, principal photography was accomplished in Portland (including the corner of Southwest

Third Avenue and Salmon Street, a doorway at the Great Northwest Book Store at 1234 Southwest Stark Street, the sidewalk outside the gay bathhouse at 303 Southwest Twelfth Avenue, the interior of Huber's Restaurant at 411 Southwest Third Avenue, etc.). Most of the Portland scenes were lensed in the squalid parts of Old Town where, at the time, homeless people and runaways were still afoot, and many of the buildings were in sad decay.

Other filming locales were Maupin, Oregon; Seattle, Washington; Twin Falls, Idaho; and Rome and Lazio, Italy. One scene filmed—which did not make it to the final cut—utilized the Seattle ferry. That sequence involved Phoenix, Reeves, and Rodney Harvey on the vessel's foredeck and depicted one of the sudden narcoleptic naps taken by River's character. On camera, Keanu and Rodney's alter egos pass a pot pipe back and forth as they study the scenic view. It took most of a very cold day to film this footage, and from the microphone boom hung a sign intended for the passengers aboard: "We are filming *My Own Private Idaho*, a Gus Van Sant movie, starring River Phoenix and Keanu Reeves, and you can't be in it. Thank you."

One of the more offbeat scenes captured for the movie occurred in the porno shop setting and involved the talking gay magazine covers. (This was shot at Portland's Film Follies bookstore at 915 Southwest Third Street.) Originally, the magazine cover for Phoenix's bit said "G-String Jesus" but, to avoid offending religious audiences, it was altered to read "G-String" and the prop cross was denuded of its cross arms. Phoenix was "tied" to the post to deliver his lines and his loincloth (his only costume) had the addition of foam-rubber padding to make the crotch bulge appropriately. After several takes River's sequence was accomplished, with the perfectionist actor inquiring, "Was that any good? Was that right? Did you believe it?"

My Own Private Idaho contained a cinema vérité section in which several hustlers sitting in a coffee shop relate their first sex-for-pay transactions. Gus advised the nonactors "to come up with their own worst scenario—they came up with these amazing stories!" All of this fascinated the filmmaker: "I'm interested in disaffected youth: the adventure side of it is interesting." (Although several subjects were captured on film, only the accounts told by Van Sant's friends Mike Parker and Scott Patrick Green made it to the final release print.)

Another scene within the movie focused on a sexual threesome between the characters played by Phoenix, Reeves, and Udo Kier. As Van Sant would note, "In *My Own Private Idaho* we were always just representing it [i.e., sex], not showing sex but giving you an idea. Not seeing it is a way to get it across. It would be interesting to do a film where you do see stuff, where you see people and it seems like they're really having sex. There's just always that area where you might not get away with it dramatically. If you're making a pornographic film, it's a totally different situation. It's a different objective." To get the suggestion of the on-film trio having intimate relations, Gus "showed it by having still images of naked bodies. You got the idea. You got to see the positions. We didn't see movements. After you saw the tableaux—this is what happened—the scene really starts after the sex." According to Van Sant: "That occurred to me as a way to present a sex scene without actually showing it, or the actors smoking in bed afterwards. It was written down that way in the script."

As in all of Gus's feature films to this point there also was the use of home movies taken by cast members. The bulk of the 16mm footage for *Idaho* was shot by Phoenix, who, despite his experience in front of the camera, was not adept behind the lens. He loaded the film improperly, which resulted in a glitch that happened to work well—it created on the homemade footage of his character's childhood a sense of a distant, far-away time.

Perhaps the movie's most crucial sequence—and the one reviewers would choose as the film's finest moment—occurs at the campfire as Mike Waters and Scott Favor motorcycle to Idaho in search of Mike's long-missing mother. Originally, as written by Van Sant, it was just an on-the-road break where a bored Mike suggests that he and Scott have sex with each other to relieve the boredom.

As Gus recollected this memorable interplay: "It was a short, three-page scene that River turned into more like an eight-page scene. He added a lot of things and changed the fabric of his character in that scene. He's a songwriter and he worked on it like he does one of his songs, which is very furiously. He had decided that that scene was his character's main scene and, with Keanu's permission, he wrote it out to say something that it wasn't already saying—that his character, Mike, has a crush on Scott and is unable to express it—which wasn't in the script at all. It was his explanation of his character."

Another time, Van Sant elaborated further on the history of the restructuring of this pivotal scene: "About three nights before we shot the scene he [i.e., River Phoenix] showed me a lot of stuff he had written and it was like 16 pages of handwritten notes with arrows and things leading to other pages and circles around words, and it was a big mess. He said he was rewriting the scene and wanted to know if he could do this. And I was really scared. It looked like he was freaking out. It was out of control. . . . Sometimes actors just want you to say NO. And I didn't think he was doing that, like he was the type of guy that wanted you to say no. So I just asked Keanu if it was alright, if he was like stepping on his turf, because when one actor starts to write another actor's lines it can get into this bad scene. And Keanu really loved River and he just said, 'Yeah, man. Yeah.'"

Phoenix's recollection of the process was, "I worked it out with Gus and Keanu and we all agreed on something. It seems real ad-libbed but it was all scripted. In pencil. But it's scripted. It's all Gus, though. It was inspired by his world." About this central on-screen exchange, River pointed out proudly about his new dialogue: "I wrote them all." He went on to explain why the newly created text was so key to his characterization: "In society there's this confusion between love and sex. People think they want love and that they'll get it through sex. Mike is very clear on the difference between love and sex because he has sex for a living. That's why his line was so important. 'I love you, and you don't have to pay me.' I'm so glad I wrote that line." (Later on, Mike Parker said, "River wrote that entire scene after a conversation with me about being able to love people, maybe even a man, without getting money for it. It was intense. River incorporated what he felt inside for real with what I felt and it just all came out in that kiss with Keanu to make one of the most brilliant scenes in the movies.")

Yet at the same time that Phoenix could so creatively enhance his character through a dialogue/character shift that he had engineered, there was a playful, childlike side to River. For example, during one of the setups for this very dramatic scene, Reeves was already feeling uncomfortable about the implications of his character holding and comforting the vulnerable Mike as they lay by the campfire. (Keanu's physical stiffness and emotional clumsiness as an actor, which worked both for and against his characterization in *Idaho*, is especially apparent in this sequence.) River chose that moment to say to Reeves, "Just think, Keanu—five hundred million of your fans will be watching this one day!" The remark threw Reeves off his mark, leading Van Sant to do what he rarely did—strongly reprimand Phoenix.

But generally on the set, Phoenix, who obviously had the film's most difficult assignment, remained strongly in character, stretching him creatively in a role that led him to take insightful acting risks. If, for example, a scene called for him to have a sleepy-eyed, drugged-out look, he would, according to the actor, "stay asleep until just seconds before the camera would roll, then I'd stagger onto the set and do the scene in a half-sleep state."

And it would be from the younger Phoenix that Reeves willingly took his acting cues. Said the reverential Keanu: "River's a heavy actor. Man, he's the best. Yeah, he helps me. He was very inspiring. He's intelligent and he had a lot of insight and I kind of like rode his wave sometimes. I don't know how much I gave him. His character, Mike, is, like, totally estranged from everything. He's overwhelmed. He knows how to hustle, though. Mike is a strong hustler."

It was not only Reeves who took his prompts from Phoenix, but an appreciative Gus as well. By now he and Phoenix had developed a close friendship that was not so much of two individuals of different generations working in tandem but of two equal people. Some years later Van Sant would say of the magical on-set experience with the young star: "River was like a person and a half, one of those very rare people who somehow have that bit of extra compassion, extra interest in the world about them. On *My Own Private Idaho* he would always get involved in calming down disputes, like if there was a sound man screaming at the props man that someone had spilled coffee on his machine, River would just go over and sort it out. He'd buy the sound man a new machine or something."

Conversely, throughout *Idaho*, the emotionally delicate Phoenix looked to Van Sant for approval—as a director, as a friend, and, perhaps in some ways, as a substitute father figure. Gus has revealed, "River was always doing things like saying, 'I just love you,' and lunging to hug me. I'd freeze maybe because my father used to grab my knee in a certain way. River didn't like that, so he'd hug me again, and I'd freeze, and he'd yell at me."

Finally, in mid-December 1990 after a few days of lensing in Seattle, the cast/crew all had a farewell cappuccino at the Virginia Inn, a trendy watering hole that had become the headquarters for Phoenix, Reeves, and Van Sant during the filming there. Then, with the rest of the cast now through with their chores, the trio flew to Italy where the final scenes were to be shot.

Assessing the fast and furious time spent making *My Own Private Idaho*, Van Sant said, "It's fun at times on the set because people really get what you're doing. The writing and the showing of it are fun. The filming and the editing are work. Filming is not fun. You make it fun. The hours are so long, and everything is set up in a certain way. Maybe someday we can get around that." Of making the movie, Reeves judged, "I probably could have used a little more rehearsal but the [*Idaho*] experience was probably the most intense filming experience I've ever had." Phoenix enthused of his director/friend/mentor: "His world is just so interesting, I can't help but be inspired when I hang out with him. Not only does he give you something that makes you think and grow, but he welcomes input. . . . Gus just has such faith in the character development, you know? Like the best artists he uses everything there [i.e., in the special creative world he inhabits]. It was so fun working with Gus 'cause in that world you can get away with everything."

18

THE VISION COMES ALIVE

All directors have to fall in love with their lead characters; the leading character is the spokesman for the universe you're making the film about. "When we're casting guys there is the extra conflict of interest of falling in love with them, but I don't allow that to happen. In France, directors say they have to make love to their actors, but they're French. [Van Sant deadpans] I'm more Calvinist.

Gus Van Sant, 2000

BY EARLY 1992 GUS Van Sant was back in Portland busily engaged in the postproduction facets of *My Own Private Idaho*. It was one of those unique periods—which happens to many creative artists—where reality and fantasy overlapped, blended, and superimposed on his life and current project.

On the *Idaho* location shoot in Italy, Van Sant has taken his boyfriend D-J Haanraadts in the capacity of assistant director. Now back in Oregon, Gus spent a good deal of time at home where he kept filmmaking/editing equipment. Young Scott Patrick Green, who was playing an increasingly important role in Gus's life, was around a good deal of the time as he observed Gus taking *My Own Private Idaho* into its next steps toward completion. Green was also learning to do still photography under Gus's tutelage. Sometimes he accompanied Van Sant on interviews about the forthcoming release of *Idaho,* which was already generating industry buzz. Scott's presence at such media question-and-answer sessions created a surrealistic situation.

For example, there was the time in 1999 when Ralph Rugoff of *Premiere* magazine came to Portland to profile Gus and to talk about his controversial new motion picture. The interview—with Green on hand—was conducted at a downtown hotel in the City of Roses. Rugoff reported: "It's an odd situation, because Van Sant has a habit of not just basing characters in his films on real people but naming the characters after them and then putting the real people in the films in other roles. Scott [Patrick Green] was a street kid Van Sant hired as a sort of consultant for [Keanu] Reeves. . . . As the real Scott chain-smokes Marlboros and glance at TV with vacant eyes, Van Sant talks about the fictional Scott. Occasionally he asks the real Scott his opinion."

Then there was the situation that, as Gus and editor Curtiss Clayton began assembling a rough cut of *My Own Private Idaho*, Van Sant could look at the celluloid frames and see the fictional Mike Waters and Scott Favor and then glance around his home workshop and observe the real-life semicounterparts— Scott and sometimes Mike Parker—doing work assignments. Making the boundaries between the "fictional" and "real" dimensions of Van Sant's life all the more fuzzy was the fact that the *Idaho* footage contained performances by Green, Parker, and many of Gus's other Portland acquaintances as well.

In addition, in approaching his fortieth birthday, Van Sant certainly may well have been in the throes of an early midlife crisis. (During the filming of *My Own Private Idaho* Gus had had a near-fatal crash while riding his motorcycle. He had passed off the traumatic incident with one of his wry witticisms: "It would've been such a good story. 'Director killed on film set.'") Perhaps this evaluating mood—if it had broken to the surface—may have prompted the director to sort out the spectrum of feelings he had for twenty-one-year-old actor River Phoenix. Their rapport during *Idaho* had turned to greater friendship and they kept in constant touch by phone. (River's next film project was to be *Sneakers* with Robert Redford and Sidney Poitier.) And, of course, at his Portland editing facility Van Sant was always "seeing" Phoenix on film as the director and Clayton worked on the amassed movie footage.

While Gus was a declared homosexual, River's sexual feelings (whether fully heterosexual or not) was focused on his current girlfriend, Suzanne Solgot. The latter had visited the *Idaho* shoot in Portland and was one of those—reportedly—whom Phoenix sought to keep in the dark about his own escalating drug usage. Whether Gus, who always kept his emotions close to the vest, really dealt with or sublimated having a rival of sorts for the attention of his actor pal can only be imagined.

Then, too, poring over the *Idaho* footage and having images of Phoenix's stoned-out, emotionally fragile screen character staring at Van Sant, most likely had some degree of subconscious effect on the moviemaker. As Gus went over the film frames, did he occasionally find chinks in his continued denial about Phoenix sampling drugs heavily during *Idaho*? Did any part of nonjudgmental, often emotionally passive Gus wonder whether he should have intervened on his pal's behalf during the shoot—or even now? (Already by this time, the national magazines and supermarket tabloids were commenting on the dramatic physical and personality changes that had come over Phoenix since he started work on *Idaho*.)

Weeks passed as Gus, often walking around his workroom in his stocking feet, went through the editing process with Curtiss Clayton. Of working with

Van Sant, Clayton would say, "Gus grows a little uncomfortable if you try to force him to say what he's trying do. He just likes to experiment and see if it happens." Clayton also observed, "You go out to dinner with Gus and you don't get the usual sort of things, like what he's upset about. Often he doesn't talk at all. He keeps a lot inside." As a tantalizing postscript to the queries thrust at him about his coworker/friend Van Sant, Clayton offered, "I know some great stories about Gus, but I could never tell them to a journalist." (Later it would be Clayton who would take a rough edit of *Idaho* to Los Angeles to show executives at New Line Cinema/Fine Line Features.)

Meanwhile, media interest was escalating in *My Own Private Idaho*. As time for the feature's fall release grew nearer, the press began snapping at the heels of Van Sant, Phoenix, Reeves, and others connected with the film, wanting their reactions to the movie's controversial elements.

Much of the prerelease attention was directed toward the homosexual aspects of *My Own Private Idaho*. Repeatedly, Gus insisted that this picture was really not a gay story, "but it doesn't bother me for people to call it that. The film was made by a gay person—me. But I don't think it's addressing a gay audience or issues in the gay world directly. It's not done from a particular point of view about sexual orientation. It's written with a general audience in mind. I hope the film will have a broader exposure [than *Drugstore Cowboy*]." As Gus reasoned, the hustlers' world depicted in the movie was one "where the men and the boys picked up by them think of themselves as straight. (The boys) are like pirates, street people." He also emphasized, "It's a film about an area of society—prostitution—that's not defined in terms of gay or straight. River's character may be gay, but you're not really sure—he's not really sure. And the hustlers and johns definitely don't think of themselves as gay. In real life, the clients for these street hustlers tend to be middle-class businessmen or construction workers with families."

On a much different tack, Van Sant informed the media about the ambiguities and contradictions in the personality of lead character Mike Waters: "Emotionally, Mike is arrested. And that means sexually, too. But it was confusing, because we changed the character a little bit, and River changed the character. In a good way, but in a way that made him normal. This whole idea that he confesses his love for Scott, that's a thing River thought up. I was all for that. It was sort of like a politically interesting thing to do, it was good. It made the character more positive. But, in fact, as written, the character was unable to say something like that, because he was arrested in his emotional development. What he did in the script was make a physical pass on Scott, because he was bored. He was just bored. He wanted them to fool around, they were in the dessert. He wanted them to s**k each other off, you know, because there was nothing to do. That was the energy behind that pass and then Scott says, 'No, man, I don't do that. . . .' But as we filled it out, he was actually in love, so all this other stuff came that's much more identifiable and normal than, you know, this arrested thing. Does that make sense?"

(Also as a part of Van Sant having Mike's character suffer a malady, this ailment has created so many gaps in Mike's memory that he remains naïve rather than becoming the typical jaded hustler. It also allows for a distinctive Gus twist, in that the lead character—through whose point of view we view much of the film—is often unconscious, in so many different ways, through much of the narrative.)

Expectedly, River Phoenix had his own viewpoint about what *Idaho* really was. "This is not a statement film about homosexuality. The characters in the film are completely at peace with their sexuality, and their sexuality is a minor element in what these characters are going through—one is dealing with his estrangement from his father, the other is searching for his mother. . . . However, it still strikes me as strange that anyone could have any moral objection to someone else's sexuality—it's like telling someone else how to clean their house. Speaking for myself, I had no second thoughts about playing this part."

Phoenix also observed: "I guess gays need a film 'cause they're a minority, because they need something like this as a social motivator. But the movie could just as easily be called an environmental film because of all the beautiful nature scenes of places that won't be around in the future."

Keanu Reeves's public take on the film was pure Keanu: "It's such an amazing story! It's so—aww! It's just different, man, it's a different sound, a different way of making a movie. I hope it's engaging; when I read it I just said, 'Yeah!'"

Meanwhile, *Idaho*'s diplomatic producer Laurie Parker offered, "Gus tackles subjects that are frightening or scary in a commercial context, but he makes them less frightening by rendering them with humor."

As it grew closer to the time for Gus to provide his employers on the project the final cut of *My Own Private Idaho*, Rolfe Mittweg, a senior vice president at New Line Cinema/Fine Line Features, was quoted in *Premiere* magazine as saying of Van Sant: "If he's going to show erect d**ks, I don't know what we're going to do." When told of Mittweg's statement, Van Sant countered, "Of course, it's only a problem because men get embarrassed when they see d**ks on the screen, and as the boss of the household, they don't want to be embarrassed." The article resolved the issue by noting that there were no pickles (i.e., men's penises) revealed in *My Own Private Idaho*.

▼

AS finalized, *My Own Private Idaho* opens on an empty Idaho road where young male hustler Mike Waters has a narcoleptic fit and falls asleep dreaming of his mother. Back in Seattle, Waters plies his street trade with his list of regular clients. One evening he is hired by a wealthy woman and she takes him to her plush home. There he encounters two other male prostitutes: Scott Favor and Gary. Scott is the arrogant son of Portland's mayor and has known Mike for nearly four years. When the client initiates sexual foreplay with Waters, Mike sinks into one of his fits. Standoffish with most people, Scott has a soft spot for vulnerable Mike, and drags him to the lawn of a neighboring estate to sleep off his latest attack.

In the morning, Mike meets Hans, a rich German who offers him a ride, but Mike refuses and suffers another spell. When Waters awakens he is back in Portland and finds Scott looking after him. Later, they learn that Bob, the once leader of their street gang, has returned to town from a trip to Boise, Idaho. They join Bob and his skuzzy followers in taking over a derelict building, which is thereafter raided by the police who are searching for the disreputable Bob. The law enforcers tell Favor that his dad, the mayor, wishes to see him. Scott visits his father but their meeting ends in the usual argument.

Scott and Mike embark for Idaho on his stolen motorcycle in a quest to find Waters's mother whom he has not seen in years. Once there they visit Mike's brother at his rundown trailer home. Richard alerts them that the parent is now working at a hotel in Snake River. Before they leave, a distraught Mike acknowledges that he knows his brother is also his dad. At the hotel (appropriately named the Family Tree Hotel) they find out that Mrs. Waters has moved on to Italy. Fortuitously, Hans is registered there. After a three-way sex scene, they sell him the stolen motorbike and use the money to fly to Italy.

Reaching the farmhouse where Mrs. Waters is supposed to be staying, they learn she has returned to America. Meanwhile, Scott falls in love with Carmella, the farmer's daughter. This deeply upsets Mike who had once told Favor that he truly loved him. Tossing him a few dollars and an empty promise that they will meet "down the road," Scott (with Carmella in tow) abandons the distraught Mike.

Once again in Portland, Mike and Bob spot a now well-dressed Scott sweeping into a chic restaurant with Carmella. They learn that Scott's father has died and that the young man has received a large inheritance. Bob, who has long awaited this moment, urges Scott to remember his friends. Favor refuses to acknowledge Pigeon, his onetime lover. That evening the distraught Bob dies of a fever. Later, on the same day and at the same cemetery, Bob and Scott's father are coincidentally buried only several yards apart.

Time passes and Mike is again on the Idaho road. Again he has a narcoleptic fit and collapses in a stupor. When a truck stops, two men take his shoes and other valuables. Thereafter, a car stops, the unseen driver carries Mike's spent body into the vehicle, and then the car speeds away.

▼

IT had been intended to have *My Own Private Idaho* unspool at the Cannes Film Festival in May 1991, but Van Sant was still tinkering with the picture at the time and the festival was reportedly unhappy with the in-progress version New Line Cinema had submitted to them. According to Gus: "They couldn't figure it out. It was a very rough cut, a different cut, and it would have screwed up our mix to try to rush it through. It's just as well it didn't play there."

In July 1991 *My Own Private Idaho* was screened in Portland, Oregon. (By then, River Phoenix had seen a work print of the feature and told the journalist watching it with him, "It's like putting a York Peppermint Patty on your heart, isn't it?") Next, in early September, it was shown at the Telluride Film Festival. It played at the Toronto International Film Festival on the twelfth of the month and it was run at the New York Film Festival two weeks later. At the latter event held at Lincoln Center, the director and cast came from a cast party at the city's China Club to answer questions after the screening. Some who attended the occasion thought many on the stage had done too much partying to be really responsive.

Two days later, the film opened officially in New York City and on Friday, October 10, it had its Los Angeles premiere. The event was a benefit for the Living/Project Angel Food and Los Angeles Film Forum. While Reeves and many of the other principals were on hand, Phoenix had been driving in from Florida and did not reach Los Angeles until Saturday morning—by which time the postshow party at the Arena Club had disbanded. Also during October, the film was viewed at the Venice Film Festival where River Phoenix won the Volpi Cup as Best Actor. At the Deauville Film Festival that year, Van Sant won the Critics Award for *My Own Private Idaho*.

Regarding Gus's new picture, Vincent Canby (*New York Times*) enthused, "*My Own Private Idaho* is essentially a road movie that, in its subversive way, almost qualifies as a romantic comedy except that its characters are so forlorn. The film itself is invigorating—written, directed and acted with enormous insight and comic élan." Canby observed, "Like the narcoleptic Mike, the movie initially seems to be without direction. It appears to drift from one casual encounter to the next, getting what it can from the passing connections, some of them very funny, others harrowing, until time runs out. When the film abruptly reaches its end, the conclusion is seen, in hindsight, to have been inevitable from the opening frame." The *Times* reviewer decided, "*My Own Private Idaho* is as blunt, uncompromising and nonjudgmental as Mr. Van Sant's two earlier films . . . but the scope is now broader and the aspirations more daring." He summed up that Gus "makes a bold leap to join Jim Jarmusch and the Coen brothers in the front ranks of America's most innovative independent film makers."

J. Hoberman (*Village Voice*) found the new entry "densely textured, beautifully shot (when not purposefully raw), and continually surprising." The critic acknowledged, "Although Reeves's callowness matches the callowness of his character, it seems likely that Van Sant, known for his upper-middle-class fascination with the lower depths, identifies with the slumming prince—even as he satirizes him."

Kenneth Turan of the *Los Angeles Times* was very impressed. "No matter what you've been used to, *Idaho* is something completely different, a film that manages to confound all expectations, even the ones it sets up itself." He admitted, "Even though it occasionally feels like the world's hippest shaggy dog story, *Idaho* invariably redeems itself when you least expect it. Edgily funny when boredom threatens, suddenly tender and heartfelt when everything seems to be on the surface, it may stumble and teeter at times, but it never quite loses its balance." Turan concluded, "Holding all these elements together is Van Sant's sensibility, such an elusive thing it instinctively squirms away from any attempt to pigeonhole it. The quirkiest notions . . . seem to leap unblocked right from his eccentric imagination to the screen."

An enthusiastic Roger Ebert (*Chicago Sun-Times*) perceived, "The achievement of this film is that it wants to evoke that state of drifting need, and it does. There is no mechanical plot that has to grind to a Hollywood conclusion, and no contrived test for the heroes to pass; this is a movie about two particular young men, and how they pass their lives." John Powers (*LA Weekly*) decided, "His [Van Sant] poetic touch lets him leap from style to style, mood to mood, carrying us along with him. Never has his filmmaking been any richer than in the scenes that gradually open up Mike and Scott's world. . . . Like *Thelma & Louise*, *My Own Private Idaho* makes us rethink the romance of the road."

Todd McCarthy (*Weekly Variety*) had a qualified reaction: "*My Own Private Idaho* gives the impression of a director so eager to make a highly personal masterpiece that he has almost indiscriminately thrown in nearly every cinematic idea he's had for the last ten years. Rather less than the sum of its often striking parts, Gus Van Sant's appealingly idiosyncratic look at a pair of very different young street hustlers is one of those ambitious, overreaching disappointments that is more interesting than some more conservative successes." As to the Shakespearean interlude that so many had cautioned Van Sant about using in the film, McCarthy determined, "Injection of such a screwy notion is so audacious that it must be considered seriously, but it just doesn't work." *Newsday*'s Jack Matthews concurred regarding the Bard: "Whenever Van Sant shifts the focus to the urban stage and fuses it with bad Shakespearean dialogue, he pushes the audience right out of the story."

Some critics, such as Terrence Rafferty of *The New Yorker*, in evaluating *Idaho*, reserved their kind words for River Phoenix: "Although the script ends up begging for sympathy for Mike, Phoenix never does. He's completely and unselfconsciously absorbed in Mike, and he's genuinely touching. . . . Van Sant has stranded the actor in a movie full of flat characters and bad ideas, but Phoenix walks through the picture, down road after road after road, as if he were surrounded by glorious phantoms." Rafferty also concluded: "*My Own Private Idaho* is the first film in which Van Sant's screenplay hasn't been based on another writer's material, and in the absence of the formal limits imposed by an existing story and cast of characters he seems to have lost control of his meanings. In attempting to give some structure to all the volatile emotions and disparate experiences he wants to capture in this picture, he has forced his drifting, suggestively muddled characters into too narrow a frame."

Much more negative about *My Own Private Idaho* was Richard Schickel (*Time*) who groused, "Gus Van Sant adores characters who are literally too sensitive for words. This recommends his work to the serious younger audience, which tends to mime its discontents by striking sullen poses. But it is not a use-ful attribute for a maker of sound movies. Neither is Van Sant's disdain for nar-rative. He got away with *Drugstore Cowboy* because its band of drugged-out dodoes were engaged in a petty crime spree that almost passed for a plot. But *My Own Private Idaho* is a different story. Or rather nonstory."

Abroad, *My Own Private Idaho* received a mixed reaction. In England, Lizzie Francke (*Sight and Sound*) bubbled, "Within the first five minutes, Gus Van Sant has re-created a synthetic American mythology that turns out to be the stuff of Mike's wet dreams. . . . Few films in recent years have kicked off with a seam of imagery as rich as this." Regarding the reaction to the picture in France, Van Sant reported that "this R-rated film is off the board for the French bourgeoisie. They have problems with the characters themselves. No one knows what's going to happen with it there."

In its domestic run, *My Own Private Idaho* grossed $6.401 million. That relatively positive financial figure is impressive when one considers that the picture had three sizeable hurdles to overcome: (1) homosexual topics not gen-erating big box-office, (2) the Shakespearean elements potentially creating neg-ative audience reaction, and (3) the lack of an obvious narrative structure in a film that switches back and forth between realism and fantasy.

As prizes were announced for 1991 movie releases, the National Society of Film Critics awarded Phoenix their Best Actor trophy. At the Independent Spirit Awards (presented on March 28, 1992, at the Raleigh Studios in Los Angeles), the picture won for Best Actor (Phoenix), Best Music (Bill Stafford), and Best Screenplay (Van Sant). From the same organization *My Own Private Idaho* received nominations for Best Cinematography, Best Director, and Best Feature Film. Ironically, when the much-lauded, much-discussed *Idaho* was re-leased on home video in 1992, the distributor chose at that late date to try to broaden the perception of the film's story line. As such, the back cover artwork of the VHS tape box featured River Phoenix and Keanu Reeves separately— each with a woman!

▼

GUS Van Sant stated once, "All the stories that I have done so far [i.e., up to 1993] have had some sort of family metaphor. In *Alice in Hollywood*, the girl falls in with a family of people on the street. In *Mala Noche*, Walt and Pepper form a couple that's more like a father-son relationship, and in *Drugstore Cow-boy*, it's like a drug family. In *Idaho*, it's a street family again with Bob as the father figure, but it's a displaced temporary family. The film's about why Mike's on the street—because his real family didn't work. That comes directly from a number of people that I've known that live that kind of life; in every case, they came from some sort of problematic family situation. One of the kids who I filmed for the interviews in the café in *Idaho*, but who didn't make the final cut, was talking about how he had a motorcycle accident and his family was sued for a million dollars and he had to leave because they didn't have the money and blamed him."

Another aspect of the family theme in *Idaho* is the search for home (a recurrent thesis in Van Sant's pictures). It ties into the shots of fish shown in the movie. Gus has said: "Mike is sort of like an embryo—I think River was playing it like that. He was doing things that I didn't even know he was doing. Interior things he wouldn't tell you about. But the fish in the beginning, those salmon are returning to their birthplace in order to spawn. . . . So River is like a salmon, he's fighting to reach his place of birth, basically. He's not an embryo, but he's going to where he was an embryo. So it's different. Where you're picking up on it . . . He's like a fish trying to get to where the fish was a fish egg . . . which is the mom. He never gets there. He even wears a salmon-colored jacket, you know?"

With the above in mind Mike's surname of Waters carries the intended imagery one step farther. One should also keep in mind that Van Sant's big Portland house at the time had been built by a salmon canner and that when the Oregon salmon head back to their breeding grounds to spawn they swim toward Idaho, which parallels Mike and Scott motorcycling to Idaho.

In a twisted variation of the 1939 Judy Garland screen fantasy, *The Wizard of Oz*, not only is *My Own Private Idaho*'s lead character wandering down assorted roads (albeit not yellow brick ones) seeking his roots, but, like Dorothy in that film musical, he encounters an airborne farmhouse that crashes to earth. Depending on one's point of view about *Idaho* the homestead smacking down into the road can be a positive or a negative image. It certainly has its irony in *Idaho*, as it occurs as Mike, the recipient of oral sex by a client, climaxes.

The spiraling structure representation in *My Own Private Idaho* was actually one of the first images that led to the eventual shaping of the picture. Years before, Gus had done paintings that featured crashing barns and houses and those, in turn, had evolved out of a book cover he once saw. For Van Sant, this was another home/family/love/relationship "image that I think represents the whole film"—just as in *Drugstore Cowboy* it had been Larry Clark's photos that sparked the feel, force, and path of the movie being made. Van Sant also notes that such a thematic image is "elusive—it's usually in your mind's eye, and you can't quite get there. And one of the big pitfalls in filmmaking is to chase that illusion—you can really screw everything up in chasing it."

Another time, in talking with actor River Phoenix about the crashing home image in his paintings and in *Idaho*, Van Sant referenced imagery in his mind that went back to his family's house in Colorado when he was a youngster: "That's my concept of home. Then we moved away, and I probably didn't like moving away. So then the house smashing in the road is like my destruction of the house that I miss. But when I painted the paintings, I never thought, 'Oh, I missed my childhood, and now I'm showing how that childhood has been smashed in 10 million bits'—though I can interpret them that way and then be sort of surprised."

In *Drugstore Cowboy* Van Sant had displayed a quirky sense of "humor" with its nuclear family of druggie thieves in which the relationships between the "parents" (played by Matt Dillon and Kelly Lynch) and the "children" (played by James LeGros and Heather Graham) have bizarre sexual interrelationships. Gus extends this conceit—now in a dramatic context—farther in *My Own Private Idaho*. There is the instance of Scott Favor having a sexual relationship with Bob Pigeon whom he later describes as more a father to him than his own dad. Then there is Mike who, while tricking with the wealthy client (played by Grace Zabriskie), finds a resemblance between her and his long-lost mom. His perplexing notion brings on another narcoleptic fit. Further into the movie, when Mike visits his trailer-trash brother in Idaho, it is revealed that the sibling is also the hustler's father. And another twist on the nuclear family is the fact that Mike is so emotionally/sexually drawn to Scott, his friend—his everything. It provides additional layers of complexity to the *Idaho* narrative. (Not to be ignored in the picture is the obsessive attachment that the German Hans exhibits for his beloved late mother—who when we see her photo proves to be homely and somewhat ridiculous looking.) Thus, as demonstrated in *My Own Private Idaho* and Van Sant's earlier films, the family, in any configuration, obviously is a major theme of quintessential importance (on and off the screen) to the complex moviemaker.

As to the highly controversial, much discussed, supposed gay themes within the gritty *Idaho,* there is much man-to-man sex but almost none of it embraces any homosexual love or emotion. In several ways, Gus uses his wry humor and unique perspective to show that male-to-male lust can be humorous. This is illustrated by the living tableau of porno magazine covers. The satiric set of cover models include a preening macho cowboy-outfitted Scott. There is also Mike garbed only in a G-string loin cloth in a Christlike crucifixion pose and seen to be half zonked and scratching his crotch.

Perhaps the most (deliberately) ludicrous gay sex escapade in *Idaho* occurs as Mike plays a game of pretend for one of his grotesque elderly clients. He is required to dress in a Dutch boy outfit and to scrub the man's apartment, which launches the freaky person into ecstasy (leading to his comedic vaudeville-type dance solo in his living room). Then there is the German Hans who, before engaging in sex with Scott and Mike, insists upon entertaining them with an ersatz avant-garde lieder routine the Teuton once performed in clubs.

With another of Mike's sex tricks near the end of the film, we learn a great deal about the emotional makeup of Waters. As explained by Van Sant: "You only get to see Mike having pleasure when he hugs the guy at the end . . . in that scene where he watches *The Simpsons* [on TV]. He was supposed to hug the guy like it was something he lost that he needed very badly. He did only have it once, it's true, but it was one of the main ideas behind his hustling, that he needed to be held, and touched. He didn't necessarily need to have sex. But he needed to be close. It was one of the reasons he liked being a hustler. We didn't really explore that, except in that one little detail, which is really too bad, because it sort of was one of the inspirations of the whole film, the emotional breakdown in the mind of a street hustler. In this particular character, one of the main things he had was his need to be wanted, and he could be wanted by men who wanted him for slightly different reasons than he wanted them to want him. He was really after attention and affection. But still what he missed was basically from a man, not from a woman. He didn't have a father."

On the opposite end of the gay sex spectrum in *My Own Private Idaho* is the mock-documentary sequences of street hustlers (featuring Mike Parker and Scott Patrick Green) clinically relating their unsavory debuts as male prostitutes. Their essentially horrific tales are compounded further by the nonchalant way in which they recall the unpleasant events.

This absence of true sexual lust within *My Own Private Idaho* led Ernest Hardy of the *LA Village View* to observe, "Another less obvious influence would seem to be the Homocore movement, a loose-knit community of young gays and lesbians within the punk/hardcore scene who have created a network of underground clubs and magazines that flourish in both the U.S. and Canada. Their influence is cropping up all over the place. . . . Van Sant has let it be known in numerous places that this fringe of the gay community holds more interest for him than the West Hollywood/assimilation crowd." Hardy points out that the Homocore movement and this film share an indifference to the issue of sexuality—making it a nonissue: "For someone as tremendously reserved as Van Sant, that must be enormously appealing."

In response to Hardy's insights about the Homocore movement, Van Sant offered, "I guess [it's] because of my social orientation. It's centered around that scene rather that the disco scene. . . . But there are a lot of different social scenes [in the gay community] right now. I didn't even know that [the Homocore network] even existed until this past year. Somebody was just showing me the magazines and I was stricken by how young it was, its youth orientation. It doesn't stress the importance of being gay.

"To me, it's embarrassing when your sexuality becomes an important political message. I think there are important political messages to be had, but it [i.e., gay sexuality] doesn't really strike me as one of the most important."

As to the reason why *Idaho*, shot at the height of the AIDS plague crisis, does not mention the horrific disease within the film, Van Sant has admitted, "We did have a reference in a scene that was cut, and Mike does have a condom in his pocket, and we see it close up. But AIDS is in the headlines all the time so just mentioning it in a movie is sort of redundant. If you don't know about it, you're not going to be in the theater watching my movie anyway—you're probably on a remote island someplace. For me to say anything about AIDS now [i.e., 1991] is beside any point I'm trying to make."

Paralleling his earlier features, Van Sant here pays a good deal of attention to visual effects. Once again, cinematographer Eric Alan Edwards provides the time-lapse photography of the almost mournful, swirling clouds used in tandem with Mike's narcoleptic spells to provide the needed shifts between several scenes. The effect—often stunningly beautiful—also adds to the movie's dreamy, expressionistic quality—one of great longing and sadness.

Another visual image that runs throughout *Idaho* is the symbolism of the smiley face. At the film's opening as Mike is on the Idaho road, he stares off into the distance and comments that the topography looks like a strange face. In another sequence, Scott lies down on a bed and stares up at a ceiling fixture that is decorated with multicolored smiley faces. At the end of the movie the legend HAVE A NICE DAY is displayed, wordage also associated with smiley faces. (Regarding such imagery, the Portland filmmaker said at the time, "I've tried to be as intimate with film as the written word is. There are all these little metaphors about how the clouds look like mushrooms. Or a writer can talk about the color of the sky for a paragraph. But how to do that in film was my big problem—how to take that imagery into a theater and have it be accessible, or at least, watchable.")

An additional visual/theme in *My Own Private Idaho* that ties into the inserted shots of salmon leaping out of the water as they swim upstream (and all that means regarding "going home" at any cost) is the film's décor, which often features such marine items as a decorative brass fish or large sea shells (one of which Mike picks up to hear the sounds of the ocean). The filmmaker also uses title cards to set a locale or explain a term. The movie opens with a close-up of a dictionary definition of narcolepsy and dissolves into a flat blue screen with the word *Idaho* in its center. Later, there are title cards to tell us that we are in Portland, Seattle, and so on. (Another intriguing trademark of Van Sant's early features is his use of messy, stuffed ashtrays that appear in *Mala Noche*, *Drugstore Cowboy*, and *My Own Private Idaho*. Carrying across the theme of characters in Van Sant's films, in *Idaho* there are the lines spoken by Waters in the coffee shop as he warns a cigarette-puffing female street person sitting at his table, "Not when I'm eating, and don't blow it in my face.")

Equally important in his new screen production, Gus the musician paid heed to the song selections used on the music sound track. The selections feature an unusual array of musical performers, including: "Deep Night" (Rudy Vallee), "Home on the Range" (Bill Stafford—the film's composer—in a steel-pedal guitar country music style), "Cattle Call" (Eddy Arnold), "Blue Eyes" (Elton John), "Cherish" (Madonna), and "The Old Main Drag" (the Pogues). River Phoenix's musical group Aelka's Attic provides the rendition of "Too Many Colors" and Portland's Conrad "Bud" Montgomery—the real-life friend of Bob Pitchlynn and has a bit in the film—composed and performed "Getting into the Outside" in this picture. Many of these numbers, as well as a version of "America the Beautiful," punctuate and prompt the sense of American icons of the old West as well as create ironic counterpoint within the movie. ("America the Beautiful" is used in one instance near the finale of *Idaho* to replace the sound effect of thunder that made the given scene too ominous.)

Also heard in *Idaho* is a Native American war chant as Mike and Scott sit by the campfire. Per Van Sant: "That's because they're traveling to Idaho, going through Indian territory. It also says 'Warning to Tourists: Do Not Laugh at the Natives' near the fire. I think that comes from the Warm Springs Indian Reservation in Oregon."

Another established routine on Gus's movies occurred during the editing process. Van Sant has said, "During the editing of the film, the editor and I mixed things around a great deal. This usually happens on my films, so that the end product differs greatly from the original intent. As the script of *Idaho* was forged, the ending had a variety of people picking 'Mike' up from the road as he lay unconscious. In the [published shooting] script . . . there is a specific person [i.e., Scott] who picks him up, but in the film the identity of this person is hidden, so that viewers can make up their own ending."

In the course of assembling *Idaho*, among the several scene switches in the chronology was, for example, the intended opening sequence of the living porno magazine covers that was restructured to come later in the narrative. Among the film's cut scenes was one set in Las Vegas where Mike Waters is mugged by a trio of young men. Badly injured, Mike tumbles to the ground in one of his fits. Scott comes to his rescue, chasing off the attackers. Another section of the movie that got severely trimmed—at the request of New Line Cinema—were the Shakespearean episodes, particularly a scene between Scott and Bob Pigeon as they are putting on a play. In the process, much of the character of Jane Lightwork was excised from the film.

Due to the sequence switching and cutting, as well as location practicality while shooting *Idaho*, a few topographical goofs and continuity gaffes occur in the movie. For example, near the film's opening, Mike Waters is in Seattle where he eludes a potential customer (Udo Kier). He falls asleep and then wakes up in Portland. However, the sequence was filmed just a few blocks from where he blanked out. Another instance is where Mike is waiting beside an Idaho highway. But from the road, Oregon's Mount Hood can be seen in the background. In the sequence where Mike, Scott, and the other hustlers spot Bob Pigeon returning to Portland, they are waking up on the rooftops of downtown buildings, yet they see Bob below—even though he is actually across the river trudging under the freeway. Later in the movie, the now establishment Scott and his entourage pour through the entranceway of Jake's Famous Crawfish Restaurant, but the inside is actually the interior of another Portland dining establishment—Huber's.

One of the script difficulties that Van Sant could never really overcome in *Idaho* was the forced parallel of Scott Favor as the haughty heir apparent to Portland's mayor being a true parallel to the Shakespearean history play where Prince Hal is soon to assume the crown of England. The moviemaker explained that this nonequivalency between the status/financial expectations and power of Scott and Prince Hal was a structural stumbling block: "We always had problems with that, and it just remained that way."

Just as *Drugstore Cowboy* ends on an uncertain note of whether Bob Hughes survives his gunshot wounds, so *My Own Private Idaho* concludes in its own ambiguity. Mike Waters is left unconscious on the Idaho roadway by the two truckers who have robbed him. A car soon comes by and the driver—seen unclearly in long shot—carries Mike into the vehicle and they drive away. It gives the film a boost of optimism for the viewer may think that somehow Scott Favor has come to Mike's rescue once again and they will ride off into the sunset and live happily ever after. It is a plot point that Van Sant, as mentioned earlier, left deliberately obscure.

Six years after *My Own Private Idaho* was released, a female customer stopped to chat with Gus at a bookstore reading of his new publication, *Pink*. She had one question that she wanted him to answer: Who is the unseen person who rescues Mike at the finale of *Idaho*?

Van Sant: I was hoping that the viewers would project themselves into the film and decide for themselves who it was.

Woman customer: Okay, then. Who picked him up in your version?

Van Sant: In my version . . . in my version, I pick him up.

19

THE NEW CELEBRITY

There are all kinds of decisions that are made, inspirations that are had, that guide you along the path. You can't be sure what you're doing. If you are really sure, then usually you're limiting yourself. Unless you're just some incredible genius, which I'm not. When I'm directing a film, I intend to have a myriad of things commenting on one another. If someone sees something I haven't consciously intended, I still think on another level it was intended. Obviously there are certain things that are accidents. But then again, everything I do is set up to create an accident.

Gus Van Sant, 1991

IN THE FINAL GESTATION period of 1990 to 1992 that led to the making, editing, release, and acclaim of *My Own Private Idaho*, Gus Van Sant, in typical fashion, remained active in other creative quarters as well. In 1990, he had been reunited with his friend William S. Burroughs Jr. when he produced a video starring the Beat poet icon. The video promoted Dead City Radio, a new Burroughs spoken-word project adorned with original music from the likes of John Cale, Donald Fagen, Sonic Youth, and Blondie's Chris Stein. During the next year, Gus and Burroughs collaborated again, this time on *Thanksgiving Prayer*, a two-minute thirty-second short shot in 35mm black and white.

Within *Thanksgiving Prayer*, the cynical antiestablishment author recited his poem that savaged the Norman Rockwell view of America—all done in Burroughs's usual mordant, witty style as he blasted the betrayal of America and its idealistic dreams. Framing Burroughs is a collage of archival footage (e.g., bread lines, burning buildings, the Lincoln Memorial, astronauts in space, the American flag), which alternately complements and counter-points the writer's sentiments. The short was shown at the January 1992 Sundance Film Festival and aired on PBS-TV on July 11, 1992, as part of the "American Flash Cards" episode of the *Alive* TV series. It was also released for home video as part of a prerecorded VHS compilation entitled *Buried Treasures, Vol. 1— Breakthrough Directors*.

On the music scene, two more of Gus's songs were released on a two-cut CD album (*Gus Van Sant*) in 1992 by Portland-based Tim Kerr Records. One was the 1984 number "Bursting Clouds" and the other, a 1992 composition, was "Lost World." As with his past recordings, he sang his own composition and played guitar (and other instruments). The cover featured a May 1990 photo (taken by Van Sant) of his young friend Scott Patrick Green.

Receiving more acclaim—and better pay—was his directing of additional music videos. He enjoyed the freedom of the form and the fact that "there are things you do with a Super-8 camera that you don't do with a bigger one." There was Tracy Chapman's "Bang, Bang, Bang" cut from her Elektra album *Matters of the Heart* and Elton John's single "The Last Song" from the MCA album *The One*. Scott Patrick Green, Gus's assistant at the time, recalls of the Elton video: "We shot it real quick, in one long night. . . . Elton wasn't there that much, but when he arrived he had a whole entourage—very dressed up, very Los Angeles." Gus's most popular music video of the time was directing the Red Hot Chili Peppers' "Under the Bridge" from their Warner Bros. album *Blood Sugar Sex Magik*. He and the Chili Peppers' guitarist Flea had already worked together (in *My Own Private Idaho*) and they were both friends of River Phoenix. (Also in this period and later, Gus, an excellent photographer, would be in demand to shoot cover photos for several musicians' albums.)

On the film scene, Gus had an uncredited cameo in Cameron Crowe's *Singles* (1992), an ensemble piece about life for the twentysomething set on the dating scene in Seattle. The cast included Bridget Fonda, Campbell Scott, and two alumni from *Drugstore Cowboy*: Matt Dillon and James LeGros. Van Sant and Mark Arm (vocalist with the group Mudhoney) can be spotted loading furniture in one sequence. The movie also boasts cameos by Crowe (as an interviewer) and filmmaker Tim Burton as a rising video director.

By now Portland-based Van Sant was being considered part of the "northwest school" of creative artists. As a *New York Times* article of mid-1991 described it, besides Gus, this group included Matt Groening, the Portland native who had created TV's *The Simpsons* and the syndicated comic strip *Life in Hell*; Seattle-based Lynda Barry who drew *Ernie Pook's Comeek* and who had authored the off-Broadway play, *The Good Times Are Killing Me*, based on her novel; and Gary Larson of Seattle who was responsible for the very popular comic strip *Far Side*.

There was also filmmaker David Lynch who had grown up in Spokane, Washington, and Missoula, Montana, and was prepping his 1992 TV series

Twin Peaks, which was being shot just east of Seattle. Then there was the 1990–95 television drama *Northern Exposure,* set in Cicely, Alaska, but shot in Roslyn, Washington. Also categorized in the same Northwest set were novelists Tom Robbins who lived just north of Seattle and Katherine Dunn, the latter being Portland-based.

Besides being lumped into the Northwest Noir group as these regional artists were also labeled, Van Sant was considered in many circles a prime exponent of the new "Queer Cinema." Primarily this was because of the themes of his features *Mala Noche* and *My Own Private Idaho,* as well as several of his short subjects—and because of the fact that he was constantly referred to as the "openly gay" filmmaker. (Van Sant joked at the time that he would prefer to be called "casually gay." Another time he said regarding the "openly gay" descriptor: "It's a political term that's printable, and so it's printed. That's fine with me. It's not exactly how I orient my life. It's not how I view myself." As to his role in gay activism, Gus has said, "I don't think you have to politically align your whole life in some quest. Unless you want to. The work itself is the political part. But me as a spokesman or a personality, no. I'm just a person behind the camera.")

Besides Van Sant, other directors of the time who were ranked as leading exponents of the American gay movie movement were Gregg Araki (*Three Bewildered People in the Night, The Long Weekend, The Living End*), Todd Haynes (*Assassins: A Film Concerning Rimbaud, Superstar: The Karen Carpenter Story, Poison*), and Tom Kalin (*Swoon*). In the late 1980s Van Sant, Araki, and Haynes had become well acquainted when they made the round of gay film festivals—often together—to promote their individual movies.

Regarding Van Sant's status as a filmmaker who was both homosexual and who often focused his camera on gay characters, reporter D. K. Holm of Portland's *Willamette Week* wrote an article entitled "All About Gus" for the November 10, 1991, issue. In the piece he said, "In Portland the great unmentionable in Van Sant's work is his consistent cinematic focus on teenage boys. According to a *New York Times Magazine* profile Van Sant is 'openly gay and has made homosexuality a theme of his work.' But Portland papers have studiously avoided this delicate subject. Critics and journalists, grappling with the conflict between Van Sant's obvious artistry and the 'unsavory' subject matter he constantly tackles either feign blindness or change the subject to Van Sant's startling camera shots. *My New Friend,* Van Sant's wry, brilliant 1984 short, comically anticipates some of the 'self-deluding john wistful over messy and indifferent street kid' elements of *Idaho,* but the new film is the apotheosis of the boy theme, and at least two actual teen male prostitutes appear in the movie. Van Sant's works are more complex than many other 'gay' films—his wit and visual style allow him perspective and distance. His obsession inspires the pictures but doesn't rule them."

On the political scene, the generally not active Van Sant did join in the cause (along with such names as Woody Allen, Robert Redford, and Paul

Newman) to support a proposed Congressional bill that would force movie theater owners to advertise that they were showing commercials before the regular
feature attraction. The bill came to naught.

▼

AS Gus Van Sant became better known to the public at large in the 1990s, he
made no effort to be anything more than he had been in the years before his
movies brought him an increasing amount of fame. If he had been of a different
mental and emotional constitution he might have utilized a public relations
specialist to channel his image into the direction of his choice. But that evidently was not his style. Thus there was no one on hand usually to do "damage
control" as he met with the press. What the combination of creative drives,
emotional repressions, antiestablishment rebellion, and public recognition of
his own gayness had rendered on this bright, multitalented individual is what
the public saw through journalist eyes.

For example, at the time of *My Own Private Idaho*, Ernest Hardy (*LA Village
View*) was one of those who had an opportunity for a question-and-answer session in New York City with the moviemaker. Hardy described, "It's easy to see
how his reputation for being aloof, edgy, even slightly vague, has taken hold. He
takes very long pauses before answering, frequently repeats the question, and
lets nothing 'accidentally' fall out. Though reclining on the [hotel suite] sofa,
and obviously worn out from a day of doing interviews, there is very much an air
of guardedness about the filmmaker." The journalist also observed, "His humor
is often so dry and understated that only in hindsight does one realize how
much of it there is in his conversation. It's that quality that comes through most
in Van Sant's films: a sly, dark humor coursing through bleak subject matter—
and a healthy dose of compassion for marginalized characters."

Hardy also chose to bring into the scope of his printed interview a recollection that someone from the *Drugstore Cowboy* cast/crew had said: "Gus is obviously very intelligent, very much on top of things but, I don't know, it's like
some wire in his head is not making its connection. It's not a major wire, but it
could sure clear up some of the fuzziness."

John Powers (*LA Weekly*) met with the *Idaho* director in Los Angeles in this
same period. He painted a perceptive word picture: "When you talk to Van Sant,
he watches you carefully—not suspiciously, carefully—answering questions with
an agreeableness that masks obvious reticence. He prefers to talk in lazy, drifting
anecdotes, and when you press him on questions about meaning, he usually slips
into a faux naïve style reminiscent of Andy Warhol's. This is not a man to give
himself away cheaply, certainly not for the sake of publicizing a movie."

Paul Andrews (*Seattle Times*) had his own slant on Gus: "A watchful observer of the human circus, Van Sant prefers to absorb rather than radiate.
When in a crowded room he seems set apart, his dark, almost swarthy mien and

probing eyes making him look somber and aloof, which he is not. If anything, he is mentally sketching the scene before him for use in one of his films." Andrews also cautioned, "Although generous and good-hearted, Van Sant is a private person who virtually never thinks out loud and tends toward monosyllables when asked about his art. He resists categorization, declining to say which directors he admires (with some prompting, David Lynch will be offered) or what films he particularly likes. Says Gus: 'I like them all, but I don't want to stay too current. You tend to get influenced too much that way. It's important to learn, but you can jeopardize your originality.'"

Portland novelist and longtime Van Sant friend/observer Katherine Dunn commented to the press about his "sublime disassociation" with events transpiring about him. She detailed, "I've seen Gus surrounded by Hollywood characters on a set, and it didn't change the way he talked or looked or worked one whit. Gus is one of those people who manages instantly to make himself at home no matter where he is." Dunn also observed, "The thing about Gus is, he sees everyone else in the world as far more interesting than he is."

In what was now his expected style, Van Sant saw no need to upgrade his wardrobe when meeting with the fourth estate. For example, when he had a meeting in Portland with a journalist writing for the trendy *Premiere* magazine, they met at one of Gus's favorite hangouts, an International House of Pancakes restaurant. As the writer detailed in his piece, the subject of the interview was dressed in scruffy levis, a "beat-up" jean jacket, and "ratty" high-top sneakers. Said the journalist, "His glazed, soft-focus eyes seem to observe life from a distance. His craggy and unshaven face unexpectedly exudes an unassuming innocence."

Van Sant seemed to thrive on presenting an air of innocence. This applied even to topics that, because of his admitted lifestyle, his interests, and his most recent film (*My Own Private Idaho*), one would assume he would have a working knowledge of its mechanics—whether or not from personal experience. But Van Sant chose to confide to *Rolling Stone*'s David Handleman: "I really don't know the streets, don't know how they work. If we went there now, you'd find that out right away—we'd probably get mugged or something. I'm the kind of person that just makes it up at home. I mean, certain people who lived that life were around during filming. It's like if you're making a film about boating, you have some boaters around or else a storm's gonna come up and drown you. But half the time, you're right anyway."

A man of many contradictions about many things, there were some topics on which he had a definite (well, almost) opinion. His favorite city was Portland, his favorite holiday was Halloween, and his dessert of choice was chocolate cake. He bought Medaglia d'Orso espresso, his favorite car was "usually the car I have [i.e., the 1982 BMW 528E his father had given him years ago]," and he liked Italian words "because they are funny." When asked who his favorite artist was, he responded, "I guess it would have to be [Andy] Warhol. He was sort of the [Frank] Capra of the pop art movement."

And as to the so-called Gus Van Sant mystique of reticence that journalists so often described, he told a Portland reporter: "I don't really get it. I think they write whatever they can find. If I seem to be a little quiet they decide I'm a mummy."

▼

IN the aftermath of *My Own Private Idaho*—which wrapped up his Portland trilogy—Gus exhibited mixed reactions to the Hollywood film establishment, an institution that continued to both intrigue and repel him. On one hand he could say, "*Idaho* is like an inch away from being a mainstream, commercial movie. Not like a mile. It's not hard to take. It just shows you how stodgy, conservative and afraid Hollywood is today to even consider a project that isn't like *Home Alone* [the 1990 blockbuster comedy hit starring child actor Macauley Culkin]. You only go this far away, and everybody thinks Keanu [Reeves] and River [Phoenix] are playing with fire. I think they're just bored with what they do." On the other hand, at about the same time (fall 1991) he could say, "I'm happy doing a low-budget film like *Idaho*, but I'm also going to make $20 million films. . . . Personally, I don't see myself as an outsider. I see myself as an A-list director." (Of playing tinseltown politics Gus admitted that he had learned a lot from the example of the late director Orson Welles who had a brash personal style: "He was hard on people in Hollywood and I'm very nice. . . . I play the game all the time. At the same time, I do try to get what I want.")

But if he wanted to be an A-list or any-list director Van Sant had to actually choose among the many screen projects that were on his plate at the time. He had already dropped the Andy Warhol screenplay (to be cowritten with Paul Bartel) and had passed on a movie adaptation of Tom Wolfe's *Kandy-Kolored Tangerine-Flake Streamline Baby* to be done with Buck Henry. Now, in short order he divested himself of such other potential vehicles as *The Wild Boys* by William Burroughs Jr. (based on a treatment by James Grauerholz), a screen version of Tom Wolfe's book *The Electric Kool-Aid Acid Test*, and an adaptation of Michael Murphy's tome *Golf in the Kingdom*. Said Van Sant: "I realized that I didn't feel comfortable facing that many commitments."

But before Gus could get back to *Even Cowgirls Get the Blues*, the movie project that he had put aside to film *My Own Private Idaho*, he had one other filmmaking commitment to fulfill—it was *The Mayor of Castro Street*.

NEW AGE *COWGIRLS*

I'll be going from the all-male cast of
Idaho to an all-female cast. In preparing to do *Cowgirls*, I've been surrounding myself with women and have been
talking to women about women a lot.
I've concluded that women are smarter
and more in tune with the universe—this
is probably a matter of biology because they are the birth-givers."

Gus Van Sant, 1991

IN 1991 AS DIRECTOR Oliver Stone (*Platoon, Wall Street,
The Doors*) was completing *JFK* for release late in the year, he was debating
what to do about a pending screen biography project. It was to be based on
Randy Shilts's 1982 book *The Mayor of Castro Street: The Life and Times of
Harvey Milk*. It dealt with government official and gay rights activist Milk who,
in 1977, beat out sixteen other candidates and became San Francisco's first
openly homosexual candidate to win election to high office (the city's Board of
Supervisors). On November 27, 1978, forty-seven-year-old Milk and San Francisco Mayor George Moscone were assassinated by former city supervisor Dan
White. Although White was charged with first-degree murder, he was only
found guilty of voluntary manslaughter and sentenced to imprisonment for five
to seven years (which led to further protests in the city). Released in January
1984, White committed suicide in October 1985.

Stone was eager to make the movie about Milk, as were his coproducers:
Janet Yang (vice-president of Oliver Stone's production company) and
Storyline Productions' Craig Zadan and Neil Meron. The Oscar-winning
director, however, felt it might be inappropriate for him to direct two assassi-
nation biographies consecutively. Stone chose to remain in a producing capacity on the project and find another director. Meanwhile, Gus happened to

casually mention to a mutual friend (a producer) of Stone that he always thought a movie about Harvey Milk could be quite interesting. When Stone heard this, he decided that the openly gay Van Sant might well be a good choice to direct it.

When approached, Gus, who already had several big-screen projects in various stages of development, was initially unsure. He reasoned, "It sounded like a film about urban politics, which doesn't interest me. I'm not that political. I'm less a gay activist than a gay pacifist." Van Sant also knew that there would be concerns at Warner Bros., which was slated to release the movie, as to whether or not he was capable of handling a $20 million production that might or might not star Robin Williams. And the new project had a lot to live up to, if it was to avoid unfavorable comparisons with the Academy Award–winning documentary *The Times of Harvey Milk* (1984) directed by Robert Epstein (whom Van Sant knew).

Despite the above, Gus reached a tentative agreement with Stone that he would direct the movie *only* if he was happy with the initial script. He had definite ideas of what he thought it should stress. He perceived that "the Harvey Milk project was about finding a new family, the Castro Street community being a family of like-minded men who had a new style of relating to one another and had sexual relationships with one another. This was a very clear bond in the new Castro Street of 1975."

As Gus explained it, he was drawn to the Milk project not because the man was a martyr or visionary or even a larger-than-life individual, but because he was an impulsive, average guy full of man's usual imperfections. Van Sant was especially impressed by the late politician's silly sense of humor. Gus wanted to "make him like Groucho Marx, the way I thought maybe he was. If you look at footage of him, you can get the energy."

In the spring of 1992 Gus temporarily moved down from Oregon to a rented apartment near the Castro district in San Francisco. He wanted to be on hand to further research Milk's life and the ambiance of the famed gay region. When Van Sant was shown the screenplay for *The Mayor of Castro Street* by Becky Johnston (riding high on her Oscar nomination for coscripting Barbra Streisand's 1991 feature, *The Prince of Tides*), he was dissatisfied because it "looked at the story from the outside." From Gus's perspective, "it didn't give a sense of where this rich, varied community that Harvey represented had come from." It prompted Gus to write his own private draft but he was so unhappy with the results that he threw it away.

As Van Sant got further immersed in the Milk story he kept telling the producers that he wanted to actually write on the project, but they said, "No, you can't, we want Becky to write." Their reason was, "She was up for the Academy Award, not you."

Gus returned to Portland to push along *Even Cowgirls Get the Blues* and to tend to other matters.

▼

Gus Van Sant, the gay pacifist, became a gay activist in the summer of 1992. It concerned a proposed measure in the Oregon legislature that, if passed, would dictate that the state and local governments could not "promote, encourage or facilitate homosexuality, pedophilia, sadism or masochism," could not give government protection based on sexual orientation, and must "assist in setting a standard" for youths of Oregon that would label homosexuality and other listed behaviors as "abnormal, wrong, unnatural and perverse." The new guidelines regarding proper moral behavior and sexual orientation would also apply to the state's schools.

The projected legislation led to the formation of a group called Campaign for a Hate-Free Oregon. Its major aim was to oppose the suggested new state amendment. Gus became involved in raising money for the fight and he also directed a public service message made for Oregon TV. The sixty-second spot featured Tom Arnold and his then wife Roseanne speaking out against the suggested state measure. A fund-raiser for the cause was held in Los Angeles at the home of Gus's agent John Burnham in mid-July 1992 with a celebrity list of attendees including Roseanne, Tom Arnold, Faye Dunaway, River Phoenix, Lily Tomlin, and record mogul David Geffen. By that fall, the Campaign for a Hate-Free Oregon had raised over $1 million and in the election that November, the initiative was defeated.

▼

At the end of September 1992, Gus received the Freedom of Expression Award from the American Civil Liberties Union state chapter because "[h]e has consistently addressed themes in his films which let us see the lives of individuals we don't often get a glimpse at."

▼

Reflecting his rising celebrity status, Gus did a TV commercial in 1992. It was for Black Star Beer. (The footage would reemerge in February 1999 as part of a seminar at the Museum of Television and Radio in New York City celebrating the creative work of David Kennedy and Dan Wieden.)

Van Sant also became a published author in 1992 with the release of *108 Portraits*, distributed by Twin Palms Publishers of Santa Fe, New Mexico. The oversized volume was an intriguing portfolio of photos taken by Gus with his Polaroid camera between 1988 and 1992, primarily in casting sessions for *Drugstore Cowboy* and *My Own Private Idaho*. The array of personalities captured in black and white included actors like River Phoenix, Matt Dillon, Peter Gallagher, Ione Skye, Balthazar Getty, Faye Dunaway, and Pat Morita. In addition, such filmmakers as Robert Altman, Francis Ford Coppola, Todd Haynes, and John Singleton, novelist Ken Kesey, and shots of such Van Sant friends as William S. Burroughs Jr., Michael Parker, and Scott Patrick Green also appeared in the volume. There is even a self-portrait of Gus as the last shot in the book, with him looking very much like famed actor Tony Perkins.

In the book's brief introduction, Van Sant writes of his "snapshots": "The day that I happened to catch them was just one little piece of time that is connected to all the other pieces of time that make up their lives. And sometimes I think I can see this in the picture itself. Somehow the camera is able to capture it. I don't know how, but it does. I swear to God."

Van Sant viewed this publication as a sort of a family photo collection of his extended family. Just over 4,000 copies were printed, of which 120 were individually numbered and signed by the author.

▼

TOM Robbins's quirky *Even Cowgirls Get the Blues* had been published simultaneously in hardback and paperback in May 1976 by Houghton Mifflin. The free-form, satirical novel told of Sissy Hankshaw, the poor Virginia girl who used her oversized thumbs to become a legendary hitchhiker and used other parts of her anatomy to headline feminine hygiene spray ads. She has an unsatisfactory marriage to a full-blooded Mohawk Native American who becomes a Manhattan intellectual. Later, Sissy lands on a dude ranch in the Dakotas that is usurped by militant cowgirls led by Bonanza Jellybeans. Sissy becomes involved with a Japanese guru called "the Chink" and, thereafter, searches for help with her chaotic life at a psychiatric clinic where she encounters Dr. Robbins (the book's narrator).

The reviews for the irreverent, even campy, and structurally quite unorthodox *Cowgirls* were mixed at best. *Publishers Weekly* opined, "This is intended as madcap, zany invention involving lust, the way things are, and Robbins's own philosophical overview. . . . Robbins's satire comes across as tedious, arch and sometimes pretentious and his puns lack timing and skill." The *New York Times* was more enthusiastic: "[The author] has an old trunk of a mind. . . . Empty spaces are filed with inventions . . . and theories on everything. . . . They add up to a primitivism just pragmatic enough to be attractive and fanciful enough to measure the straight society."

Booklist's critic decided "Robbins' alliterative, idiosyncratic, and inventive language is a great help to his hilarious profile" and that his tale of sexual liberation "moves along with the zany momentum and madcap adventure of an offshoot of the 1960s." Ann Cameron (the *Nation*) lauded, "With the agility of a mad photographer, taking quick shots from a hundred unexpected angles . . . Robbins dazzles the reader. . . . Truth and beauty, like magic and poetry, are not found but reinvented [here], and beyond more familiar novelistic truths are others that shine brighter."

Robbins's offbeat counterculture novel became a best-seller. Among those who bought a copy was Van Sant. Years later, Gus spelled out just what appealed to him about Robbins's nonconformist work. "I think my attraction to *Cowgirls* is that it's a kind of New Age novel. It was, as Robbins wrote it, setting up a new bunch of rules as to how to tell a story and it mixed in a lot of different techniques on top of one another. That was what really struck me. It also plays with a couple of different genres, one of them being the romance novel. It seemed Robbins was using the form of the romance novel to write a new fiction. He has the lead character going in and out of different sexual situations to create this very grand, *Gone with the Wind* type of journey. As she's a hitchhiker, it could also be a road movie, which I think my other movies are, too, including *Mala Noche*, although I read *Cowgirls* before I read *Mala Noche* or considered any of the other movies. . . . It'd take too long to describe specifically what the message of the movie is because there's a lot of different characters who explain their philosophies of life and Sissy experiences each different one. Then she has her own philosophy, one specific idea, except maybe 'time' itself, rhythm itself, is a kind of metaphor within the overall scheme of the movie. Time measured by travel, distance, practices; time measured by literal time, historical time, philosophical time, or religious time." He also pointed out, "I liked the method that Tom used to write the book, which was to employ a lot of different formats and then mix them up. That's something that I've been doing a lot in visual form."

Meanwhile, also in 1977, Robert Wunsch, who had produced the successful ice hockey movie *Slapshot*, optioned the screen rights to *Even Cowgirls Get the Blues*. He signed screenwriter Stephen Geller (*Pretty Poison*, *Slaughterhouse-Five*, *The Valachi Papers*) to adapt the book for the movies. But, before a studio could be found to enter into a deal with Wunsch, his option expired. In 1980 Warner Bros. inked actress Shelley Duvall (3 *Women*, *The Shining*, *Popeye*) to both adapt and star in *Cowgirls*. Two years later she admitted defeat. Thereafter, several others attempted to corral the wide-ranging Robbins work into a suitable conventional scenario, but nothing ever gelled.

During the 1980s as the Portland-based Van Sant gained repute as an emerging American filmmaker, others with more financial backing came and went on the *Cowgirls* property. Gus remained convinced that he could lick the structural problems of transferring the book to film. By mid-decade as Gus was struggling to make and release *Mala Noche*, he took time out to visit Portland's Looking Glass Bookstore where Tom Robbins, who lived about 135 miles north of Portland, was signing copies of his latest book. Van Sant bought a copy and waited to have the author autograph it. Gus introduced himself to Robbins, said how much he liked the book, and that he, as a budding filmmaker, wanted to bring *Even Cowgirls Get the Blues* to the screen one day. He asked the author about the movie rights to *Cowgirls*, although at the time he was hardly earning $100 a week and had no available capital to option the property. Polite chitchat ensued, and that was that.

Later, as *Drugstore Cowboy* made Van Sant a name to reckon with on the film scene, Gus came to know director Alan Rudolph (*Remember Me, Choose Me; The Moderns*). Rudolph (re)introduced Van Sant to Tom Robbins. Gus and Tom met at Seattle's Café Sport to discuss *Even Cowgirls Get the Blues*.

When asked by a reporter how that pivotal dinner meeting had gone, Van Sant said with his usual reticence: "We just discussed life and the Northwest. We just had a normal dinner where we talked about, uh, current events." Robbins told the same journalist: "We talked about casting, we talked about parts of the book that could be left out. I said to him from the very beginning, 'It's my book, it's your movie. I'll stay as far away or stand as close to it as you prefer.'" (When Robbins saw an early draft of the movie he said, "Gus, the problem I have with this first draft is that there's too much of me in it and not enough of you.")

As Gus shaped and reshaped his *Cowgirls* script he asked for Tom's feedback. Robbins has recalled that Van Sant "took some of my suggestions and some he didn't. Which is fine. That's the way it ought to be."

Eventually, Gus and Tom peddled their property around Hollywood, but no one seemed interested until they met Mike Medavoy, a top executive at Orion Pictures. The cigar-smoking Medavoy said he remembered that hippie book as once being very popular. Some months later when Medavoy made the switch to TriStar Pictures, he called Van Sant in Portland.

Medavoy: *Cowgirls*. I want to do it.
Van Sant: Well, okay, but I'm busy and I don't know if I can come and pitch it.
Medavoy: You don't have to pitch it to me. Just do it.

▼

IT was in May 1990 that a deal was struck for TriStar to distribute *Cowgirls* when everyone was happy with a final screenplay. But then a new career priority took hold for Gus—*My Own Private Idaho*, a heartfelt project that suddenly found funding at Fine Line Features. Thereafter, off and on, Van Sant continued with his *Cowgirls* rewrites. As usual, there were more professional interruptions as Gus got drawn into and out of other screen projects (e.g., *The Mayor of Castro Street*).

By early 1992, after finishing with *My Own Private Idaho* Van Sant discovered that TriStar was having serious second thoughts about funding *Even Cowgirls Get the Blues*. They wondered at the present viability of this quirky novel to mainstream audiences nearly twenty years after its publication (and even in 1976 some of Robbins's notions on feminism, ecology, etc., were already considered dated). It was suggested to Gus's producer on the project—Laurie Parker—that they, perhaps, find foreign financing to help cover production costs. By May 1992 TriStar had put *Cowgirls* in turnaround. Within several weeks Gus and Laurie had sealed a deal with Fine Line who had been quite pleased with the critical and commercial response to their release, *My Own Private Idaho*.

In the usual rush-rush, wait-wait, rush-rush-rush process of Hollywood moviemaking, the Van Sant team prepped the property for an early September 1992 shoot and a projected July 1993 release. Meanwhile, Van Sant—still tagged the "openly gay filmmaker"—was asked if *Even Cowgirls Get the Blues* would have a strong lesbian theme since *My Own Private Idaho* had dealt with homosexual coupling. He responded, "No, not really—they're almost opposite. although *Idaho* has characters that are perhaps gay and perhaps not, I don't think it's specifically talking about homosexuality. . . . *Cowgirls* has a much more organized sort of agenda, presenting philosophies that are feminist. Maybe *Idaho* is a nongay film made by a gay director and *Cowgirls* is a feminist film adapted from a book by a nonfeminist or a nonfemale writer, Robbins, and also directed by a man; me. The philosophies and the discussion in *Cowgirls* are extremely pro-feminist or pro-female, and pro new life. There're all kinds of things that go on within it that address that."

At another time, Gus enthused that with *Even Cowgirls Get the Blues* "the challenge will be the sex. You can't sort of gloss over it. It's the way that Robbins writes about it that dictates a certain attitude toward sex: freely. It's a little freer than we're used to watching, which will be really fun, and people are really scared of it, too [laughs]. The people who make the film, the studio executives, say: Geez—there is so much sex! And she keeps f**king him in the butt!"

And, as Van Sant was pleased to point out, the new cinema project also dealt with an extended family, this time "a family on a ranch, a family of women that she [Sissy Hankshaw] ends up staying with."

While Gus began the casting process he allowed publicly that he was a bit daunted by having to direct such a predominantly female cast. But, he said, "I did have a lead character in *Alice in Hollywood* who was a girl. So the first feature I ever made had a female lead. It is an interesting situation, though." He concluded with a typical Van Sant comment. "I don't see a real difference, except that, you know, ultimately girls are girls. There are certain emotions and things they have that you don't. But you can ask them what that's like and then use it."

21

RAIN AND RIVER

In *Cowgirls*, though, you don't really get this sex-object angle, although at the same time you can get the feeling that the writer [Tom Robbins] is living in a fantasy in sex-object land. It's sort of this other world, a city of women. . . . The whole project is a great women's film. It's a chance to make the ultimate remake of *The Women*, which is a beautiful [George] Cukor [MGM] film from the 1930s.

Gus Van Sant, 1992

NOW THAT GUS VAN SANT was rising in status within the film industry he had less difficulty attaching big-name talent to his new screen projects. With *Even Cowgirls Get the Blues* there was a merry-go-round of major film personalities interested, at one time or another, in starring in this satirical feature. One of the earliest to express enthusiasm was Madonna. This was in the pre-May 1992 period when TriStar was still involved with Gus's project. It did not seem to matter to TriStar, according to Van Sant, that the Material Girl was considered box-office poison when she acted (rather than in her documentaries or her unique music videos) on the big screen. (She had not yet made her acting comeback in 1992's *A League of Their Own*.) Said Gus, "They just wanted the most famous woman in the world to be in the movie. They claimed they needed something big to announce, which is probably why Madonna mattered. She would have impressed the Japanese who just bought them [i.e., TriStar]."

Other stars interested in appearing in *Cowgirls* were Elizabeth Taylor, Jodie Foster, and Uma Thurman. Then when Madonna could not come to terms with Van Sant and his team as to which part she would play in the movie, she dropped out. So did Jodie Foster. Apparently, former megastar Taylor left the potential cast line-up when she realized that the film's story championed the over-

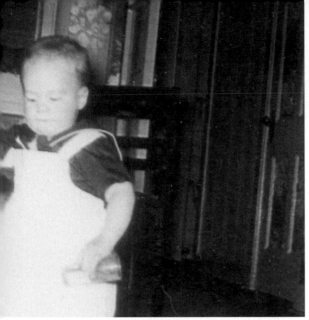

The very young Gus Van Sant Jr. in 1953.
[PHOTO COURTESY OF BETTY AND GUS VAN SANT SR.]

A jovial "Van" with his mother Betty, sister Malinda, and father Gus Sr.—Denver, Colorado, 1957.
[PHOTO COURTESY OF BETTY AND GUS VAN SANT SR.] ▶

The future filmmaker with his sister Malinda—Denver, Colorado, 1957.
[PHOTO COURTESY OF BETTY AND GUS VAN SANT SR.] ▶

The musician at age eight—Mt. Prospect, IL, 1960.
[PHOTO COURTESY OF BETTY AND GUS VAN SANT SR.]

**Gus Jr. and his classmate John Howell
—Darien, CT, 1963.**
[PHOTO COURTESY OF JIM EVANS.]

Gus Jr. at age eleven, with Dixie, his first dog—Darien, CT, 1963.
[PHOTO COURTESY OF BETTY AND GUS VAN SANT SR.]

The Van Sants (Gus Sr., Gus Jr., Betty, and Malinda) skiing at Aspen, Colorado—December 1969.
[PHOTO COURTESY OF BETTY AND GUS VAN SANT SR.]

Ready to attend the senior prom at Catlin Gabel —spring 1971.
[PHOTO COURTESY OF BETTY AND GUS VAN SANT SR.]

Gus on summer vacation from Rhode Island School of Design—Darien, CT, 1972.
[PHOTO COURTESY OF BETTY AND GUS VAN SANT SR.]

Gus Van Sant's Portland home and office in the 1990s—at 1883 SW Vista Avenue.
[PHOTO BY RICHARD A. SCOTT]

The Van Sants (Betty, Malinda, Gus Jr., and Gus Sr.) at the Oregon coast—1995.
[PHOTO BY PAIGE POWELL COURTESY OF BETTY AND GUS VAN SANT SR.]

The filmmaker/musician performing at a Portland, Oregon club in 1994.
[PHOTO BY PAIGE POWELL COURTESY OF BETTY AND GUS VAN SANT SR.]

Co-star (Matt Dillon) and the director (Gus Van Sant) conversing at the *To Die For* premiere in 1995.
[CREDIT: FOTOS INTERNATIONAL/ARCHIVE PHOTOS]

Director Gus Van Sant at work on the set of *Psycho* (1998). ▶
[CREDIT: FOTOS INTERNATIONAL/ARCHIVE PHOTOS]

Director Gus Van Sant on the New York set of *Even Cowgirls Get the Blues* (1994) with actress Carol Kane.
[CREDIT: FOTOS INTERNATIONAL/ARCHIVE PHOTOS]

Filmmaker Gus Van Sant with Sean Connery (center) and Rob Brown (right) at the Los Angeles premiere of *Finding Forrester* —December 2000.

◄ Music composer Danny Elfman (left), a frequent collaborator on Gus Van Sant films, with the director at the Miramax Films' Oscar Party in March 1998—Los Angeles.

Filmmakers Gus Van Sant, Curtis Hanson, James Cameron, and Francis Ford Coppola at a Directors Guild of America function in Beverly Hills—1998.

throw of a cosmetic empire—an ideology that conflicted with her own profitable perfume business.

Another problem in getting the production green-lighted was TriStar's mounting concern over the lesbian scenes in the revised script. According to Van Sant, TriStar's executives were "really scared of the sex. Before we made the movie, the script was really pretty graphic. As we made it, it wasn't very graphic at all. But they were afraid we were going to show what was in the script. So we took the graphic stuff out just to make them feel better." But that still did not appease the film company and TriStar withdrew from the project. At that point Gus felt that *Cowgirls* "was dying on the vine."

However, in mid-1992 New Line Cinema/Fine Line Features agreed to back the project to the tune of $7.89 million. With the game now back on, Van Sant solicited other big-name players to join the cast roster. For a time Irish-born Peter O'Toole was touted as considering the role of the transsexual countess, but the star of *Lawrence of Arabia* soon went off to other filmmaking tasks. There was talk that Willem Dafoe or Daniel Day-Lewis might take on playing the countess, but the colorful acting assignment eventually went to Britisher John Hurt (*Elephant Man, 1984, King Ralph*), who had already played fey gay characters on screen (e.g., 1982's *Partners*).

Famed funny lady and dramatic performer Lily Tomlin was interested in appearing as Delores Del Ruby, the whip-snapping cowgirl, man-hating, peyote queen. Tomlin vanished from the project, however, and it was Lorraine Bracco (*Sea of Love, The Dream Team, Switch*, and Oscar-nominated for 1990's *GoodFellas*) who captured this celluloid assignment. Another of the contenders to play Miss Adrian, who runs the Rubber Rose Ranch, was Oscar-winner Faye Dunaway. But it was eventually Angie Dickinson, the onetime star of 1970s TV's *Police Woman* and such movies as *Rio Bravo, Point Blank*, and *Big Bad Mama*, who accepted the featured part.

To interpret the key role of Sissy Hankshaw, Gus selected twenty-two-year-old Uma Thurman, the six-foot ex-model who had quit school at age fifteen and had made her screen debut in 1987's *Kiss Daddy Goodnight*. Since then the willowy blond had been in such movies as *Dangerous Liaisons, Henry & June*, and *Final Analysis*. The beautiful Thurman could be affecting on-screen but she had marginal drawing power at the box office.

The part of Bonanza Jellybean, the Rubber Rose Ranch head cowgirl whom Sissy is greatly drawn to, went to a twenty-year-old actress. She had the appropriate fleshy look described in Robbins's book original but had limited acting experience to that date. She had made her big screen debut in the comedy *Maid to Order* (1987), but had not made a feature since. Seemingly it didn't matter to Gus Van Sant who was used to working with novice actors. Besides, this fledgling performer had one of the best qualifications of all for Gus—she was River Phoenix's younger sister, Rain. (River, busy elsewhere making movies, had agreed to do a cameo in *Cowgirls* as a pilgrim and/or a heavily disguised birdwatcher near the finale. River's former girlfriend—and now a pal—Suzanne Solgot also was given a bit in the Van Sant screen production.)

Rounding out the main cast of *Even Cowgirls Get the Blues* was Noriyuki "Pat" Morita, a veteran of many films and TV shows, but who was best known for playing Arnold the diner owner in the TV sitcom series *Happy Days*. Morita was set to play the enigmatic, supposedly spiritual "the Chink." Acerbic script writer/actor Buck Henry, who had considered collaborating on a screenplay (*Kandy-Kolored Tangerine-Flake Streamline Baby*) with Van Sant several months earlier, was contracted to be Dr. Dreyfus.

Past Van Sant actors were also tapped for other *Cowgirls* on-camera assignments. To impersonate the full-blooded Mohican Julian Gitche, Gus asked Keanu Reeves, whose career was in high gear (*Much Ado About Nothing, Dracula*), to handle this part. Keanu's response was, "Oh I gotta play this role." Heather Graham (*Drugstore Cowboy*) joined the team as a cowgirl, while Grace Zabriskie (*Drugstore Cowboy, My Own Private Idaho*) agreed to portray Sissy's mother. Udo Kier (*My Own Private Idaho*) returned to the fold, this time as the temperamental director of TV commercials. Two other *Idaho* participants— Michael Parker and Scott Patrick Green—were cast in the new movie as visitors making a pilgrimage to see "the Chink." Oregon-based actor Eric Hull, another Van Sant movie alumnus, was contracted to be the White House Undersecretary, while Portland's Tom Peterson, the appliance dealer/TV spokesman, was on hand again, this time as an on-camera crewman.

Established talents like Carol Kane, Ed Begley Jr., Sean Young, and Crispin Glover were employed to portray the far-out New York intellectual set orbiting around Julian. Roseanne agreed to a cameo (as a fortune-teller) at scale pay ($485 a day), as did such others as Edward James Olmos (barbecue musician), writer Ken Kesey (Sissy's dad), and Gus's friends William S. Burroughs Jr. (pedestrian) and Wade Evans (cameraman). It was arranged for Tom Robbins, the author of *Cowgirls,* to be the film's narrator.

On *Cowgirls*, Gus technical crew regulars included Beatrix Aruna Pasztor (costume designer), Missy Stewart (promoted here to production designer), Curtiss Clayton (editor), John Campbell and Eric Alan Edwards (cocinematographers), and Jane Goldsmith (script supervisor).

▼

IN developing his screen adaptation of *Cowgirls*, Gus kept the story set in the 1950s to the 1970s, the time frame of the original book. He must have felt if he changed the ambiance to a contemporary setting, he would not be true to Tom Robbins's literary work. Moreover, Van Sant must have also believed that if he started readjusting the flavor of the narrative too severely, the screenplay could easily tumble apart like a house of cards. As Gus explained, "It's also part of those times, the seventies, when there was an insistence on feminine hygiene. Body odors and feminine odors, in particular, were to be covered up. At the time, the Food and Drug Administration had found problems with the hygienes that were being marketed. This is why there's a character, the countess, who owns a feminine-hygiene company that has a staff of females who are standing up and speaking for themselves, and overthrowing the beauty ranch because of the products it's making. The book is very hippie-esque in its point of view: let the body smell the way it smells."

But not everything in the *Cowgirls* book was sacred to Van Sant. As Gus allowed, "There are a lot of things that he [Robbins] just talks about, his own reveries, which are beside the things the characters are doing and talking about. Those went. I followed what the characters were saying, not the things Robbins speaks about."

In the process of the adaptation, Van Sant realized, "Sissy is more of a character apart from the audience's point of view. You are experiencing things along with her, but they're not necessarily told from her perspectives. *Mala Noche*, *Drugstore Cowboy*, and *My Own Private Idaho* are definitely films that are told through the characters' eyes. Less so with Sissy. She's an object that you're watching as opposed to someone you're watching the world through."

As Gus configured *Even Cowgirls Get the Blues* for the screen, the movie focuses on 1950s southern girl Sissy Hankshaw who is "blessed" at birth with abnormally large thumbs. She grows up to not only become a champion hitch-hiker—the best in the world—but also a very beautiful woman. For five years in the late 1960s she is the chief model for the countess, a transsexual from Mississippi who has made a fortune in the feminine hygiene industry. In the 1970s the countess summons the retired Sissy to Manhattan to meet Julian Gitche, a young Native American artist. When plans fail to have Sissy—still technically a virgin—mate with the asthmatic Julian, the countess dispatches her former employee to the Rubber Rose, a health ranch in the Dakotas. There the cowgirls—led by appealing Bonanza Jellybean and urged on by the peyote-hallucinating Delores Del Ruby and a mysterious, cave-dwelling sage (the Chink)—take over the ranch spa. Sissy and Bonanza become lovers.

Later Sissy, who has one of her oversized thumbs amputated, resumes her travels but keeps in touch with Bonanza. At the Rubber Rose, the cowgirls are holding hostage the last surviving flock of whooping cranes in the United States. Sissy arrives as the cowgirls and local ranchers are holding off federal authorities who want custody of the whooping cranes. Relying on the advice of Delores, having another peyote-induced vision, the cowgirls and ranchers decide to surrender, but in the process Bonanza Jellybean is killed by the trigger-happy government men. Eventually, the Chink, who had been living with Sissy and Delores, leaves for Florida.

▼

ACTUAL production on *Even Cowgirls Get the Blues* began on September 12, 1992. There were exteriors to be shot in New York City where Sissy visits the

countess, meets aesthete Julian Gitche, and has a sexual encounter with
Warholian social set friends of Gitche. During the filming in the Big Apple, the
increasingly affluent Gus took time out to visit a Mercedes-Benz showroom.
Said an assistant to the filmmaker, "Gus is into cars."

Much of the movie takes place en route to, away from, and around the
Rubber Rose Ranch in the Dakotas. Van Sant chose to film these scenes in
Oregon. In his adoptive home state, Gus shot in Bend, Portland, at the John
Day Fossil Beds National Monument (about 180 miles east of Portland, near
the small town of Clarno), and in Sisters (in the Willamette National Forest
near Redmond). A good deal of this location work was done at a ranch (about to
be converted into a resort) near Crooked River and Smith Rock. Part of the local skyline there was the three-hundred-foot-high Monkey Face. The cast
stayed at the Eagle Crest Resort, the film's headquarters about eight miles outside of Redmond.

As on *My Own Private Idaho*, one of the unique aspects of the *Cowgirls'* production was its use of two directors of photography. Said Eric Alan Edwards of
his collaboration here with John Campbell: "It was like inviting two painters up
to a canvas and giving each of them a brush. It was like going up to Fidel Castro
just after the Revolution and saying, 'Look, we got this other guy we want you to
work with.'" Campbell detailed, "When Gus first asked us to co-photograph the
film we were confused—shocked even. . . . My own fears were that the relationship would be based on power struggles. I'd have to fight to get what I
wanted, and I might not always get my voice."

Low-key as always, Gus described the setup: "John does the shooting, Eric
does the lighting. . . . Some European directors split between a camera opera-
tor and a lighting cameraman." Van Sant's explanation for the strange situation
was, "Well, Eric is great at what he does. But he can sometime be, uh, stub-
born. If he gets an idea in his head, about how a scene should be shot, you can't
talk him out of it. Nobody can. But with John there . . ."

The astute Edwards, a longtime Van Sant buddy, noted, "Gus is in his own
right a very strong visualizer. Very often he knows exactly where he wants the
camera and what lens should be on it. His vision is pretty single-minded and
forceful. By hiring the two of us, I figured he wanted to divide and conquer,
keep us both in something of a quandary, a befuddlement." Edwards continued,
"After *Idaho*, John wanted to light more and I wanted to operate more. But once
Cowgirls started, it was bang! Right back to the old *Idaho* mode." Edwards also
discussed the downside of the working arrangement: "Every time Gus does a
scene, he has to talk to two people who ultimately have a certain say over the
image; it becomes committee decision-making. And when you have a committee, it takes longer and you tend to muddle over things. It's just better if one
calm dictator dispenses with it quickly."

Campbell amplified further on the dual cinematographer condition: "I con-
struct the shot physically and Eric does most of the light placement. Once
we've roughed it in, we come back together and talk about it. I look at his lights,

he looks at my camera. We do our tweaking; we check each other's work. Then I shoot it." But, conceded Campbell, "it sure seemed odd when I first did it. I suppose at times it seems cumbersome and I do resent it, [but] I've known Eric for eight years. We've collaborated together long enough to work things out. In the best situations, I feel the emotional support of an old friend."

In actuality, having both Eric and John on hand proved useful in other ways to Gus. For example, during *Idaho*, Edwards had come down with the flu during the shooting of the Italian sequences, while in *Cowgirls* Campbell had a car accident in Portland. Thus, during these emergencies Van Sant had a spare director of photography sitting on the warm-up bench. (Furthermore, regarding the *Cowgirls* lensing, Gus experimented technically by shooting bits of the continuity on a Sony Handicam with the footage then blown up to 35mm to test its clarity. Although pleased with the results, Van Sant admitted, "I was still afraid to go all out and do a full-scale production on DV [digital video]."

One of the fast-in, fast-out celebrity visitors to the *Cowgirls* set was Roseanne. She flew to the Oregon location on her personal jet, accompanied by husband Tom Arnold and her entourage. The comedian shot her fortune-teller sequence in one day and then left. Other guests on the set included Rain Phoenix's younger brother Joaquin (formerly Leaf), as well as River (to see Gus and to do his cameo in the film). Another occasional observer present was Tom Robbins, the book author of *Even Cowgirls Get the Blues*. He quite openly voiced his concerns about the shooting script: "My dialogue—particularly in the earlier books—tends to be purposefully mannered, which can work on the page but doesn't work coming out of the mouths of actors. Had I written the screenplay, I probably would have used far less of my own dialogue. But that was Gus's decision and I respect his choice. After all, it's his baby."

Regarding the free-spirited shoot of *Cowgirls*, Gus assessed, "We had more time to do stuff, though we had a smaller crew than we did on *Drugstore Cowboy*. I haven't really run into the sort of thing that could have happened if I'd made the Harvey Milk film [*The Mayor of Castro Street*] or in a situation where there's a lot of studio involvement." As to working with Uma Thurman, the film's star: "She was really steady. Even though she comes from a modeling background I always thought she had a little more experience than myself. . . . Yeah, for whatever reason I always got the feeling that she really had the beat on acting."

Angie Dickinson, as Miss Adrian who operates the Rubber Rose Ranch, acknowledged she had never read the film's book original: "It missed me by 10 or 15 years. But that's why when I read the script I was laughing so hard, because it was all fresh to me. It was just clever, and a very different kind of writing than I'm used to." As to working with Van Sant, she informed the press, "He's marvelous. There's not a lot to tell because he's so agreeable. Some directors can be very specific. . . . Gus is very fun, very patient, and also very vague about what he wants. He has a way of suggesting, without actually making specific suggestions. Kind of like Howard Hawks [for whom she made 1959's

Rio Bravo]: they don't say much, but they get across what they want—or at least what they don't want."

While guiding acting novice Rain (who facially resembles Joaquin more than River), Gus did his usual thing of providing the others on the shoot with an atmosphere of near autonomy to develop their characterizations. Already, however, Van Sant was questioning a creative choice he made while developing the *Cowgirls* movie adaptation. It concerned the plot line structure.

As he viewed it in hindsight: "The problem was that Julian is only a passing character in the movie. In the novel, there's a whole engaged kind of life that Sissy has with Julian, who is a gentrified Mohawk Indian living in New York. He represents traditional marriage and she ends up marrying him and becoming dissatisfied with her life because she feels pinned down. All this is going on while she's hitchhiking to the ranch and back again, and eventually he loses her. It was evident when I was writing the script that these were two different stories. There was one at the ranch with Bonanza Jellybean and there was one in New York with Julian. As time went by, we favored the ranch instead of New York, and the way the script ended up Julian became a less important character.

"What happened when we shot the movie was that Keanu found a section of the book that he thought was really interesting, and we worked on it and rehearsed and shot it. It was actually very nice in the movie, but it was a long scene that took away for Cissy's involvement with Jellybean at the ranch because it makes Julian's character larger. It was a close decision in the end. We wanted to keep it in and for a while we did, but eventually we took it out."

After the sprawling movie wrapped principal photography in November 1992—just before Thanksgiving—Van Sant would say, "There are two kinds of jobs in filmmaking. There are jobs for dreamers and jobs for doers. As a director, I get to dream up a vision. I might say, I want a red carpet stretched across two miles of Oregon wheat fields and it is the producer's job to make it happen. Laurie [Parker] has never said, 'We can't do that,' and she has always managed to do it within the budget. At the end of *Cowgirls*, cast and crew told me that they couldn't recall a more friendly, efficient shoot, which I think is another tribute to Laurie. The fact is, though, I've never worked with another producer, so I don't know good or bad things could be."

▼

REGROUPING back in Portland, Van Sant began the postproduction phase of *Even Cowgirls Get the Blues*. As he and editor Curtiss Clayton reviewed the footage it appeared that it would be an even more laborious task than anticipated to carve something cinematically cohesive out of Tom Robbins's parody of the 1960s–1970s cultural revolution. Everything went extremely slowly on these stages of completing *Cowgirls*, a situation that had to be causing great concern at New Line Cinema/Fine Line Pictures.

One piece of good news for the production was that singer/songwriter k. d. lang and her longtime associate Ben Mink, another Canadian, had agreed to do the score for *Even Cowgirls Get the Blues*. With her background in classical country music and other genres, as well as her being openly lesbian, lang was especially appropriate to help create the score for the film and the sound track album to be released on the Sire label. Lang was one of River Phoenix's favorite performers, which must have made it even more enticing for Gus to use this popular musician on his current movie.

▼

DURING part of the summer of 1993, Van Sant was frequently doing double duty: editing *Cowgirls* and being once again involved with *The Mayor of Castro Street*. By this point Becky Johnston was completing her revised screenplay. When she submitted it, according to Van Sant, the production team said, "Perfect, we love it."

But Gus was still not satisfied with the script: "I think on page 45 Harvey kissed his boyfriend and that was the first time you saw anybody touching the other. And I said, 'Well, I want to open with Harvey screwing his boyfriend in his bedroom and then looking out his window.' And they were saying, 'Well, shoot it that way.' But I could just see myself at a rough cut and Warner Bros. saying, 'Well, this scene we didn't want. It wasn't in the script. Get rid of it.' I wanted it to be in the script so that everybody was on the same page about what you were going to do. If you don't start out that way, it's just a mess."

So, Van Sant bowed out of the big-budgeted project that he envisioned as a smaller, more intimate production. As he reflected later: "I never had an argument with Oliver [Stone]. I don't think Warner Bros. was particularly excited about doing that story. I think Oliver talked them into doing it. I was saying, 'If I were Warner Bros. and I was thinking of making a film with a gay subject, I wouldn't make this film.' I mean, I might make it, but I'd never design a film like this to make money. I think it was Oliver's willfulness that said, 'Dammit, this is gonna make money.' I was interested only because it was happening. But, in fact, it wasn't really happening. It was only happening in Oliver's head. And Warner Bros. let it happen in Oliver's head. Warner Bros. was just kissing Oliver Stone's ass."

▼

INCREASINGLY anxious to see a financial return on the long-in-post-production *Even Cowgirls Get the Blues*, New Line Cinema/Fine Line Pictures entered it at two September film industry gatherings. The movie played at the Venice Film Festival in Italy on September 2, 1992, and eleven days later was screened at the Toronto International Film Festival.

The reviews and audience reaction were far from promising. After the Venice showing, *Weekly Variety*'s Deborah Young warned readers, "Unless the Fine Line release takes off as a cult item itself—which is doubtful—it will have trouble expanding the minds of those who lack a hippie past." She thought the film's themes (mystical utopianism, female sexual freedom) "look about a century old." Young judged the picture "at best amusing, at worst, uninvolving, often confusing and sometimes a little boring."

Roger Ebert (*Chicago Sun-Times*) was among those who caught *Cowgirls* at the Toronto confab. He recorded, "As one of the witnesses to that occasion, I remember the hush that descended upon the theater during the screening; it was not so much an absence of noise as the palpable presence of stunned silence." Van Sant had been at the Canadian unspooling; in fact, it was the first time he had seen his movie on a big screen with an audience present. As he acknowledged later in what has to be regarded as a colossal understatement: "We tried to cover all the bases, get all the characters in, and there were a lot of them. There wasn't a focus on specific characters."

As the mostly negative feedback poured back from these two dismal festival showings, New Line Cinema had no option but to delay the planned October 1992 opening of *Cowgirls*. The ramifications of this decision were many. There would now be heavy reediting costs and other new postproduction fees (an estimated $200,000 before the salvage/fine tuning process would be over). But even more costly was the effect of the delayed release within the motion picture industry and on the entertainment world at large. It established firmly in the minds of critics and the public alike that *Cowgirls* was a troubled production, a taint that nothing could likely counteract. There were even worse problems, primarily with the preplanned marketing for the picture, including ancillary products (namely the sound track album, as well as a new paperback edition of the book).

Everything had been geared for an October 1992 release and several magazines (including *Rolling Stone, Harper's Bazaar, Interview,* and *Out*) had feature articles on the movie already incorporated into issues that had gone to press. Under ordinary circumstances, these pieces would have supported the film's release campaign—now they would be read and forgotten by the time the movie made its belated debut. The same applied to the well-produced sound track album (which had k. d. lang singing, among other numbers, "Sweet Little Cherokee") that bowed in October 1993. It earned its share of air play as did the music video of "Just Keep Me Moving" with k. d. lang that Gus directed. But, like the magazine articles, the sound track album would be out of the public's mind by the time the movie was finally distributed.

It must have been a nerve-wracking and embarrassing situation for Van Sant—one that went well beyond the extensive amount of editing/tinkering that had gone on to get *Drugstore Cowboy* and *My Own Private Idaho* to the marketplace. The good professional news for Gus during this period was that he, based on past reputation (certainly not *Cowgirls*) had already signed a deal to direct a new movie (*To Die For*), based on a Joyce Maynard novel. That meant, because of the time frame established for lensing the upcoming film, Gus would be working further on *Cowgirls* while prepping and then directing *To Die For*.

▼

AS Halloween 1993 approached, forty-year-old Van Sant had too much on his mind to really appreciate, let alone enjoy, one of his favorite holidays. By Sunday, October 31, he had even less cause to celebrate. A tragedy had occurred. He heard the news from a pal who called him in Portland around nine A.M. It was so upsetting that he began to cry. "Then," said Van Sant, "I went out to the beach to Sauvie Island and walked around." The devastated director was trying to cope with the death of one of his best friends.

At 1:51 A.M. on that weekend day, twenty-three-year-old River Phoenix was pronounced dead at Cedars-Sinai Hospital in Los Angeles. Piecing together the events of the day before, River had been filming interior sequences in Hollywood on a new movie entitled *Dark Blood* under the direction of Dutch filmmaker George Sluizer. That evening, after partying at a few locations, the actor, his sister Rain, his brother Joaquin, and River's actress girlfriend Samantha Mathis had arrived at the Viper Room, a hip rock club at 8860 Sunset Boulevard in West Hollywood. This was the trendy youth-oriented venue partially owned by actor/musician Johnny Depp. In the club that evening River exhibited strange behavior. Later, when he said he was having difficulty breathing, he was helped out to the street in front of the club. He soon collapsed, went into convulsions, and was in cardiac arrest by the time the paramedics arrived in their ambulance. He was dead by the time they reached the hospital.

Once it was announced that River had passed, gossip spread fast that it must have been a fatal drug overdose. This, so the grapevine insisted, was the tragic result of Phoenix's drug problem that had supposedly escalated at the time of *My Own Private Idaho* and only gotten worse thereafter. While the results of the autopsy were not announced for days, there was little doubt in most anyone's mind that River's self-destructive substance abuse had led to the disaster. (When the coroner's autopsy report was made public, it stated that Phoenix had died of acute multiple drug intoxication, resulting from the use of cocaine, heroin, marijuana, and Valium.)

One of the few persons *not* to accept the emerging picture of the late star's severe drug problem was Gus Van Sant. He told Portland's *Willamette Week* that he had spoken with Phoenix just a week before his death. "River had been working hard on *Dark Blood* and there were a lot of politics and ego-clashing happening on the set that really got to him. Though he wasn't new to wild partying, I really don't think the overdose was a result of addiction. It was an isolated incident, like at a frat party when somebody goes overboard."

In short order, there were a mounting number of media accounts that substantiated the actor's history of drug abuse. Several of the reports put the final blame on River's alleged heavy-duty experimenting with heroin during the making of *My Own Private Idaho*. Van Sant, however, insisted, "Just because of River's excellent portrayal of Mike Waters, people see River's *Idaho* character as being River and he was not like that all." The director protested that while shooting *Idaho* and thereafter he would often share a drink of sake with the actor, but that he never saw Phoenix doing illegal drugs nor did he discuss drug use with him.

Manifestly, Gus was devastated by River's death. Said Heidi Snellman, one of Van Sant's Portland friends, "The most unhappy I've seen him was when River Phoenix died and that was awful."

As time passed, Gus would come to terms—to a degree—with River's passing. ("I thought it wasn't drug related until the medical support came out. I thought it was like an aneurysm. To the bitter end I assumed that it wasn't drug related.") In late 1997, over four years after the young star had died, Van Sant told *Venice* magazine: "I never really saw his death as a self-destructive death. I see it more as a sort of calamity. A sort of mistake that was made on a wild bender that I don't think was related to self-destructiveness. He really wasn't a self-destructive person. . . . River had a certain public image that went against the grain of how he died. It was like 'how can a vegetarian possibly do drugs.' It's like they [the press] felt they'd been cheated and lied to by this guy. If he had been hit by a truck it would have been different—which is really how I look at it, as a tragic accident. To me River really was a symbol of hope and good cheer. He was probably one of the greatest persons I've ever met."

▼

IN the winter of 1993, it was announced officially that *Even Cowgirls Get the Blues* would debut on April 29, 1994. By now several things had happened to the restructured film. A good deal of the New York City sequences featuring Sissy's relationship in Manhattan with the urbanized Mohawk Native American (played by Keanu Reeves) had been sliced out. So had most of the movie's references to the Clock People (the keepers of the keys to the cosmic consciousness), and a good deal of Pat Morita's role as the Chink had hit the cutting room floor. Paring down (or nearly eliminating) these plot aspects allowed more emphasis to be given to the ranch scenes, the lesbian cowgirls, and, in particular, to Sissy's growing emotional rapport with Bonanza Jellybean. The film's ending was now benign with the Chink leaving for Florida. (An earlier version featured a close-up of pregnant Sissy's belly in which the unborn baby—a product of her coupling with the Chink—is "all thumbs.")

The revamped *Cowgirls* now carried an on-screen title-card dedication, "To River." Said a still-grieving Gus: "River was a great friend of mine. We had a lot of projects planned [including one in which Phoenix would play Andy Warhol] in the future and now they won't ever be made. It was very important to me to dedicate this movie to him."

Then came the last-minute news on April 13, 1994, that *Even Cowgirls Get the Blues* would not be released on April 29. Instead, it would be issued on May 20. The reason given was that there were too many other movies opening at the end of April. By mid-May 1994, a Fine Line executive was telling the *New York Times*: "I think there is no film that is not born out of chaos. They are born in postproduction, and few turn out as planned." So much for damage control.

Meanwhile, Van Sant had flown into New York City from Toronto where he was making *To Die For*. He was on hand in the front of the firing line to discuss the long-awaited, revised *Even Cowgirls Get the Blues*. He insisted in his disarming, offhanded way: "All my previous films have gone through similar stages that *Cowgirls* has. It's just that, this time, the film was much anticipated. It played festivals in what I would consider 'rough-cut' form. I very much wanted to go back and make some changes. Nobody forced me to do this or that, or took it out of my hands. It was, like all my films, an ongoing creative process—but with this movie it was more public."

Now reduced from 106 to 96 minutes, the R-rated *Even Cowgirls Get the Blues* opened to generally disastrous reviews on May 20, 1994. (It led nationally syndicated gossip cocolumnists Marilyn Beck and Stacy Jenel Smith to quip, "Giving a whole new meaning to thumbs down, *Even Cowgirls Get the Blues* was panned by 43 critics in New York, Chicago, Los Angeles and Washington, D. C.") Many of the reviewers commented that the new edition was no better than the aborted fall 1993 version of *Cowgirls*, although they acknowledged that the movie contained some splendidly lensed vistas. (This time, however, Van Sant stayed away from using much time-lapse photography.)

Of this road movie, Caryn James complained in the *New York Times*: "The 70s haven't aged well, especially if you take them seriously. . . . One of the many problems with Gus Van Sant's tortured, worked-over *Even Cowgirls Get the Blues* is that Sissy Hankshaw talks like a novel, and a dated one at that." James pointed out, "Much of the liveliness of Mr. Robbins's novel comes from the way it scatters all over the place. . . . Mr. Van Sant's movie is all over the place, too, but that strategy makes the film scattershot instead of vibrant." For James, "The central problem is Sissy. Uma Thurman looks the part. But she has a strained backwoods Virginia accent and is carried along by a script that tries to cram in so much of Sissy's life that she careens from one city to another without becoming more than a character sketch. It would have taken some serious rewriting and reshooting to give Sissy the substance to carry the film."

John Anderson of *Newsday* reported about the film that "the viewer comes away from the film with the distinct sense that the director had lost his vision and decided to make light of his own project. There are moments of sweet, ethereal and perhaps winsome Van Sant . . . but where and why they occur seems sophomoric. What the book portrayed as mischievous or spirited generally comes off as rude, and the lyrical has become ponderous."

Jack Kroll (*Newsweek*) registered his negative opinion of the movie with regrets. He mentioned that Van Sant "has become a one-man counterculture in the movie industry. That's a tough job, as his new film, *Even Cowgirls Get the Blues*, demonstrates." But, Kroll reasoned, "There are just too many half-cooked ingredients in this utopian stew of a movie."

Kenneth Turan of the *Los Angeles Times* also panned this tale of the funky Sissy and her cowgirl cohorts: "Like many films that arrive on screen more dead than alive . . . *Even Cowgirls Get the Blues* contains its own built-in epitaph. 'Playfulness ceases to have a serious purpose when it takes itself too seriously,' someone says, a theory this unfortunate movie goes way out of its way to prove." According to Turan: "[W]hat Robbins' smug whimsy doesn't need is a dose of Van Sant's deadpan aesthetic of knowing, way hip boredom. Though the director's sensibility worked extraordinarily well when applied to hard-edged subject matter . . . combining it with Robbins' flimsy jokiness has resulted in a film whose tedium is painful."

Joe Brown (*Washington Post*) was also not a fan of the flat-footed new release: "Saddled with leaden lead performances, hobbled by an arch, incoherent script and pokey pacing, the new, improved *Cowgirls* is a miscarriage—misconceived, miscast, miserably boring. And misogynistic too—perhaps the queerest thing about this adaptation of Robbins's freewheeling feminist 1976 novel, which celebrates rebellious cowgirls and their lighthearted lesbianism." Brown concluded, "In a reverent panic to cram in all the key plot points of Robbins's psychedelically enhanced story, Van Sant misses most of its sweet, sunny spirits."

Michael Medved (*New York Post*) was among the many who found Rain Phoenix badly wanting in a key screen role. In Medved's estimation, this was "the most unspeakably awful all-star extravaganza of this (or any other) season: a movie so breathtakingly bad that it actually leaves the viewer in a state of numbed disbelief."

Even Roger Ebert (*Chicago Sun-Times*), a great enthusiast of Gus's past features, skewered the new entry: "What I am sure of is that *Even Cowgirls Get the Blues* is one of the most empty, pointless, baffling films I can remember, and the experience of viewing it is an exercise in nothingness."

One of the few American critics to have anything positive to say about *Even Cowgirls Get the Blues* was Marjorie Baumgarten of the *Austin Chronicle*. She allowed, "[T]he pleasure of seeing Van Sant's impeccable imagery makes *Cowgirls* worth seeing for fans. His New York sequences that owe a debt to Warhol, the Western landscapes that resemble Ansel Adams photographs, the lithe image of a woman guiding her freakish thumbs through a roadside ballet—all are stunning moments that exist only inside this film."

The much-lambasted *Even Cowgirls Get the Blues* disappeared from first-run limited distribution fairly rapidly. It grossed a paltry $1.71 million. The misguided campy film received two nominations for the 1995 Razzie Awards: one for Worst Actress (Uma Thurman) and one for Worst Supporting Actress (Sean Young). Booby prizes should also have been bestowed on John Hurt for his one-note, over-the-top performance as the outrageous countess, and, for sheer dreariness on camera, on Lorraine Bracco's whip-snapping cowgirl. Sad to watch in this tribute to antimale chauvinism were such veteran personalities as Angie Dickinson who seemed bewildered by the chaotic plotline and seemed awkward on-screen.

When the trounced-upon picture finally made its way to England in January 1995, the response was equally negative. *London Time Out* lamented, "Watching *Cowgirl* is a melancholy experience, but only by default: it's sad to see arguably the most intuitive American film-maker to emerge in the late '80s barking so strenuously up the wrong tree. In aiming for the small loopy, off-the-wall humour and pop-art sensibility which distinguished *Drugstore Cowboy* and *My Own Private Idaho*—only more so—Van Sant has neglected to provide any counterbalance."

As to the fiasco of *Even Cowgirls Get the Blues*, Van Sant said, "I can't explain why it didn't work. We all thought it was off-kilter enough to be interesting, and I can't explain the reaction. But you can waste a lot of time trying to figure it out, and in the end, they either get our material, or they don't. I make these films for myself, anyway." He did have a theory as to the adverse critical reaction: "Actually, I think a lot of critics didn't like the previous films, but they felt obligated to give them a good review. . . . *Cowgirls* offered critics an opportunity to give me the bad review they wanted to give before."

But for Van Sant, *Even Cowgirls Get the Blues* would always remain a favorite project. "Sometimes you like the more enfeebled child best. It's the most loved child."

A PROJECT *TO DIE FOR*

I don't have any gripes with
Hollywood. I can't accuse Hollywood
of inhibiting my vision. It depends on
how you go about making your film. If
you don't think things will work out,
then you just don't do it under those circumstances.

Gus Van Sant, 1994

IF CHUNKS OF 1993 AND the first quarter of 1994 had
been consumed with the ill-fated *Mayor of Castro Street* project, the making
and remaking of *Even Cowgirls Get the Blues*, and coping with the sad loss of
River Phoenix, Gus Van Sant's life at the time was nevertheless bursting with
other activities. He traveled the United States and Russia to shoot portraits for
a Gap Clothing campaign. He had *Mala Noche* transferred to 35mm for its
showing at the San Francisco Lesbian and Gay Film Festival. He continued to
direct and/or do special photography for the music videos of such artists as
Chris Isaak and Deee-Lite. Gus also brought together two unlikely artists for a
collaborative album: William S. Burroughs Jr. and Kurt Cobain, the latter
touted as "the voice of his generation."

Rock stars Cobain and his wife Courtney Love lived in Madrona, Washington, and through mutual friends had come to know Gus. Tim Kerr of Portland's TK Records asked Van Sant to introduce Cobain to Burroughs. He did so
and their joint effort led to a short disc entitled *They Call Him "Priest"* in which
the author/poet provided the voice on selected Burroughs pieces and Cobain
contributed the eerie guitar background. Gus and Mark Trunz did the photo
shoot that was used for the album covers. Although Van Sant never got to know
the rock superstar that well, he, like millions of others, was shocked when

Cobain was found dead at his Washington home on April 8, 1994, with a bullet through his head. Along with River's death, it thrust Van Sant into a more sober mood during this period.

It was also in this reflective time that Van and his boyfriend (D-J Haanraadts) broke up, but remained friends. The six-year relationship was the longest one Gus had experienced so far. As Van Sant told *Monk* magazine, "Maybe we'll get back together. We made a really great team. He's really outgoing and I'm really quiet and non-adventurous. I mean in my art I'm really adventurous, but in life . . ." Van Sant acknowledged that his new special friend was Scott Patrick Green, who had been involved with *My Own Private Idaho* and had worked as Gus's assistant since then. With Green and Michael Parker (another *Idaho* alumnus who had become part of the director's circle) Gus formed a new musical group called the Dots. The players rehearsed at Van Sant's home and even did a benefit gig in Portland for a local record company called Dogfish that had burned to the ground. However, because of the filmmaker's hectic schedule, the Dots never were able to take their group to the next level.

Also in this decade, the filmmaker continued to experiment with hallucinogenic-type drugs. As he informed James Crotty and Michael Lane for a 1995 issue of *Monk* magazine, on one occasion: "I had this reoccurring trip in which I thought that people were going to deliver to me the secret to life. I thought that's what was going to happen to me that night, that people were going to bring me to a place in which I was going to receive a knowledge that was the key to history, time travel, civilization." Another time, Van Sant remembered, "I was tripping at this suburban home with some friend and I'd taken three hits and they'd all taken one and we were all watching *Roller Derby* [on television] and I just thought that I was going to receive this knowledge. And someone else showed up, another friend came, and I said, 'Well are we going to go now?' and they said like 'where?,' and I said, 'Well you know, I don't know where, whatever the next place is.' And they were sort of 'what's wrong with Gus? He's waiting for the secret of life.'"

Another influence in Gus's life at this time was photographer Larry Clark, whose books of photos had helped to inspire *Drugstore Cowboy*. Clark wanted to expand his creative output and Van Sant encouraged him to try directing music videos. He did one for Chris Isaak with Gus serving as producer and cinematographer. Clark now wanted to direct a feature film and Gus agreed to serve as executive producer, offering his contacts and filmmaking savvy. The project was *Kids*, budgeted at less than $1.5 million and to be scripted by a teenager named Harmony Korine.

Yet another venture mentioned for Gus was a sixty-minute television drama, *Christmas on Stark Street*, an AIDS drama to be produced in conjunction with PBS-TV's *American Playhouse* for a series entitled *Red, Hot & Film*. It was supposed to feature Michael Parker and Scott Patrick Green. It would tell of a movie director with AIDS who is living on the streets of Portland. In the plotline, a $40,000 money order from Hollywood—a lure to get the director back to work—is misdelivered to two street kids (Green and Parker), who cash it and set off on a cross-country road trip.

If often during this hectic phase of his life Van Sant rightfully seemed preoccupied, there were occasions when he could shake off his reveries and take action when it was needed. For example, at the August 1993 symposium of the American Association of Physicians for Human Rights being held at Portland's Benson Hotel, Gus was to be the recipient of an Achievement Award along with such honorees as Bob Hattoy (the White House staffer who movingly addressed the 1992 Democratic convention as a gay man with HIV), educator and Ph.D. Joseph Fernandez (who championed gay-inclusive curricula in public education, which had recently cost him his post as chancellor of the New York Board of Education), Sari Staver (who had chronicled the challenges of lesbian and gay physicians for more than a decade), and Jeff Levin (director of public policy at the AIDS Action Foundation).

As writer Steve Taravella, who was then associate director of the organization (now called the Gay and Lesbian Medical Association), detailed for this author: "It's late August, 1993, at the Hotel Benson, an elegant, historic old hotel in Portland. . . . One of my responsibilities was organizing . . . [the group's] annual membership conference, which drew about 500 physicians and medical students from around the U.S. (and a few from Canada) for three days of educational meetings and social events.

"I am in the hotel's ballroom, which is packed with doctors for our main luncheon, where several people were to receive the organization's annual Achievement Award. A brief slide show had been hastily arranged to introduce one of the awardees and I was to operate the projector, which was front and center of the room. Wouldn't you know—at the very moment the program was to begin, the projector jams. I was unfamiliar with the machine and the harder I try to fix it, the more nervous I become, since everyone in the room is watching me fiddle with this lever and that button and this light, etc. To my great relief, one of our members steps up to help me, and he seems to know what he's doing. I'm intently focused on the machine, so—while I thank him for trying to help—I don't really look up to see exactly who was lending a hand. In a flash, he gets it working and, with great relief, I look up to see that the fellow who just made everything OK isn't a physician after all. It's none other than Gus Van Sant.

"He was there to receive one of the awards but—although we had corresponded prior to this event—I had not met him and he had not been introduced. He apparently was running late; he was supposed to have been seated at the same table I was, with a few other honored guests, but hadn't arrived when the event began. I think he just walked in, realized what was happening and put his AV experience to use. I don't think most folks recognized him. I was terribly grateful that he was such an unpretentious, roll-up-your-sleeves kind of guy. And he sat beside me for the lunch and presentation."

▼

AS the 1990s approached its midpoint, Gus, who for so many of his Portland years had lived relatively frugally, acknowledged, "I spend a lot of money now. . . . I've been buying a lot of stuff recently. A lot of cameras, cars, guitars and motorcycles. . . . [But] recently I've been getting paranoid that maybe it'll stop, which it might. Like maybe in a slow way. Like maybe I should save money because someday the tables might turn and they may not finance the films I want to make."

▼

BACK in July 1993, as Gus continued to work on the edit of *Even Cowgirls Get the Blues*, his agent John Burnham, cohead of the motion picture department at the William Morris Agency, came to Van Sant with a offer to direct an upcoming picture. The project, based on a published novel, was to be adapted to the screen by another of Burnham's clients, Buck Henry. Gus already knew Henry from their abortive screenplay collaboration and from the fact that Henry was to play a small acting role in the upcoming *Even Cowgirls Get the Blues*. The new picture was to be made at Columbia Pictures, which meant that Van Sant would have to operate within the confines of a big-studio project. Was Gus interested?

Up until now Van Sant had been making movies that he had written, co-written, or adapted. Here he would have no part in the screenwriting process. He would be a "hired gun" to direct the vehicle and he would have to function to a large degree within the studio system. It led him to the following consideration: "Not being the writer starts to make a more defined difference in the producer's and director's minds. When you're the director and the writer, too, you often feel that you have to protect the script from the producer and other sources to have as much leeway and spontaneity in actually forging the film. That would have happened on an independent project, too, if I was just the director."

Despite the downsides of the assignment, it was an opportunity to expand his professional horizons. Van Sant accepted the challenge. By late August 1993—a few weeks before he started filming *Cowgirls*—the deal was solidified with Columbia Pictures. The movie would go into production in the first half of 1994.

The news took many in the Hollywood film community by surprise. Said one unnamed producer at Columbia, the movie lot making the project, "It is hard to believe Van Sant would work at a major studio. He's an extremely independent artist. My guess is that he's negotiated a filmmaker's deal . . . [that gives him] things like the final cut in exchange for a lower budget, no [management] notes and leaves him alone."

What was important to Van Sant and his management team, however, was that Gus was now in the major leagues of moviemaking. Not an easy accomplishment for the maker of such nonmainstream projects who refused up till now to play the Hollywood games.

BACK IN BUSINESS

Fortunately, I was already shooting *To Die For* when *Cowgirls* came out. If you're looking for work when a movie gets shot down, you're in trouble. . . . I did have a moment of panic on the set the morning the *Cowgirl* reviews came. I'd never received such public ridicule, so I went to work that day convinced that no one would listen to me. I wondered, "Are the actors going to come to work? Is the crew going to forget to load the film?"

Gus Van Sant, 1995

ON AUGUST 1, 1990, Gregory Smart was shot to death at his condominium home in Derry, New Hampshire. In the ensuing high-profile trial, the jury determined that sixteen-year-old William "Billy" Flynn was the killer. Smart's wife, Pamela, twenty-two, was found guilty of "capital murder" for "hiring" Flynn to do the task. At the murder trial, it was brought forth that Pamela, director of media services at Winnacunnet High in Hampton, New Hampshire, had been having a sexual relationship with student Flynn and that allegedly she had threatened to break off their relationship if he did not commit the murder. Smart was sentenced to life in prison without possibility of parole, while Flynn (through plea bargaining) was sentenced to a twenty-eight-year prison term that was subject to the possibility of parole.

The sensational case received tremendous media coverage that included having Court TV air the trial in depth. Months later, on September 24, 1991, a CBS-TV network movie on the notorious killing debuted. Entitled *Murder in New Hampshire: The Pamela Wojas Smart Story*, it starred Helen Hunt, with Chad Allen as the love-struck student who shot Gregory Smart in the head reportedly at the demand of Pamela. It was a straightforward, well-acted presentation in the established movie-of-the-week format.

The next year, Joyce Maynard authored *To Die For*, a fictionalized version of the Pamela Smart case. As recast for the book, it was the tale of a ruthlessly ambitious young woman who persuades a trio of high school misfits to eliminate her spouse when he seemingly stands in the way of her unfounded goal of becoming a media star. A Literary Guild selection, the well-constructed book was popular in hardback and paperback.

One of those who read an early review of Maynard's novel was film producer Leslie Morgan who had a working relationship with Hollywood producer Laura Ziskin. Morgan suggested to Ziskin that Maynard's book would make a good movie. A deal was made to acquire screen rights for *To Die For*. Veteran scenarist Buck Henry, then going through a dry spell in his screenwriting career, was recommended to adapt the property for filming, possibly because he and Ziskin had professional links through their agents. After a few top choices to direct the murder case picture passed on the offer due to scheduling problems, etc., Van Sant was suggested to helm the vehicle. It was reasoned that he had demonstrated a knack for turning out movies about disaffected people. Therefore, the argument went, he was qualified to handle this tale of oddball youths lured into committing homicide by a beguiling, ambitious (albeit vapid) young woman. As Ziskin stated in retrospect for the *To Die For* press kit about pairing Van Sant and Henry: "Gus is a real visual artist. He has a fabulous eye and, I say this in the best sense, an idiosyncratic way of shooting and a somewhat idiosyncratic design sense that is very strong, defined and clear. His style and Henry's writing talents seemed like a good mix for this project." Gus's agent made the deal for him to guide *To Die For* to the screen.

▼

WHAT had initially attracted producer Ziskin to Maynard's satirical novel was one primary ingredient: "What I generally look for are good characters and here was this amazing character in the form of Suzanne Maretto. This is a woman whose entire value system is based on television and the desire to be famous."

What had intrigued Gus to sign on for the project—besides working with quick-witted Buck Henry and the healthy fee attached to direct—was the fact that the story "was about a neighborhood which was like the one I grew up in. A sort of portrait of a small East Coast town where the different ethnic groups came together in a particularly awkward way." He thought the story unfolded an interesting look at the messed-up class relations in the United States where friendship between the classes "were looked upon as a problem." Van Sant also had his own take on the narrative's sociopathic lead figure: "I saw the character as more like Gloria Swanson was in *Sunset Boulevard*. . . . [Suzanne's] character has created her own space and world in this small town due to her vanity."

What struck a chord with Buck Henry about the planned vehicle was "[e]veryone's avocation in America is show business. Television captures the imagination more than anything else in people's lives. The country is somehow held together by celebrities. Celebrity actors. Celebrity talk-show people. Celebrity designers and politicians. It's this jungle of junk. Junk information, junk misinformation. Half-baked knowledge. Received opinion. It's like a huge orchestra with everyone playing in a different key." As to Maynard's lead character: "Her brain has been short-circuited by all this stuff. Her ambition is crossed with a kind of dopiness. She'll do anything to get that instant fix of fame."

As Henry began structuring his script, he came to an important conclusion: "Since one of the central themes of the book is the siren call of public media, and its effect on the participant and the viewer, how could I make that part of the structure? So I came around to the idea that all of these people are telling these stories for a reason other than just telling the stories. I don't like voice-overs. I think, with a few exceptions, when movies have voice-overs it's because the filmmaker has failed to find a dramatic course to take that covers the information. . . . But a straight voice-over is the same thing as a straight talk-to-camera: it's a fallback position. Anyway, in a flash of either inspiration or obviousness, I thought, 'Oh, yes, of course. They're all entertaining on different media.' The problem, then, was finding a reason for Suzanne to talk to the camera, since I knew she was dead. That's why I devised her taping her story, which in itself becomes part of the plot."

Working within this frame, Buck constructed a wry black comedy (more so than the Maynard book had been) that took full advantage of Buck's mordant humor. To play the ruthless female would require a performer of physical charisma, one with the necessary talent to credibly combine blind ambition and naïveté. In addition, the actress playing the part must never forget that this was a dark comedy and her histrionics must be kept in check.

Among the actresses who registered interest in the challenging project were Jodie Foster, Bridget Fonda, Nicole Kidman, Meg Ryan, Patricia Arquette, Holly Hunter, Mary Louise Parker, Susan Sarandon, and Jennifer Jason Leigh. Those in the top running at first included Sarandon, Arquette, and Ryan. For a brief time Sarandon was "attached" to the project, then she went on to other screen commitments. As a result, Ryan and Arquette became the likely contenders. As everyone pondered their options, Ryan dropped out of making *Beyond Rangoon,* another picture she was considering at the time. This led to Arquette being offered and accepting the *Rangoon* role, at a healthy $1 million fee, making her unavailable to do *To Die For* in the spring of 1994.

Ryan, especially noted for her cheery screen persona in such movies as *When Harry Met Sally . . .* (1989) and *Sleepless in Seattle* (1993), continued to debate the wisdom of starring in *To Die For.* Eventually she vetoed doing the role. Van Sant said later: "I don't know why she changed her mind, but perhaps it was because the character was too dark for her. The character is annoying at some point and you might feel the audience is going to hate her."

Meanwhile Kidman went into overdrive regarding the *To Die For* casting. The twenty-seven-year-old Honolulu-born actress had grown up in her parents' native city of Sydney, Australia. She had dropped out of high school to pursue a full-time acting career. Her debut was in an Australian TV movie, *Chase Through the Night* (1983). She made her first impact on American films audiences with the 1989 thriller *Dead Calm*. While shooting *Days of Thunder* (1990), she fell in love with her costar (Tom Cruise) and the couple married in December 1990. Such subsequent features as *Far and Away* (1992—with Cruise) and *Batman Forever* (1995—as Dr. Chase Meridian opposite Val Kilmer's caped crusader) had highlighted her pulchritude more than her acting acumen. On the other hand, in *Malice* (1993), a sexy, twisted tale, she had displayed a flintiness opposite Alec Baldwin.

One day Van Sant, juggling his time between *Cowgirls* and the upcoming *To Die For,* received an unusual phone call at home. It was from Kidman who quickly introduced herself. She mentioned she knew she was not his first choice to play Suzanne Maretto. Then she said, "I'm just obsessed with this story. I love the script and I love your work [especially *Drugstore Cowboy*] and I was destined to play this part."

Van Sant was taken aback by her remarks, especially by her announcement that "I am destined to play Suzanne." As her words registered on him, he decided, "In a way, it's just something you would say. But I took it a different way, like she really was destined to play the role." Gus knew little about Kidman, but he had liked her in *Malice* because "that showed she could be very direct in her portrayal of a character who is evil." He reasoned further, "I felt that if she felt destined to play it, she would work harder than you normally would. She was so convinced that she would be the best choice that that was enough. I figured we could work it out."

Gus offered Nicole the pivotal role without first screentesting her—just from the impact of her phone call to him. In doing so, Van Sant was actually following the guidelines set out by the author of *To Die For.* In that fiction, Maynard had her character Suzanne Maretto say should her life ever be filmed, she'd want it to be played by "that actress that just got married to Tom Cruise." (The director later insisted—which might have been an engineered publicity gimmick—that he was not aware at the time that Kidman was wed to box-office champion Cruise.)

Naturally, the studio's higher-ups had to be convinced of the director's casting choice. There was some concern whether Nicole could drop her Australian accent for this very American character and if she had the necessary acting resources to meet this acting challenge. For Buck Henry, who had no performers in mind when he wrote the screenplay, "My problem with Nicole was her [five-foot ten-inch] height: I'd always imagined Suzanne to be a dangerous, short time-bomb, and not an overwhelming, beautiful, tall she-demon." But he also agreed with Van Sant that Nicole was a talented individual.

With the Kidman decision approved by the producers and Nicole signed for the feature in December 1993, it was decided to postpone the shooting schedule from March to April 1994. Now Van Sant had to fill the other key parts.

To play opposite tall, svelte Kidman, Gus turned to his unofficial stock company—in particular, to Matt Dillon. Since the well-received *Drugstore*

Cowboy, Dillon's career had not maintained the expected upward progression. While the ensemble feature *Singles* (1992—in which Matt had costarred and Gus had had a cameo) had done decently at the box office (a gross of over $18.47 million), Dillon's follow-up pictures (*The Saint of Fort Washington*, *Mr. Wonderful*, *Golden Gate*) had not registered well with the public. It took persuasion on Van Sant's part to convince the studio to use Dillon for the assignment, even with the credential of the good work Matt had done for Van Sant in *Drugstore Cowboy*. The director's task may have been eased by the fact that Dillon's character is killed partway through the feature and is not the movie's main thrust.

As to the trio of losers who become pawns in Suzanne's murderous game plan, the pivotal one is sixteen-year-old Jimmy Emmett. He is the inarticulate son of trailer trash who lives in a dream world of rock music, drugs, and sexual fantasies. He does not have a clue about what he wants from life; he has enough trouble navigating through his adolescent confusions and inertia.

Many names were suggested to play Jimmy, and many auditioned for Gus. One of those who read with Gus was Matt Damon. Born in 1970, the good-looking Damon hailed from Cambridge, Massachusetts, and had made his screen debut in *Mystic Pizza* (1988) and gone on to *School Ties* (1992) and *Geronimo: An American Legend* (1993). He was ambitious and resourceful, but so far he had not enjoyed that breakthrough screen role needed to push him to the next career level. He did his best to persuade Gus that he could be Jimmy Emmett.

Van Sant was impressed by Damon's talent, drive, and appearance. But, said the director: "Matt looked like the football quarterback, not the emaciated kid from the other side of the tracks. . . . Matt was an extremely adept actor, very quick, and he really wanted the part. Probably more so than anybody I interviewed. . . . Matt tried hard to get it to the point where—he was 23 and I said, 'You're just a little too old,' and he said, 'No, no. I can act younger if you give me a couple weeks'—and he starved himself so he was real skinny and he somehow focused his eyes so he looked not as intelligent, and a little green, not as worldly, about six years less worldly. He really did look 16, and I said, 'God, that's amazing.' And I kind of forgot to say, 'But you're too all-American.'"

In any event Van Sant already had another actor in mind to be the malleable Jimmy. It was Joaquin Phoenix who had just turned twenty. Born in Puerto Rico, he had followed his older siblings—River and Rain—into show business and had used the name Leaf Phoenix. He had already been in such TV series as *MorningStar/EveningStar* (1986) and such features as *Space Camp* (1986), *Russkies* (1987), and *Parenthood* (1989). Questioning whether he wanted to further pursue an acting career, he had gone to Mexico with his father for a bit. When Rain had starred as Bonanza Jellybean in Gus's *Even Cowgirls Get the Blues*, Joaquin had come on the Oregon set to visit. Joaquin was in Los Angeles with River on October 31, 1993, when the latter died of a drug overdose in front of the Viper Room club. In fact, on that traumatic night it had been Joaquin who phoned 911 for medical help for his convulsing brother. (Joaquin's recorded hysterical plea for assistance would be played over and over by the media on national TV.)

With the death of River, Joaquin was understandably in a highly emotional funk. His pals and peers urged him to return to acting as therapy. In was in this mode that he auditioned for the part of the obsessive stooge Jimmy in *To Die For*. With Gus's close past relationship to River and, to a lesser extent, with Rain, it must have seemed like excessive favoritism when he began touting Joaquin for this key assignment. There certainly must have been those on the Hollywood scene who thought Van Sant's championing of the younger Phoenix was a payback of sorts. It was, after all, so the gossip mills insisted, the supposed drug scene on *My Own Private Idaho* that had allegedly so enticed River into the world of heavy substance abuse and in turn, so the theory went, had contributed to his demise. Another supposition could be that by casting Joaquin in the *To Die For* assignment, Gus was showing the film industry and the world that River's family did not hold Van Sant responsible for their relative's death.

In any event, Gus was extremely responsive to Joaquin's movie audition. It led Van Sant to say later, when reflecting on his having to choose between Phoenix and Matt Damon for the part of Jimmy: 'It was really neck and neck. But Joaquin was the obvious favorite.'" Another time, Gus acknowledged, "I thought Matt was very good, although Joaquin was more of a name than Matt Damon." The filmmaker also said of the process in making this casting decision: "It was a tough story. His character kills somebody, and I didn't know if it was too freaky, if it was something he could handle. But he decided he wanted to do it. He thought the script was very funny." Then, according to Gus, "I didn't want the producer or casting director to think it was nepotism or something, so I let them say, 'He's the best, first.' I knew already that he was my first choice, but this was right after River died, and there was a question as to whether he wanted to act in anything."

So Joaquin said yes, the production executives said yes, and Phoenix joined *To Die For*.

It was Matt Damon who suggested that nineteen-year-old Casey Affleck try out for *To Die For*. Matt was best friends with Casey's three-years-older actor brother, Ben, and the trio had grown up together in Cambridge, Massachusetts. Casey's earlier screen credits included a role in the Kevin Bacon–directed TV movie *Lemon Sky* (1987). In the TV miniseries *The Kennedys of Massachusetts* (1990) young Affleck had played Robert Kennedy from ages twelve to fifteen. As both Matt and Ben gained roles in show business, the profession had become more appealing to Casey. Van Sant sensed a talent in the teenager and hired him to be Russell Hines, the other male of the high school trio of outcasts.

The last of the screenplay's scruffy threesome was Lydia Mertz, the tag-along character in the group of nonconformist loners. The dumpy girl is so anxious for attention that she is an easy prey for Suzanne who showers the pliable Lydia with beauty tips, apparel gifts, and, best—or worst—of all, a role model.

Reportedly it was at a mass audition for the important role that Alison Folland came to Gus's attention. She had supposedly never acted before, but went to the casting call with friends as a lark. She was sixteen years old at the time and was attending private school in the greater Boston area where she was known for her habit of dying her hair strange colors. Supposedly Alison was so convinced that she didn't get the part that she had already departed with her family for a vacation in the Bahamas when the casting directors put out an S.O.S. for her.

Having selected his five principals, the rest of the *To Die For* cast fell into place. To play Janice Maretto, the sister of Matt Dillon's character, Illeana Douglas was singled out. She was the granddaughter of past screen and stage star Melvyn Douglas. After training at New York's Neighborhood Playhouse, Illeana began getting screen roles: *GoodFellas* (1990), *Cape Fear* (1991), and *Household Saints* (1993).

Veteran actor Dan Hedeya (*Wise Guys, The Addams Family, Boiling Point*) was already known to Van Sant, having auditioned for past Gus feature films. He had also acted with Matt Dillon in *Mr. Wonderful* (1993). Hedeya was contracted to play the Italian restaurateur father of Dillon's character. Other familiar faces to join the *To Die For* cast were Holland Taylor and Kurtwood Smith as Suzanne's pampering parents, and Maria Tucci as Dillon's on-camera devoted mama. Chunky Wayne Knight—known to millions as the conniving postal worker Newman on TV's *Seinfeld*—was picked to be the film's small-town cable station manager.

One *To Die For* screen role proved rather easy to fill. It was the part of the sarcastic high school teacher, Mr. Finlaysson. It had been a female figure in Maynard's book original, but had been changed to a male for the screen presentation. This job went to the film's scenarist Buck Henry, whose acting résumé included many screen roles: *The Man Who Fell to Earth, Heaven Can Wait*, and *Defending Your Life*. According to Henry: "I modeled Mr. Finlaysson after a teacher I had had in school whom I'd always wanted to write about. I didn't know I was going to play him. I never know I'm going to play a certain character in any movie I've ever written. That's always come up sort of halfway through the casting session, when somebody says, 'Why don't you play one of these?' And they almost always think I want to play someone other than I do, although in this case I would have been happy to play several characters—Hal Brady, the network guy that George Segal plays, for instance—but I thought Mr. Finlaysson was someone I really knew."

It was now spring 1994. Van Sant had survived the ordeal of the hugely disappointing festival prerelease showings of *Even Cowgirls Get the Blues*. Currently he was reediting the feature yet again to meet its much-delayed play date. Completing the preproduction on *To Die For* was intermingled with the *Cowgirls* chores. Working on the fresh project—so different in every way from *Cowgirls*—must have been a godsend for the beleaguered Van Sant.

A MURDEROUSLY FUNNY MOVIE

All of my films are black comedy. But this one [*To Die For*] is more outwardly funny. There are a lot of jokes and funny situations that make it light. . . . But while there are both satirical moments and funny moments, I've never consciously tried for either or tried to keep it any one way.

Gus Van Sant, 1995

WHILE NEW LINE CINEMA was announcing to the world that the much unanticipated *Even Cowgirls Get the Blues* would have its debut postponed yet again (from April 29 to May 20, 1994), Gus Van Sant was away from the brouhaha. He was in Canada, in Toronto, directing *To Die For*.

Like many runaway Hollywood movie productions, *To Die For* was taking advantage of the more economical labor, services, and equipment rates available in Canada. (Van Sant had wanted to shoot the movie in Oregon, around Astoria, but finally yielded to the studio's budgetary decision to film outside of the United States.) By mid-April 1994 a few days of preliminary shooting had already been accomplished in Florida. There Van Sant and a small crew and the coleads captured on film the plot line fragments of Suzanne and Larry Maretto's honeymoon.

Despite this being a big-studio project with all the bureaucracy that that entailed, Van Sant was allowed to assemble much of the same creative team from his recent independent pictures: Missy Stewart (production designer), Beatrix Aruna Pasztor (costume designer), Eric Alan Edwards (cinematographer—without the collaboration of John Campbell), and Curtiss Clayton (editor). (Also aboard the shoot was Van Sant's former boyfriend, D-J Haanraadts, in the capacity of Gus's assistant.) Among those new to the director's squad would be

Danny Elfman (the composer), Pablo Ferro (title designer—who had frequently worked for director Stanley Kubrick), Vlasta Svoboda (art director), Carol Lavoie (set decorator), and Patricia Green (makeup artist). The latter group would bring additional slickness to Van Sant's project.

The thrust for the new picture had already been established by scenarist Buck Henry. He saw the murderous tale as "partly [Andy] Warhol's prediction that 'in the future everybody will be famous for fifteen minutes.'" In addition, Buck drew inspiration from a quote in the obituaries of President Richard Nixon that said, "Americans don't believe anything unless it's on TV." Henry also had in mind a particular imagery that would carry throughout the motion picture: "I always wanted to use ice as a kind of theme: it's cold, the town is cold and gray, Janice [Maretto] can skate on it. It also has to do . . . with Suzanne's personality. It's also like a mirror, and a television screen, all that stuff. It seemed to me to be an interesting way to begin and end the film." (And, of course, Suzanne Maretto's fate is indelibly tied into the ice theme, one that leaves her in frozen perfection looking out through a thin filmy protective cover—like television—at the world.)

For *To Die For* the filmmaker and his team relied on a new visual point of reference. According to production designer Missy Stewart: "Gus was particularly taken by the work of a woman photographer called Joyce Rabin who had done these amazing hand-colored photos that portrayed a certain sadness. I had lived in New England for a long time and I knew how those small communities worked, how hard it was to move out of your strata or even out of the town."

Stewart continued about Gus: "He likes little details that are often jokes or visual tricks. I think it comes from that basic instinct of his that there is always something funny even in a very sad scene. There are definitely a lot of those things in this film and in all the films I've worked with him on since *Drugstore Cowboy*."

In setting the movie's visual character, Stewart noted, "We decided to dress Suzanne in pastels. I think it was in Gus's mind that pastels could trick you because they are pretty—like Suzanne. It was much more subtle than simply dressing her like a femme fatale in red and black." As a result, the lead character of *To Die For* wore short, tight-fitting suits in pinks and other outfits—with eye shadow to match—that were in unrelentingly cheery shades (e.g., canary yellow, powder blue, foam green, lavender). Even her small dog, Walter, named after TV news journalist Walter Cronkite, is dressed on winter days with a pink coat and tiny hat.

This color scheme within *To Die For* was reinforced by costume designer Beatrix Aruna Pasztor: "The Stone family are like the American dream so we kept them in pastel colors. The Marettos are Italians. A little more flamboyant, a little bit more aware they know more about life so we put them in purples, blues, and blacks. You can see the contrast particularly well in the TV studio [talk show scenes]." Further on the subject, Pasztor said, "Gus looks at life through different lenses. I can put somebody in a louder print which still fits the character and to him it seems perfectly normal."

As had become his custom, Gus devoted approximately two weeks for pre-production rehearsals, with two hours of such in the morning and again in the afternoon. "Sometimes there's some going off the page and just doing the character without going from the script—just inventing things. Also during that time there's costuming and gearing up and getting ready. I'm totally in favor of keeping out of the way of the performance, because you can definitely jump in there and screw things up. I always let the actors sort of come up with a bunch of things, and maybe there's an editing process or advising process, but there's not a whole lot of monitoring the performance or the actor. Unless they really want it. Sometimes an actor will really want you to sort of explain exactly what to do, and you can do that."

As to plotting appropriate camera angles for each scene: "I'd often find out that you'd put the cameras say, in point A, and since you couldn't stand in point A, you'd have to stand over here. But during the shooting, you'd realize that point B was a better angle! Then, you'd move the camera over to point B. It was really frustrating. Then you'd realize that, OK, you have this side and that side and you're sort of starting to create a philosophy of that particular scene which you're drawing from sort of a history of all kinds of things: storyboards that you've done in the past, films you've seen. There's sort of a dictionary you've built up in your head by the time you've done three or four films so that you start to be able to think on the set pretty fast. And you can do pretty tricky things, even though you are just thinking them up on the set."

For Van Sant: "You are channeling everybody's energy—the cinematographer's, the actors', and trying to channel something to make the scene come alive." He also has said about the director's responsibilities on the set: "I think for me, it's mainly keeping everybody comfortable, very comfortable, where they can make a mistake and it's OK to try something new, or don't be afraid to goof because you can always roll again. And once everybody's really comfortable, the different styles and the different experiences kind of equal out, and then people can have fun together. I like to do just a couple takes if it's appropriate, depending on the actor." In essence, according to Van Sant, as a director "I have to be like a dentist. When you go to the dentist's office and he's really nervous, you're really nervous, so I try to have a good dentist's vibe: confident or friendly or reassuring. Even if I get concerned inside, I wait and see what comes around before I get panicky."

Of all the cast, the one requiring the most preparation was Nicole Kidman, since the entire plot line revolved around her and she is on camera nearly all the time. As part of her groundwork, Nicole had left Los Angeles with her husband Tom Cruise and registered at a plush hotel up the California coast. There she immersed herself in watching the boob tube nonstop for three days, relying on room service to provide food breaks. According to Kidman: "I found out that TV deadens you, and it's hypnotic. I would get involved in the talk shows, yelling back at the screen."

She and Van Sant also conferred about her characterization. By then Gus had formed his approach to the film's lead figure: "There are people like Nicole Kidman's character that I knew who wanted to escape from their environment and become something in the big world. What was special about their life living in a town where they knew everybody and people talked to them daily, was what the big city lacked." He also told her his theory about Suzanne Maretto: "This character is really scary because you don't like her and she's the lead. Some actors' natural reaction in that situation is to say, 'I know the audience is going to dislike me, but how do I get them to like me?' That's not the solution. You have to like to dislike the character." (While Kidman saw a naïveté in Suzanne's character, Van Sant had a more objective viewpoint, interpreting this figure as a savage woman with an extremely warped sense of how to get ahead.)

To help Nicole dig even further into her challenging characterization, the filmmaker had her wear extensive cosmetic touches, ranging from extended fingernails to heavy eyeliner and including a hairpiece. He reasoned, "She's in almost every scene, so she had to have this kind of interpretive openness. I also think the wig that she wears helps a lot. She said it did. Even a slight disguise can bring out something unpredictable in someone." (Much of the look of Nicole's on-camera character was derived by studying small-market TV broadcasters, Barbie dolls, and such plastic screen icons as Kim Novak.)

After the fact, Van Sant would say of working with Nicole: "You can always do good work even if you're only half into it, but she put in extra time." He added, "She was obsessed with perfection, which is definitely in contrast with my personality. I got to Hollywood and I see these people waking up at 5:30 to read 10 international papers, then have a power breakfast, read a script, have another breakfast, and then spend two hours on the phone to London. You have to be like that if you're going to be successful in Hollywood, and Nicole is that way. She'll be on top."

Years earlier on *Drugstore Cowboy* Van Sant established a good rapport with Matt Dillon and the two had remained in touch. Now it was easy for the duo to slip back into their working relationship. Said the moviemaker: "Matt always had a good take on his role because he grew up in a town like ours [in the film]. He seemed to slip into that mentality very easily. In many ways we were both reexamining our childhood in *To Die For*." An amused Van Sant also commented that Dillon told him that his "character and his [own] father probably told each other everything about their lives. Matt also said he thought the two of them would go shopping and buy matching jumpsuits." For his part, Dillon would assess of his *To Die For* experience: "Gus definitely seems more clear now about what he wants as a director, and that's something that happens with experience."

Working now with Joaquin, the third member of the Phoenix tribe, must have been a surreal experience for Van Sant—part déjà vu and part wonder at the range of talent within River's younger brother. Said Joaquin of the shoot: "A director can have a lot of power, but you never feel that way around Gus. I think any authority can be intimidating. But with Gus it feels like you're working with a friend on a student film, and that you can do no wrong."

In Canada, the first few days of lensing occurred at Jackson's Point at Lake Simcoe (about fifty miles north of Toronto) where the temperatures dropped below zero. Thereafter, besides shooting on Toronto sound stages, location work included time spent in Brampton, King City, and Port Hope—all within the province of Ontario and not far from Toronto. Since Canadian moviemaker David Cronenberg was Toronto-based, Gus convinced him to do a cameo in the picture—as the Mafia hit man who resolves the Marettos' thirst for justice. (It had been Cronenberg, the director of *Scanners*, *Dead Ringers*, and *The Fly*, who had helmed a 1991 screen version of *Naked Lunch*, based on the book by Gus's literary idol, William S. Burroughs Jr.)

Joaquin's sister Rain made a brief return in an unbilled cameo in *To Die For* as a patron at the Marettos' restaurant who watches Larry and his dopey rock band perform. Another Gus stalwart, Tom Peterson, made one of his customary brief appearances in a Van Sant picture—this time as the Portland appliance dealer seen in a TV commercial. As a lark, Joyce Maynard, the author of *To Die For*, played the small part of Suzanne's attorney. Van Sant himself filled in as an off-camera voice of a TV news interviewer. And then there was veteran movie/TV star George Segal. He provided an extended unbilled appearance as the smarmy celebrity newscaster who encounters Suzanne at a broadcasting convention. He is the randy man, one who is as drawn by her beauty as he is bemused by the airhead's blind ambition.

One person *not* on the set during filming was Kidman's celebrity husband Tom Cruise. It was not by the superstar's choice, but Nicole's. As Van Sant clarified, "She wouldn't do her best work with him in the room." Gus elaborated, "It's a pretty major disruption on the set, like having the Beatles there. It was accepted that he wasn't going to be there, though he came on the set instantly when we were done. A lot of it has to do with his stature. He's too large a presence. It would affect me, it would affect everybody."

By the time principal photography for *To Die For* ended, experienced scripter/actor Buck Henry had absorbed fresh pointers from Van Sant about the necessity of keeping a movie within a reasonable running time. Later, Henry said, "Actually, quite a few things of the [trio of high school] kids in the shooting script are missing [from the release print], due to exigencies of time during production. No, I never got much input from Gus before we actually sat down and started putting the production together. He did keep saying to me, 'It's too loaded up at the beginning; it takes too long to get started and we're not going to have enough time.' I should have listened to that more carefully. You know, I'd cut a couple of pages out, and he'd say, 'No, we need 30 pages out.' And I'd say, 'Oh, Lord,' and I'd cut out 10 pages, and finally I just didn't cut enough, which is why several big sections of the [final shooting] draft . . . are missing from the film, even though they were shot." As to whether this paring down of his writing generated on-set problems, Henry allowed that there had been "minor skirmishes, mostly having to do with trying to fill in a hole, or, for instance, putting something in like her [Suzanne's] last speech about television at the end of the murder, just things that I thought of to make it more interesting."

By June 1994, as *To Die For* was reaching its wrap, Gus's *Even Cowgirls Get the Blues* premiered in the United States, was lambasted, and quickly died. On one of the last days of shooting the new picture, the Toronto-based crew sat glued to a sound stage TV set. They were avidly watching the spectacle as alleged murderer O. J. Simpson drove wildly along a Los Angeles freeway in his white Ford Bronco as he led pursuing law enforcers on an amazing chase. This sensationalized event—and the circus of the televised Simpson homicide trial to come—would reinforce to all involved in the film how valid their movie about a TV-dominated society actually was.

▼

HAVING made this his fifth feature film, Gus Van Sant should have been used to the give-and-take of the arduous editing process, especially after the protracted reshaping of *Even Cowgirls Get the Blues*. Expectedly after the *Cowgirls* debacle he must have been concerned how his new releasing company—this time a major Hollywood studio—would react to his latest work. He was too experienced not to know that he was probably in for another long haul with Columbia Pictures executives once they viewed a rough cut of *To Die For*.

To begin with, right after *To Die For* had been purchased in 1993 and the scripter and director confirmed, there had been a management change at Columbia Pictures. The new regime was not as enthusiastic about this screen project as their predecessors had been and wanted to protect their investment. As a result, it became one of the pictures that Columbia's head honchos agreed to be part of a deal between *To Die For* executive producer Jonathan T. Taplis (Trans Pacific Films) and Rank Film Distributor. It gave the latter international rights for the release of *To Die For* in return for providing half of the budget for the under-$20-million picture.

Later, during production of *To Die For*, reportedly there were pointed disagreements between Gus and producer Laura Ziskin that continued into the postproduction phase. At one point Van Sant said, "Relations are extremely bad." He, however, declined to be more specific. On the other hand, Ziskin insisted, "I have no beef whatsoever with Gus." With so many production forces already negative toward Van Sant's new movie, he must have felt at times like the odd man out. It only got worse as *To Die For* moved into postproduction.

When Van Sant and editor Curtiss Clayton made their initial assemblage of footage, *To Die For* clocked in at about two hours and forty minutes, which was excessively long. In the give-and-take of excising and trimming scenes there was a lot of sequence reshuffling. What had started as a chronologically told story now became a pastiche of flashbacks, flash-forwards, and present-time continuity. Doing this could easily cause difficulties. As Henry analyzed after the fact,

"It's a terrible problem when you put together a complicated story, complicated in its structure. The danger of it is, if a piece falls out, everything else begins to clank. Sometimes there's very little one can do about it, except pray."

In the continuity reassembly, for example, the troubled high schoolers do not appear until nearly one third of the way into the movie and thus they lose weight as points of view in the narrative. Also, while Buck Henry had plotted the screenplay to have breaks between scenes of a character speaking to the camera—to avoid giving any one figure a stronger presence in the story—as the narrative was re-sorted several interview snippets with the Janice Maretto character (played by Illeana Douglas) were telescoped together. On its own, this gave more weight to Janice's position as a sharp observer to what was transpiring between her brother and Suzanne.

The patching together of the Janice sequences (and other cuts in footage/dialogue of her character) created another unintended inference—that this klutzy ice show skater was actually a lesbian. This led Henry to tell one reporter, "In fact, a critic made a complimentary note of the fact that I had turned her into a lesbian without having made a big deal of it—making good use of a gay theme, which, of course, was never intended on my part. But one takes whatever gifts one is given."

As the editing proceeded, a sequence was discarded in which a deer is hit accidentally by one of the characters driving out in the woods; it showed the spark of life leaving the animal's eyes (which tied in visually with the later death of the Larry Maretto character). In addition, a lengthy encounter between Suzanne and policemen after Larry is killed was dropped. Also excised were interchanges between the Stones and Marettos in the TV studio as they discuss how the tragedy has bound them together. In the film's restructuring, the first time the audience witnesses Suzanne and Jimmy Emmett (played by Joaquin Phoenix) having sex is at the Marettos' home while Larry is away. (A written scene of the pair's first coupling under the boardwalk at the ocean was never filmed.)

Most noticeably changed from Buck Henry's original script to the reassembled cut was the place within the narrative sequences when viewers actually see that Suzanne has been killed and that her body is now frozen beneath the surface of the icy pond. This change was indicative of the studio's feeling that the movie should be more of a romantic lark (!) than a dark comedy. This bothered Henry: "When that disappeared, I just thought it made it much more like a TV movie. I also thought it was really in Gus's idiom to do it my way, with the shots at the beginning of the various houses closed up for the funeral in this silent, spooky town. The image of the reporters running through the snow from this draft is still in the beginning of the film, but that's about it." (As it turned out, a few minutes into the film there is an inserted sequence at the pond where a woman's screams are heard. It is not until near the picture's finale that the contested shot of Suzanne's corpse frozen in the water is flashed on-screen. Also cut in the final release continuity was footage of the police discovering

Suzanne's body and then destroying clues that might lead others back to the Marettos who had contracted their daughter-in-law's murder.)

As the weeks dragged on, the Columbia executives were still convinced that the overall film was far too bleak. They resorted to more test screenings. One who opposed this decision making by a lay jury was Buck Henry: "I don't think storytelling is helped a lot by test screenings, in most cases. Here, it was clear that we were wading in some kind of murky water that I never understood. I was only at a few of these screenings, but the audiences, by and large, seemed to really like the film. They laughed in the right places, bought it in the right places, and then, in the end, said terrible things about it."

Finally when all the tinkering with *To Die For* was nearly done, Danny Elfman's music score was fine-tuned to fit the new running order of scenes. Part of the final score also included sound track performances by Billy Preston ("Nothing From Nothing"), Strawpeople ("Wings of Desire"), Lydia Rhodes ("Live It Cool"), and Donovan ("Season of the Witch"). There was also a main title sequence created by title designer Pablo Ferro. It tied in visually with what Suzanne's character says about television: "If you get too close to the screen, all you can see is a bunch of little dots. You don't see the picture until your stand back. But when you do, everything comes into focus."

Now *To Die For* was ready to meet the public. Happily it could retain its original pun-filled title. (A British-made gay film, *To Die For*, directed by Peter Mackenzie Litten and starring Thomas Arklie and Ian Williams, had played at the 1994 Los Angeles Gay and Lesbian Film Festival. That movie import was persuaded to change its American release title to *Heaven's a Drag* so as not to confuse audiences regarding Van Sant's film.) Gus's new offering was set to debut at the May 1995 Cannes Film Festival, even though Columbia Pictures was still unsure how and when to distribute the much worked-over product.

At the Cannes hullabaloo, *To Die For* was shown out of competition on May 19, 1995, at a midnight screening. Its play date revealed how little faith many parties had in the completed product. Gus Van Sant and Nicole Kidman were among those in attendance that evening to promote their film. *Variety*'s Todd McCarthy judged the results "[a] quirky comic study" that "delivers continuous pinpricks of irreverent humor and subversive cultural commentary. Witty, energetic and splendidly acted, this handcrafted curio will find support among the specialized, adventurous-minded audiences who have patronized the director's work in the past." But, cautioned McCarthy, it "doesn't look to break out to a wider public." Fortuitously, other industry sources at the showing liked the film even better and the movie quickly generated positive word-of-mouth.

With the favorable buzz created at Cannes the picture's release pattern was shifted. Columbia Pictures no longer intended to open it in only a few small markets before shunting it to home video. The movie's release was pushed from June 2 to July 21 (and then to late September 1995). At the Seattle International Film Festival that May, Nicole won the Golden Space Needle Award for Best Actress. (Gus was runner-up at the festival in the Best

Director category.) The movie earned a favorable response from audiences at the Toronto International Film Festival on September 8, 1995, and also did well at the Telluride Festival.

▼

IN its final edit version, *To Die For* opens with headlines of Suzanne Stone involved in the high-profile case surrounding the murder of her husband. She is a glamorous weather forecaster on local cable TV in Little Hope, New Hampshire. As her relatives, in-laws, and others who are caught up in the killing are interviewed on TV, Suzanne relates her story to an unseen listener.

Pretty, pampered, and empty-headed Suzanne, with a junior college degree in electronic communications, has always dreamed of being a celebrated TV newscaster like Barbara Walters or Katie Couric. She is sidetracked from her career goal when she becomes involved with hunky Larry Maretto, whose parents own the local Italian restaurant. Larry is warned about predatory Suzanne by his sister Janice, an Ice Capades hopeful. He, however, is blinded by love and weds the beauty. On their Florida honeymoon, Suzanne sends her husband off fishing, while she plays up to a horny network TV newscaster.

Refusing to yield to pressure from her husband or in-laws to become a housewife, Suzanne strong-arms her way into a minor post at local cable station WWEN. She pressures station manager Ed Grant into having her present the evening weather show. Later, Grant reluctantly allows the unrelenting Suzanne to launch a cable program (*Teens Speak Out*). In the process of interviewing high schoolers for the show, she makes allies of a trio of student losers: Jimmy Emmett, Lydia Mertz, and Russell Hines, who fall under her spell, each for different reasons.

When Larry pressures Suzanne to abandon her media "career" to become a mother and to help out at their restaurant, she panics. Desperate for a way out, she seduces druggie Jimmy and lies to him that her spouse is abusing her. Under her constant prompting, Jimmy and Russell borrow a gun owned by Lydia's parent, and steal into Larry's home and shoot him on his and Suzanne's first wedding anniversary. Just as the heinous deed is carried out, Larry has been watching Suzanne deliver the weather report on TV.

It is not long before the local police use Suzanne's cable station footage on *Teens Speak Out* to track down the student conspirators. Confessions are easily drawn from the dazed youths. Playing up to the huge media attention she is attracting, Suzanne insists she is innocent and is released on bail. She lies to the pursuing press that Larry had been a drug addict and that it was Jimmy and Russell who supplied him. (Eventually both youths are sentenced to long prison terms.)

Having completed her account, Suzanne removes the VHS tape from the camcorder and rushes to meet a man who claims to be a Hollywood producer interested in filming her notorious story. It proves that he is a Mafia hit man hired by Larry's parents. Suzanne is killed at the local pond and her corpse dropped into the icy water. While Lydia prepares to fly off to be interviewed on yet another talk show, Janice Maretto cheerfully skates over the lake and Suzanne's submerged body.

▼

THE R-rated *To Die For* bowed in New York on Tuesday, September 25, 1995, with a premiere at the Sony Village Cinema on Third Avenue at Eleventh Street. It was a fund-raiser to benefit the National Gay and Lesbian Task Force. Said Van Sant: "The film is not a gay story, but I've supported the task force and its work in Washington and in politics, and they need money." In Portland the movie debuted on October 5, 1995, at the Broadway Metroplex as a benefit for ArtAIDS. For $25 one got admitted to the screening and to hear the live introduction provided by Gus; for $50 the ticket holder gained admission to the movie as well as to the reception being held in the lobby of the Portland Center for the Performing Arts.

Janet Maslin (*New York Times*) cheered, "There are times when we get exactly the satire we deserve, and this is one of them. *To Die For*, an irresistible black comedy and a wicked delight, takes aim at tabloid ethics and hits a solid bull's-eye, with Ms. Kidman's teasingly beautiful as Suzanne the most alluring of media-mad monsters. The target is broad, but Gus Van Sant's film is too expertly sharp and funny for that to matter; instead, it shows off this director's slyness better than any of his work since *Drugstore Cowboy*. Devilish wit sets *To Die For* worlds apart from the unwatchable fiasco that was his last effort, *Even Cowgirls Get the Blues*." Maslin concluded, "Both Mr. Van Sant and Ms. Kidman have reinvented themselves miraculously for this occasion, which brings out the best in all concerned."

Kenneth Turan of the *Los Angeles Times* championed, "A smart black comedy that skewers America's fatal fascination with television and celebrity, it employs an unerring nasty touch to parody our omnipresent culture of fame." He observed, "Working with a tight, classically structured script is definitely a departure for Van Sant, known for loopy, eccentric films like *My Own Private Idaho*. But the director was unexpectedly charged by the experience, adding his trademark absurdist sensibility to the mix as well as an empathy for inarticulate, inchoate teenagers that turns out to give this film a good deal of its impact."

Newsweek's David Ansen endorsed the movie: "It's a surprising movie from Van Sant. . . . Gone is the wiggy lyricism of *Drugstore Cowboy* and *My Own Private Idaho*, replaced by a remarkably disciplined black-comic edge. The imprint of [Buck] Henry's sardonic intelligence is obvious, but you can feel Van Sant's touch most strongly in the spooky pathos of [Joaquin] Phoenix's odd and affecting performance (he's literally blurry with lust) and newcomer [Alison] Folland's poignant portrayal of the abused Lydia." Ansen decided, "'In another director's hands, *To Die For*'s satirical venom could have turned sour and obvious."

Roger Ebert (*Chicago Sun-Times*) was impressed by Gus's new release. "All this could be done broadly as farce, but director Gus Van Sant uses Henry's wicked screenplay as a blueprint for quieter, crueler comedy. . . . *To Die For* is the kind of movie that's merciless with its characters, and Kidman is superb at making Suzanne into someone who is not only stupid, vain and egomaniacal . . . but also vulnerably human."

In contrast, a displeased Amy Taubin (*Village Voice*) argued, "But for all *To Die For*'s cutely intimate asides to the camera and slightly elliptical editing, its parody of a TV-obsessed culture is tired, and its slagging off on Hollywood's favorite target—the ambitious woman—is misogyny at its lowest. . . ." Taubin continued, "Van Sant revels in making Smart—here named Suzanne Stone and played by Nicole Kidman . . . [a] grotesquely camped figures. He hates her and he envies her small seductive power. (The barely hidden message of the film: A boy who allows a woman to get her mouth on his c**k will wind up doing life plus 30 years.) Kidman plays right into Van Sant's game by telegraphing her contempt for Suzanne at every opportunity. Didn't anyone ever teach her that the first rule of acting is to find compassion for your character?" On a similar tact, David Denby (*New York*) noted, "Henry and Van Sant have hollowed Suzanne out, as if an ambitious, driven woman needed to be exposed as a jerk. Vaguely feminist emotions stir in my breast; would they have done this to Matt Dillon if he were the ambitious one?"

According to a disappointed Mick LaSalle (*San Francisco Chronicle*): "The murder plot is a cheap turn that says absolutely nothing about the unique nature of Suzanne's ambition. She could be any kind of sociopath and plot to kill somebody. When *To Die For* loses Suzanne's media obsession as its point of focus, it ceases to be a pointed satire and becomes just another fairly good black comedy about a deluded person." Barbara Shulgasser (*San Francisco Examiner*) concurred. She thought Van Sant "has directed a movie that is half snappy, sardonic and incisive and half slow-moving, goofy and dense."

Elizabeth Pincus judged for *Harper's Bazaar*: "[T]he film is cold, predictable, and as void of subtlety as the name of the fictional New England town in which it's set, Little Hope. Even Suzanne's outrageous getups seem a bit forced—another ruffle or flounce and she'd be mistaken more for a pop-art sofa than for Deborah Norville, presumably her role model of choice." Pincus concluded, "*To Die For* is salvaged from artifice by Kidman's dazzling performance, a wickedly deft comic turn."

Finally, Jack Matthews (*Newsday*), who thought the film to be "a wicked and very, very funny satire about the effects of television on our culture," could not resist highlighting, "Van Sant was clearly a gun for hire on this project. It's a major-studio movie, and after last year's disastrous *Even Cowgirls Get the Blues*, he needed to prove that he could be trusted with an investor's money." Matthews suggested, "Van Sant's faithful, who prize his scruffy looks at the victims of society's underbelly, may be disappointed by the slickness and commercial narrative of *To Die For*." The *Newsday* critic decided "the film really belongs to Buck Henry, an elfin wit."

As the movie awards for 1995 releases were announced, *To Die For* had additional victories beyond the Seattle festival. Nicole Kidman won Best Actress Awards from the Boston Society of Film Critics, the Broadcast Film Critics Association, the Golden Globes, and the Southeastern Film Critics Association. (She was nominated as Most Desirable Female on the 1996 MTV Movie Awards.) When the movie opened in England that October, its 106-minute running time had been shorn to 103 minutes apparently to appease the British censors. The picture was well received and Kidman won the London Film Critics Circle Award as Actress of the Year. Gus received no awards for his work on *To Die For*.

In its domestic release, *To Die For* grossed $21.2 million. (Van Sant, in retrospect, thought it could have done better in the marketplace but that the studio had pushed it to fit within one of their standard release campaigns—romantic comedy. "They didn't have dark comedies. They didn't have that side to their marketing concept.")

▼

IN many ways *To Die For* is a continuation rather than a departure from Gus Van Sant's past screen work. Once again he showcases morally reprehensible characters but maintains his standard objectivity in presenting them. In fact, when dealing with the irresponsible teenagers—and especially in his sensitive presentation of Joaquin Phoenix's dazed killer character—Gus offers them in a sympathetic light.

As in his prior films, color motifs and sounds (wonderfully upgraded by the professionalism of Danny Elfman's deft score) create thematic contrasts (and ties) between the characters and plot points. It is a case of shades and tones stirring emotions in viewers that are contrary to what the scene and characters at hand indicate. For example, the cotton candy colors of Suzanne's outfits suggest a childishly happy person, but beneath lurks a lethal sociopath. When something tragic has happened on-screen to a character (e.g., Larry's death), the score sardonically rises up with "America, the Beautiful." At Larry's funeral, Suzanne, who feels no remorse over engineering her husband's death, pretends to be a martyr and turns on a recording of "All By Myself," much to the amazement of the attendees.

Relying on Buck Henry's biting script, Van Sant smartly uses the television medium in its many aspects to unfold his tale of a deranged woman unrealistically hoping for a career as a media journalist. In her crazy obsession with TV and instant fame, she reasons, "You are not anybody in America unless you're on TV. On TV is where we learn about who we really are. Because what's the point of doing anything worthwhile if nobody's watching. If people are watching it makes you a better person."

To draw the viewer into her vortex and present the amazing story line Van Sant utilizes a variety of visual presentation formats for his faux documentary: talk shows, news interviews on the street, and even Suzanne's lengthy camcorder chronicle. Cutting back and forth—with flashbacks and flash-forwards—the unreality of the characters' lives are revealed through "unreal" television where so often the gullible public accepts live footage as valid, no matter the source.

Another contrast between the perceived and the actual is the seeming homogeny of the suburban New Hampshire town (ironically named Little Hope) where the chronicle unfurls. Suzanne is a microcosm of the bigotry and class distinction that festers within this apparently benign New England village. In her monologues she casts aspersions, among others, against Jews and Asian-Americans, while her father—on national TV—suggests that because his in-laws are Italians they must be tied to the Mafia. But this is not just an upper-middle-class problem, for trailer trash teenager Russell Hines has foul words to say about Italians, overweight people, etc.

In *To Die For*, Van Sant also indulges his passion for close-ups of objects as well as for splintering the vista into abstract objects, such as when a single image of Lydia being interviewed splits into two and keeps subdividing until the screen is filled with postage-size shots of the sloppy young woman.

This movie also embellishes a constant in Van Sant films, that of unsatisfactory love relationships—sexually and emotionally. Larry adores Suzanne but is too much in love to see how poorly she regards him. Eventually he discovers how little their love life or potential parenthood means to her. In Suzanne's twisted world, the only man she cares for is her dad (as she whispers in his disbelieving ear on her wedding day). Even her sexual coupling with the besotted Jimmy Emmett is a mechanical thing to gain her murderous goal. As for the boy—who always addresses his beloved as "Mrs. Maretto"—he seems more satisfied dreaming about her or masturbating to images of her on television.

Once again in a Gus screen work, none of the characters has a fulfilling family life. Suzanne's parents dote on her while nearly totally ignoring her older sister. Mrs. Stone remains subservient to her spouse and oblivious to the flaws in her damaged younger girl. Similarly, the Marettos are another patriarchal group, with a submissive wife, an opinionated father, and two not so bright offspring. Susceptible Larry is way over his head in life—whether in helping to run the family restaurant or dealing with overly ambitious Suzanne. His ice-skater sister, Janice, has the intuition to see through Suzanne's sham but not the depth of character to follow through on her beliefs and stop the wedding. As for the three teenagers, each one has a more pathetic home life than the next, each having had enough unsavory experiences to delight any TV talk show host for many episodes to come.

Much discussed at the time, but now part of pop culture history, is the fact of how timely the release of *To Die For* was, coming on the heels of the Tonya Harding case and the O. J. Simpson murder trial—both of which demonstrated the amazing power of the media and the frequent lunacy of media fame. Then, too, there is a connection of sorts between *To Die For* and Oliver Stone's 1994 movie, *Natural Born Killers,* based on a Quentin Tarantino story. Stone's earlier-released picture, starring Woody Harrelson, Juliette Lewis, and Robert Downey Jr., also dealt with the infamous becoming famous and the penchant of obsessed journalists to mold the new American "heroes." *Natural Born Killers* is a much more violent and heavy-handed picture. Van Sant (and Buck Henry) must have noted carefully its pitfalls as they shaped their own scathing indictment of TV as a starmaker and omnipotent source of all that is "real" and "true." Meanwhile, other analyzers of *To Die For* have found thematic associations between it and such movies as *Double Indemnity* (1944), *Pretty Poison* (1968), *Heathers* (1989), *The Positively True Adventures of the Alleged Texas Cheerleader-Murdering Mom* (1993—TV movie), and *The Last Seduction* (1994—cable movie).

With the generally favorable critical response and decent, if not huge, box-office returns on *To Die For*, Gus Van Sant could rightfully boast, "Actually, my stock is going up. My phone rings a lot now."

IN THE *PINK*

Making a film in a studio environment tended to be more along corporate procedures. It's kind of like having an interesting collective mind in charge where nobody shares responsibility. The system is in place and you have to campaign within the entity and that way you make the corporation feel good. . . . Things can get out of control easily if the system is challenged. Then the corporation is set up to deal with that assignment, using more authority to take care of the problem. The setup is made so that you not have one guy control the money. Otherwise, strange things can happen. People can make dangerous decisions.

We independent filmmakers revel in our status as mavericks. But the studio system is good. It has a white-collar bureaucracy. I grew up in a white-collar town, Darien, Connecticut, a suburb of New York. So, I was comfortable with that atmosphere.

Gus Van Sant, 1995

WHEN GUS VAN SANT attended the Cannes Film Festival in May 1995, it was not merely to talk about *To Die For*, being shown out of competition at the French-hosted conclave. He had other projects to promote. One was *Binky*, about a mathematician who drops out as a university professor to find the son he was disconnected from years ago. The potential film would be based on Van Sant's own script. Also Gus was at Cannes to support *Kids*, Larry Clark's controversial feature film debut for which Van Sant had served as executive producer.

As Van Sant had promised Clark back in 1993, he had done his best to help the photographer-turned-moviemaker find backing for the potential picture. The financing had eventually come through Cary Woods, one of Van Sant's former agents. Meanwhile, while photographing teenagers in New York's Washington Square Park, Clark had met nineteen-year-old Harmony Korine. They began talking and before long Clark convinced the young man to draft a script about his friends and their contemporary world. What Korine conceived was a nihilistic narrative of New York young teens caught in a negative spiral of sex, drugs, and AIDS. Clark was impressed with the screenplay and chose to film it. Ironically, it was just the type of tale Gus himself might have made in his earlier days—like *Drugstore Cowboy*, which had been inspired by Clark's photo book of junkies.

The graphic *Kids* was photographed by Van Sant veteran Eric Alan Edwards. It featured a cast of unknowns (including a young Chloë Sevigny) as they spend twenty-four hours on a hot Manhattan day/night and, during which, one of the teen girls discovers she is HIV positive. When completed, the $1.5 million *Kids* was shopped around to distributors and gained the interest of Harvey Weinstein, head of Miramax Films. He acquired the movie because of its highly controversial nature, which made the industry wonder how this would affect Miramax's relationship to the squeaky-clean, family-product-oriented Walt Disney Studio, which had acquired Miramax. (Eventually Miramax chose to take the film back from Disney and to issue the gritty drama through its own newly formed subsidiary.)

Reviewing the much-hyped feature at Cannes, *Daily Variety*'s Todd Mc-Carthy found it "disturbing precisely because it is so believable" but wondered as to "the extent to which the picture seems voyeuristic and exploitative of its young subjects." The critic enthused that for Larry Clark, then in his fifties, to have "understood the characters so well and won the trust of his young cast to such an extent is most impressive."

Back in the United States Van Sant put forth his best effort to build interest in *Kids*. Wherever he went, he told the press that *Kids* would "blow the lid off filmmaking, [it is] the film that we have been waiting for." This hype proved greater than the reality for many critics. For example, when Kenneth Turan (*Los Angeles Times*) evaluated *Kids*, he complained, "Authenticity is no guarantee of interest, and once the initial jolt of observing kids who look barely out of diapers talking dirty and having sex wears off, what remains is more tedious than shocking or even involving." Nevertheless, *Kids* went on to gross $15 million in worldwide distribution. A few years later, when asked if he still thought *Kids* was the best film ever made, Gus responded, "I think what I meant by that was that it was the most inspiring to me. It was new, but it learned from past films. It was an amalgamation of all that previous knowledge."

More important for Gus, the *Kids* experience brought him into contact with young Harmony Korine whom he came to admire as a new voice in American independent filmmaking and as an individual. Van Sant also learned that perhaps his talents did not lie in being a producer, even in his basically no-hands-on status on *Kids*. He reasoned, "I don't have the sort of energy a producer has. I'm not on the phone all day long. Usually, I'm writing. I understand the business, but I'm not the sort of guy who goes out and leaves no stone unturned."

As 1995 progressed, Van Sant became discouraged about the fate of his self-written *Binky*. A few years later, one of the reasons for its nonsale would become evident. Said Van Sant: "I had this small one called *Binky* that I had been shopping around but the money fell through. I didn't want to show the company the script and I didn't want them to have anything to do with it. I just wanted them to give me the money and then I would give them the film when it was done, so the bargain was difficult." Indeed!

For a time it seemed Gus might take over the directing chores on a $35 million actioner entitled *Speed Racer*. If so, he would replace Julien Temple who had exited the project. Joel Silver was one of the producers, Johnny Depp was expected to star, and the shoot was projected to launch in October 1995 on location in Australia and Japan. Because of the good word-of-mouth on the upcoming release of *To Die For*, Van Sant had been considered for the project. The film eventually did not get off the ground. Nor did Van Sant's *Cowboy Nemo*, his planned adaptation of a Jack Gibson story.

Meanwhile, Gus thought again of doing a movie on Harvey Milk, still unable to let go of his past efforts on Oliver Stone's to-be-produced *The Mayor of Castro Street*. But Van Sant's Milk biopic concept went nowhere. Then, in mid-1996, he became involved with Stone's *Castro Street* once again. Said producer Janet Yang, still part of the Oliver Stone-Storyline Entertainment (Craig Zadan and Neil Meron) team on the vehicle, "I believe it will be made, and it's time. The times have changed, and what was shocking and daring in the script back then [several years earlier] is not an issue anymore. Gus is contemporizing the project, because we want something a bit edgy." Van Sant turned in a script to the producers, but to date that vehicle has not become a reality.

As Gus looked about for a new screen property to make happen, he had an opportunity to reassess his career objectives. For one, he still intended to remain based in Portland and not relocate to Hollywood. He reasoned, "You sort of become wrapped into some viewpoints if you recreate within the business. It takes over your life. I'm not interested in Hollywood or in sales. Staying in Portland keeps me out of the hunches down there—hunches on what will be a good idea, good sell, good film. The bad side is that I have to fly there a lot. But when I do fly there, I tend to get things done in person."

Regarding his role as a filmmaker: "Pretty much my attitude as an independent filmmaker and as even a mainstream filmmaker is that I look for something new and unusual. Independent filmmaking to me means that you're trying to make something that isn't going to look like *Batman*. . . . As an independent, I've always looked to things that Hollywood wouldn't make because their stories didn't conform to the status quo or conventional politics or ideology or religion. A lot of stories caught my interest in particular because they were labeled 'wrong.' I don't mean wrong in a literal context, but wrong in that the challenge to make them work was great. To make a script that can obviously be a great movie isn't the challenge I'm looking for. I see no reason to make that movie. . . . To me, a group of people making a picture independently means without restrictions, meaning creative restrictions. That's my definition of an independent movie. The true independents also sell the film themselves."

Asked whether he kept up-to-date on alternative lifestyle movies, Gus answered, "As for gay films, I just don't pay that close attention. But if somebody says, 'This film is really great,' then I'll go see it. I do that for gay films just as I would for regular market films."

Realizing he was frequently spreading himself too thin professionally, Van Sant also had concluded that, if he wanted to get more movies made and released into the marketplace, he might well have to abandon his practice of being so heavily involved in the editing process. He now accepted that his time-intensive approach to that step of postproduction often slowed down the completion of his pictures.

▼

IN the fall of 1995 Van Sant was contentedly entrenched in Portland where he emphasized, "I don't get infected by certain modes of Hollywood thought. It's a high-stress business, not unlike banking, where senior people tend to disappear only to get replaced by 30-year-olds. I certainly don't want that to happen to me." Through his projects, he was extending a helpful hand to young (would-be) moviemakers as previously he had been assisted by an earlier generation of Oregon filmmakers. He was also considering setting up a new postsound facility for the Northwest region. As to his visibility in his adopted hometown: "I'm not a movie star, so people don't really recognize me. I think that what they do like, though, is that there is this guy from their community that's doing well. Maybe not necessarily the films themselves. My films are pretty odd."

By now, as he informed Dale Reynolds for an interview in the gay publication *Au Courant*, Gus and his unnamed (for the article) current boyfriend (presumably Scott Patrick Green) "don't live together any longer. That makes it easier." Van Sant allowed that he still found time to jam in the basement of his house with his short-lived music group the Dots (which included Van Sant, Green, and Michael Parker) and such other musicians as Thomas Lauderdale of the Portland cocktail band, Pink Martini. (There would be a recording of Gus and Lauderdale doing "Moon River" on the 1996 benefit CD entitled *Fabric of Life*.)

Predominantly a shy man, Van Sant's manner of socializing derived from his unusual point of view. For example, he owned up to *US* magazine: "I'm addicted to something that teeters on embarrassment. I often find myself surrounded by people who embarrass me. It's probably how I make up for being quiet. I have good friends who always get thrown out of restaurants. They're yelling and screaming and throwing chairs, and I'm just sitting there. I guess

I'm interested in sociopathic people, in life and in my movies. I'm probably one of them, you know?"

On the subject of offbeat behavior, Gus told about a recent trip to Manhattan: "I don't even know if it's neurotic or just true, but some friends told me all the hotel rooms in New York have cameras in them, because they saw a [TV] show where Donald Trump found a camera in his hotel-room lamp. So I was looking for this camera. That's kind of neurotic. Never found it. I figured it was behind the mirror."

▼

DURING 1996, Gus had an opportunity to work with another of his counterculture idols, Allen Ginsberg. The famed Beat poet and peace activist, who turned seventy that year, had long been prolific in the recording field. Ginsberg had a new album coming out in the fall of 1996 from Mouth Almighty Records and it was decided to release a video short of him reading his poem "Ballad of the Skeletons" (from the upcoming disc). The selection dealt with the apathetic nature of contemporary society. Said Ginsberg, "Everybody's walking dead—a lot of these right-wing people are even more dead." *Ballad* was performed to the accompaniment of the music of Paul McCartney, Lenny Kaye, and Philip Glass. Gus directed the video, which was filmed by Eric Alan Edwards. The four-minute short was shown at the Seattle International Film Festival in mid-1997 and won the Golden Space Needle for Best Short Subject. (By this point in time, Ginsberg had passed away.) In 1998 *Ballad of the Skeletons* won an honorable mention for Gus at the Oberhausen International Short Film Festival in Germany.

▼

ALSO in the mid-1990s Gus briefly turned screen actor again. He agreed to play a small role in *Roughcut*, written, produced, and directed by Simon Babbs. (Babbs had worked locations on *Even Cowgirls Get the Blues*.) The movie, shot on 16mm film, was made in and around Eugene, Oregon, and featured an eclectic cast: Ken Babbs, Ken Kesey, Dr. Timothy Leary, Pedro Shanahan, Jason Crum, and Gus Van Sant. In the plotline Gus plays a scientist known as Herr Doktur. As Simons Babbs told this author, "The only problem I had with Gus was trying to get him to say his lines properly. It needed to be 'I don't care, inject more Psycho Subliminal Anilzine!' Gus kept saying, 'I don't care, inject more Psycho Subliminal Analzine!'" The scene with Gus was shot in Ken Kesey's Bus Barn Studio that he put together years ago for the filming of *The Further Inquiry. Roughcut* was shown in local Oregon theaters but never made it to television. It is available on VHS.

▼

IN the early 1990s Gus was not only writing screenplays, he was also venturing into novel writing. One such effort was entitled *How to Make Good Movies*. Conceived as a pseudo-autobiography it was, as Van Sant described it in May 1994, "the distorted account of a filmmaker. . . . I've been writing it for a year on weekends. It's like a hobby, but the more I write it, the more I want it to be really good. Last winter, I was ready to go to press and then I realized I should really work on it some more. It's at that stage where I want it to be really great, not just dashed off like a journal."

An excerpt of the book appeared in *Projections III* (1994), an annual anthology series dealing with movies and filmmakers. Entitled *The Hollywood Way*, the piece was mostly a thinly veiled account of Van Sant's misadventures with moviemaker Oliver Stone during the abortive *The Mayor of Castro Street* project from 1992 to 1993. Knowing the facts behind the narrative makes the sarcastic text more fun to read, and it clearly shows that Gus was still smarting from that episode.

By 1995, Van Sant decided that the now-completed *How to Make Good Movies* just did not pass muster. (Discarding that full manuscript, which he had not submitted for consideration, led him to observe of book writing, "With a book, it's a lot easier to get stuff done and throw it away. . . . Once you make a movie, you don't throw it away.") Invigorated by his book writing, he switched to a new literary project, one he described as "a novel about an infomercial producer who meets a pair of dimensional travelers posing as film students." (It was an expansion of a series of letters he had written to a friend in Montreal to amuse the recipient.) The new manuscript concerned itself with teen stardom, addiction, death, reincarnation, and spirits moving between different dimensions of "life." When it was completed Gus showed it to his talent agent John Burnham at the William Morris Agency. Burnham in turn passed it on to Owen Laster, the head of the firm's literary department.

Before long, a six-figure deal had been negotiated with Nan A. Talese Books (an imprint of Doubleday & Co.) to publish Van Sant's book—called *Pink*. Gus was jubilant about the impressive sale: "I don't think I've ever been that happy before. I don't think I've ever had that experience before—they call it walking on air. I really felt like I was walking on air for about a week. I don't think movies can have that."

In the fall of 1997 three American filmmakers had books in the stores: Tim Burton (*The Melancholy Death of Oyster Boy & Other Stories*), Oliver Stone (*A Child's Night Dream*), and Gus Van Sant (*Pink*). Each of the books received a good deal of publicity because its author was venturing away from filmmaking into the world of literature.

In typical Van Sant idiosyncrasy, *Pink* is filled with clashing typefaces, explanatory footnotes, random doodles, line drawings, and page-flipping cartoon animations. Its unconventional format and style, a trademark of Gus's self-written screenplays, only enhanced the thematic focus in *Pink* on alternative universes.

Van Sant offered that his literary influences for *Pink* included James Joyce, Kenneth Patchen, William S. Burroughs Jr., Joseph Heller, Jack Kerouac, and Samuel Beckett. In addition, Gus was inspired by the style of George Roy Hill's 1972 movie, *Slaughterhouse-Five*. Van Sant also acknowledged what had prompted a great deal of the tome—his meaningful friendship with River Phoenix and the director's grieving over the actor's death in the fall of 1993. Said Van Sant: "It's true that the inspiration for a lot of the book—and its sentimentality—stems from River dying, but things kind of dissipate from there." Gus also noted that the character of Jack in *Pink* was based on an actual film major Gus had met named Jack. The latter's resemblance to Phoenix had astonished the director: "When I met him that's all I could think about. He was talking to me, but I didn't really hear what he was saying. I said, 'You look just like River Phoenix.' And he said, 'I know,' and he carried on talking, because he just did. There was nothing he could do about it."

Another time, Gus expanded further on the River Phoenix connections to *Pink*: "This book is very much influenced by River. It's a documentary of my life and existence through him. The reason I don't like to say that is that a lot of the stuff, you could say, is a reaction to his death. The impetus of me writing is him dying. But the book is not about that, so I don't like to bring that up." He also explained, "I don't feel like masking that sort of inspiration for the book. The book could be about anyone dying. It's really about a character that's grieving. It's not necessarily even grieving, it's just that you can't figure out what happens, you know, where you go when you die. So everything is centered around that investigation. It's hard to talk about the book in terms of real people, because then it becomes this other thing, like, 'Who are the real people?' and 'What happened to the real people.' And that's not really the intention of the book. It's more about what happens to people as opposed to what happens to *those* people."

In *Pink*, Spunky Davis, who lives in Sasquatch, Oregon, is middle-aged and gay. He makes infomercials and is working on a screenplay that he hopes will jump-start his Hollywood career. He is also mourning the loss of his close friend and favorite infomercial star, teenage idol and drug burnout Felix Arroyo. (Arroyo means a small, steep-sided watercourse or short-lived river, which has its obvious implications within the plot of Gus's novel.) One day two young slackers and would-be filmmakers, Jack and Matt, come into his life. These strangers seems peculiarly familiar to Spunky—not just because Jack has an amazing resemblance to the late Arroyo and Matt to the dead rock legend Blake. It develops that the duo are messengers from a dimension beyond time known as "Pink." Often they disappear for days at a time. Later, they ask the perplexed Spunky to join them on their amazing trek of transcendence and recovery.

Within *Pink* the title color has other associations. As the Matt character states, "Pink is a color that marks the highest degree of awesomeness or perfection." It is also the shade film turns when it fades and decays, which, according to Van Sant, is then "destroyed cruelly, like drowning a little puppy after you are tired of playing with it." Besides Arroyo's resemblance to River Phoenix in the book, Spunky is of course a variant of Van Sant himself who had made TV commercials in New York in the early 1980s and then, a few years later, hung out with indie filmmakers in Portland. Other characters in *Pink* are also drawn to some degree from Gus's own life. They include Blackie and Blake (rock stars Courtney Love and Kurt Cobain), J.D. (Van Sant friend D-J Haanraadts), Dewey Cyrus (cinematographer Eric Alan Edwards), Buzz Post (Claymation filmmaker Will Vinton), and Todd Truelove (German moviemaker Werner Herzog).

But it was not Gus's intent to make *Pink* a roman à clef. Instead, he wished to reshape events into truths that have more constructive value than, perhaps, the painful actual facts (i.e., the death of River Phoenix). Above all, it allowed Van Sant to vent his frustration and anger at the media who had for so long insinuated that the supposed substance abuse by some of the cast on the *My Own Private Idaho* project was somehow Gus's fault and that the alleged excessive drug taking had led Phoenix on a death spiral.

When published, *Pink* received mixed reviews: Ray Olson (*Booklist*) reported: "Imagine a William S. Burroughs extravaganza without the grotesque sex, the drug taking, and the wild-and-woolly humor. That is *Pink*. How odd." *Kirkus Reviews* was *not* impressed with "this self-indulgent fantasy." The review continued, "Van Sant cheapens his offbeat effort to grieve his young friends (and imagine their lives on some other, happier plane of existence) with a number of gimmicky effects—amateurish line drawings, different typefaces, footnotes, and a cartoon flipbook in the corner of the pages. The grossest conceit is Van Sant's linkage of his own passing troubles and anxieties with filmmaking and the deaths of two young superstars—his rant against the tabloids seems particularly lame given his own exploitative tendencies here."

Robert L. Pela (*The Advocate*) decided, "While Van Sant has made splendid movies—among them the very gay *My Own Private Idaho*—his first contribution to literature is awkward and artless." According to the "Bookworld" column of the *Washington Post*: "It's clear that Van Sant was hoping to tackle the larger issues of life and death in this novel, but he's wholly convincing only when he's writing about film and the film industry. . . . The best few pages in this book are actually written as a description of a film about rock star Blake's experience in detox. . . . It's a powerful scene, stuck in without warning or explanation toward the end of the book. It's as if someone randomly slipped a few pages from an excellent screenplay into a decent but less-than-excellent novel. Van Sant might want to stick this scene into a film sometime."

Jeff Baker reviewed *Pink* for Portland's *Oregonian*: "Van Sant makes a worthy attempt to spruce up the form with drawings, different typefaces and footnotes, but as a novel, *Pink* is a failure. It reads like bad science fiction, hastily written and full of pointless digressions and flights of fancy that never leave the ground. The language is pedestrian, the plot (such as it is) goes nowhere, and the characters never engage the reader or come across as anything but sketchy, dashed-off representations of real people." Baker reasoned, "[I]f this book is Van Sant's way to remember [River] Phoenix and deal with his death, it can be respected as such. If it is to be taken as anything more than that—a fair presumption considering Van Sant had it published and wants people to read it—then it is natural to wonder what the author was trying to say about himself, his life, Phoenix's life and death, Cobain's life and death, and the world they all live in."

As for Van Sant, despite the book's critical reception, creating *Pink* had been a refreshing change of pace: "Yes, writing the book was much more fun. Screenwriting is like a roadmap—you read it as you're going, you're looking at the finished thing as you're working on it. One thing you don't ever do when working on a film is go to a place unless you're shooting, and even then you're not really experiencing the place. When you're writing a book, you can go to this place—even if it's Paris, France—while you're still sitting at your desk. I talked to other writers about this, and they were like, 'Yeah, of course.' But I thought it was an amazing thing."

FINDING *GOOD WILL*

When I read a screenplay, I'm looking
for a number of things: character and setting, dialogue, and a good first act, second act, third act, and then an ending.
And all these things are really crucial
when I'm reading a screenplay, and they
don't have to just be there, they have to
be good ones! It's very easy to find a
screenplay that has great character and
setting. And you get through the first act
and you find out that there's not really a
second act or there's not really a third act
or not really a great ending. Dialogue is
important as well.

Gus Van Sant, 1998

TO SOME, IN RETROSPECT, it may have seemed
merely a fluke of good luck that Gus Van Sant ended up directing 1997's *Good
Will Hunting*. While good fortune played its role in the process, there were
other factors at work. These included Gus's creative intuition, his past screen
work, and his reputation in the film industry for bringing out the best in actors.

In reconstructing the genesis of *Good Will Hunting* and how Van Sant became attached to this highly successful screen property, the director once offered his quick version of the events: "There are a lot of scripts floating around
Hollywood and it's easy to get swamped by them, so I have a policy of not taking submissions. I don't have the time to read a thousand a month, and anyway,
I like to develop my own material. But occasionally a friend will give you something, and that's how I got *Good Will Hunting*."

That condensed account is by no means the full story.

It actually began in the fall of 1992 when twenty-two-year-old Matt Damon
was entering his senior year at Harvard University. Ordinarily Damon, who had

matriculated at the Ivy League School in September 1988, would have already graduated, but he had taken time out for acting assignments, such as the movie *School Ties* (1992). Now back on campus, Damon chose his curriculum for the semester. One of his selections was a course in creative writing taught by Anthony Kubiak.

In Kubiak's class, Matt wrote a tale about Harvard students who intersect/clash with the contrasting world of "townies." The instructor advised Damon that his short story was really the kernel for a full-length piece. He encouraged Matt to expand upon it. As Damon was reshaping the narrative, he adapted it into a one-act play for the theater directing course he was taking with David Wheeler. That December (1992), Damon's best friend was home from California. He was twenty-year-old Ben Affleck, Matt's longtime pal and Cambridge neighbor. Affleck had been in Los Angeles filming *Dazed and Confused*, directed by Richard Linklater. Matt showed Ben his story-turned-play and Affleck thought it had potential. He agreed to do a two-character scene with Damon for Matt's director's class.

Also that same December, Damon auditioned for a new Western, *Geronimo: An American Legend*. To his delight he won a supporting part in the project that was to star Wes Studi, Robert Duvall, and Jason Patric. Again, Matt took a leave of absence from Harvard. When the movie was finished, he remained in Los Angeles, hoping to ride a wave of career momentum once *Geronimo* was released. Again he put his university life on hold.

Time passed and Damon continued to lose out on key screen parts he wanted badly or to reject movie roles he felt would not further his career. By now, Ben Affleck had dropped out of Occidental College in Los Angeles to focus on movie roles. Through much of 1993 as both actors waited for long-overdue acting breaks, they reworked Matt's Harvard story/play. They envisioned completing the screenplay, finding backers, and making a low-budget independent feature with themselves in the lead roles—it would their big-screen showcase.

During this writing period, acting assignments occasionally came their way. For example, in 1994 Affleck was back East making Kevin Smith's *Mallrats*, while Damon was in Texas shooting a made-for-cable Western (*The Good Old Boys*) directed by and starring Tommy Lee Jones. Not to break the creative momentum on their dream screenplay/acting project, the two twentysomething actors took to faxing each other rewrites of scenes for their ever-expanding screenplay.

In the summer of 1994 Damon and Affleck were sharing a one-bedroom bachelor digs in a rundown West Hollywood building. Nothing positive was happening with their acting careers. (Earlier in the year Matt had auditioned for Gus Van Sant's *To Die For* but lost the role to Joaquin Phoenix. Damon, however, had been able to refer Affleck's younger brother, Casey, for a casting call for Van Sant's film. Casey had won a part in the movie that was shot in Canada from April to June 1994.) Waiting impatiently for that big acting break, Matt and Ben continued with their screenplay, which was getting inordinately long and more complex. By now, their mutual friend, Chris Moore, a struggling talent agent who aspired to be a film producer, had seen and liked their in-progress script. He demonstrated his faith in the project by quitting his daytime work to focus on finding the money to back their independent production.

In the fall of 1994, Matt showed the script to his acting agent who, in turn, gave it to a literary agent at the same firm. The latter made a suggestion that made sense: Why not sell the project to a film studio? Damon and Affleck agreed with the idea, adding one caveat—whoever bought the picture *must* use Matt and Ben in the lead acting roles.

On Sunday, November 13, 1994, copies of *Good Will Hunting* were dispatched to studio executives as part of an auction bid that had a four-day deadline. In the final hours of bidding on Thursday, November 17, Castle Rock Entertainment offered more than $500,000 for this first screenplay. Damon and Affleck were agog at their "sudden" success. The news became the talk of Hollywood and was featured prominently in the industry trade papers. One of those who read the articles was Gus Van Sant. He already knew a bit about the script from Casey Affleck who, during the making of *To Die For*, had told Gus about the fantastic screen project his brother Ben and their pal Matt were whipping together. Having already met Damon through *To Die For* auditions and having been introduced to Ben through Casey, Gus was pleased with their "overnight" triumph. He appreciated, from his own Hollywood experiences in the late 1970s, how tough it was to sell a screenplay, let alone to a major player in the film business.

Director Rob Reiner (*This Is Spinal Tap, Stand By Me, When Harry Met Sally* . . .), a partner at Castle Rock, later met with Damon and Affleck. In the process of their lengthy discussion, he told them to remove all the extraneous material that had accumulated into their over-thousand-page screenplay (nearly ten times the length of most filmed scripts). Months passed as they rewrote and rewrote, but nothing seemed to bring their project any closer to pre-production. Later, the scripters were told the movie would shoot but, for economy's sake, it would have to be lensed all in Toronto. That was upsetting enough to these two New Englanders who wanted the flavor of the actual Boston setting to come forth in their picture. The second stipulation announced by Castle Rock was even more of a deal-breaker. Castle Rock mentioned that one of the company's other partners, producer Andrew Scheinman, intended to direct the vehicle. (Scheinman's only movie directing credit to date was 1994's indifferent *Little Big League*.) This, along with other creative differences the two actors had with their benefactors, led to *Good Will Hunting* being put in turnaround. The screenwriting partners had thirty days to sell their property to another studio (and reimburse Castle Rock for its expenses thus far) or the project would revert to Castle Rock. At that point, the company would be free essentially to do with the screenplay as they wished.

As the month's grace period evaporated, Affleck took the screenplay to director Kevin Smith who had guided Ben through *Mallrats* and was now directing him in *Chasing Amy*. Smith, in turn, promptly showed it to Harvey Weinstein, the head of Miramax Pictures. Weinstein was so enthusiastic after reading the script that he immediately put in his offer—just under $1 million. (Ironically, a Miramax staff reader had earlier rejected the property when it was going through the bidding wars in November 1994.) By Christmas 1995, at Weinstein's instigation, Matt and Ben met with superstar actor/director Mel Gibson in New York. The *Braveheart* star liked their vehicle and was inclined to direct it, but he was already committed to starring in the upcoming action movie *Ransom*. As such, it would mean delaying the start of *Good Will Hunting* for at least nine months. Convinced this would be a disservice to the two young men who had gone through so much already to get their project to this point, Gibson soon bowed out of consideration as director.

While the Mel Gibson linkup was failing, Gus Van Sant was in New York on business. He took time out to have lunch with a friend named Mark Tusk who was then working for Miramax. During their meal chatter, Tusk mentioned that Miramax had just acquired the screen rights to *Good Will Hunting*. He told Van Sant who had never read the screenplay that it was "about Boston kids." Gus said he would like to read the script. Mark sent it to Van Sant's hotel that very day and the director read it there and then.

According to Van Sant: "Halfway through, I was so positive about it I called Joaquin Phoenix, who had Casey [Affleck]'s telephone number—Joaquin and Casey had remained friends after *To Die For*. Casey had Ben's mom's number. Ben's mom had Ben's number. So I eventually got to Ben, told him that I really loved the screenplay, and that I would do it. And I would do it right away, too, which made them really excited."

Affleck recalls the situation and his first conversation with Gus as follows: "Gus Van Sant knew of us—my brother Casey had acted in *To Die For*—and we heard he wanted to direct *Good Will Hunting*. We loved the idea, because we respect him so much. Gus has this way of delivering earth-shattering news in the most disarming, nonflustered flat monotone. " 'Yeah, I want to direct it,' he said. 'That's if you want to do it. OK. Bye.' "

When asked later what he thought had appealed to Van Sant about *Good Will Hunting*, Affleck responded, "We didn't offer the kind of street kids Gus is used to [presenting in his films]. But it's still young guys trying to find an alternate home for themselves. It played into one of Gus's favorite themes: the notion of a person trying to create his own family."

On his part, several key ingredients drew Van Sant to *Good Will Hunting*. As he has elaborated, "What attracted me was the balance of the story. The thing that I'm usually skeptical about in a screenplay is the sense of story. *Drugstore Cowboy* was similar in that it was extremely funny, it had a very strange setting . . . it had unique characters, amazing dialogue, intriguing ramps that the lead character, Bob, would go on. But I knew that could only last so far before the audience—me as an audience—would say, 'Okay, so where are we going?'

"If you don't have the story, and the unfolding of the trajectory of the saga, it's like getting in a car and not having any gas. In this case, as in *Drugstore Cowboy*, it had the arc, which is to me the most important thing. Because all the other stuff—the dialogue, the photography, the light, the set decoration—all the fun stuff is . . . just fun. The hard thing is just that core journey that the story is traveling on."

For Gus, "I liked the cohesiveness of the story: Everything fit together, and the journey of the lead character, Will, is an intellectual puzzle that gets unraveled slowly. Will's not sure why he resists certain things in his life until he is actually presented with them, and then when he is, it's a surprise to him, and also to the audience." He also noted, "It was probably the best-written screenplay I had ever read. We called it a color-by-numbers script: if you just filled in the scenes as they were written, it would come to life."

Van Sant analyzed further, "I always thought *Good Will Hunting* was a beautifully told story about a guy making one decision, one major decision in his life to take responsibility for his actions and not be overly concerned with thinking things through to the nth degree. He makes one decision in the movie, and I think everybody can relate to that."

Once Gus had registered his strong interest in *Good Will Hunting*, Damon and Affleck were jubilant. They assumed their last tough battle on the property was now over. But that was not to be the case. Miramax was just not that excited about having Van Sant—he of the very offbeat films—direct the vehicle and things stalled for bringing Gus aboard the project. Van Sant has recalled, "There were people like [Miramax top executive] Harvey Weinstein who weren't sure. I tried to sell myself by saying that *Ordinary People* was my favorite film, which it is. Ben and Matt, however, had faith. Maybe it was hard for . . . [the studio executives] to make a leap, because Hollywood people put you in a category. Ben and Matt never had those preconceptions."

Meanwhile, Miramax had brought in experienced producer Lawrence Bender (*Reservoir Dogs*, *Pulp Fiction*, *White Man's Burden*) to shepherd *Good Will Hunting* into eventual reality. He met with the scripters/actors and a new cycle of rewrites began. Whenever the novice screenwriters brought up the name of Van Sant as their prime choice to direct their work, the response was tepid. (Van Sant would later assess the possibility that he had erred in showing his great enthusiasm for the project from the start; perhaps he should have played harder to get.)

With no big-name director attached to *Good Will Hunting* and no important stars involved (since the two leads would, by stipulation, be played by Damon and Affleck), the project seemed to bog down at Miramax. But when Damon was signed to star in *John Grisham's The Rainmaker* for director Francis Ford Coppola, Weinstein and Miramax immediately perked up about *Good Will Hunting*.

They reasoned that if Coppola's courtroom thriller should make a screen star of Damon, then Miramax and *Good Will Hunting* could take advantage of the situation.

Suddenly, *Good Will Hunting* was a priority of sorts. After such name directors as Robert Redford and Sydney Pollack turned down the project, Miramax finally came to Van Sant and made a deal. In Gus's words: "Then they turned to me and said, 'Look, these other guys don't want to do it, so if you want to do it . . .'" Later, producer Bender would explain why he and Miramax finally went with this indie director on this very mainstream tale: "If you look at his other movies, all right, this doesn't seem like the right movie for Gus. But then you look at several things: He's amazing with actors and this is an actors' piece. It's full of people that hang around and talk. Two, he's a visualist. He's always interesting, camera wise. Three, he has a sense of the blue collar, the underclass group. And the script has that element of it. It also has . . . I hate to use the word 'edge' it's so overused, but it's the only one I can think of; the emotional parts of it had an edge to them, and so had the comedy part. And I felt that Gus really could hold that edge, and that he'd really relate to these guys."

At this juncture, Damon and Affleck took the next important but highly emotional step, which meant letting go of the control of their "baby." They told Gus: "This is your movie now." As Damon reasoned, "We had to have a director who was going to heighten it and make it better, otherwise the film would have been a total failure for us."

One of the first meetings Van Sant, Damon, and Affleck had on their script was at a Denny's restaurant on Sunset Boulevard in Hollywood—a place where each of them had spent countless time in the past dawdling over coffee while figuring out how to make something happen in their stalled careers. Later, as Matt and Ben became involved with shoots of other movies, the trio spoke by phone, faxed one another, or had script conferences in Nashville where Damon was filming *The Rainmaker*.

As the three participants collaborated on the revisions, Gus came up with all sorts of suggestions to smooth out the scenario. Some were fruitful exercises, while others were ideas that he later agreed were taking the story line in unnecessary directions. One such inspiration was Van Sant's proposal that Matt and Ben revamp the plot to have Affleck's character killed in a construction site accident. The acting team were taken aback by this thought, but they had so much respect for Van Sant that they complied. (The actors referred to Gus as the "indie Guru.") When they all read the new version in which the character of Chuckie is "crushed like a bug," Van Sant was the first to admit that it was a "terrible idea. It was quickly agreed by all to drop that notion.

By now, Damon and Affleck were accustomed to the perpetual delays that seem to haunt *Good Will Hunting*. As 1996 moved onward, Miramax still had not yet green-lighted the project. Then everything suddenly changed.

When the duo had been crafting their debut screenplay for Castle Rock they had been told by veteran scenarist William Goldman that it helps to write characters by mentally imagining appropriate real-life actors in the roles. Among those Damon and Affleck visualized to play Sean McGuire the therapist, who breaks through Will Hunting's emotional barriers, were the likes of Robert De Niro, Robert Duvall, Ed Harris, and Morgan Freeman.

These were all fine choices, but not feasible alternatives in the real world due to salaries required, prefilled schedules, etc. While Miramax was submitting the script to several name contenders, Gus sent it to Robin Williams whom he knew from the days when they had both been involved in the aborted *The Mayor of Castro Street*. It was also a natural fit since Williams had played a vaguely similar role as the shepherding teacher in *Dead Poets Society* (1989), for which he had won a Best Actor Oscar nomination.

In more recent years Robin's résumé had been filled more often with light screen fare like *Being Human, Jack,* and *The Birdcage,* instead of meaningful projects. He was looking for an acting challenge, if it did not interfere with his big-salaried movie assignments. In the midst of his hectic schedule in 1996–1997 to make *Deconstructing Harry, Father's Day, Flubber,* and then *What Dreams May Come,* it developed at the last minute that he actually had time to fit in *Good Will Hunting.* The role resonated with him and he was even willing to take this essentially supporting part at a lower up-front salary (but with a heftier back-end percentage participation) to accommodate Miramax. But *Good Will Hunting* had to work its start date around Williams's availability.

For Van Sant there was no need to test Williams for the crucial part. The star was, per Gus, "slotted in. I don't really require readings, not like the top on my list. It's mostly the visual, like what the person is like. And then I figure I can get the performance out of them in some way. I trust that I can, usually, and the visual is hugely important." Williams was signed for the part.

With Robin Williams aboard the project, Miramax immediately gave the go-ahead to *Good Will Hunting.* But to adjust to Williams's crowded timetable it was obligatory that the movie get under way in short order. Knowing what comedian/actor Williams could bring to the table in terms of talent and ticket sales, Van Sant, Damon, and Affleck shuffled their own priorities to make *Good Will Hunting* happen—now. As such, the film had less than two months for a prep period that forced everyone to move at intense speed to meet the fast-approaching production start date. For Van Sant this long wait and fast go-ahead was nothing new. He seemingly thrived on the pressure of thinking on his feet to meet the demands of the telescoped preproduction period.

Casting the two other major roles for *Good Will Hunting* gave everyone initial pause. Who was to play Professor Gerald Lambeau, the former classmate/rival of the Sean McGuire character? Who would be right to handle the role of Skylar, the Harvard premed student who falls deeply in love with Will Hunting? (The character was loosely based on Damon's former college sweetheart—named Skylar—as well as other women he had dated over the years.)

Harvey Weinstein suggested that Van Sant consider Swedish-born Stellan Skarsgärd (*The Unbearable Lightness of Being, The Hunt for Red October,*

Breaking the Waves) for the role of Professor Lambeau. Stellan was already set for a role in Steven Spielberg's *Amistad*. After meeting with the resourceful actor, Van Sant was agreeable to his joining the cast.

Many ingénues would be considered and/or tested for the crucial role of Skylar. (Gus, for example, was interested in Kate Winslet for the part, but she was exhausted from making *Titanic* and was thus unavailable.) As it would turn out, one of the first to be actually auditioned was Barbados-born, London-raised Minnie Driver (*Circle of Friends*, *GoldenEye*, *Sleepers*), a chameleon-like talent who seemed to change in size, weight, and character from one movie role to the next. She had just flown in from England when she met with Van Sant, Damon, Affleck, producer Lawrence Bender, and coproducer Chris Moore at a Manhattan hotel. Self-confident Driver did her scene readings for the assemblage, one time with a British accent, another go-round as an Irish lass, and the third run-through using a flawless American dialect. They were extremely impressed with the dimension she brought to the audition. Although they all felt she was great in the part, it was decided that they must test others for the assignment. (Meanwhile, Damon, who was smitten with Minnie's abilities, did further revisions to the script, tailor-making the on-screen Skylar role to Driver's capacities.) Eventually, Driver was cast in the key role and it was agreed to have her use her natural British accent in the part.

To play the remaining two members of the South Boston (the "Southies") quartet who function in the narrative, Damon and Affleck had casting suggestions. One was Affleck's brother Casey. Having worked with Casey on *To Die For*, Gus was impressed with his talents and approved the choice. Casey was auditioned and signed. The other part, that of the fourth wheel, went to Cole Hauser (*A Matter of Justice*, *Dazed and Confused*, *Higher Learning*) who had worked with Matt and Ben in 1992's *School Ties*. (At one point, Gus had been considering using actor Rodney Harvey for one of these *Good Will Hunting* assignments. By then, however, the *My Own Private Idaho* cast member had sunk again into deep substance abuse and was not capable of handling such a part. Thirty-year-old Harvey would die of a drug overdose in a fleabag Los Angeles hotel in April 1998.)

To perform the roles of the therapists who try and fail with Will Hunting before Sean McGuire takes over the case, Van Sant displayed his typical offbeat casting. He hired writer/experimenter/blue blood celebrity George Plimpton to play one, and well-known painter Francesco Clemente to portray another (the hypnotist). Producer Lawrence Bender, with whom Gus had a few clashes on *Good Will Hunting* about creative control, took on the role of a third therapist in these sequences, but his scene was later edited from the too-long film.

Now, with all the principal parts filled, production was to start on April 14, 1997, with most of the interiors to be filmed in Toronto and exteriors/atmosphere shots in Boston. Thus, almost three years to the day since he began *To Die For* in Canada, Gus Van Sant was making a new movie in the same city.

THE ROAD TO OSCAR

I've actually heard some interesting comments. Some people who'd seen the film [*Good Will Hunting*] said, "It's really good. I'm surprised Gus made this." Did I change my style consciously, if at all? I don't think so. It was the screenplay, really, as was the case with my other films. They were screenplays that I really liked; they were stories that I liked; I went in and made them without regard to anything other than my own reaction to it.

Gus Van Sant, 1998

IN ACTUALITY, *Good Will Hunting* was Gus Van Sant's first mainstream-themed picture. While *To Die For* had been made for a major studio, it was still the type of quirky movie fare that one could associate easily enough with Van Sant from his prior features and short subjects. But the characters and themes of *Good Will Hunting* were in many ways so traditional that one could easily have imagined a more conventional director helming this screen project. Nevertheless, Gus proved, as he had before, that he could adapt successfully to new work situations. If he had uncertainties about his leap into the major leagues of filmmaking, he was wise enough to keep them to himself or to share these concerns only with confidants.

While Melissa "Missy" Stewart (production designer), Beatrix Aruna Pasztor (costume designer), Pablo Ferro (title designer), and Danny Elfman (music) were again working in tandem with Van Sant on *Good Will Hunting*, both the director of photography and the editor were new to Gus's creative team. For years Van Sant had relied on his friend Eric Alan Edwards to be (co-)cinematographer on his movies. But Edwards was busy on other projects (*Flirting with Disaster, Cop Land*) so Van Sant turned to Jean-Yves Escoffier (*Dream Lover, The Crow: City of Angels, Grace of My Heart*).

French-born Escoffier had recently worked with young Harmony Korine on the latter's feature *Gummo* and Gus had great respect for Korine's enthusiasm for this cinematographer. (Per Van Sant, using the new director of cinematography "was a chance to see what it was like to work with some new people. And it was different. They have totally different ideas about working.") Nevertheless, Gus and Jean Yves utilized the approach Eric Alan Edwards had employed when he shot *Kids*—the movie Van Sant had executive produced—for director Larry Clark. There Eric had used a minimum of unnatural lighting on the sets and this technique was adopted on *Good Will Hunting*. In addition, Italian film editor Pietro Scalia (*Little Buddha, The Quick and the Dead, Stealing Beauty*) took over the technical assignment so often handled in the past for Gus by Curtiss Clayton. (On *Good Will Hunting*, Gus's past boyfriend D-J Haanraadts functioned as an assistant editor while Van Sant's newer friend, Scott Patrick Green, was Gus's assistant.)

Because the new picture would be filmed in two different cities within two different countries, there was a problem in hiring the crew. To find on short notice people experienced with what each city had to offer that was unique, and how to best handle other problems, including local filming regulations, was not easy. As a result, the director noted, "Our Boston crew was mixed with Toronto crew as we also shot half the film in Toronto, and it was tough because there's not a lot of filming done in Boston."

As Gus prepared for the start date, he had to accommodate two main thrusts of the screenplay. One of these, according to Van Sant, was "Will has extraordinary mathematical abilities which he keeps a secret. These abilities are something that all the other characters in the story either want a part of, or want to know more about, or want him to do something with. This story device is our [Alfred] Hitchcockian 'maguffin'—the thing that all the characters in our story care desperately about but we as an audience don't particularly care about, at least not directly. What interests us as viewers is watching and listening to the characters discuss and fight over Will's good will."

The other aspect was that "in almost every scene, there is the construction or observation of an educational class structure. The young South Boston kids are the uneducated, poor, scrappy lower-class laborers with bleak prospects for a scholastic future, while the Cambridge teachers and students play in a privileged upper class. There is a particularly East Coast orientation to these distinctions of class and also an exaggeration between these differences. The lower class is the hero, the upper class the antihero."

The director had a particular concern about the wordy screenplay. Van Sant described this obstacle: "The *Good Will* staging was usually two people sitting in chairs across from each other and talking. Only the backgrounds and the characters changed, and usually only one of the characters changed since Will is in virtually every scene. We wondered if this might become tiring, but as we forged ahead and began to shoot the film it became captivating, just as it was on the page."

Then, too, because Damon and Affleck had labored over their screenplay for years, it was up to Gus to find creative ways on a daily basis to keep the on-camera interchanges fresh and real for the two actors who had lived with every word of dialogue and each scene situation for so long.

As filming got under way Van Sant kept to two of his own important guidelines. One was, "There's one feeling I always try to instill on the set, which is, 'Don't worry about the words too much.' Because you can get really tripped up with whether you said this line right, or which line comes after it, if you missed your cue, or what have you. To me, once you're on the set and once you're going, you could almost make it up. If you go by the script, that's okay. If you stray a bit, that's okay. If you forget something, the other actor will pick up from you or maybe something new will develop. I really welcome that."

The other was, "I let my actors choreograph every scene, because they're the ones who are getting up and going to the window. They have their own motivation for going to the window. If it looks weird, I'll tell them. If they need something to do, I'll give it to them. Actors generally show me what their ideas are, and then I say, 'That's great. Can you try this?'"

On *Good Will Hunting*, Van Sant might easily have had legitimate apprehensions about exerting his authority on a set in which the two lead actors knew the subtle ins and out of their story far better than he. That, however, did not prove to be a stumbling block during filming. Damon and Affleck were so genuinely thrilled that their years of work were finally coming to fruition that they were quite amenable to Gus's low-keyed channeling of their performances. (On the first day of shooting on *Good Will* the actor duo were so overcome with emotion at having their movie come alive after all this time that they were teary-eyed.)

With the supertalented, hyperenergetic, and quite mercurial Robin Williams, Van Sant quickly discovered that the star was fully prepared to play out his emotional characterization and that he was not planning to be excessive in his delivery. Moreover, Robin was a perfectionist who never tired of redoing a scene with a different shading that had suddenly occurred to him. Describing his working relationship with the celebrated performer who chose to be bearded and mustached for this assignment Gus said, "Oh, he was a dynamo, all right, in the way the ideas came sort of fast and furious. But at the same time, he was really subdued and on his own when he showed up. He was a certain way with the script and what he thought he wanted to do with the character of Sean McGuire, which was unlike anything he might be doing in films like *Flubber*. Although he's a professor in *Flubber*, too . . . Well, one is completely like a certain kind of Robin Williams, and Sean McGuire is another type of professor in Robin's imagination, which had really little to do with his stand-up comedy life. But it came from him. . . .

"At times, during production, Robin would say, 'Let me do a few more takes like this and then I'll do a really wacky one.' And I'd go, 'Great.' So I'd get ready for this huge thing to happen, and it would be like a little ad lib. And I'd go, 'So that was the really wild one, huh?' And he'd go, 'Yeah?!' He was totally contained with the Sean character—except between takes, of course: he would liven up the set, to put it mildly."

It did not come as a surprise to Van Sant that Stellan Skarsgård would be inventive in his role as the M.I.T. professor with the superinflated ego, but he was amazed to the degree that this veteran talent would jump deeper into every aspect of his characterization. One day, for example, the Swedish actor arrived on the set moaning and groaning, announcing that he must lie down immediately. When concerned cast and crew members rushed to see what the problem might be, Stellan explained that *he* did not have a headache, but that his character, Professor Lambeau, did in this sequence. In addition, there were all sort of little touches that the actor and Van Sant played off each other to enhance the role: making Lambeau a womanizer who utilizes any given opportunity to charm a young woman, or the scarf the famed mathematician wears as a badge of his celebrity status at the university.

What made an interesting contrast in the execution of the plotline was having Skarsgård work in tandem with Canadian teacher/mathematician/ occasional actor John Mighton. The latter played Lambeau's meek assistant who delights in pleasing his mentor and must overcome his jealousy of the much brighter Will Hunting, who so quickly gains the professor's admiration and interest. Said Gus of Mighton, "He sort of had this whole presence that he brought to the screen. He could ad lib, he could do all these great things and Stellan would just be amazed."

As to the correctness of math equations and professional jargons the teacher characters discuss within *Good Will Hunting*, as well as the on-screen campus ambiance at Harvard and M.I.T., Gus reached back into his college years at the Rhode Island School of Design. As he explained, "A lot of the classes at the School of Design were very technical, involving math. Most of the students in my school were in different states of being very advanced in their field. A lot of them had back stories similar to the characters that we have in the film. My school had the same kind of vibes, intensity and level of study. So I just applied that to this particular screenplay."

Still not convinced that they had the dynamics of the scenes involving math correctly, Van Sant wanted a consultant with expertise in the area. In that search, he lucked out. He and Missy Stewart were dining at a Vietnamese restaurant in Toronto one evening as they prepared for the shoot. Gus spied a scholarly type leaving the bar. Too shy to pursue the diner himself, he sent the more outgoing Missy to chase down the stranger to see if he might like to be an extra in the film. (The production was already flying several extras from Boston to Toronto to provide verisimilitude to the various Boston scenes.) As it turned out the man, Patrick O'Donnell, was not only willing to be an extra in an upcoming barroom scene as well as to play a member of the janitorial staff at M.I.T., but he was a math professor and became a technical consultant on the picture.

As filming began, it quickly became evident that the two Affleck brothers had a special dynamic that could enhance the movie's ambiance. In real life, not only was Casey the younger sibling who knew exactly how to irritate Ben, but he had a daring, wild streak as an actor. He was fearless about making his screen character more outrageous at a moment's notice. It was quickly decided—reportedly on actor Cole Hauser's prompting—that Cole's character of Billy should be the quiet one in group scenes and that Casey's Morgan would be the rambunctious member. Several of Hauser's dialogue lines were given to Casey.

Another unexpected aspect of the cast interaction was the real-life romance that bloomed during production between Matt Damon and Minnie Driver. It made their joint scenes more tangibly real, just as having longtime buddies Matt and Ben and to a lesser extent Casey and Cole play friends on camera gave the film that extra dimension of truth.

A daily production challenge was to find new ways to shoot intimate scenes. For example, there are several sessions between therapist Sean McGuire and patient Will Hunting in the former's small, cluttered office. It required a lot of ingenuity on the part of Van Sant and Escoffier to devise fresh camera angles and scene setups to keep the interchanges interesting and nonrepetitive.

While Van Sant had already lensed heterosexual love scenes in *To Die For*, they were primarily moments of Nicole Kidman's manipulative character exploiting the beguiled teenager played by Joaquin Phoenix. On the other hand, *Hunting* required romantic sequences of tenderness with accelerating degrees of sexual spark, so rather than shoot such moments between Will and Skylar in wide focus, which would have meant extended nudity, these sequences were handled in fairly close shots. It gave an intimacy to the footage as well as sparing possible embarrassment on either side of the camera.

(On the subject of directing heterosexual love sequences, Van Sant has said, "A gay director who is directing a straight sex scene is removed, which helps. He can objectively see what the dynamics of the two characters are. But when you're making movies, it's like designing a building. If you're designing a room and you're gay, there are some things that will be affected—maybe the shape of the room, the interior decoration. But when you're talking about just getting people through doors with the right kind of perspective, your sexuality doesn't necessarily apply. . . . And a sex scene is architecturally rendered by the filmmaker. The actual sexuality of the characters is the last thing you come in contact with.

"First of all, you're just trying to get across to the audience that two people are in bed. When you're learning to make movies, it's hard just to set up your first camera angle. You realize, Oh, the audience doesn't know we're in a room if I shoot your face too close. You get into very basic graphic representation of things. Eventually you get to a state where you want the characters to be intimate. Their sexuality is the last thing to be manipulated.")

One scene early in the emotional exchanges between Will and Sean McGuire has the math whiz examining a painting on McGuire's wall, one that the therapist character did himself, and one that Hunting, the mental genius, uses to poke chinks in the older man's emotional armor. It was key to have an appropriate painting—one that suggested insights into McGuire's troubled nature. Van Sant, production designer Missy Stewart, and costume designer Beatrix Aruna Pasztor were all art school graduates. They had a competition among themselves to create the most appropriate symbolic painting to be hung in Sean's office. Gus won with his painting of a lone man rowing a boat as he struggles against a stormy sea with dark clouds rolling overhead. It was used on-camera in the pivotal scene.

Technically, a film innovation on this Gus Van Sant production was the use of video monitors. As Gus detailed, "I was really fighting against it on this film. Our Director of Photography [Jean-Yves Escoffier] wanted to have a tiny one on the dolly so that the crew members could actually see what the camera was doing. The boom guy may need it to figure out where his cut-off line is: if there's a monitor, he can find it; if not, the cameraman would have to say 'In, in, in, out' as he's riding the whole shot. Similarly, a dolly grip can see what the camera is doing so that when he moves the dolly one way, he understands what the shot is trying to accomplish, he can see it unfolding. So there are time-savers involved with a monitor within the crew."

However, the presence of a video monitor on the set had repercussions for Gus. "As a director, unfortunately, I was drawn to that. I caught myself many a time staring right at the monitor. I'm not supposed to look, but whenever it's around—even a small little one—I tend to get sidetracked. In other words, it was a good thing for the crew, a bad thing for me."

▼

WHEN *Good Will Hunting* returned to Boston for additional location work, Matt Damon and Ben Affleck felt like prodigal sons back on their home turf. Here their years of growing up in the Hub paid off as they could suggest locales, costuming, local characteristics that enhanced the film's Massachusetts ambiance. Frequently, the costars' friends and relatives were among the crowds gathered to watch the outdoor scenes being shot in Harvard Square or the rough-and-tumble Irish neighborhoods of South Boston. In some scenes, such as the one in which Will and Skylar sit at a park table discussing his genius ability to learn so quickly, Damon's parents can be seen as background extras. The stars' former classmate Derrick Bridgeman—actually the one who had created the title *Good Will Hunting* for his own novel and whose three words he gladly sold to Damon/Affleck for their vehicle—is seen momentarily as an M.I.T. student.

In the South Boston courthouse sequence where Will is being arraigned, the judge is performed by Jimmy Flynn, a local, well-known teamster. Beantown policemen were hired to play themselves, as was a local landlady. (Not that Van Sant did not work a few of his own friends into the proceedings: Harmony Korine was visiting the *Good Will Hunting* set and agreed to play the effeminate prisoner who asks fellow inmate Will if he'd like a "piece of a**." *To Die For*'s Alison Folland is seen briefly as an M.I.T. student conversing with Professor Lambeau.)

▼

BY June 1994 principal photography on *Good Will Hunting* had wrapped. Matt Damon would enthuse of working with Gus: "Actors want to work with him because of the moment-to-moment honesty that he gets out of interaction with people. Whatever they are, he always has a great idea as to where to put the camera, and he gets good performances out of the actors because he shoots around them. He rehearses them, then very calmly decides where to put the camera, in a very unobtrusive place. It's just amazing. I felt like my acting process—whatever you want to call it—was nurtured by him. I would very much like to work with him again." Matt also said of his director, "It's always about what you're doing, he's never telling you what to do."

Affleck confirmed, "You see these naturalistic performances in his films and wonder what he does and I found that I was never more at ease—it was never about the fact that it was a movie, it was easy to forget that and do your thing."

As for Robin Williams's take on Van Sant, he quipped: "Gus is so mellow he could turn a teamster into a Buddhist."

Gus's reaction to working with stars/scripters Damon and Affleck was couched in typical Van Sant understatement: "I think they were also very happy with the way it was being done. If we'd screwed it up, maybe it would have been different, especially because they had years invested in it, but I stuck pretty closely to what was on the page." He did allow, "Sometimes there'd be dialogue changes, but those were encouraged by them. They wanted the freedom to come up with stuff while we were shooting."

▼

PAST Gus Van Sant feature film productions—especially *Even Cowgirls Get the Blues*—had endured long, laborious, often painfully tense editing periods that lasted for many, many months after principal photography had concluded. *Good Will Hunting* was a different situation. It was edited, tested, and fine-tuned in comparatively short order. For one thing it was a very linear story so there really could be little switching around of scenes in the continuity. (A scene that was altered in the time line was the one when Skylar embarks on her flight to California.) So, largely, it was a matter of trimming scenes that were too long or deleting any unessential sequences (e.g., Skylar visiting Chuckie to talk about Will, a few construction site interchanges, a Saint Patrick's Day parade that Will and Chuckie attend, a cat joke told in a barroom by the Southies, Sean McClure drinking on the roof of his apartment building).

Most important, the editing process on *Good Will Hunting* was speeded along by the production executives, due to several factors. One was that almost everyone had much more faith in the project now and wanted to get it to the marketplace. Miramax and producer Lawrence Bender had been pleasantly surprised when viewing the rough cut to discover that the drama of emotional unblockage had turned out so warmhearted, so funny, and so dramatically effective. Then, too, with Paramount planning a November 1997 release for Matt Damon's first starring vehicle, *The Rainmaker*, Miramax intended to roll out *Good Will Hunting* into movie theaters on the heels of that rival picture, which was already getting good word-of-mouth. In addition, there was always the potential of Academy Award nominations for some/every aspect of *Good Will Hunting*; to qualify, the picture had to play in Los Angeles and New York City movie theaters for seven days before the end of the calendar year.

As indicated previously, Danny Elfman provided the original music for *Good Will Hunting*. To contribute several songs to the production, Gus turned to Elliott Smith. The Dallas-born Smith, then in his late twenties, had spent several years in Portland where the singer/songwriter often performed. Van Sant's friend D-J Haanraadts had worked with Smith's girlfriend and had been one of the individuals to bring Smith to Gus's attention. By this point, Smith had three independently produced albums in release and had a small cult following. He contributed several songs to the *Good Will Hunting* score including such old numbers as "No Name #3" and new items like "Miss Misery." Also used on the sound track score were cuts performed by the likes of Gerry Rafferty ("Baker Street"), the Dandy Warhols ("Boys Better"), and Al Green ("How Can You Mend a Broken Heart?"). (Gus would serve as coexecutive producer on the sound track album along with the film's producer Lawrence Bender and its music supervisor, Jeffrey Kimball.)

Meanwhile, as part of Miramax's preparations for releasing *Good Will Hunting*, the company rushed out a paperback volume of the film's script with an introduction written by Gus. It was released under their Miramax Books imprint and distributed by Hyperion.

▼

IN the final print of *Good Will Hunting*, twenty-year-old Will Hunting is a janitor at M.I.T. whose off hours are spent drinking with his South Boston buddies, Chuckie, Morgan, and Billie. One night, outside the math classroom Will, who keeps his genius I.Q. hidden from one and all, scribbles the answers to a difficult math challenge posted by Professor Gerald Lambeau for his students. By the time Lambeau tracks down this anonymous genius, combative Will has been arrested for brawling and sentenced to a jail term. Lambeau persuades the judge to suspend Hunting's sentence if the young man (1) works with Lambeau on math equations, etc., and (2) undergoes counseling.

Meanwhile, one night while Will and his cronies are drinking in a Harvard Square bar, Hunting meets Harvard premed student Skylar. When he puts down ("how do you like them apples!") a snotty rival for her attention, she is impressed with the brash, handsome, and extraordinarily bright newcomer. They soon have a pleasant date together but he does not call her back. Some days later he asks her out again and they begin a romantic relationship.

While Will demonstrates his astonishing mental acumen in solving math equations for Professor Lambeau, he does poorly with his therapists whom he deliberately embarrasses. As a last resort, Lambeau persuades his former college roommate, Sean McGuire, to meet with Will. Both therapist and patient have a lot in common: they are from South Boston, have had bad childhoods, love baseball, and are extremely bright. As it develops, each is suffering from severe emotional blockage: Will because of his abusive foster father, Sean because his longtime wife had died a few years earlier of cancer.

Lambeau's efforts to find Will worthwhile employment—at least from his own viewpoint—riles McGuire, who feels that the professor is thinking more of himself than of Hunting's actual needs at the moment. Will overhears their painful battling over his future and shortly thereafter has an emotional breakthrough in his session with Sean.

Skylar leaves to study medicine at Stanford University in California. She asks Will to take a chance on life and join her, but, out of fear, he refuses. Later, Chuckie convinces his best friend that he owes it to his pals to make something of his life. Just as Sean has learned from his sessions with Hunting, Will departs on an adventurous trip to experience life once again. Thus Will Hunting breaks free of his emotional shackles and heads to the West Coast to reconcile with Skylar.

▼

GOOD *Will Hunting* had its premiere in Westwood, near UCLA in Los Angeles, on Tuesday, December 2, 1997. By then, Matt Damon had become the media's new dream boy (replacing the prior year's Matthew McConaughey), which heightened the excitement that evening. The screening, with a party afterward at the Westwood Brewing Company, was a benefit for the American Film Institute. Among the celebrities attending the $250 per ticket event were Matt Damon, Ben Affleck, Minnie Driver, Dustin Hoffman, Jennifer Aniston, Claire Danes, Matthew McConaughey, Courteney Cox, and director Wes Craven. Robin Williams, busy filming elsewhere, was not present, but Gus was very much in evidence. He had on a sort of furry Technicolor dreamcoat. When asked where he had found the unusual apparel, he replied, "Uh, in a store . . . in Portland." The movie had its debut in Gus's adopted home state of Oregon on Thursday, December 11, 1997, with Van Sant in attendance. For $35 a ticket, one could attend the prefilm party and the showing of *Good Will Hunting*, while for $200 a pop, one also got to enjoy a postfilm dinner at the Heathman Hotel. Proceeds went to the Northwest Film Center.

In January 1998 *Good Will Hunting* had its most unique showing. President and Mrs. Clinton requested a screening of the picture at Camp David. Among those invited to the command screening at the first couple's retreat were the film's stars, plus Gus and producer Lawrence Bender. When Bill Clinton asked Van Sant why he had dedicated the picture—with a special title card on-screen—to William S. Burroughs Jr. and Allen Ginsberg—both of whom died in 1997—the director answered, "They were both friends of mine." The chief executive's response was, "Yeah, right on!"

▼

REGARDING the much-hyped feel-good picture, Janet Maslin (*New York Times*) wrote, "Two young actors with soaring reputations have written themselves a smart and touching screenplay, then seen it directed with style, shrewdness and clarity by Gus Van Sant. There couldn't be a better choice than the unsentimental Mr. Van Sant for material like this." Furthermore, Maslin enthused, "Mr. Van Sant demonstrates how entertainingly a real pro can direct a strong if not especially groundbreaking story. . . . Never one to condescend to restless young characters, Mr. Van Sant . . . neither romanticizes the angst of the film's college-age hero nor finds anything maudlin in his relationship with a middle-aged psychotherapist."

Amy Taubin (*Village Voice*) pointed out, "Long on charm, short on logic, *Good Will Hunting* is a movie to love in spite of your better judgment. . . . The difference, however, between the sentimentality of *Good Will Hunting* and that of, say, *Phenomenon* (another movie about unlikely genius [starring John Travolta]) is that the people involved in making *Good Will Hunting* depict the world as they wish it were, while the people involved in *Phenomenon* depict a world they think audiences will lap up." As to the moviemaker, Taubin decided, "Working as a director-for-hire, Gus Van Sant mixes high spirits with lyricism while soft-pedaling the aching sense of loss and abandonment that colors his best films. . . . Van Sant's camera gazes perhaps too adoringly at Damon's beautiful, slightly clownish face, with its toothy, mocking grin, and his hunky, slightly bowlegged body (if this sounds like boy porn, the film, at moments, is right on the edge). But he also taps into Damon's volatile emotional range, into the violence that underlies his antic humor."

According to Roger Ebert at the *Chicago Sun-Times*: "The film has a good ear for the way these characters might talk. . . . It was directed by Gus Van Sant . . . who sometimes seems to have perfect pitch when it comes to dialogue; look at the scene where Matt and Skylar break up and say hurtful things, and see how clear he makes it that Matt is pushing her away because he doesn't think he deserves her." Ebert also underscored, "The outcome of the movie is fairly predictable; so is the whole story, really. It's the individual moments, not the payoff, that make it so effective. " Andrew Sarris (*New York Observer*) focused on the movie's plot: "The situation is clearly contrived and not a little fantastic.

Yet the film works as a character-driven narrative because Mr. Van Sant and his coscreenwriters are not afraid to unlock the psychological mysteries of their five major characters with clear and concise dialogue."

Although Kenneth Turan (*Los Angeles Times*) found the film's premise "a clever and delicious one," he had reservations. "The result is an uneasy hybrid of old and new Hollywood, where the engaging and independent spirit the actors provide coexists shakily with the kind of traditional sticky sentimentality that characterized films like *Dead Poets Society, Awakenings,* and *Mr. Holland's Opus.*" Turan judged, "[E]ccentric director Gus Van Sant is apparently determined to become the next Frank Capra. While it's nice to see Van Sant challenging himself (no one in their right mind wants to see *Even Cowgirls Get the Blues: The Reunion*), it would be nice if some of the edge he brought to the mainstream *To Die For* found its way to the screen here."

David Denby of *New York* magazine concluded, "Gus Van Sant may no longer be as original a hipster-artist as he was in the days of *Drugstore Cowboy* and *My Own Private Idaho,* but he has gained in coherence and accountability. In the end, however, he's betrayed by the script, which takes a disastrous turn toward conventionality." As for *Newsday*'s Jack Matthews: "The performances are all solid, and Van Sant . . . has guided it with a fluid, transparent style, allowing the relationships to run their course at a seemingly nature pace. But in the end, *Good Will Hunting* is less a great movie than a great opportunity. For Matt Damon, it's *A Star Is Born.*"

And when *Good Will Hunting* bowed in England in early March 1998, Alexander Walker provided Gus with a backhanded compliment when he wrote in *This Is London*: "The invasive presence of anti-intellectualism in *Good Will Hunting* is smartly disguised by director Gus Van Sant's desire to entertain folks by giving them what they think they want and giving himself what his own career has so far lacked, a mainstream hit."

And indeed *Good Will Hunting* was a hit. Made on a budget of less than $16 million, it grossed $138.339 million in domestic distribution and almost half that amount more abroad. As the yearly awards for filmmaking were being tallied, *Good Will Hunting* was on several top-ten lists and was nominated for and/or claimed many prizes. For example, at the Golden Globes, it won for Best Screenplay—Motion Pictures; the National Board of Review bestowed on Matt Damon and Ben Affleck its NBR Award for Special Achievement in Filmmaking. At the Berlin International Film Festival Damon won the Silver Berlin Bear for Outstanding Single Achievement, while Gus was nominated for a Golden Berlin Bear as director. Van Sant was also nominated by the Directors Guild of America for Outstanding Directorial Achievement in Motion Pictures.

But, of course, the king of all prize events was the Academy Awards. On February 10, 1998, the nominations were announced. *Good Will Hunting* received nine nominations: Best Director, Best Picture, Best Actor (Matt Damon), Best Supporting Actor (Robin Williams), Best Supporting Actress (Minnie Driver), Ben Original Screenplay, Best Music, Best Song ("Miss

Misery"), and Best Editor. In nearly every category, *Good Will Hunting* was competing against the talent involved with the year's four other nominated best pictures: *As Good As It Gets, The Full Monty, L.A. Confidential,* and the blockbuster *Titanic.*

On Monday, March 23, 1998, the Academy Awards were presented at the Shrine Auditorium in downtown Los Angeles. By this point most of the nominees had been to an assortment of prize-giving events over the previous several weeks. (These happenings gave Van Sant a tremendous high profile within the filmmaking community and with the public at large.) Gus escorted longtime Portland friend and journalist Paige Powell to the Oscar ceremonies. They drove to the event in a big rented recreational vehicle—stocked with goodies and a TV—so his parents, sister, aunt, and Portland friends who were in the entourage could enjoy the festivities. Because he was not arriving in the typical chauffeur-driven limousine, the parking attendants almost did not let Gus's vehicle into the proper parking zone to disembark for the Oscar festivities.

Always a bit outrageous in his apparel, Van Sant was dressed in black and wore a long dark Edwardian outer coat that boasted vertical colored stripes. The garment, designed by Jean-Paul Gaultier, gathered much attention from the hosts of the televised preshows who were greeting the celebrities as they paraded down the red carpet. (Gus's companion, Paige Powell, who had worked for Andy Warhol and his *Interview* magazine, was wearing a low V-cut Warhol original gown that night and during the walk on the red carpet found herself coming out of the loose-fitting dress. When she voiced her problem to preoccupied Gus, he chirped in, "Well, put it back in!")

When Van Sant was asked later how he felt on this night of nights, he ventured, "I was really nervous because it's a big party and I don't like parties. It's like a wedding, or something, so you're worried about how everybody's doing. It was fun but it wasn't my happiest moment."

Early in the Academy Award proceedings hosted by Billy Crystal, *Good Will Hunting* had its first victory when Robin Williams won his Oscar. Overwhelmed by the win and by the audience's thunderous applause, the comedian/actor admitted, "Oh, man! This may be the one time I'm speechless." In the course of thanking everybody responsible for his win, he said of his director: "Thank you Gus Van Sant for being so subtle you're almost subliminal."

Later in the star-studded evening, an amazed and jubilant Matt Damon and Ben Affleck clambered up to the stage to accept their Academy Award in the Best Original Screenplay Category. Ecstatic to the point that they could hardly stand still to speak to the crowd, Ben confided, "I just said to Matt, 'Losing would suck and winning would be really scary.' And it is really scary." Rarely have the stagers of this premier show been so indulgent with allowing recipients precious extra moments at the podium as Affleck and Damon rattled off the names of *all* those to whom they owed thanks—which ranged from Gus to the people back in Boston.

Much further on in the globally televised program came the segment devoted to announcing the Best Director. Facile Warren Beatty stepped to the microphone and listed the five nominees: James Cameron (*Titanic*), Peter Cattaneo (*The Full Monty*), Gus, Curtis Hanson (*L.A. Confidential*), and Atom Egoyan (*The Sweet Hereafter*). As the camera panned to the directors in the auditorium, Van Sant sat with a bemused look in his eyes and a near deadpan look on his face. He was chewing gum, as was often his habit.

Given the coup that James Cameron had already pulled off in pushing the mammoth *Titanic* to completion and the fact that the epic had already become such a huge box-office champion, few pollsters doubted that he would claim the director's award, as the film had already gathered in several other Oscars. (Gus and his companion Paige Powell had a tip-off to how the evening would go prize-wise when they first entered the auditorium and saw a *Titantic* ship motif on the presentation stage.)

As anticipated, Cameron won the director's nod from the Academy. As Gus and the other losers politely applauded the victor, Cameron strode up onstage and in the midst of his acceptance speech asked the throng, "So this does prove, once and for all, that size does matter?" (Earlier in the evening as Cameron, sitting across the aisle from Gus, amassed his pile of Academy Awards, Gus had reached over with his camera and snapped a shot of the stack of prizes.)

After the ceremonies, because Gus had relatives and friends awaiting them in the Winnebago, he chose not to attend the Academy's Governors' Ball with Paige Powell. Instead, the group took a nighttime drive about the city and eventually ended at the lavish party hosted by Miramax Films.

Although Gus had lost the trophy of all trophies for a moviemaker, he would now be listed in his credentials as the Academy Award–nominated director of *Good Will Hunting* (the film that claimed two Oscars). No longer would he be described just as "openly gay filmmaker Gus Van Sant."

More important, Gus had demonstrated to the Hollywood filmmaker community that he could make a crowd-pleasing mainstream picture. As he perceived of *Good Will Hunting*, "I was trying to make it not like something that I would do. But because you're making the decisions it ends up being like one of your movies." As to any potential Van Sant–type on-screen quirkiness: "I tried to keep all that kind of stuff out of there. The script was very straight-ahead, very *American Playhouse, Hallmark Presents*. . . . I knew the kind of movie that was like that so I tried to make it one of those movies. I can still see the presence of myself in there. I was just trying to present it like something I had seen elsewhere."

▼

LIKE his past works, *Good Will Hunting* contained striking examples of dysfunctional family life with the characters creating their own versions of a bonded group: Will, Chuckie, and their South Boston pals; Professor Lambeau, his flunkies at M.I.T., and fellow mathematicians; etc. In the midst of these special groups there is therapist Sean McGuire, widowed and alone, as well as Skylar, whose father died when she was thirteen and whose mother (if alive) is not mentioned.

The ties that bind some of these individuals to their peer groups are explained as male bonding. However, the texture of these relationships suggests that within the film, there could be more implications beneath the surface. Take for example, the sequence in which Lambeau and Will are seated in front of a blackboard filled with math equations that they have just worked on together. The seemingly heterosexual Lambeau places his arm on the back of Will's chair and then pats the boy with an "affectionate" gesture. Such instances as this or the extreme closeness of Will and Chuckie, who both date women but have yet to have a satisfactory emotional relationship with one of the opposite sex, led critic Andrews Sarris (*New York Observer*) to point out, "The quantity and intensity of male bonding in the movie made me a little uneasy about other possible subtexts."

As in all Van Sant features, there are stunning shots of the landscape, here including the Boston skyline, boaters on the Charles River, the Boston Common, and Harvard Square. There are not only the director's typically unique perspectives in camera setups for the many one-to-one sequences, but Gus occasionally interpolates one of his specialty shots. For example, the opening title sequence, executed by Pablo Ferro, boasts a swirling collage of mathematical equations superimposed in and around close-up shots of the film's lead character reading. (These images were attained by having six-foot-high blow-ups of math text pages standing on a set as they are photographed.) In a flashback sequence as Sean McGuire and Will Hunting relate how their (foster) fathers had beat them viciously as children, there is a shot of a man climbing the stairs, which fragments into kaleidoscopic shapes.

Another visual that is blended with meticulously executed sound effects is the schoolyard fight scene between Will, Chuckie, and their followers versus some former neighbor enemies. Part of the sequence was shot in slow motion and as Van Sant describes proudly in his director's commentary to the DVD edition of *Good Will Hunting*, there are over one hundred sound-effect tracks overlayed to create the proper audio accompaniment.

Good Will Hunting, despite its formula ingredients, took Gus in new directions. Rarely had his characters emoted with such depths of feelings before. While, obviously, he was working with a well-crafted, albeit emotionally manipulative screenplay, Van Sant still did not hold back in allowing his screen figures to register crowd-pleasing pathos. Examples range from Skylar's crying scene as Will refuses to accept and return her great love, to McGuire recalling the wonders of his late wife, or to the film's most highly charged scene at the therapist's office. There Sean prods Will to let loose the pain he has bottled up from his past years as an abused child. The interplay of McGuire repeating over and over, "It's not your fault. It's not your fault" may not be high-level therapy at work, but it is effective screen drama.

And, if over a toss of the coin way back when, Ben Affleck agreed to play Chuckie and Matt Damon to take on the showcasing role of Will Hunting in their movie, Affleck has a shining moment when he arrives at Will's house one morning to find something different. He discovers that his friend has finally broken out of his rut and has left town. In pantomime, with his mouth slightly agape, Ben registers a variety of emotions that include joy at his pal's liberation and great pain at losing his best friend in the world.

Such sequences as the above reveal an intriguing new dimension to Van Sant the filmmaker. Gus could now say, "With this film I learned about speaking to the audience. When I go to the theatre, I'm looking for something that is moving. The audience is basically there to be moved, like an audience that goes to hear a symphony. . . . I've learned the value of that, paying attention to audiences' needs, why people actually go. It's not so much about manipulating, but imparting something of value to the audience. In our case, it's like a lesson; Will Hunting is learning something that applies to all of us. We all have reservations about doing a certain thing because that will jeopardize what we already have. We're conservative with our directions in life. If you make this one move, you might endanger things you already feel safe with. Will takes a chance on getting to know someone that he's attracted to, but following his emotions jeopardizes his relationship with his friends. The film is saying, don't be afraid of change. It's something that I run across every day in my own decision-making."

28

WANTED: NORMAN BATES

Good Will Hunting changed everything for me. And for Ben [Affleck] and Matt [Damon]. For all three of us, I think. It changed our lives, you know.

Gus Van Sant, 2000

IN THE WAKE OF HIS tremendous success with *Good Will Hunting* in late 1997 and early 1998, many movie critics and reporters around the globe bemoaned the apparent defection of independent filmmaker Gus Van Sant to mainstream cinema. For example, in *Variety International Guide: 1999*, in her essay on the quirky director, Sheila Johnston described him as "a strikingly original talent with a penchant for unconventional subjects, a unique, hip but poetic sensibility and a highly idiosyncratic storytelling style. His emergence coincided with the revival of American independent cinema in the mid-1980s, sparked by directors like Spike Lee, Jim Jarmusch and, subsequently, Hal Hartley, Steven Soderbergh, Richard Linklater, and Quentin Tarantino. But with *Good Will Hunting*, like so many before him, he appeared to be surrendering his maverick status."

When Van Sant was questioned why he had veered into the ultracommercial arena, he explained, "I had this notion being mainstream was easier, and that what I was doing was very hard. . . . I was thinking, maybe that my association with the anti-heroes in my first films was something I needed and shouldn't—so I made *Good Will Hunting*. . . . The only difference is in how people define entertainment. My early films were more challenging; the new ones are what films are like for most people. William S. Burroughs told me he tried and failed

100 times to write an ordinary detective novel. I just wanted to know if I could do the other stuff."

When Gus was asked if he would indeed continue in mainstream cinema, he told Peter Keough of the *Boston Phoenix* in early 1998: "I probably would if the price is right. No, I probably wouldn't because of Michael Lehmann. He made *Heathers*, which is brilliant. Then he made *Hudson Hawk* because he was doing that thing of 'I really want to make a bunch of money so that I cannot worry about my future.' And something went wrong. So I would probably be cautious of certain types of movies. But I would make a James Bond movie."

Meanwhile, those who knew Van Sant personally appreciated that he was the same individual as before *Good Will Hunting* and that he continued to march to his own beat both in moviemaking and in his private life. Writer Katherine Dunn described her longtime friend Gus in 1998 as he mingled in the city they both called home—Portland: "The waiters and bartenders here know him even when he's disguised by ragged sweaters, a battered flasher's raincoat and a three-day beard as scruffy as any of his characters. He trails around like that for weeks sometimes. The locals say, 'Gus has gone native.' The idlers debate whether he's submersing himself in the lives of his characters or trying for invisibility among the roving detritus of the pavements. But he doesn't explain and nobody asks."

She goes on to detail, "He's a hometown hero, of course. The tuxedo set shows him off to visiting dignitaries as a municipal asset, like a scenic view or a winning NBA team. If the civic boosters wish he'd stop depicting their town as a sleaze-pit, they won't mention it to him. He's a nice guy, after all, a ready supporter for good causes. His film openings are AIDS benefits. He never forgets a friend, they say, and his friends range from chic to seedy. He leans in the shadows at gritty club concerts, tavern readings, and alley art shows. He sips counter coffee at the greasy spoon."

As far as upcoming film projects, Gus still preferred topics that were offbeat and touched his unique sensibilities. Just before accepting *Good Will Hunting* he had planned a picture based on David Schneider's book *Street Zen*. It told the true account of Issan Dorsey, a junkie transvestite hooker who became, among other occupations, a Zen teacher. The project was now in limbo due to lack of funding. On another front, Gus agreed to executive produce *Burn*, to be written and directed by young filmmaker Nick Perry. It was a tale of a runaway teen who dreams of becoming a professional race car driver. En route to North Carolina, the lead character hitches a ride to Las Vegas where he is befriended by a veteran street hustler. Later retitled *Speedway Junky*, the $1 million–budgeted feature was set to shoot in 1998.

Van Sant was also quite enthusiastic about adapting John Callahan's life story for a film to headline Robin Williams, and TriStar was interested. The drama dealt with Portland-based Callahan who was a quadriplegic as the result of a car accident. The narrative related how Callahan coped with his major handicap and undertook a tough path to become a successful and controversial politically incorrect cartoonist and writer. The proposed film was to be based on the subject's 1989 book, *Don't Worry He Won't Get Far on Foot*.

Another item on Gus's agenda was *Brokeback Mountain*, based on the Annie Proulx novella that would later appear in her 1999 collection *Close Range: Wyoming Stories*. Sony Pictures/Columbia Pictures had the screen rights, Larry McMurtry and Diana Ossana were to coadapt the story, and Gus was announced to possibly direct the vehicle. The tale by the Pulitzer Prize–winning Proulx dealt with two bisexual cowboys who have an occasional but intense sexual relationship over a two-decade period.

While Gus weighed his several filmmaking choices, he was also preoccupied with other types of projects. He contributed a drawing for the book *Signature Flowers: A Revealing Collection of Celebrity Drawings* put together by Victoria Leacock. Well-known individuals in such media as music, film, theater, literature, and television each provided a floral drawing they had done. Besides Gus, the others who volunteered included Madonna, Francis Ford Coppola, Cindy Crawford, Robert Altman, Celine Dion, Barbara Walters, and Bette Midler. The volume was a fundraiser for AIDS research.

Reflecting his growing prominence in the film industry, Van Sant was asked to participate in a panel discussion at the Directors Guild of America in Los Angeles. In March 1998 he joined James Cameron, Curtis Hanson, James L. Brooks, and Steven Spielberg for the session, which drew a full house. When Gus described for the audience his well-known habit of taking Polaroid shots at casting sessions and then spending hours and hours poring over the shots, "mixing and matching," Cameron quipped, "Did you ever spend time in jail?"

▼

IN early 1998 a journalist who was interviewing Gus Van Sant commented that the director seemed to be consciously surrounding himself with young people, both on- and off-camera. Gus replied, "It seems to be an age I'm stuck in. The age between 14 and 25 is to me where the most inspirational thinking comes about in our culture. The establishment doesn't take ideas from that age group seriously. Society says they're inexperienced—something that's said in *Good Will Hunting*. A lot of the ideas are worth pursuing. The germ of an idea is the thing of value."

One set of youths he had professional contact with at the time was the teen pop group Hanson. He directed the music video to "Weird" from their Mercury label album *Middle of Nowhere*. It was shot over a four-day period in mid-February 1998. Van Sant supplied the musical short with its garish look, but the thematic concept came from the boy band. Gus had first met the enormously popular trio (whose fame had already peaked) in late 1997 when he approached their managers about starring the boys in a feature film. Van Sant had no particular concept in mind beyond making it something like the Spice Girls' 1997 feature *Spice World*. When that idea found no favor in the Hanson camp, Gus suggested directing a music video for them.

Regarding the Hanson video shoot, which included location work in Manhattan, Van Sant has detailed with boyish enthusiasm: "My favorite moment was when we had the band walk into the middle of Times Square, Saturday at midnight singing to their playback—their song 'Weird'—and walking by regular people on the street. The first take was successful and we tried it again, but just as we started out, there were these partying fraternity brothers who were coming out of a subway stairwell and they recognized the band. They screamed 'Hanson!' . . . and the first A.D. [assistant director] said, 'No boys, it's not Hanson,' but they screamed 'We're Delta Phi from Oklahoma State. We know Hanson when we see them!' And 25 blustery, plastered and loud jock-type guys surrounded the band. From where I was standing all I saw was a complete mob scene moving its way across Broadway. I began running toward the crowd with newspaper headlines flashing behind my eyes: 'Hanson Ripped Apart by Drunk Oklahoma Fraternity Brothers.' But when I got to them the band was skipping away from the mob laughing and exclaiming, 'Wow!! Male energy!!'" (Later, for a mid-2000 issue of *Interview* magazine, Van Sant would do an extensive photo layout/interview of Hanson. No film project between the group and Gus ever materialized.)

▼

THERE'S an old saying: "Be careful what you wish for, because it might come true." Perhaps, in retrospect, Van Sant may have regretted not heeding that sage advice. Gus, however, could always find a satisfactory rationale to explain why he was about to launch into a fresh activity. Then he would have the same or additional reasons why he was doing the new thing as he actually undertook it, and later, after the fact, he would have an explanation of why all along it had made sense to do what he had done, even when it seemingly did not. Rarely, at least publicly, did he voice discernible regrets about what paths he had taken.

In the frenzied aftermath of *Good Will Hunting*'s box-office bonanza, Oscar-nominated Van Sant and his agent were besieged with Hollywood job offers. Many were of particular vehicles such as *Brokeback Mountain*. Others resulted from schmoozing, the time-honored Hollywood tradition of power makers gathering to chat about possible movie projects. Now that Van Sant was coming off a huge mainstream film success, he was not only admitted to more such meetings, but he was on a far more equal footing.

Since the days in 1989 when *Drugstore Cowboy* had first given Gus prominence and respect within the American film industry, he had made periodic visits to Universal Pictures. During these conferences in the executive tower, he had undergone the ritual of answering executives' question, "What do you want to make?" with his wish list of offbeat film projects. Typically the recitation brought a polite but stony silence. Sometimes it would lead to a studio suit pulling out a list of company-owned past films and suggesting that Van Sant direct a modernized remake of one of those. Gus had, at such times, raised his own suggestion—redoing Alfred Hitchcock's *Psycho*, but *not* in a new variation but a scene-by-scene remake. (It should be remembered that back in 1977 Van Sant had contributed the "Psycho Shampoo" filmed skit to the satirical stage revue, *Rabies!*)

It was Gus's rationale that "[i]t's stupid to remake bad movies. One should remake the good ones. Any numbers of remakes are made, but they never preserve the original, they all play with the logic and language of the actual filmmaker. They're not interested in remaking the original but robbing it. This is a remounting of the original piece."

Such "madness" on Gus's part had always brought to a quick close any negotiations between Universal and Van Sant. Now, it was a different situation. Academy Award–nominee Gus had sudden status. His project ideas—even if others might think them bizarre—carried weight and received due consideration.

This time around, in 1998, when Gus returned yet again to Universal for a new battery of meetings, highly successful producer Brian Grazer was involved in the confab. (Grazer and his filmmaker partner Ron Howard at Imagine Entertainment were based on the studio lot.) Almost immediately Grazer was intrigued by Van Sant's high concept notion of treading into sacred Hitchcockian waters to do a complete remake of *Psycho*. Said Grazer, "Hearing how passionate he was and knowing he wanted to make it in a respectful way, it seemed like a smart bet. It gives the movie a new pedigree: *Psycho*, as told by Gus Van Sant. And if it works, it will prove there's a fascinating way to re-create films from our library."

Reportedly, Grazer advised the studio decision-makers, "You have a chance to do something really unique. I told them you can make one more crappy movie for $40 million or you can take a chance. It could be a huge disaster, a big mess, and the critics could hate it. At least you're doing something really different, and if it works, something profound may emerge from it."

Part of Grazer's enthusiasm, undoubtedly, was the economics of doing the remake. Since the new edition would be following exactly the master's storyboards, a defined, contained budget could readily be created. Since, presumably, it also would follow an essentially preedited continuity, the editing of the new *Psycho* could be swift.

Casey Silver, Universal's head of production, seconded Grazer's motion, although he would admit later of Gus's proposal: "I thought it was a very strange idea. The idea of remaking a classic like *Psycho* just seemed like a dangerous business to get into." So why did he okay the project? As he reasoned in the postshoot period: "Gus is a more mature filmmaker than he was 10 years ago. That made us more willing to take a chance."

As for Van Sant, he must have been taken aback at the unexpected change in reaction to the off-the-cuff idea about *Psycho* that he had first thrown onto the discussion table nearly a decade ago. It gave him a quick lesson in the power of power: "That's usually the reason things get done in Hollywood nowadays. It has nothing to do with the *idea* for the movie." Out of the blue he had a new film going into production almost immediately, without the usual long delays. As the moviemaker phrased it, "Suddenly I was using my 'Get Out of Jail Free' [Monopoly] card for this project." His salary for *Psycho* would be twice what he had received for *Good Will Hunting*. (The fee was probably in the million-dollar range.) He also would be a producer of this film along with Brian Grazer.

With Universal having given him the go-ahead, Van Sant devised a game plan: "I've always had a great appreciation for Hitchcock. But I never really knew how he made his films. So the challenge was to follow his footsteps, to go back and figure out how he set up his shots."

▼

DOING remakes of feature films was not in itself alien to American studios: in fact, during Hollywood's golden age, a picture frequently would be refitted at economy rates into a budget vehicle from the same studio (e.g., 1936's *The Petrified Forest* to 1945's *Escape in the Desert*, 1941's *The Strawberry Blonde* to 1948's *One Sunday Afternoon*). Many classics had also been redone: e.g., *Ben Hur*, *It Happened One Night*, *The Virginian*, *The Front Page*, *The Nutty Professor*. Sometimes a director like Cecil B. De Mille would take one of his own earlier Hollywood pictures, such as *The Ten Commandments* (1923), and revamp it to a new edition (1956's *The Ten Commandments*). Or French filmmaker George Sluizer might use his own European-made *Spoorloos* (1988) for an American redo as *The Vanishing* (1993). But to venture into the sacred territory of Alfred Hitchcock, the king of suspenseful thrillers who was in his own pantheon, was another matter. Or was it?

Several properties of the late Hitchcock had already been revamped into new feature films or TV movies, including *Shadow of a Doubt*, *Strangers on a Train*, *Notorious*, *Dial M for Murder*, and *Rear Window* (scheduled as a fall 1998 telefeature with Christopher Reeve and Daryl Hannah). Hitchcock had actually restaged his own 1934 British-made chiller *The Man Who Knew Too Much* as the glossy, widescreen, color Hollywood feature of 1956. Universal had already turned out such sequel distillations as *Psycho II* (1983), *Psycho III* (1986), and the made-for-cable *Psycho IV: The Beginning* (1990), besides the telefeature offshoot *Bates Motel* (1987). So what was so off-the-charts about Van Sant's plan for *Psycho*?

It was the fact that Gus intended the new edition to be a shot-by-shot match of the original, with *no* change in plot, characterization, ambiance, or even Bernard Herrmann's gilt-edge musical score. (The only difference Van Sant envisioned was shooting the new version in color, rather than the black-and-white of the original.) Van Sant's game plan was a marked departure from the usual

Hollywood remake where typically the story line or the gender of the leads or the genre or the locale would be altered—or even perhaps songs added—to give a new spin to an old property.

But in Van Sant's unique way of thinking, just redoing *Psycho* in color—and obviously with a new cast—was sufficient grounds to tackle the beloved property. He reasoned that, since the original *Psycho* was in black and white, many of the younger generations since its release had never watched the movie (on the theory that young people will not sit through a noncolor film). This, argued Van Sant, created a huge new audience for his edition of the thriller and everyone knew, said Gus, that teenagers and twentysomethings made up a preponderance of moviegoers. Van Sant also concluded that a goodly number of potential ticket buyers who had seen *Psycho* back in 1960 had not rewatched the classic in the subsequent thirty-eight years. They were also candidates for attending the new big-screen edition.

Convinced his estimations were on target, Gus envisioned this movie project as a high-class, high-profile test of whether, like a stage play, a film could be restaged (not revamped). It led him to expound excitedly on this great new twist in the aesthetics of filmmaking. To his way of thinking it would help him—and other filmmakers to follow—to isolate the greatness of a "classic" picture and to recapture that essence in a mirror new edition. Intellectually, Gus was tremendously excited by the daunting task ahead.

For him, redoing *Psycho* was an extension of his visual arts education at the Rhode Island School of Design in the 1970s: "They teach appropriation your first year at the school. You're supposed to go out and find your found object and make it your own. Draw it, become obsessed with it."

And in his newfound fervor, he began to talk up the project. His rationale for doing the movie seemed to alter from announcement to announcement or from interview to interview. As *Entertainment Weekly* noted later with a tinge of bewilderment, "Every time he's asked, Van Sant gives a different reason for why he's remaking *Psycho*. Other answers include 'It's never been done before,' 'A lot of people have never seen the original,' 'I've never dabbled in high-concept before,' and the always conversation-stopping 'Why not?' His marketing-scheme explanation isn't any more convincing, but it does at least have some resonance with the suits at Universal." (Later *San Francisco Examiner* journalist Walter Addiego would point out, "Van Sant has had a great time with the press, offering up scores of different answers—evasive, facetious, tantalizing—as to his motivation in faithfully remaking a classic [my favorite: 'Why are they asking why?']. The real answer is in the movie itself, a virtual textbook in using sardonic and macabre humor to make subversive observations.")

One of the first announcements of Gus Van Sant's daring new cinema project appeared—ironically enough—on April Fool's Day in the *Hollywood Reporter*. It might have been more appropriate if the information had leaked out in the trade press on Halloween—All Saints' Day—for all hell was about to break loose.

▼

BY April 2, 1998, Liz Smith was mentioning *Psycho* in her syndicated newspaper column. She referenced that hip young movie star Drew Barrymore was interested in taking on the female lead role of Marion Crane, the part made famous by Janet Leigh in the original film. By then, the avalanche of publicity, conjecture, disdain, shock, anger, rebuttal, and so on had begun about this upcoming remake of Hitchcock's classic, which had grossed about $32 million (a lot of money in the 1960s) since its original release and had been placed on the National Film Preservation Board's National Film Registry in 1992.

The tenor of complaints registered by film critics in print and by "outraged" Hitchcock purists on Internet web sites and news/user groups was, essentially, how could Gus Van Sant dare to display such hubris as to think he could remake the most memorable of the master's entire screen oeuvre. (Original *Psycho* star Janet Leigh, who had recently written a book on the making of Hitchcock's masterpiece, was initially drawn into the fray but quickly withdrew to the diplomatic sidelines.)

The depth and range of the virulence must have amazed both Van Sant and Universal. In response Gus argued, "We're not trying to show off. We're taking a story that's antiquated, in the sense that it's not in color, and we're updating it." That did not satisfy the dissenters. Nor did they care that Gus's reason for taking on *Psycho* rather than some other lesser Hitchcock celluloid exercise was because *"Psycho* was barebones enough" —in its austerity and simplicity—in contrast to, for example, the "complicated" *North by Northwest*. To no avail, the director reasoned, *"Psycho* is like *Waiting for Godot*. You can put anybody in the places of the characters, stage it indoors, outdoors, it's going to do its thing. The puzzle has been so worked out it almost wants to be redone. It's very much like an opera, something you should restage and celebrate."

It also fell on mostly deaf ears when Van Sant reflected, "But as cinema grows older, these things will start happening more and more. To shut the door and say 'blasphemous' seems to me a very strict and old-fogy way of thinking." He also suggested (in vain) that relatively few people today had seen the original *Psycho*. "They only know about the shower scene, little glimpses of this or that. I think it'll be suspenseful because people don't know what's going on. Even if they know the surprise ending, my guess is that that's not what keeps you in suspense. Hiding of information is not the thing—Hitchcock let people know about the danger and the danger kept them in suspense."

Finally, worn out by the ongoing, unproductive contretemps, Van Sant told the *New York Times*: "It's impossible to defend myself against questions like, 'How dare you remake *Psycho*?' When the critics see it, I hope they'll change their minds. But I know some people will be hoping I get bad reviews."

Along the way, the beleaguered director had a few defenders. One such was Anthony Timpone, the editor of the popular horror film magazine, *Fangoria*. In the November 1998 issue, Timpone wrote, "Hitchcock fans are reeling. Horror fans are seething. Film nerds are screaming! . . . Gus Van Sant is remaking the greatest horror film of all time, and on December 4 a new version of *Psycho* will be unleashed for the *Scream* generation. . . . Many fright fans are justifiably appalled by Van Sant's bold move. Those with too much time on their hands have even put up anti-*Psycho* 1998 websites! Lighten up, people. Let's wait until the movie is done before we start throwing rotten tomatoes at it." The editorial continued, "It will take genius in line with the master to pull another *Psycho* off, but the eccentric Van Sant may be up to the task." Timpone reasoned further, "Its success or failure will not diminish Hitchcock's masterpiece in my eyes. If anything it will help others rediscover it or turn to it for the first time, or even pick up Robert Bloch's original novel. All those readying a boycott on December 4 should take a cold shower instead."

▼

BY the end of April 1998 Gus had begun to assemble his cast or, at least, to narrow down the options. One of his top choices to play the ill-fated Marion Crane was *To Die For*'s Nicole Kidman. But her schedule did not lend itself to the projected summer shoot. Others Van Sant considered were Winona Ryder and Claire Danes but, like Drew Barrymore who wanted the part, casting one of them would have meant rewriting the part to be several years younger than in the original.

In characteristic fashion, Gus came up with a more offbeat choice—Anne Heche (*Donnie Brasco, Wag the Dog, I Know What You Did Last Summer*). A veteran of the TV soap opera *Another World* where, from 1987 to 1991, she played a dual role, Heche had become the center of off-camera controversy when the actress acknowledged that she was having a live-in relationship with comedian Ellen DeGeneres. (Heche's previous longterm romantic connection had been with comedic actor Steve Martin.) The revelation had occurred while Heche was filming a romantic comedy, *Six Days, Seven Nights,* with Harrison Ford. The big questions at that time revolved around whether Heche could perform convincingly on camera with her leading man in a heterosexual story line, and, more important, would the public buy the charade at the box office. (The answers were yes and yes, and when released in June 1998 the feature grossed over $74.29 million in domestic distribution.)

Gus remembered his reaction to Heche auditioning for the Marion Crane role: "Anne had so many nuances. Janet Leigh seemed to have this complete, rock-hard solidity that '50s women had. Anne wasn't as direct. She played the character's strength, but with a kind of ditsiness, like she didn't know she was getting in so far over her head." The actress later said that she had never seen the original *Psycho* until the night before her scheduled meeting with Gus.

By early May 1998 Heche had committed to the new *Psycho*. Gus had also found the talent to portray the secondary female lead of Lila Crane, the sister of Marion. In the original the assignment had been handled demurely by Vera

Miles, a Hitchcock protégée and an accomplished performer. In the new rendition it would be Julianne Moore (*The Fugitive, Nine Months, The Lost World: Jurassic Park*). Like Heche she had begun her career playing a dual role on a daytime drama (*As the World Turns* from 1985 to 1988). The prolific Moore had recently been Oscar-nominated in the Best Supporting Actress category for her performance in 1997's *Boogie Nights*.

While these casting choices were key to the film, the all-important decision was who would play Norman Bates, that seemingly benign mama's boy who wouldn't hurt a fly. In the famed original the part had been handled to perfection by tall, gangling, twenty-seven-year-old Tony Perkins in a performance that forever typecast him and essentially sidetracked his once promising acting career. Out of resignation, disgust, and a desire to work the decades thereafter, Perkins had made three *Psycho* sequels and even directed *Psycho III*. Perkins had died of AIDS in 1992 and his memory was still attached like holy water to the sacred original *Psycho*.

With so much controversy resonating in Hollywood about the role of Norman Bates and the fame/career damage it had brought to Perkins, there were real obstacles to finding a suitable actor willing to tackle the assignment. For some, to compete with the ghost of Perkins in a remake of that defining horror role was too daunting. For others, the fear of having their acting future narrowed into playing variations of the deranged keeper of the motel from hell was an overwhelmingly scary consideration. As candidates for the part weighed the risks of taking the job, Van Sant kept pondering the decision whether to find a similar type to Perkins or go in a new direction with the enigmatic Norman Bates. Being Gus, he chose to take a fresh route.

To break away from the Tony Perkins image so associated with the part, Gus initially approached Leonardo DiCaprio, then riding high on the crest of *Titanic*. The director also discussed the job with Matt Damon and Joaquin Phoenix, both alumnae of past Van Sant films. When none of these choices worked out (lack of interest from DiCaprio and Damon, a too-full schedule on the part of Phoenix), Gus had to look elsewhere.

The man of choice proved to be Vince Vaughn, the six-foot five-inch beefy actor from Minneapolis, Minnesota. After small guest roles on episodes of TV series, he had made his big screen debut in a bit in 1991's *For the Boys* starring Bette Midler. Five years later he had his breakthrough part in *Swingers* and since then had done good work in *The Lost World: Jurassic Park*, *The Locusts*, and *A Cool Dry Place*. More recently he had acted in two movies with Joaquin Phoenix: *Clay Pigeons* (as a serial killer) and in *Return to Paradise*. The latter film was photographed by Gus's good friend and cinematographer Eric Alan Edwards, and the drama had featured Anne Heche.

In retrospect, it made solid sense to have considered seriously twenty-eight-year-old Vaughn for the Norman Bates screen part. Vince was a virile actor who had already demonstrated an appealing acting range. On the plus side, Vaughn had already performed on camera with both Anne Heche and Julianne Moore. Thus, from conversations with the actresses and/or studying the footage, Van Sant could surmise how their chemistry would work on-screen together.

Yet, said Gus, "Vince was not even in my imagination as being close to right for Norman Bates. But he's a good friend of Joaquin's, and when I met him, he had a really interesting quality I wasn't expecting. He has a certain presence that's friendly, but there's an undercurrent. It had nothing to do with Tony Perkins, and that opened up a way to avoid a stereotype."

The director envisioned that Vince, with his hair cropped short and wearing a simple T-shirt and slacks, could well be the new Norman Bates. "It's not something you can really explain," Van Sant said. "Sometimes you can just read the story in an actor's face." Gus also responded to the actor's ordinary yet edgy demeanor and because Vaughan had, as Van Sant described, "that ability to snap." Then, too, noted the filmmaker, "like Anne [Heche] he seemed very excited about doing it, which was a big thing."

After the casting of Vaughn was announced the actor was subjected to a battery of queries of why he wanted to be in the new *Psycho:* "The most important thing for me was to work with Gus. And my feeling was that songs get remade all the time. Plays get reinterpreted time and time again. So when friends and the press said to me, 'How can you do this?' my take is, 'Acting comes from a childhood place, to a religious place.'"

Within the next weeks of late spring 1998 Gus rounded out his *Psycho* cast. To play the role of Marian's married lover Sam Loomis—performed in the original by handsome, but detached John Gavin—Van Sant contracted New Yorker Viggo Mortensen (*The Indian Runner, Crimson Tide, G.I. Jane*). The wiry Mortensen, also a professional photographer, had recently played the second male lead in *A Perfect Murder*, the 1998 remake of Hitchcock's 1954 *Dial M for Murder*.

The final key member of the new *Psycho* cast to be chosen was the actor to play Milton Arbogast, the private detective who meets his fate on the creaky staircase of the Bates home. In Hitchcock's rendition the part had been handled in superior fashion by veteran character performer Martin Balsam. If anyone could be said to be a modern counterpart to the gifted Balsam, it was William H. Macy. The latter had been in films since the early 1980s, gaining recognition with roles in such movies as *Homicide, Benny & Joon*, and *Ghosts of Mississippi*. Macy had been with Julianne Moore in *Boogie Nights* and Anne Heche in *Wag the Dog*. As the low-caliber schemer in 1997's *Fargo*, Macy had won an Oscar nomination as Best Supporting Actor.

Rounding out his cast ensemble, the director selected Chad Everett as Tom Cassidy, the randy rich home buyer. Rance Howard, the father of filmmaker Ron Howard, took on the role of Mr. Lowery, the real estate man, and Philip Baker Hall signed up as Sheriff Al Chambers. Robert Forster—who was nominated for Best Supporting Actor Oscar for 1997's *Jackie Brown* and was featured in 1998's telefeature remake of *Rear Window*—was picked to be Dr. Simon, who delivers the monologue at the end regarding Norman Bates's mental problems. Rita

Wilson, actress wife of superstar Tom Hanks, was chosen to be Caroline, the co-worker of Marion at the real estate firm. (In the original *Psycho*, Hitchcock's daughter Patricia had played Caroline.) Character actress Anne Haney was added to the lineup as the sheriff's wife, Mrs. Chambers. Former fitness model and drag racer Stephanie Reaves was hired to play Mother Bates in a portion of the knife-wielding shower sequence and in the footage when she is shown in a long shot pacing back and forth at her bedroom window.

Also given subordinate parts in *Psycho* were three Van Sant cast veterans: James Remar as the patrolman, James LeGros as Charlie (the used car dealer), and Flea as Bob Summerfield. Whereas Van Sant had not been on camera in *Good Will Hunting*, he gave another nod to Hitchcock by creating a special cameo for himself in the same shot—outside the real estate office—that Sir Alfred had performed back in 1960 for the first *Psycho*. To carry the conceit one step further, actor Roy Brocksmith, bolstered by appropriate body padding and makeup, was assigned to replicate Hitchcock in the same sequence, so Van Sant as the Man in the Cowboy Hat outside the real estate office, could be seen briefly chatting with "Hitchcock."

29

PSYCHO REDUX

We started out being really fanatical about doing it [*Psycho*] exactly the same. But there were a couple of scenes we just couldn't get right. We just couldn't see how [Alfred] Hitchcock did the blocking, where people were supposed to be standing in relation to the camera. So all we could do was loosely base them on the original.

Gus Van Sant, 1998

BACK IN 1959, FILM DIRECTOR Alfred Hitchcock had read a review in the *New York Times* of a new book by Robert Bloch entitled *Psycho*. The tome was suggested by a rash of grisly murders in Wisconsin. In the real-life homicides the culprit turned out to be Ed Gein, an ostensibly average individual who was actually a terrifying serial killer. (Among other horrendous misdeeds, after Gein butchered his mother he made table lampshades from her skin.) Bloch said later of his intent in writing *Psycho*, "I based my story on the situation, rather than on any person, living or dead involved in the Gein affair. I decided to write a novel based on the notion that the man next door may be a monster, unsuspected even in the gossip-ridden microcosm of small-town life."

At the time Hitchcock, who had a production deal with Paramount Pictures, was actively preparing a new motion picture to star actress Audrey Hepburn. When that production did not materialize, he turned back to *Psycho*. The director paid $9,500 for the screen rights to Bloch's novel. After Paramount, who thought the tale too grim, agreed to distribute the film but not to finance it, Hitchcock accepted their distribution deal and backed the project through his own production company. He shot the vehicle at Universal Pictures where his then current weekly TV series was being produced. Anxious to maximize his profits on the picture, he filmed the feature in economical black and white and established a compacted thirty-six-day shooting schedule. When initial adaptations of the novel did not please the very particular Hitchcock, he turned to writer Joseph Stefano who drafted a new version that met with the master's approval. The provocative script, which dealt with schizophrenia (and other topics), incorporated many Freudian themes as subtexts since Stefano was then undergoing Freudian analysis.

In Alfred Hitchcock's published conversations with French filmmaker François Truffaut in 1966, Hitchcock said of making *Psycho*: "I didn't start out to make an important movie. I thought I could have fun with this subject and this situation. The picture cost $800,000. It was an experiment in this sense: could I make a feature film under the same conditions as a television show? I used a television crew to shoot it very quickly."

From the start, the astute director understood that his new movie would not appeal to establishment movie reviewers. After all, it was breaking many filmmaking conventions of the day as well as mores of the time with its mix of sexual taboos, gore, and a leading lady who dies partway through the narrative. So, when the picture was to be released in March 1960, the filmmaker and Paramount decreed that there would be no advance screenings for movie critics. When the initial reviews of *Psycho* appeared, Hitchcock's intuition proved correct. *Newsweek* dismissed the entry with "*Psycho* is plainly a gimmick movie whose suspense depends on a single, specific twist." The *New York Times* noted disdainfully that the film was "[a] blot on an honorable career." Nevertheless, the public thoroughly endorsed the daring movie. (As a gimmick to stimulate audience curiosity, Sir Alfred and the studio told theater owners that no one was to be seated once the film began and to urge patrons not to reveal the movie's surprise ending to others.) *Psycho* eventually grossed a then-astounding $32 million. The movie received four Oscar nominations: Best Director, Best Supporting Actress (Janet Leigh), Best Cinematography—Black and White, and Best Art Director—Set Decoration—Black and White.

By the mid-1960s, Hitchcock considered *Psycho* not only his most commercial vehicle to date but perhaps his finest artistic achievement. He told Truffaut: "I take pride in the fact that *Psycho*, more than any other of my films, is a film that belongs to filmmakers, to you and me."

After Hitchcock's death in 1980, Universal Pictures, which now had rights to the property, made the previously mentioned three *Psycho* sequels plus *Bates Motel*, a spin-off of sorts.

▼

AS Van Sant and Universal prepared to launch their cinematic revisit to *Psycho* it was essential—especially to appease the mounting outcries from horrified Hitchcock purists—to have the approval of two particular parties. One was Patricia Hitchcock O'Connell, the deceased filmmaker's daughter who represented her father's estate. An agreement was reached, and Patricia served both as technical adviser on the remake as well as an occasional spokesperson to endorse the venture.

The other party of interest was seventy-six-year-old Joseph Stefano, the original *Psycho* scribe. Since that landmark adventure he had produced the 1963–64 TV series *The Outer Limits* and written such movies as *Futz!*, *Snowbeast*, *The Hidden*, and *Psycho IV: The Beginning*. When contacted, he was agreeable to the new *Psycho*. His blessing on Van Sant's production included being brought aboard to modify his original screenplay for the sensibilities of late-1990s moviegoers.

As to Gus's creative crew, among the regulars to return for *Psycho* was Beatrix Aruna Pasztor (costume designer), Pablo Ferro (title designer), Kelley Baker (sound designer/supervising sound editor—this was his fifth Van Sant movie), Amy E. Duddleston (editor—she began as assistant editor on *My Own Private Idaho* and thereafter was associate editor on *Even Cowgirls Get the Blues* and *To Die For*), Jane Goldsmith (script supervisor), and Danny Elfman (music producer/supervisor/adaptor). Initially, the much-in-demand Elfman was not interested in the *Psycho* assignment because it required replicating Bernard Herrmann's original score which curtailed the amount of new creativity he could bring to the task. But Van Sant persuaded him to accept the aesthetic challenge and Elfman would work with a seventy-two-piece string orchestra (twice the size Hitchcock had) to provide the new music track.

For *Psycho* Gus chose Australian-born Christopher Doyle as the director of photography. (Originally, Van Sant had considered using a cinematographer well versed in shooting television to approximate the style used by Hitchcock in the original, but he dropped that notion.) Fluent in French and Mandarin, Doyle had a sterling reputation from having photographed many Hong Kong–made features in the 1980s and 1990s, including *Chungking Express* and *Temptress Moon*. This was his first American-made feature and he was excited at the challenge of replicating a masterpiece from a modern sensibility. Britisher Tom Foden, who had designed many music videos and had been the production designer on *The Hunger* TV series in 1997, was contracted to handle similar chores on *Psycho*. This time, it was Gus's young friend Ben Alexander who served as Van Sant's general assistant, while the director's past boyfriend, D-J Haanraadts, functioned as the director of *Psycho Path*, a promotional short subject about the making of the new film.

▼

BY summer 1998 as the new *Psycho* commenced its shoot, there was great interest all around as to what possible alterations had been made to the original script. Although Van Sant had initially stated it would be a shot-by-shot and word-for-word revisit, rumors had circulated that the screenplay was being doctored to (1) modernize the dialogue and (2) to create new on-screen surprises.

Because Gus and Universal Pictures were not forthcoming on this topic, the press turned to scripter Joseph Stefano. In July 1998 the scribe appeared as a guest speaker at a screenwriting seminar in West Hollywood where he happened to talk about the new *Psycho;* a *Los Angeles Times* reporter just happened to be in attendance.

According to Stefano, when he and Van Sant met to discuss the project it had become evident that "some things in the script would have to be changed. [For example], in the original movie there was some sense that being in a hotel room on your lunch hour was morally wrong. I didn't think that would fly today. And then some minor things, like increasing the amount of money that [Marion Crane] steals from $40,000 to $400,000. And not being able to make a phone call for a dime today. Things like that . . . I felt that some of the talk of [Norman Bates'] mother—when you hear her calling him 'Boy'—I felt you had to be more subtle now. A mother calling her son 'Boy' and asking if he has any guts doesn't work today."

Stefano pointed out, "Janet Leigh was a big star who had been in pictures for almost 15 years at the time of *Psycho.* The whole point of casting her was because the audience would come unglued by the fact that Janet Leigh was supposedly dead 25 minutes into the movie. That's something that I don't think will work today. I don't think that anybody will go to the movies today and be shocked that somebody gets killed early in the movie . . . whether people will be surprised that Anne Heche is killed, I kind of doubt. . . . But a lot of young people will be seeing it for the first time—*Psycho* to them is a funny bit . . . [i.e., the famed but much satirized shower stabbing]. So it may be a shock to them."

Stefano commented on his updated script: "I've made Sam [Loomis—played by Viggo Mortensen] a little different in the new version—a little more open. A little more, frankly, sexual. I think he's a little more interesting this time around. . . . He was the only character in the [original] movie that I wasn't really terribly pleased with. I felt he was almost being a little flippant at times. Putting myself in his place, if you told me that your sister has disappeared and I loved her, I would stop being flippant damn soon. Maybe John Gavin [the original film's Sam Loomis] had something to do with that tone. That happens sometimes. But it was in the script, or he wouldn't have been able to do it."

At the West Hollywood lecture, the scriptwriter allowed that as far as the premise of *Psycho* went, "not that much has changed. The suspense that the movie generated—Why was she in this room talking to this man? And why was this man's mother so nasty to him, not allowing him to bring a woman in the house?—to me, I think, that still plays on the same nerves today. I don't there's anybody today who won't recognize it."

For Stefano, "My feeling about *Psycho* was I had two jobs. One was to make you love and mourn a wonderful young woman. The other was to make you feel sympathy and sorrow and friendship for the person who was the killer. I don't think audiences ever had any trouble doing that."

The veteran scenarist, who was being paid more for the polish/update than he had been for the full script of the 1960 thriller, stated diplomatically he felt that Van Sant was the correct individual to helm the remake. "The nightmare would be if some other directors I could name had done it who had been doing it, as a matter of fact, for most of their careers. That would worry me. Gus is oddly like Hitchcock just in his way: kind of reserved and yet friendly and forthcoming."

▼

THE new *Psycho* (which would cost approximately $25 million compared to the original's $800,000) was shot on closed sets—to maintain an aura of secrecy—at Universal Pictures in Los Angeles. The shoot began on July 6, 1998, and for the duration Gus was stuck living in Los Angeles, a situation that did not please him. For the filming, they used sound stages twelve, twenty, and twenty-two, as well as the back lot's Colonial Street and New York Street. Even before actual production had begun, there were elements that had already changed from the original thriller movie. For example, the famed Californian-Gothic *Psycho* house—so indelibly etched in people's memories and long a featured part of the Universal Studio tour—could not be used because of its juxtaposition to the tour route and the Bates Motel edifice, which had been moved several times over the years to accommodate the tour course. A new Bates home façade was constructed adjacent to the old, but this time the fronting was made of red brick and there were pointy metal dormers. To keep this revised Bates residence masked from tourists' view, a wire fence with camouflage netting was constructed.

Since the Bateses now had a different residence, it was agreed to update the famed Bates Motel. The new version was more 1990s contemporary (they even take charge cards and there's a satellite dish on the motel's roof). The establishment boasted a new sign: AIR CONDITIONED * CLEAN ROOMS * NEWLY RENOVATED * COLOR TV. But in all other physical aspects of the movie, Van Sant's team did their best to duplicate the original, even to finding the same stretch of road in Gorman, California, where, in the 1960 plotline, Marion Crane had spent the night in her car sleeping. (Also the eerie swamp scenes for the new *Psycho* were accomplished in Gorman because Universal's back lot Falls Lake area had been so overexposed in movies shot over the years since the first *Psycho*, plus the site had grown unwieldy in size.)

As for costuming, because this was a color production and nearly forty years had elapsed since Hitchcock's rendering, it was resolved to make the outfits worn—especially by Marion—more timeless than either vintage or contemporary. But like the shading motifs for the sets themselves, the color saturation in the scenes became more vivid and harsh once Marion has stolen the money and reached the Bates Motel.

Because Van Sant had full access to Hitchcock's *Psycho* production notes and the original shooting script, he had the option of utilizing plotline bits that his predecessor had discarded for one reason or another (e.g., censorship, timing). To ensure that camera setups and cast choreography would duplicate the original whenever possible, not only did the crew have copies of Alfred Hitchcock's original storyboards (executed by famed Saul Bass) to reference, but blowups of freeze frames from the original movie were tacked up on bulletin boards around the Universal sound stages being used by Gus. (To help with this meticulous approximation Gus kept a DVD player and monitor near the camera at all times, so he and the others could reference the original whenever possible.)

Occasionally there was a scene setup from Hitchcock's *Psycho* that could not be dissected properly for blocking and the new technical team had to use their own best judgment. On the other hand, in the film's opening shot where the camera pans in from a wide view of Phoenix, Arizona, and closes in on a hotel room where Marion Crane and Sam Loomis are having their rendezvous, Hitchcock had intended to make this a helicopter shot done in one unbroken flow. Technology at that time did not allow for that to be executed properly. In 1998, however, the take was quite feasible and Van Sant ordered it done.

In Van Sant's analysis of the original *Psycho*, the sexist way in which Marion Crane's character was dealt with did not require alteration for the new edition. Gus reasoned, "I think such treatment is still commonplace today in the places Marion finds herself—car lots, real estate offices. Marion is locked in this weird world where all the men may as well be the same guy. They all seem to be somewhat menacing and oppressive, and then Norman is ultimately the crazy one—the one who seems the least dangerous until the last minute. We just played the way the guys came on to Marion in the manner it was originally written. Men still act the same."

The director also realized that, "Reflections are a major theme in the original, with mirrors everywhere, characters who reflect each other. This version holds up a mirror to that film; it's sort of its schizophrenic twin." (Yet another theme within the shock movie is birds: Norman stuffs them, he is essentially a bird of prey, Marion's surname is "Crane." To carry this motif one step further, costume designer Beatrix Aruna Pasztor used a bird design on the inner lining of Marion's purse. Another instance occurs in the motel sequence, where Marion's hair is ruffled and birdlike.)

While most of the original *Psycho* dialogue remained essentially unaltered (except for the updating of money figures, etc.), there were textual and structural changes evident in the opening hotel sequence. Marion Crane is still in her bra and panties (considered very shocking and titillating indeed for a mainstream movie in 1960) but Sam Loomis, who was clothed in the 1960 edition of the scene, is buck naked in the 1998 counterpart. This required altering the choreography for the interchange and allowing new nuance for the text.

In the same vein, most of *Psycho*'s principal cast—with the approval of Gus—revamped the past interpretation of their characters. This not only helped make the new *Psycho* more accessible to late-1990s audiences, but it gave the performers an opportunity to bring freshness to their roles rather than merely imitate their on-screen predecessors.

Thus, in Van Sant's *Psycho*, the performances have a new vigor. Anne Heche's Marion Crane is much more femininely soft—even a bit giddy—compared to Leigh's heroine. According to Heche, "I looked at the character and thought, What a lamebrain. She pays no attention to what she's doing. She doesn't think about the consequences. Who is this doofus? So I kind of went with that. I went with her flightiness." As to the difficulty of doing a scene-by-scene remake, "It was actually one of the simplest things ever. You already had the blueprint of what had to be done. You only had to worry about your personality."

Julianne Moore chose to give her Lila much more bite, making her a variation of a lesbian stereotype: aggressive manner, strident walk, wearing a Walkman, having keys on her waist belt, etc. Said Moore, "I think that makes her an even greater threat to Norman. I didn't do it to be shocking. I think it benefits the story. It's another level of sexual tension in a film seething with sexual tension." She also elaborated, "The movie was made in 1960 so it was a little anachronistic, and you have to translate it into your own vernacular. Instead of just being kind of upset, I tried to make her kind of angry and aggressive. It wasn't a matter of being feminist or not; it was a matter of making it work in a somewhat modern setting." As the actress detailed, "Everybody [in the cast] has gone in their own direction. Viggo [Mortensen] is doing this cowboy thing, and I'm kind of a vinyl-head. There's a reference in the movie to me working in a music store, so we took that to another level with my wardrobe and attitude."

Viggo Mortensen's Sam Loomis is far from the button-down type that John Gavin essayed for Hitchcock. This Sam, a Texas-accented cowboy, has sex on his mind all the time—whether it be bedding Marion or contemplating doing the same with Lila. As for William H. Macy's private eye, his approach in the 1998 *Psycho* is more low-key midwestern than Martin Balsam's New York abrasive had been. But beyond that, Macy's performance replicates the original.

In contrast, in interpreting Norman Bates, Vince Vaughn "didn't see a value in mimicking what they did the first time. But I didn't try to do things totally differently. I just tried to use a truthful interpretation." But, according to Vaughn, "There were some things I did as a tribute to Anthony [Perkins]. I liked what he did with [his] stuttering and body language . . ."

Vaughn also observed, "Norman is actually more like most people than people realize. Except he goes into a very extreme place." The performer conceived his Norman to follow Gus's guideline: "He's sort of like a suburban guy at a barbecue. His reality is so fragile he has to push away anything that threatens it. So he's always trying to make like everything is great." Another deviation in Norman's character from the original film is that there is no subtext that he is gay. In the new *Psycho* rendition, the Bates character, who favors wearing tight jeans, is seen/heard (to some degree) masturbating as he voyeuristically watches Marion disrobe for her shower. Later, heterosexual porno "skin" magazines are seen in his bedroom along with his childhood toys.

As for actor Robert Forster, he was stuck with the thankless role of Dr. Simon: "When I got the part I wondered what Van Sant was going to do with it. My character is pretty small—he basically explains to the audience why Norman does what he does—but I certainly assumed there would be *some* change. But then someone pointed out that they don't change *Hamlet* whenever some new company puts on a production. So, I gave myself the task of doing my character *precisely* the way it was done in the original. Every word, down to the very last syllable." But unlike Simon Oakland's embarrassingly unsubtle performance in the 1960 version, Forster brought modulation to his screen assignment. During one take of the expository speech, Forster was clocked at delivering it in seven minutes and twelve seconds, whereas Oakland had done it in five minutes flat in the first *Psycho*. Forster's version was redone until the timing was a near match with Oakland's because of the concern that if the length of one sequence changed noticeably it would have a domino effect on the impact of the rest of the movie.

Then came the time to lens the movie's famed shower scene—the one so vividly recalled by so many from the original. About this sequence, which required over seventy camera setups, Van Sant revealed, "We found out a lot of things about the shooting of the shower sequence that made it less of an icon. I think the iconography of that scene has to do with the end result rather than the creation of it. There's something about the day-to-day making of that scene that brought the way they dealt with it more to light. We couldn't find in their original schedule the legendary six days [Hitchcock] took to shoot it. There were maybe two days. We figured maybe a lot of those shots were done second unit. But I might have it wrong, too."

What made the new version different, to a degree, besides Van Sant's decision to insert moments of storm clouds in his rendition and the glimpses of the nude Marion's buttocks and—ever so briefly her pubic hair—was "partly because it's in color. In 1960 it was perhaps the first time that particular kind of murder had been done in such an elaborate way in a movie. I'm sure if Hitchcock had cut his footage and done the sound differently, and had shot in color, it would have been way more gory. What happened with us is we could use the ends or beginnings of some of the shots that he had cut down. That made it more grisly, not particularly more gory."

Gus also explained what heightened the intensity of his *Psycho*'s bloody shower scene: "We put back the things that got cut out of Hitchcock's movie because of the censors. It's very similar to the original, but we don't have the knife slashing this way and that way as much. And there's more nudity and blood."

As for Heche, whose character Marion is the subject of the deadly shower, she had to be nude for portions of this filming: "It was fun but tedious. I mean, three days of going in the shower, drying off, then going back in. It was dry, wet, dry, wet, wet, wet, dry. 'O.K., scream.'" Heche has also admitted, "I was kind of worried about the dead-eye shot. But it turns out I have big pupils, which is what you want for that scene [with its big close-up of her orb]. I guess my eyes look sort of dead even when I'm just walking around. So it wasn't difficult at all. We did it on the first take."

One section of *Psycho* that caused production difficulties was the near-finale sequence in which the decayed, preserved corpse of Mrs. Bates is finally revealed to the audience. Producer Brian Grazer had been urging Van Sant all along to make the new offering more gruesome than the original to meet the demands of late-1990s young moviegoers. When Grazer saw footage of the crucial scene, he was dissatisfied with the look of the dummy being used. Special effects guru Rick Baker was brought in to create a new Mrs. Bates and the scene was reshot in October 1998. Pleased with the revamped results, Grazer enthused, "She's horrific, she'll shock you."

▼

THE end of August 1998 saw the completion of principal photography on the latest *Psycho*. It had taken Van Sant thirty-eight days to do his version of the thriller, two days longer than Alfred Hitchcock's on the initial one. By then the cast had had ample opportunity to observe Gus at work on the set—one that had been closed to visitors to preserve the secrecy of how closely the production was or was not adhering to the original script. Even Anne Heche's then significant other, Ellen DeGeneres, could not get a pass to come on the set. (One of the few unannounced guests on the set—which caused a brief security alert—was the unexpected arrival of Julianne Moore's eleven-month-old baby. Quipped Moore, "I was like, 'Who's he gonna tell?'" Another quasi-member of the production who visited the set was Patricia Hitchcock O'Connell. She had chosen to drop by the sound stage the day the real estate office scene was being shot, the one in which she had appeared in her father's production. Unfortunately, it was also the day that the quick cameo of the Alfred Hitchcock look-alike was being captured for the film. Reportedly, once a startled Patricia had observed her dad come to life, she departed the set.)

Typical director's garb for Van Sant was blue T-shirt, jeans, white socks, and thickly soled Doc Marten shoes, along with his trusty glow-faced wrist watch. Said one observer of Gus (who frequently sipped tea—preferably Earl Grey—on the set), "He resembles what he probably once was: your most unathletic, introspective, sensitive, hypertalented friend from high school."

Anne Heche observed of her director: "This was a chance for him to see what it might have been like to be Hitchcock and make this historical thriller. To play out what Hitchcock went through. After all, this whole movie is about psychological duplicity—what goes on inside somebody else's mind, how much can we step into another person's brain. It's all very trippy."

Vaughn perceived of Van Sant: "His vibe is beyond mellow. He just kind of lets things unfold. You never really know what he's thinking. He's kind of like—

water." And of Gus's passion for this remake: "I think he sees it as going back and playing with the stuff that inspired him to be a filmmaker in the first place. It's sort of like a musician doing a cover of another artist's song."

Julianne Moore felt that "he's a little opaque. But I think that's interesting in a person and a director. I don't want anyone spelling it out for me all the time and I don't think it's necessary. I don't think he's being elusive. I honestly think that's the nature of his personality. He's kind of a quiet guy." She opined, "It must be the ultimate head trip for a director. For Gus to get inside Hitchcock's mind like that—it must be so much fun for him."

As to the director's demeanor on the set, coplayer Viggo Mortensen remarked, "At first, I thought Gus was having a terrible time. He sits there on the set not smiling. Then I realized that Gus has his own way of smiling."

▼

AS Danny Elfman prepared to adapt Bernard Herrmann's original *Psycho* score for the deluxe fidelity sound track for the new edition, Elfman announced, "I'm going to attempt to do as respectful a re-creation as I can, acknowledging the fact that it is a different movie and no scene is exactly the same length as the original. I would say that half to two-thirds of the cues won't even be a note different. They're just going to be rescored. Maybe a third of the [music] will get jostled, shirted, stretched, abbreviated, but in a way that will stay very much true [to the original]."

Elfman also detailed, "My approach is going to be contemporary and retro at the same time. I'm going to attempt to record in a smaller room with close miking to re-create the presence and energy [of the original] but it's still going to be a contemporary stereophonic recording. . . . There's no way I'm going to pollute it by trying to make it more modern or pumping it up with drums or anything else. It is what it is and I'm going to try to make it as effective as possible."

▼

MEANWHILE, all through this accelerated postproduction period of the new *Psycho*, Van Sant still was uncertain about the ramifications and results of his great cinematic experiment. He confided, "This concept is still under the watchful eye of executives and critics, so it's not to say it's a good idea. It could be a horrible idea." He also allowed, "It's going to be a bummer if people really hate it."

▼

BY September 1998 the marketing campaign for *Psycho* had already been launched. Producer Brian Grazer enthused, "*Psycho*'s image is hard-wired into moviegoers' genetic memory. It doesn't feel old to them. I've even heard lyrics about Norman Bates in hip-hop songs. It has what you want when you're marketing a movie: a huge awareness factor. Even if kids haven't seen the movie, they know the idea of it—it's cool and it's scary."

In the post–Labor Day period of 1998 billboard ads were already promoting the December release of *Psycho*, a film that Hitchcock purists loudly threatened to boycott. One such ad featured a hand pressed against a shower curtain with the tag line: "Check in. Unpack. Relax. Take a shower." (There was no reference to the film's title in this advertisement.) In Boston, a variation of this ad campaign caused a mild uproar. Several of the posters hung at local rapid transit stops were torn down. After several complaints, the Massachusetts Bay Transportation Authority removed the rest of the *Psycho* posters on display. Producer Brian Grazer, cochairman of Image Entertainment, responded, "I guess they thought it was too sexy or erotic. I love the eroticism of it. I approved the poster." One of the TV ads released that month showed snippets of Anne Heche and Vince Vaughn's characters and brief bits of the re-created legendary shower scene. The catch phrase used was, "We'll leave the light on for you." Another fragment of the ad was a large question mark that turned into exclamation points.

Marc Shmuger, Universal's then new marketing president, stated that the object of the TV spots was to "impact the consumer much like a recurring nightmare does. It comes out of nowhere, it's everywhere, it's haunting you, then it's gone. And then it's gonna come back." Grazer explained that this early teaser ad was to challenge scream-worthy competitors due for fall theatrical release, such as *John Carpenter's Vampires*, *Apt Pupil*, *Bride of Chucky*, and *I Still Know What You Did Last Summer*. According to Grazer: "We wanted to be in people's consciousness. The idea was to say 'Hey, we're the movie to wait for.' . . . We're trying to appeal to the people who haven't ever seen *Psycho*—all the kids and twenty-years olds."

(This marketing thrust was in contradiction to what the old/new *Psycho* really was about—primarily a slowly paced, character-driven psychological thriller with several plot twists and two gory scenes. As Glazer had been concerned during production, now Universal was fearful that this celluloid revisit to Alfred Hitchcock's masterpiece would be considered too tame by the new generation of young moviegoers whose genre tastes had been sharpened by the likes of *Scream*, *I Know What You Did Last Summer*, *The Silence of the Lambs*, and many other such graphic entries filled with fast-paced horrific violence.)

Like the original *Psycho*, it was decided that Gus's new film would not be reviewed in advance by critics, on the theory that if Hitchcock had followed the no-screenings-for-the-critics rule, so should the new edition. It was also resolved to hold no special premieres for the film going on the same theory. (Some wags suggested that if Universal was seeking to really replicate the 1960 debut of *Psycho*, why not return box-office admission prices to those less expensive days.) Meanwhile, Universal promoted a *Psycho* trailer on the Internet, the first time a preview of a Universal movie had aired in that media *before* the trailer played at movie theaters. To lessen the comparison factor, the original *Psycho* was taken out of home entertainment release.

By the end of November 1998, Universal was becoming even more skittish about the upcoming bow of *Psycho*, a film still taking a great deal of heat from the antiremake sector. The studio had just suffered two major box-office flops: *Meet Joe Black*, a costly remake of *Death Takes a Holiday*, and *Babe: Pig in the City*, a high-priced sequel to the hit *Babe*. As a result Casey Silver, chairman of Universal Pictures, had been ousted. He had been the one to ultimately green-light Van Sant's current opus and would not be in office when *Psycho* debuted.

As for Van Sant during this prerelease period, he was participating in many media opportunities trying to defuse the antipathy to his scene-by-scene re-make. He was also dealing with continuing rumors promulgated on the Internet that insisted his *Psycho* was this, or that, or had changed Hitchcock's plot line in these ways or that manner. To Stephen Rebello (*Movieline*), Gus insisted he had no misgivings about having remade *Psycho*. He added, "I never did. Until now, after I've done it. But I feel this way after I've done any movie. Because you're locked in."

▼

WITHIN *Psycho*, Marion Crane and her financially challenged lover Sam Loomis have a noontime assignation at a Phoenix, Arizona, hotel. Returning to her job at a local real estate office, Marion is entrusted to deposit $400,000—from a new sale—in the bank. Instead, she takes the money and drives toward Fairvale where Loomis lives and has his hardware store. En route, she stops at the Bates Motel. She is greeted by young Norman Bates who shares a nearby house with his mother. After having conversation and sandwiches with Norman in the motel office, Marion goes back to her room, planning to return to Phoenix to repair somehow her money-stealing matter. While taking a shower she is stabbed to death by Bates's mother. Later, a horrified Norman cleans up after the gruesome killing and disposes of Marion's corpse and her car in a nearby swamp.

Marion's sister, Lila, arrives at Sam Loomis's store to question him about her missing sister. They, in turn, are interrogated by Milton Arbogast who has been hired to recover the stolen funds. Later, Arbogast tracks Marion to the Bates Motel. There Norman is helpful to Arbogast but is not informative about the missing Marion. When the now suspicious private eye is refused the opportunity to question Mrs. Bates, he sneaks into the Bates home. He has a surprise encounter with the mother who stabs him to death. Once again Norman covers up the crime. He carries his parent to the cellar.

Lila and Sam Loomis arrive at the Bates Motel, already having been ap-prised by Arbogast of his hunches about the case. Earlier, Lila and Sam learned from Sheriff Chambers that Norman's mother died several years ago. At the motel, Norman knocks Sam unconscious and runs up to the main house; Lila follows. She discovers Mrs. Bates's preserved corpse in the basement and is then attacked by Norman, the latter outfitted as his mother. Lila and Loomis subdue the knife-wielding Bates and he is taken into police custody. Later, from a psychiatrist, they are told that years before Norman had murdered his mother and her boyfriend and that the deranged Norman has buried his own personality and taken on his mother's persona.

▼

ON Friday, December 4, 1998, the R-rated *Psycho* debuted in 2,447 movie theaters around the United States. The critics had mixed reactions to the much-discussed, much-maligned aesthetic experiment by Gus Van Sant.

On a relatively positive note Janet Maslin (*New York Times*) reported, "It turns out the apparent rocks in Mr. Van Sant's head are mere pebbles. If he isn't Hitchcock, neither is he crazy. His film is an artful, good-looking remake (a modest term, but it beats plagiarism) that shrewdly revitalizes the aspects of the real *Psycho* (1960) that it follows most faithfully but seldom diverges seriously or successfully from one of the cinema's most brilliant blueprints." Although approving of the performances of Anne Heche, Julianne Moore, and William H. Macy, Maslin argued, "While Vince Vaughn gives the role its share of creepiness, his beefy presence and mechanical recitations also throw off the material's exquisite balance." (Maslin was referring to the physical/emotional resemblance between Norman and Marion on one hand, and Lila Crane and Sam Loomis on the other.") The *Times'* critic pointed out, "And another of Mr. Van Sant's new ideas, having Norman masturbate just before he kills Marion, would seem to dispel the very tension that matters most in the story." She concluded, "However interesting these modifications are, they won't make *Psycho* any more *Scream*-like for viewers who like fast, easy fright."

Owen Gleiberman (*Entertainment Weekly*) rated the new *Psycho* a "B." He reasoned, "Unique among studio-system films, *Psycho* is a movie that invites you to watch yourself watching. In killing off his lead character . . . (and, along with her, our entire sense that a Hollywood movie would always unfold in an ordered dramatic universe), Hitchcock teased the audience's elemental desire for identification and, in the process, undercut the notion of identity itself. It was his ultimate ghoulish prank to make a movie about a monster—Mrs. Bates—who literally doesn't exist. The monster is in Norman's head—and, as we watch, in our heads as well. To see *Psycho* is to experience a thriller as a test for the limits of rationality. That's why a remake seemed so seductive. What could be juicier, or more appropriate, than this post-postmodern *Psycho*, a movie that asks us to sit back and meditate on our self-conscious response to it?" But Gleiberman analyzed of the remake, "There's really only one difference—but it turns out to be a major howler. The film is now set in the present day, and so a great deal of it no longer makes sense."

Many critics agreed with Roger Ebert (*Chicago Sun-Times*) who voiced, "The movie is an invaluable experiment in the theory of cinema, because it demonstrates that a shot-by-shot remake is pointless; genius apparently resides between or beneath the shots, or in chemistry that cannot be timed or counted."

Kenneth Turan (*Los Angeles Times*) had a far more negative response: "There's a word for Gus Van Sant's colorized version of Alfred Hitchcock's *Psycho*, a word that so dominates today's marketing-driven movie culture it probably deserves to be written in capital letters. It's not sacrilege, not travesty, not profanation or desecration. The word is gimmick." According to Turan, "What Gus Van Sant has done . . . [is] simply boring, a waste of time and money, and doomed to be the failure it is."

And on Van Sant's home turf of Portland, Shawn Levy reported in the *Oregonian*: "The truth is, the march of film history, for good or ill, hasn't been kind to this landmark that Hitchcock devised and Van Sant replicated. Our pop culture has inured us to the sight of murders, even explicit ones. The shock of the old, it turns out, is no shock at all. It's a fate, finally, that this *Psycho* cannot overcome. Though it's well-acted and shot with wit and style, the film never sweeps you up."

Levy allowed, "But, clever media creature that he is, Van Sant has allowed for this possibility in the film itself. Take a careful look when Marion enters her office at the beginning of the film. That Hitchcock look-alike who's repeating the late director's cameo in the film. He's sticking a finger in Van Sant's chest, as if to tell him a thing or two about making a thriller. And Van Sant, bless him, has the grace to be smiling."

During its key opening weekend of release in December 1998, *Psycho* grossed only an estimated $10.5 million. By the time it had faded from U.S. distribution at the end of January 1999, its box-office take was a relatively mild gross of $21.38 million. The critical and audience response abroad was no better for the new *Psycho* than it had been in the relatively unresponsive United States. (For the foreign cinema runs, 2 to 5 minutes of deleted footage was added to the film's 104-minute U.S. running time.)

In the annual tally of film awards, *Psycho* received little recognition. William H. Macy won a Best Supporting Actor Award from the Boston Society of Film Critics for his work in *Psycho*. Both Anne Heche (Best Actress) and Joseph Stefano (Best Writer) were nominated for Saturn Awards by the Academy of Science Fiction, Horror, and Fantasy Films. *Psycho* won two Razzie Awards: Worst Director and Worse Remake or Sequel. (Anne Heche was nominated for a Razzie in the Worst Actress Category.)

▼

IN evaluating Gus's audacious cinematic experiment, one can only wonder how other film directors might have approached the task—if they had even deemed it prudent or viable to tackle such an artistic and intellectual challenge. Would these other moviemakers have opted to revamp Joseph Stefano's screenplay to a far greater extent to bring it more in alignment with modern times? Or, would they have chosen to freeze the story into a 1960 ambiance and not have used so many (if any) modern physical trappings such as 1990s cars, TVs, etc.? Then again, would they have instead chosen Stephen Dorff, Billy Crudup, Christian Bale, or Eric Stoltz to portray the unhinged Norman Bates?

But, returning to what Gus Van Sant did with *Psycho*, was it a worthwhile lab test? Do we gain new values and perceptions regarding the plot line and characters of *Psycho* from what the director replicated? Unfortunately, in this author's estimation, the answer is "not much." After all, so much of what was intended on the surface and buried within the film were conscious and subconscious choices on the part of Hitchcock, Stefano, and the cast. They, in turn, were responding and reacting to the mores of the times, which dictated what was allowable on-screen, what common assumptions a viewer of 1960 would make about the characters and the plot twists. Above all, a large number of moviegoers had no idea of what surprises lay in the story line of *Psycho*. These disclosures and shocks were already passé to 1990s audiences, either because they had long known the story or the new presentation hardly amazed them given what they had already seen of violence on-screen.

Most of any intellectual interest in *Psycho* is what it may tell about Gus Van Sant. It is his decisions and choices on when to vary from and when not to veer from the original script and film that provide stimulating thoughts. While one cannot burrow into another's psyche or stand in his shoes, especially when the person is as bright and intellectualized as Van Sant, one can only ponder questions regarding this deliberately enigmatic filmmaker and his *Psycho*.

As a young adult—and even later—many commentators observed and noted a physical resemblance between Van Sant and Anthony Perkins, the star of the original *Psycho*. What special attraction had *Psycho* held for the young Gus when, years ago, he first watched Perkins in his most famous screen role? Was there some connection of visual identity that drew Van Sant to *Psycho* because of this? Then, too, Alfred Hitchcock was extremely voyeuristic in his approach to filmmaking. (One of the great voyeuristic movies of all times is Hitchcock's 1954 entry, *Rear Window*). Did Van Sant, long-noted as a greater observer of life and people, respond, as Hitchcock had, to the voyeuristic aspects of *Psycho*?

What inner amusement drew Gus, the avowed gay director, down the path to (sub)consciously gender switch genders of his lead cast in his thriller? Why cast Anne Heche, the world's then most visible bisexual, to play the lead female role? How come Van Sant allowed Julianne Moore to alter her characterization from a typically submissive screen heroine of 1960 to a rather butch lesbian of the 1990s? Why reshuffle Norman Bates's sexual identity from a seemingly or actual closet gay/open transvestite (forgetting what the psychiatrist says at the end of the movie) to a quite masculine, hunky persona?

Also, what factors led Gus to focus so much attention on the anatomy of his stud star, Vince Vaughn, or to have the well-built actor outfitted in such tight jeans and to have the camera well-positioned to capture his backside whenever he bends over or walks away from the camera? This led Ella Taylor of the *LA Weekly* to observe in her *Psycho* review: "Just as when Vaughn's Norman, freaked by all the snooping, bounds upstairs to haul Mother down to the fruit cellar, there's nothing for us to do but appreciate, along with Van Sant, that the actor is a fine piece of ass." And why play out Norman's masturbation/voyeurism scene so graphically just before the shower homicide occurs? Then, too, why did Gus have trim Viggo Mortensen's Sam Loomis parade around in the buff in the film's opening hotel room assignation scene, but leave Anne Heche's Marion semiclothed in her bra and panties? The naked Loomis jarringly announces from the film's start that this new *Psycho* is not the same as Hitchcock's presentation. Yet Gus's version then reverts back to a methodical replication of the original thereafter. Who was Van Sant trying to entice and entertain with this opening sequence?

As for trademark Van Sant touches, each of the two murder sequences contain cut-away images from the death site as the victim—we assume—sees swirling clouds or other imagery and objects pass fleetingly by in the tradition of *Drugstore Cowboy* and *My Own Private Idaho*. There are also the wonderful vista shots of Phoenix and within the sequence of Marion Crane fleeing the city. Another Gus favorite are the close-ups of a fly on a sandwich or, later, that of the crawling spider on the mummified face of Mrs. Bates. Perhaps the most famous up-close shot in *Psycho* is the one of the dying Marion Crane's eyes as she lies on the bathroom floor expiring with her spark of life evaporating.

Thematically, as in so many past Van Sant film productions, *Psycho* contains plot threads of a character fleeing a scene and embarking on a road trip. There is also attention to autos, here with Marion's trade at the user car dealership and the closing images of the film as her automobile is pulled from the swamp.

▼

GUS Van Sant was less critical of his own work than usual. Looking back on his *Psycho*, he would admit, "Boy, that really taught me a lot, that film! It didn't teach me anything about Hitchcock. But it taught me a lot about the press. Because when you work long enough you see all sides of it. And I've seen the bad side and the great side. My film of *Even Cowgirls Get the Blues* got bad reviews, too, but that was more ordinary. The critics saw it, and simply didn't like it. This was different. With *Psycho* critics had it [in] for me from before the beginning!

"The lesson that I learned is that the press is very conservative. I wasn't aware of that. They had always been the ones who had paved the way for me. In this case the pavement totally ended. . . . It really hurt."

However, Van Sant allowed, "I learned a lot about myself as a filmmaker. Because the images in my films and the things in my films tend to be sentimental. And Hitchcock is not about that. He's about suspense and austerity and separating everybody. And I'm about including everybody."

ON THE FILMMAKING MERRY-GO-ROUND

I like to be surprised. And I like something to be maybe something that I hadn't thought of before. My general process is to start working on my own ideas and screenplays and then somewhere along the line . . . something shows up, like *Good Will Hunting* sort of like showed up, the same with *To Die For.*

Gus Van Sant, 2000

IN REVIEWING THE 1998 *Psycho* Mike Clark (*USA Today*) wrote, "The only real fun here apparently was Van Sant's. So now that playtime is over, how about if the director of *Drugstore Cowboy, To Die For* and *Good Will Hunting* gets back to his career?"

Truthfully, Gus Van Sant was eager to get back to business. Just as thankfully he was already at work on *To Die For* when *Even Cowgirls Get the Blues* was bombing in movie theaters, so now he was anxious to start a fresh project that would take away the sting created by his poorly received *Psycho* remake.

In January 1999 Van Sant was already prepping two screen ventures. One was the gay-themed *Brokeback Mountain* for which he was to direct the movie for Columbia Pictures. It was slated to film in the summer of 1999. There was also the pending cinematic account of quadriplegic cartoonist John Callahan in which Robin Williams might star. Gus now added *Standing Room Only* to his filmmaking roster. The movie was budgeted at $70 million and was to be released through Touchstone Pictures domestically. It would shoot in April 1999 for a Christmas release. Most important, it was to star movie comeback king John Travolta.

Daily Variety headlined the news with "Travolta croons again." (It would be the star's first musical since 1978's *Grease.*) The musical biography would encompass the life of Jimmy Roselli, a lounge singer who was a favorite of the

Mafioso. When Jimmy later rejected his association with the underworld he was targeted for elimination. Only the intervention of the mobsters' wives—who adored him—saved the crooner from certain death on several occasions. Billed as "Hoboken's other great singer," Roselli never achieved the popularity of Frank Sinatra because he passed up golden opportunities for national exposure and had this ongoing love-hate tie to the mob. Travolta's actress wife Kelly Preston would have a featured role in *Standing Room Only,* playing Donna Roselli. Besides directing, Van Sant was to be one of the film's producers.

A script had already been drafted for *Standing Room Only* and things looked quite promising—at least on the surface. Travolta's manager, Jonathan Krane of the Krane Group, bragged of his client: "He'll be the *Raging Bull* of lounge singers, but with the humor John brings to the role. John will be singing the standards the way Roselli did." Filming was to commence in Atlantic City in the spring and then continue in Los Angeles. Marvin Hamlisch would arrange the musical numbers.

There were, however, two major wrinkles to this big deal. One was for the producers to locate sufficient financing to cover the production's hefty budget and the other was Travolta's commitment to star in the upcoming science fiction epic *Battleship Earth,* based on the L. Ron Hubbard novel. Being a committed Scientologist, John was unflinchingly determined to make the long-discussed project a reality—and soon. In fact, *Battleship Earth* was announced to shoot later in 1999 once all the final details had been worked out.

When *Standing Room Only* jumped into the trade paper headlines, there were many observers in Hollywood who wondered why Gus Van Sant had been selected to direct a musical. While he had helmed several music videos and was a musician, he had never guided a song-and-dance screen production and certainly not one on this grand a scale. In fact, in an interview with David Ehrenstein for the *Los Angeles Times* Van Sant was asked directly why he had been chosen to direct the movie rather than, say, Martin Scorsese, who had directed a big-budgeted musical (*New York, New York*). Gus replied that Travolta "saw me as an original choice, I suppose. Either they asked Marty [Scorsese] and he had another project or maybe they just thought . . . If I were them, I would have asked Marty. But they asked me. So it was me doing a genre I'd never done. And [Walt Disney Studio's Touchstone Pictures] said, 'Let's go.' And so we went ahead because we didn't have any time not to."

While Gus was gearing up for this extremely demanding major studio screen project, the producers were scrambling madly to attract the necessary bankroll to meet the sizable costs. They were also creating the usual media publicity to keep the buzz on the venture going at full thrust. This too cost money to perpetuate. The result was that the not yet consolidated production was expending a healthy quantity of money before any new cash was realized. This was not a unique situation in the creative financing circles of Hollywood moviemaking but it was one that could explode in the producers' faces.

Initially *Standing Room Only* was established to begin filming March 15, 1999. Soon that was moved to April and then changed to May 3, 1999. Those delays gave star Travolta dangerously little time to complete the musical before he embarked on *Battlefield Earth,* which now had a firm start-up date of July 15, 1999, in Montreal. After the science fiction entry, it was touted that Travolta and his wife would next costar in *Shipping News,* based on the book by Annie Proulx, the author of Gus's *Brokeback Mountain* project. While superstar Travolta soon became unattached from *Shipping News, Battlefield* remained a solid go for July.

By early May the prospects for *Standing Room Only* did not look good. Word was out on the industry grapevine that the producers had peddled their planned Roselli vehicle at the American Film Market and it had received what one trade paper termed "an underwhelming response." More to the point was the producing company's lack of visibility at the annual Cannes Film Festival later that month. It was a tip-off that the Travolta musical was no longer a sure bet and that the production company probably did not want to expend money or time at the French film market/festival to hunt out possible backers when so many other money sources had evidently already rejected the property.

By June 1999 Van Sant was no longer attached to *Standing Room Only.* As he described it, "All of a sudden it's like 'We're not really going anymore.'" According to Gus, the Disney studio had pulled out of the venture because "they had a disappointing year, and they decided that they would do some trimming. And we were one of those trims."

▼

WHILE *Standing Room Only* was quickly becoming a what-might-have-been footnote in Hollywood history, one of Gus's other screen projects reached the next step toward fruition. *Speedway Junky*—the movie Van Sant was executive producing—did get made in 1998. Directed by young Nickolas Perry, it was financed by Menahem Golan and Yoram Globus's First Miracle Group. Along the way, actor Balthazar Getty, who was playing a Las Vegas street hustler who shelters a cute young would-be race driver (Jesse Bradford), left the cast after three weeks of production. He was replaced by Jonathan Taylor Thomas. The latter, leaving the TV sitcom *Home Improvement* after several years on the hit show, wanted to change his squeaky-clean show business image. Others in the eclectic cast of *Speedway Junky* included Tiffani-Amber Thiessen (formerly of *Beverly Hills 90210*), rapper Warren G, actress Daryl Hannah, and Jordan Brower playing a young scam artist.

Speedway Junky had a brief release in Germany in February 1999 and that April the R-rated feature was screened at the Los Angeles Independent Film Festival, where it impressed Kevin Thomas of the *Los Angeles Times.* In detailing the low-budget entry, which he found "tender, heart-wrenching," Thomas described the plot as characters seeking "solace in supportive relationships that transcend traditional ties of family, biology, and heterosexuality." As to the caliber of acting, the critic for the *Times* rated both Jonathan Taylor Thomas and

Daryl Hannah as "impressive." That was the last media news on this intriguing, little-seen feature until early January 2001, when an interviewer for the Los Angeles gay-based newspaper *Frontiers* asked Gus about *Speedway Junky*. He answered, "That's a good question. I thought it was going to come out a year ago, but then something happened with the company, I think. I'm not sure where it's at right at the moment." Four months later the independent movie debuted on home video in the United Kingdom, a few months before Regent Entertainment released the picture in the United States to very mixed reviews.

▼

BY mid-1999 the resilient Van Sant had a wide array of potential film projects on his plate. *Brokeback Mountain* had delayed its start-up, but was still in the works. In his low-keyed manner the director explained its latest postponement: "I think casting on this is going to be a hard one. You can go high profile or you can go unknown. And I'm very, very torn about who the characters are and how to cast them." (At one wild point in time, it was rumored that Gus was considering Matt Damon and Ben Affleck for the co-leads of *Brokeback Mountain*.) In the interim, Van Sant had not abandoned the handicapped cartoonist tale (*Don't Worry He Won't Get Far on Foot*), nor had he given up on doing *Street Zen* about the once San Francisco transvestite hustler.

Gus was now talking about producing, along with Andrea Sperling, *Heatstroke*. The project was to be made by experimental filmmaker Nina Menkes (*The Great Sadness of Zohara*, *Queen of Diamonds*, *Bloody Child*) and dealt with longterm rivalry between two sisters and also concerned the mysterious disappearance of one of their husbands. It would be filmed in Cairo, Egypt, and Los Angeles. Menkes detailed, "Gus has been a big booster of my films and said he wanted to be involved after he read the script. His participation has opened up a lot of doors in terms of financing and interest for actors. It's also opened me up about reaching a larger audience." (But in time the *Heatstroke* project seemingly stalled and has yet to reach the big screen.)

Van Sant was also touted to direct the film adaptation of Francine Du Plessix Gray's 1998 book *At Home with the Marquis de Sade*. The picture was to be produced by USA Films. However, at the same time Fox Searchlight Pictures at Twentieth Century-Fox was pushing forward with making the screen production of *Quills* based on Doug Wright's play. The latter also dealt with the infamous eighteenth-century Frenchman de Sade. *Quills*, which was to feature Gus's friend Joaquin Phoenix in this period drama starring Geoffrey Rush, Kate Winslet, and Michael Caine, was made and released in 2000. The projected *At Home with the Marquis de Sade* faded from sight.

Also up for Gus's consideration was *Satyricon*, which revolved around a hot evening at a punk rock club. The director was also considering a story set at a commune in Northern California or Oregon, and an adaptation of the stage play *Wit*. Also, not to be overlooked was Van Sant's intention to participate in

Jokes, to be made up of three short films. He was to direct one, his friend Harmony Korine another, and a third filmmaker (not yet chosen) would do the remaining one.

As if these projects were not sufficient to occupy all of Van Sant's time, Gus was set to receive the Outfest Achievement Award in July 1999 at the Pantages Theater in Hollywood. He was to be presented the trophy on the opening night of Outfest (the new name for the annual Los Angeles Gay and Lesbian Film Festival) by his friend, singer k. d. lang.

Through all this rise and fall of screen projects that seemed not to materialize, Gus remained a viable commodity in the Hollywood film game. The Oscar-nominated director of *Good Will Hunting* had additional cache from his past personal films (*Mala Noche*, *Drugstore Cowboy*, and *My Own Private Idaho*). As far as the residue from his commercial defeats (*Even Cowgirls Get the Blues* and, to a far lesser extent, *Psycho*), they were offset in many people's minds by the huge success of the mainstream *Good Will Hunting* and the popular response to his quirky *To Die For*.

Nowadays it seemed mandatory for interviewers when meeting with Gus to comment that he was still the same shy, reserved person with a dry wit, that he would likely forever be on the top ten wanted list of the fashion police, and that he had interesting companions. For example, when David Ehrenstein broke bread with the director for a question-and-answer session at Hugo's Restaurant in West Hollywood, Van Sant was accompanied by nineteen-year-old Ted Jan Roberts (aka T. J. Roberts), a then rising martial arts youth-film star (TV series *Masked Rider*, films like *Magic Kid I* and *II*). Ehrenstein described the tag-along actor as Gus's "latest protégé." Throughout the meal/interview, when Van Sant was not resounding to Ehrenstein's remarks, the filmmaker bantered frequently with T. J., especially on the topic of how the teen actor could become really successful in films.

Some months earlier, when Van Sant was being profiled for *Monk* magazine by James Crotty and Michael Lane, they met in Portland at one of Gus's favorite restaurants (Wildwood) and then adjourned to Van Sant's big house. Present at the hearthside meeting was Scott Patrick Green whom Crotty labeled as Gus's "longtime companion/photographer." A few months before that, Michael Musto (*Village Voice*) reported in his column "La Dolce Musto": "Over in L.A., Gus Van Sant and a young man named Ben Alexander seem unbreakable to the point where Mr. Jealousy, Ben, protects Gus against anyone hunting for too much goodwill." (Alexander would serve as Gus's assistant on the *Psycho* set in July/August 1999.)

By fall 1999 *Don't Worry He Won't Get Far on Foot* still seemed no closer to actualization than before. The subject of the potential movie, Portland's John Callahan, was not unused to such postponement on the bumpy path to turn his life story into a picture. Earlier, actors Billy Crystal and William Hurt had expressed an interest in picturizing his book. That was before Robin Williams and his wife had optioned the vehicle and interested Gus in directing the venture, which was still in development. Said the wry, handicapped Callahan who created the Nickelodeon network cartoon series *Penswick,* which featured an animated character in a wheelchair, "I told Robin Williams, 'Just get Chris Reeve to play the part.'" But Callahan thought the paralyzed Reeves "has got such a clean image, a noble kind of white knight–type guy. By contrast, I consider myself the Anti-quad[riplegic]." When Callahan was asked in the fall of 2000 about the progress of the film, he commented, "By the time Robin and Gus make the movie, we'll all be in wheelchairs."

As far as *Brokeback Mountain* went, it was still in the planning stage. Finally in 2001, Gus would admit, "I think through my own negligence it was something I never really got cast, or approached it the way I thought it would work. It also came in conflict with some of the other projects as far as being the next one. I think it might be considered by other filmmakers right now. . . . *Brokeback*'s problem wasn't financing; we actually got financing for that."

Then there was Van Sant's long-cherished filmization of *Street Zen* about the Zen teacher Issan Dorsey whose past history included being a cross-dressing San Franciscan prostitute and later running an AIDS hospice. Gus pinpointed the problems on getting that venture launched: "If you're traversing four decades it's hard to imagine doing it for $1 million, but you could get $1 million to do it. It's a trade-off. When you're asking for $10 million, it's different than asking for $1 million."

▼

IN late 1999, a year after *Psycho* had been released, Gus Van Sant still had no new screen project ready for immediate production. The frequent traveler chose to attend the Calcutta Film Festival in November 1999. While in India, he received a lengthy fax from Los Angeles. It was from Dany Wolf who had produced Gus's *Ballad of the Skeletons* short, and several commercials and music videos directed by Van Sant, and had been the producer/unit production manager on *Psycho*. The transmission required nearly five hours to complete. When collated, Gus had in hand a new script that Wolf wanted him to read at once. It was titled *Finding Forrester*.

31

FASHIONING *FORRESTER*

I knew it [*Finding Forrester*] would be kind of similar, with a similar audience. I thought *Good Will Hunting* was successful in making education sexy. That's a good thing. I had a lot of teachers comment about that. There's enough room for another film like that. . . . I didn't mind going into the same territory, as long as I thought the audience wouldn't mind. That was the only question—would the audience care. In screenings we've had, it's clear they don't mind at all.

Gus Van Sant, 2000

THE SCREEN PROPERTY THAT had grabbed Gus Van Sant's attention while in India was *Finding Forrester* written by Mike Rich who, it turned out, was also from Portland, Oregon. The drama dealt with a gifted African-American teenager who encounters a reclusive, aged Pulitzer Prize–winning novelist and how each benefits emotionally from the friendship. It was set in the battered Bronx as well as at an exclusive coed prep school in Manhattan.

Despite the change in setting from Boston to New York City, *Finding Forrester* might easily be a close cousin to *Good Will Hunting*. Both properties concern a student/teacher relationship and how the dynamics of their interaction prompt great life changes for each. The obvious parallels between the two screenplays struck Van Sant at once, making him ponder the wisdom of directing this new screenplay. Did he really want to be "repeating" himself with a vehicle similar to his greatest box-office success to date? More important, he wondered whether he could bring a freshness to his directorial approach to such a similar story line. After all, the *Finding Forrester* plot line also concerned a super bright younger man being mentored by a wise older person and the two engaging in several one-on-one discussions. In many ways it was *Good Will Hunting* all over again, and it presented a dilemma for Van Sant.

But as with Gus's decision to redo Alfred Hitchcock's classic *Psycho*, Van Sant's unique perspective on life came into play. This outlook allowed him to intellectualize such a career decision in a manner completely unlike how most people might analyze the situation. Gus has recalled of his reasoning process regarding *Finding Forrester*, "I think I thought because it wasn't that different from something I'd done before, that in itself was different." Besides, he concluded concerning the plot parallels between *Good Will Hunting* and *Finding Forrester*: "The details of how that was happening were different enough that I felt, 'Well, so what?'"

Having argued those points in his mind, the director considered whether the new screenplay was edgy enough in its story premise and in the characters who peopled it. According to Van Sant, "I didn't know whether, without the controversial material, would I still be standing? If I wasn't able to wield the freaky characters in front of the viewers, would I be interesting anymore?"

In his most rewarding early movies Gus had always spotlighted what he called "dispossessed" people: illegal Mexican immigrants (*Mala Noche*), druggie robbers (*Drugstore Cowboy*), male street hustlers (*My Own Private Idaho*). Were there any "scapegoated" groups represented in *Finding Forrester*? Van Sant concluded: "I supposed in *Finding Forrester* it would be the African-American community as a whole. It's kind of an ingrained injustice that is hard to get under control, but it is an injustice."

That resolved to a degree, Van Sant had to admit that *Finding Forrester* was, as *Good Will Hunting* had been, an example of "the type of movies that I would go see in the '70s, human dramas that I liked a lot—my favorite type of movies . . . *On Golden Pond*, *Ordinary People*, *Julia*. I liked the craft of the Hollywood human drama. I studied it and was obsessed by it when I was in my twenties. But by the time I actually made a movie I was relying on other influences. And I couldn't write a story like that. It would be impossible for me. It's not in my nature. The stories that I write are things like *My Own Private Idaho*—not these Hollywood dramas." It led him to realize, "I'm not going to be stuck in the Hollywood drama forever, but it's connected to something that is part of my past and part of my interests. And it is, probably, part of selling out. I mean, my agents are really happy that I do these bigger budgets."

In his final evaluation Van Sant decided, "I had to admit it also was as well put together and as sharp as *Good Will Hunting*. So I had to go ahead and say 'yes' just for fear that I wouldn't see another script like that. And partly because I hadn't done a film like that twice." What also entered into the equation was, "I decided just to do it before someone else did. I would've been jealous and thought, 'I should have done that.'"

Another reason for Gus giving John Burnham and Gaby Morgerman, his William Morris Agency representatives, the go-ahead to negotiate the *Finding Forrester* contract was that megastar Sean Connery had already agreed to star in the new picture, thus making it a very commercial venture. To celebrate that they would be working together, Van Sant would send fellow golfer Connery a new driver club.

Within three days of giving his acceptance on *Finding Forrester*, Gus Van Sant returned to the United States.

▼

MIKE Rich was in his late thirties when he wrote the *Finding Forrester* screenplay. A lifelong radio disc jockey, by the late 1990s he was the news director for KINK, a Portland FM radio station where he also reviewed movies and books. Over a period of time he had interviewed several established authors and wondered why so many of the breed, especially the older ones discussed in these chat sessions, tended to be reclusive types. As he mulled over that thought, he also kept having flashback memories of a English teacher (Sharon Forster) at Enterprise High School in Eastern Oregon who had greatly influenced his life. For example, when she gave him a "C" on a class assignment paper, he argued over the grade with her. He said, "You can't tell me that this isn't the best work in the class." She answered, "It is. But I'm not grading you on a curve. I'm grading you against yourself." Rich also has recalled, "She would take us to Shakespeare festivals and really challenged us. So, in effect, this film [i.e., *Finding Forrester*] is a tribute to her and what she meant to me."

Melding these plot ideas together over a three-month period, the Portland radio personality began writing a screenplay in early 1997. He worked a bit each day between the time he completed his early shift at the radio station and the afternoon hour when his three children returned home from school or when he did not have to shepherd them to activites like Boy Scouts and soccer practice. At this point Rich knew little about proper screenplay formatting and just worried about completing what to him was an acceptable screenplay draft. Although he set his story in two of New York City's boroughs, Rich had never been to Manhattan, let alone the Bronx. He based his descriptions on what he discerned over the years from watching films and TV shows as well as from reading about the Big Apple. He finished his script in the spring of 1997 and spent the next six to eight months revising its dialogue.

Being a novice at the film business and not having an agent to represent him, naïve Rich did what every seasoned screenwriter knows *not* to do: he tried making direct contact with Hollywood producers and agents, but to no avail. He mailed copies of his script to many Hollywood studios and production companies. The unsolicited packages, as is industry custom, were generally returned to him unopened. Disappointed but undaunted, Rich sought procedural advice on the Internet. Someone suggested he enter his work in a screenwriting competition, reasoning that if he should win a contest, it would attach importance to his work and thus attract the attention of potentially interested movie producers.

In early 1998, Rich submitted *Finding Forrester* to the Nicholls Screenwriting Fellowship, a contest sponsored by the Academy of Motion Picture Arts and Sciences. The only stipulation for entering the competition was that the screenwriter must never have sold a screenplay before. Out of forty-four hundred entries submitted, Rich's offering was named one of the five finalists. As a result he received a $25,000 prize as well as a gala award presentation night to officially celebrate the victory. After being chosen a finalist, a friend of a friend put Rich in contact with United Talent Agency, who took him on as a client. His representatives there quickly sold the script.

The script deal called for Rich to receive a mid-six- against a high-six-figure salary fee. Among the terms of the negotiations, he was to deliver the script, plus complete two later rewrites. The buyer was veteran producer Laurence Mark (*The Black Widow, Jerry McGuire, Romy and Michele's High School Reunion*), who was based at Sony Pictures Entertainment's Columbia Pictures. Soon thereafter Rich began reshaping and refining his screenplay.

Meanwhile, John Calley, president/chief executive officer of Sony Pictures Entertainment, took great interest in the property. He discussed *Finding Forrester* with his actor friend Sean Connery, who was always looking for new film projects in which to star/produce. The Oscar-winning Scotsman, most famous for his hugely successful forays into the cinematic world of James Bond, was impressed with Rich's screenplay. Connery explained that he responded to the lead figure in *Finding Forrester*, "because underneath is lurking a rather nice, marvelous person and there is a great arc to the story." The vehicle intrigued him because it would be the first time that he had played in a male bonding story since 1975's *The Man Who Would Be King* opposite Michael Caine. Also *Finding Forrester* was an opportunity for the performer to portray an introverted soul on-screen rather than his usual man of action: "I suppose that was what appealed to me about it . . . trying to get the mix between what this character would be and how he would ever come to have a working relationship with this kid."

As a result of negotiations between Sony Pictures Entertainment and Connery's United Kingdom–based Fountainbridge Films (which included production partner Rhonda Tollefson), Connery was signed to star in and be one of the producers of the project. (By the end of 1999 he was actually Sir Sean Connery, having been knighted by Queen Elizabeth.)

One of the studio's first choices to direct this new Connery vehicle was Mimi Leder. She had made her industry reputation directing multiple episodes of TV's *ER* (for which she won an Emmy) as well as such features as *The Peacemaker* and *Deep Impact*. She might have accepted the offer, but it conflicted with her prior commitment to direct Kevin Spacey and Helen Hunt in the drama *Pay It Forward*. Thereafter, in the process of finding a new director for *Finding Forrester*, the script was faxed to Gus Van Sant. (Later, producer Laurence Mark stated Gus had been considered for the project because "he's a filmmaker with a distinctive voice who doesn't seem to have his eyes only on the marketplace.")

▼

AFTER the fact, Van Sant would acknowledge several reservations that cropped up when it truly sank in that he was about to direct *Finding Forrester*: "I was trying to avoid getting sucked into the type of film that *Forrester* was. A studio film, a star attached, a star producing. . . . It was way out of my desire. I was just trying to work on films that were coming more from myself." That understood, and reweighing the reasons for having accepted the offer, he pushed ahead with preproduction on his latest assignment. Almost immediately upon returning home to Portland from India, he met with Mike Rich, the ecstatic scriptwriter of *Finding Forrester*. Their first get-together took place at the Bijou Café in the heart of the City of Roses. It was the first of several breakfast conferences the two Portlanders had there to discuss refinements to the screenplay.

It was now nearing the end of 1999 and *Finding Forrester* was scheduled to shoot in Toronto (and later New York City) as of April 3, 2000. While Rich continued to revamp his screenplay at the direction of Laurence Mark, Sean Connery, and Gus Van Sant, the latter began casting the film. F. Murray Abraham, who had won an Academy Award playing the frustrated, jealous composer Salieri in *Amadeus* (1984) and who had shown his versatility in such diverse pictures as *The Big Fix, Baby Face Nelson*, and *Star Trek: Insurrection*, was cast as Professor Robert Crawford, the catalyst for much of the plot tension within *Finding Forrester*. Sixteen-year-old Anna Paquin, who had earned a Best Supporting Actress Oscar for her film debut (*The Piano*) and since been in such movies as *Amistad, A Walk on the Moon*, and *X-Men,* was set to portray Claire Spence, the private school classmate of the African-American teenager Jamal Wallace.

To play Jamal's older brother, Terrell, Brooklyn-born rap singer Busta Rhymes was hired. He had previously appeared in such features as *Who's the Man?, Higher Learning*, and the remake of *Shaft*. To appear as the mother of Jamal and Terrell, April Grace was selected. She was, perhaps, most noted for several recurring appearances on such TV series as *Star Trek: Next Generation* and *Chicago Hope*. Michael Pitt, who had displayed an acting presence in the TV series *Dawson's Creek* as the young boyfriend of Michelle Williams's character, was selected to be Coleridge, Jamal's classmate at the prep school (Mailor-Callow). Michael Nouri (*Flashdance, The Hidden, Captain America*) came aboard to enact the snobbish father of Anna Paquin's character who is a member of the private school's board of trustees.

The toughest casting chore for *Finding Forrester* was locating the right performer to play Jamal Wallace. Van Sant grew concerned as time was running short and auditions held around the country had yet to turn up a suitable talent.

Gus asked the studio, "What happens if we don't find this guy?" They said, "Oh, you'll find him."

Auditions to locate their Jamal Wallace were conducted in Los Angeles, Boston, Chicago, Philadelphia, and New York. It was in the latter city that fifteen-year-old Rob Brown was discovered. Growing up in Brooklyn and now living in Queens, he was then an A student in his junior year at Brooklyn Polytechnic High School (as part of a program for bright public school youths to be placed in prep schools), where he was on the football squad as a wide end receiver and had plans to major in engineering in college. Like many others he learned about the open auditions for the *Finding Forrester* role through a flyer distributed at school. Needing quick cash to pay a $300 cell phone bill, he decided on a whim to audition for the movie. (His only previous acting experience was in a third-grade production of *Pocahontas*.) Brown thought, "[at the least] I had a good chance of getting hired as an extra."

At the audition, six-foot-tall Rob, who had neither a clue who Gus Van Sant was nor had seen any of the filmmaker's work, was convinced that producer Dany Wolf was the film's director "because he's bald and he looks stressed out." In contrast, the teenager appeared very relaxed at the casting call. When it was his turn to read, he quickly gained everybody's attention just by the way he spoke his name when the preliminary introductions were made. (According to Van Sant: "It was sort of like he said, 'Paul Robeson.' It was this very intense sound that came out.") Rob registered a strong impression on Gus and he videotaped a test with the teenager. ("He handled himself so beautifully that I'm not sure how he did it with no previous acting experience—not even a lesson! We were all amazed. We felt it at once. Here was Jamal.") Gus's main concern was that Rob looked too perfect, "too much the Hollywood version of the South Bronx kid." Later in the selection process, as Van Sant mulled over the final contenders for this pivotal film role, he showed the footage to two friends who happened to drop by his lower Manhattan digs where the director was based for the duration. The visitors were Matt Damon and his actress girlfriend Winona Ryder. They were both impressed by Brown's test, which confirmed Gus's hunch about his latest discovery.

Meanwhile, back in Scotland, Connery was watching the tests of likely candidates to play his vis-à-vis in the picture. Later Sean flew to New York to meet with the finalists to play Jamal Wallace. The seasoned actor did a reading with Rob Brown and with James Williams III, the latter being the youth who eventually played Jamal's pal Fly in the picture. Connery described the situation: "Gus Van Sant had one of those handheld Sony digital cameras and we talked about a scene, kicked it around a bit and shot it. Both of them gave interesting and different readings. Afterwards Gus and I had a conversation and I thought, without question, that Rob had that feeling, that center which was what we wanted for the piece. He had a very capable stillness. Actors have a tendency to act to get that, but he had it from the start. Gus agreed. Now we just had to tell Columbia we wanted someone who's never acted before to play the lead in the movie."

Columbia Pictures eventually agreed and Rob Brown was contracted to make his screen debut. Two others added to *Finding Forrester* were alumnae of Gus's movies. Alison Folland (*To Die For, Good Will Hunting*) was asked to play a contestant in a specially filmed segment of the quiz show *Jeopardy*, and Matt Damon (*Good Will Hunting*) agreed to take on a cameo as a Manhattan attorney who delivers crucial news to Jamal near the finale of *Finding Forrester*.

While the extensive casting process was under way, Mike Rich continued to refine his screenplay. At one point, the studio dispatched him to New York for further project conferences. The novice screenwriter assumed it was going to be merely more rounds of give-and-take meetings with involved film executives. Instead it was to work directly with Van Sant and Connery. The trio spent a weekend going over the script line by line. By now, Connery's character had already been tailored to fit the star's real-life Scottish background, age, and such other niceties as making him a bird watcher. In his notes to the screenwriter, Connery also declared about William Forrester: "He's got to be ingratiating on one page and infuriating on the next."

As the preparations for the shoot continued it must have been hard for Van Sant to be helming a major film where not only had he *not* written the script, but one in which he was taking orders (to one degree or another) from both Laurence Mark (and Columbia Pictures) and superstar/producer Connery. The full impact of serving several new masters at once must have made for a strange period of adjustment for the self-contained director.

And equally odd for Gus was that the vast majority of this studio-engineered vehicle was peopled by a creative staff totally new to working with Van Sant. There was no Missy Stewart (production designer), no Beatrix Aruna Pasztor (costume designer), no familiar cinematographer such as Eric Alan Edwards or John Campbell, no longtime editor such as Curtiss Clayton or Amy E. Duddleston, no often-employed associate like Danny Elfman to provide the music. Instead, on *Finding Forrester* it was Jane Musky (production designer), Ann Roth (costume designer), Harris Savides (cinematographer), Valdis Oskarsdóttir (editor), and Bill Frisell (original musical). About the only holdovers from past projects were Dany Wolf (executive producer/unit production manager) and Kelley Baker (supervising sound editor). This was typical of working for a big studio, plus the fact that the movie was being made away from Hollywood in the environs of Toronto and New York City. (At least Gus had already filmed twice—*To Die For* and *Good Will Hunting*—in Canada and was somewhat familiar with filmmaking conditions there.)

But there was a consolation to being many miles from Los Angeles. Van Sant grew increasingly appreciative of being far away from the Hollywood studio lot and its ever-present array of corporate executives micromanaging projects. Gus explained, "We would never have had the control we had up in Toronto. In the studio, there's always noise and distractions. You don't get to do that kind of exploration. That would have made it harder for Rob [Brown]. But up there nobody came near us."

In mid-March 2000, *Finding Forrester* cast rehearsals began in earnest in Toronto, with scripter Mike Rush on hand to provide any last-minute script changes. By then, Van Sant and his production squad had the key William Forrester apartment set constructed. The pre–World War II Bronx setting was built to be oversized—as was the furniture—so that six-foot two-inch Connery would not feel physically confined or awkward in these sequences. To everyone's relief, the star pronounced he felt "very comfortable and very much at home." Since he did not know how to type, he was pleased that the manual typewriter his character uses within the story had been rigged to make it seem like he was hitting the keys properly. As rehearsals progressed, props were added, dropped, and changed in the Forrester apartment set to accommodate the new refinements brought to the writer's character.

To carve out his characterization, Connery revealed, "I based him on J. D. Salinger and William Burroughs, literary favorites of mine." (On the point of reference for Forrester's eccentric nature, Van Sant offered, "It was vague. J. D. Salinger is famous for being reclusive, but not agoraphobic. He was simply shut off from the media. He traveled around the world. I don't know a writer specifically like Forrester. Somebody mentioned James Purdy as someone similar.")

Connery told of building his William Forrester alter ego: "I didn't want it to be sentimental at all, and Gus agreed with that. And the handling of the black-white situation could always get kind of dodgy, so we wanted to deal with that immediately and go from there into a relationship that developed believably. And we didn't want to get bogged down with the educational stuff or the literacy of the script, but find a way to play it dramatically and get humor out of it."

To prepare for his dramatic role, young Rob Brown had acting coach Barry Papick to tutor the newcomer in the many tricks of the acting trade. Brown also had the benefit of instruction from twenty-five-year-old Russell Smith who was the film's basketball consultant. Rob's biggest concern as he launched into his acting debut was the intensity level of his character: "I did think about not being too big. We worked on that a lot, me and my coach."

In Canada, after more than two weeks of scrupulous rehearsal, the crew shot the sequences set inside the apartments of Forrester and Jamal. Then everyone involved relocated to Hamilton, Ontario's Copps Coliseum, where Forrester's massive anxiety attack occurs in the screenplay. They also filmed the Mailor-Callow versus Creston basketball play-off game.

Each day, Connery—who had a financial as well as artistic stake in the production—vigilantly studied the rushes. He explained, "There are a lot of actors who avoid the dailies. To me it's the stupidest thing because if you're trying to do something, you don't know if you're accomplishing it. When I get the rushes, I look at everything. I look to see what I did wrong and what I did right, so if need be I can say I have to do it again. We never had to do that. I think there was only one retake, a scene in which I smashed a glass."

Very much in control of the situation during the shoot, Connery said of working with Rob Brown: "It's one thing for someone to appear to be able to do something, and then when the camera's rolling it disappears. But that wasn't the case with Rob. He's very smart. We spent a lot of time together, and he just got better and better. He never appeared to be nervous or in doubt or apprehensive, so it was a very manageable and compatible relationship." It was Brown who instructed Connery on the ethnic lingo of the "hood." Thus it was Rob who suggested the dialogue line "You're the man now, dog" that William Forrester says as Jamal pounds away at the typewriter.

As for Brown, the newcomer seemed unfazed that he was working on this A-list film with a quartet of Oscar winners or that he was sharing many one-on-one scenes with the screen's legendary James Bond. Rob would insist later that he felt no pressure on the set from his far more experienced coworkers: "I just thought, I must be doing something right. So I just went ahead and did it." As for the way Van Sant dealt with Brown on the shoot, Rob noted that "Gus just let me go" and that the director would let the novice know "when he had a problem."

On his part, Van Sant revealed, "Rob seemed to know instinctively how to play a scene. It didn't seem difficult for Sean to work with him. Rob seemed somehow practiced and natural. His imagination was such that he could walk into a scene and fit right in, despite no experience." At one point in the production, however, Brown evidently was so relaxed that he offered co-star F. Murray Abraham acting advice on a particular scene. Gus related this breach of professional decorum: "Rob saw me (telling people what to do), so he thought he just had an idea, you know? Also sometimes professional actors like Murray like to establish their turf, so Murray put him in his place when he did that."

When Gus was questioned if he felt any intimidation interacting with Connery on *Finding Forrester*—or for that matter with any star he had directed—he replied, "No. So far, I've never felt threatened. I think that you could be. It's possible. If you don't get along with an actor like Sean you could really feel threatened emotionally or physically. But part of it is he doesn't want his director to feel threatened. He wants his director to direct the movie as best he can." As to dealing with Van Sant, the generally unflappable Sir Sean allowed, "Oh, Gus can handle himself, he's passively aggressive. He's very much his own kind of instrument. I had a very compatible relationship with him. Besides, we'd done 75% of the work on the script before we got to the rehearsals."

Actually, there were *rumors* of one supposed miniclash between Connery and Van Sant during *Finding Forrester* that both parties later passed off as a matter of miscommunication. Allegedly this occurred when the superstar read that Gus had supposedly suggested that the Forrester character might be gay and have a "subliminal" desire for the youth he is mentoring—referencing that the writer figure is seventy and has never married. Later in 2000, Connery would admit of his screen role: "I suppose there could be an undercurrent that [my] character is closeted. It depends on the response of people, and who's watching. As they say in France, you buy a ticket, you're allowed to be a critic." Then, too, Gus would elaborate further to the press of the potential gay angle to

Finding Forrester: "I'm sure that my sexuality plays into that kind of friendship between two [male] characters. That always has a kind of subliminal overtone for me."

While on the Canadian phase of making *Finding Forrester*, Gus took occasional work breaks for relaxation. For example, he had dinner with pal Joaquin Phoenix at the Teatro Bar on College Street, when the actor happened to be in Toronto.

By May 3, 2000, after a month of filming in Canada, *Finding Forrester* moved to New York for six weeks of work. The logistics of shooting in the Big Apple were quite complex, not only for crowd control but for just moving around the traffic flow. In Manhattan, there were scenes filmed at the New School in Greenwich Village (standing in for Mailor-Callow's cafeteria), the Boy's Harbor Community Center (used as Mailor-Callow's gym), Regis High School (to represent Mailor-Callow classrooms and hallways), Seward Park High School (substituting for the Coolidge High School cafeteria and hallways), the Science Library (the sequence where Jamal Wallace requests a copy of Forrester's book), Park Avenue (where Forrester takes his daytime bike ride), the General Theological Seminary (to stand in as Mailor-Callow's main auditorium), and a spacious penthouse apartment near Carnegie Hall (as the Spence family's party site).

In the Bronx, filming was accomplished at Yankee Stadium, DeWitt Clinton High School (to represent Coolidge's classrooms and hallways), John F. Kennedy High School (Coolidge's main entrance and the principal's office), Park Avenue at 158th Street (site of Forrester's building and the nearby basketball court), and finally Clay Avenue (the location of Jamal's apartment building).

Being THE star, Connery had a spacious trailer to repair to during filming breaks. Gus had a less luxurious one. There he housed his video playback and editing equipment so during lunch breaks he and actor/friend Casey Affleck (serving as an assistant to Gus and also as technical adviser on this picture) could review the most recent scene takes.

For Connery one of the more difficult aspects of the shoot was executing his on-camera bicycle ride along Park Avenue. He described, "It was crazy, because the temperature was unbearably high and the humidity was 98 or something, and I had a three-piece suit on, and a black shirt and tie and a wig like a buzz-bee hat. I was cycling up and down and people would jump up and try to take pictures, which was really not conducive to getting good results. I think I changed the shirt six times with perspiration."

On the other hand, one of the most challenging aspects of making *Finding Forrester* for Gus was handling the picture's several basketball scenes. It did not help matters, Van Sant admitted, that "I don't even know the rules of basketball. I probably did at some time, but I forgot them." Yet he acknowledged of the game footage, "That was fun to shoot, but it's also hard. It's like doing action in a film. We'd work out different plays for them to run, but then they'd improvise on the court." There were often sideline observers to the sports scenes who thought they could add something athletically appropriate to the sequence. For example, when they were shooting the footage of Jamal and his friends playing pickup ball on the outdoor court up in the Bronx, frequently neighborhood kids would be on hand and they often begged, "Gus, put me in the movie, please. Gus!"

For Gus who had never previously featured African Americans in his films, *Finding Forrester* was a learning experience. It was a chance to avoid the stereotypes of so many inner-city screen dramas where so many characters seemed to be armed with weapons. As he pointed out, "In urban neighborhoods everyone's not carrying. The kids who are in the movie are from the same neighborhoods we're shooting in. They're exposed to a lot more of that kind of life, they can show you what a guy looks like when he has a gun and walks down the street because he walks differently, which is something I was not aware of. They can show you what the walk is like."

On *Finding Forrester* Gus relied on his standard directing technique: "They can see I'm relaxed so it makes them relax. A lot of times when we're behaving in real life, everything is tossed off. We're just making things up. On the set, I try to make them not worry about lines. It's better if they screw it up sometimes. The whole vibe on the set is trying to fool itself into being real."

Producer Laurence Mark said of working with Gus on this production: "He seems genuinely to like showing up and making it happen. It's the most civilized party." Rob Brown detailed about making *Finding Forrester*: "Everybody tells me I've been really spoiled to work with Gus. I think that's true because seeing how directors are depicted on TV and in other movies, they're real harsh and, like, jerks. That's not Gus at all. He's really laid-back and knows what he's doing. It was just his whole attitude toward me and how straightforward he was with what he wanted." Veteran talent F. Murray Abraham praised Gus: "I'd work for him for the rest of my life. His quiet insistence, his integrity, his trust and faith in you—it's, I'm sorry to say, unusual. But it draws out the best in you; you've just got to give him your best."

Production on the $42 million *Finding Forrester*—Gus's most expensive film to that date—wrapped on June 10, 2000. As with *Good Will Hunting* and *Psycho*, the postproduction phase was telescoped to meet an end-of-the-year release schedule. The movie was targeted to open in December 2000 for two prime reasons: for potential Oscar consideration and because the Christmas/New Year holiday period is appropriate for a feel-good type of movie like *Finding Forrester*.

During the extensive but relatively quickly executed edit of *Finding Forrester* Van Sant made an important decision regarding a key scene near the movie's finale where William Forrester reads a sample of Jamal Wallace's writing to Mailor-Callow students. It was Gus's choice to use music on the track instead of letting the viewer hear much of what Forrester is reading. Van Sant reasoned, "There were words but I never felt like we got the words that were really going to blow you away. That's sort of what was necessary for that scene. For whatever reason, the words that we were always trying to find always seemed so specific, that there was nothing that ever captured your imagination as much as what you thought he was saying. And that's what the music was there for, for you to put in your own words, and in that way, satisfy everybody as opposed to something that might be seen as for part of the audience and not for another part. It was so subjective that it was a way to use the subjectivity itself by letting people imagine it."

At one juncture during the editing process, Van Sant showed the latest cut of *Finding Forrester* to filmmaker Mike Nichols. Gus remarked, "He said it wasn't sentimental, which is the key to this film. I hate sentimental films. Mike said it reminded him of an old athlete teaching a younger man."

Of editing *Finding Forrester*, whose continuity had been carefully structured before the shoot, Gus noted, "It was the only film I've worked on where we didn't change the order of the scenes." During the later test marketing and final tinkering phase the lengthy picture was trimmed from over 140 minutes to 136 minutes.

As *Finding Forrester* was being edited, Gus worked with Hal Willner (music supervisor/original score producer) on the prerecorded material to be utilized on *Finding Forrester*. It was Van Sant's decision to use six Miles Davis tracks (including "Little Blue Frog" and "Black Satin"). Said producer Laurence Mark, "Gus had a yearning for jazz as far as this score was concerned from the beginning. I guess because he felt jazz was the best way to get New York across, to suggest various culture clashes." According to executive producer Jonathan King: "Not all the Davis songs are totally approachable, and I think that works particularly well in this movie with Forrester (played by Sean Connery) not being totally approachable." The Davis recording sessions used came from the musician's classic quintet period of the 1950s. "Over the Rainbow" from the classic movie *The Wizard of Oz* was used twice in the film: first in a guitar arrangement by *Finding Forrester*'s composer Bill Frisell, and then over the closing credits, using the late Israel Kamakawiwo'ole's rendition. Producer Mark noted of using this famed number: "'Over the Rainbow' is sentimental but not the way it's used here. Gus didn't want to go the standard route, so he took the most sentimental song imaginable and used a unique arrangement."

▼

ONCE *Finding Forrester* had been announced for filming under Gus Van Sant's guidance, movie industry wags, having noted the movie's plot similarities to *Good Will Hunting*, jokingly referred to the new project as *Good Will Hunting II*, *Ghetto Will Hunting*, *Good Will Writing*, *Black Will Hunting*, etc. (These satiric titles led Gus to say, "You can't make anything without it getting named things. Howard Stern used to call *Psycho Dyko*. What are you gonna do?") The puns aside, the studio did little to discourage this association to a past box-office champion. In fact, in their ad campaign one of Columbia Pictures' key tag lines was "From the director who brought you *Good Will Hunting*."

As the film's ad campaign was finalized, Columbia Pictures' marketing department came up with two choices for the movie's key poster. According to Van Sant: "One looked really, I thought, cool, and one looked really bland. And everyone, because they were afraid that the film would look 'independent,' didn't think that the cool-looking poster would be good." Gus did not battle that marketing decision. He reasoned, "It's their own gig. It's their chance to make money and if I screw it up for them, then I screw it up for them. And if they do exactly what they want, then at least it's their responsibility. I think the answer is in getting it up front rather than bolting in at the end and saying, 'This is unacceptable and I absolutely will not support this movie unless you change your marketing campaign.' That's not my style."

▼

WITHIN *Finding Forrester*, Scottish-born William Forrester, who has lived in the United States for many decades, is the author of the great American novel, *Avalon Landing*, which is his first and only published fiction. The eccentric Forrester has been existing as a recluse in his Bronx apartment since the 1950s. Because he frequently stares out the window—using binoculars to bird-watch and to chart neighborhood activities (especially the locals playing basketball in an outdoor court across the street), Forrester has been labeled by the basketball players as "Window" or "Ghost."

African-American Jamal Wallace is a sixteen-year-old Bronx high school student. He has great talent on the basketball court and uses this to disguise his dazzling writing talent and high I.Q., fearful that his neighborhood friends will not relate to his academic prowess. One evening, on a dare from his pals, he breaks into Forrester's apartment. Surprised by the occupant, Jamal—not convinced that rumors of the place being haunted are not true—flees, leaving his backpack behind. Inside are notebooks full of Wallace's diary entries and thoughts. Forrester corrects them before tossing them/the bag out the window to Jamal. Later, Jamal returns to ask the irascible novelist for further guidance. In the thawing process, the two develop a warm teacher-student rapport.

Because of high state aptitude test scores, Jamal is awarded a scholarship to Mailor-Callow, a Manhattan prep school. There he meets student Claire Spence, whose dad is on the board of trustees. As part of his scholarship duties, Wallace goes out for the school's basketball team and becomes a member of Professor Robert Crawford's creative writing course. After seeing Forrester's photograph on the cover flap of an edition of *Avalon Landing*, Jamal confronts the novelist about his real identity. On condition of remaining anonymous, crotchety Forrester helps Jamal with his entry in the school's annual prose contest. Jamal uses a supposedly unpublished piece by his mentor as his starting-off point for his own writing of the piece. He submits the finished results at school.

During a conversation, Forrester tells Jamal that he went into seclusion after his brother's death years ago. One evening, to celebrate the writer's birthday, the student convinces the hermetic Forrester to leave the apartment and to join him at a baseball game. Later, in the classroom Wallace embarrasses Crawford by showing his own knowledge of sundry literary quotes. The vengeful teacher then accuses his pupil of plagiarism in the competition since he has found Forrester's original published writing (in an old copy of *The New Yorker*). With Jamal under the threat of expulsion, Claire's father offers to have the matter overlooked if Wallace leads his team to a championship on the courts. Instead, Jamal throws the game.

Forrester makes a surprise appearance at Mailor-Callow's prize ceremony for the writing competition. After reading a new work—which receives hearty applause—the novelist reveals that the piece was actually written by Jamal.

Now ready to face the world, Forester departs for Scotland where he later dies of cancer. A lawyer advises Jamal that William has left him his apartment as well the manuscript to a new novel.

▼

THE PG-13-rated *Finding Forrester* premiered in Los Angeles on Friday, December 1, 2000. Sean Connery was among the film's stars to attend the festivities, but, as duly noted by the attendees, he slipped away in the time between the screening and the dessert reception at the Academy of Motion Picture Arts and Sciences in Beverly Hills. Gus, garbed in slacks, striped tie, and jacket, was on hand to answer questions, as was screenwriter Mike Rich. At the special New York opening of *Finding Forrester* on December 5, the cast was there, as were Gus and his family and friends (although Rob Brown was forty-five minutes late due to the traffic). Also present were such celebrities as film director John Waters, screenwriter/director Nora Ephron, screenwriter/actor Buck Henry, and ABC-TV News political analyst George Stephanopoulos. After the showing, there was a party hosted at the nightclub Laura Bell. Commenting on the differences between the film's two coastal debuts, Connery observed, "They cheer in L.A., but no clapping and here there was clapping but no cheering."

Reviews for *Finding Forrester* were mixed at best. Besides being bothered by the thematic resemblance to *Good Will Hunting*, many critics found the new Van Sant entry reminiscent of the Al Pacino–Chris O'Donnell 1992 drama *Scent of a Woman*. Stephen Holden (*New York Times*) labeled the drama the "latest in a rising tide of shameless male weepies." He decided of Connery: "Had anyone else played the role, this dubious character would probably have come off as clinically insane." The unimpressed review alerted, "Now for the bad news. *Finding Forrester* is 100 percent bogus, from its high-concept characters whose resemblance to real human beings is distant at best, to the 'lessons' it imparts on everything from courtship to writing." As to the filmmaker, Holden judged, "The director Gus Van Sant, who with the far superior *Good Will Hunting* staked his claim to being king of the surrogate father-boy genius subgenre, does what he can to gloss over the movie's absurdities. But the screenplay by Mike Rich is so far-fetched and riddled with holes that Mr. Van Sant's urban realist touches only underscore the falseness of what's on the screen."

An unsatisfied David Denby (*The New Yorker*), who acknowledged that "Connery, though schlurping [*sic*] his 'S's more than ever, gives a performance that can only be called bristling," decided the film "for all its high-culture references and its respect for writing, is essentially old Hollywood corn." Denby saw that "the picture represents twin fantasies—a desire for the J. D. Salinger types to publish again and for the emergence of a young black male who is Michael Jordan and Ralph Ellison rolled into one."

Laura Miller at the salon.com Internet site observed, "Of course, just as *Good Will Hunting* wasn't really about mathematics, *Finding Forrester* isn't really about writing. Neither film seems interested in the nature of intellectual or creative passion, the particular joy to be found in what's essentially a solitary, internal quest, or the fact that genius is often accompanied by an alarmingly cold-blooded willingness to sacrifice personal relationships in pursuit of its fulfillment."

For an underwelmed Kenneth Turan (*Los Angeles Times*): "One more time, as well, we're presented with a well-oiled piece of Hollywood machinery, pat and overly familiar but tolerably entertaining until it piles on the contrivances at the close." As to Connery's participation, Turan suggested, "His I'm-crankier-than-you-are performance, though glib and entertaining, feels like a reprise of a lifetime of greatest hits. More affecting, and more surprising, is the debut work done by a 16-year-old actor named Rob Brown."

More impressed with *Finding Forrester* was Glenn Whipp of the *Los Angeles Daily News,* who decided "the film is so finely crafted that you don't really care that you've seen it (and not all that long ago) before." On the other hand, Whipp reported, "But Van Sant brings his considerable skills to the film, giving the movie a stylish restraint that keeps the proceedings from venturing into *Patch Adams* country."

Daily Variety's Emanuel Levy asked, "When was the last time a Hollywood movie portrayed the acts of reading and writing in such a gratifying and fulfilling way that it made you want to read a real book rather than an 'airport' bestseller? And when was the last time you saw an interracial mentor-pupil relationship presented as mutually rewarding, and interracial teenage romance depicted without punitive condescension or parental disapproval?" The scribe assessed, "With the notable exception of *Psycho*, his futile 1998 remake, Van Sant's technical work continues to improve in a way that doesn't call attention to itself. His work has always shown a fondness for outsiders, but rather than merely depicting them sympathetically, Van Sant places his outcasts in crisis, forcing them to confront their relationship to society and its rules. Two of the filmmaker's most-used motifs are highlighted in the new film: the moral odyssey of outsiders and the casual randomness of urban life."

Los Angeles' *Entertainment Today* reviewer Brent Simon highlighted, "As a director, Van Sant brings some of his typical visual style (off-center framing, et al.) to *Forrester*. There's a long, silent stretch in the middle of the film that is delightfully at odds with the typical overblown, spell-it-out verbosity of most student/mentor cinematic relationships. Jamal learns mainly in silences . . . [and] we witness his maturation not through cheap set-piece drama, but reflection and reaction." Simon indicated, "Van Sant only stumbles in the weird, loose staging of a crucial state play-off basketball game. Captured mostly in medium shots that give the sequence an offbeat, voyeuristic bent, it feels like the work of a man who is a casual fan of the game's beautiful rhythms but isn't particularly familiar with the specifics."

Later, when *Finding Forrester* opened in England, Peter Matthews (*Sight and Sound*) labeled Gus's new screen entry a "moist hunk of humanist uplift that sets a caesura on Van Sant's once-promising indie career." In making the by-now-standard critical comparison between *Finding Forrester* and the earlier *Good Will Hunting*, Matthews weighed, "both films present an idealized cartoon of the creative process rather than dramatizing its sweat and frustration," and that "Van Sant seems to have cornered the market in a new kind of upscale male-bonding movie where the partners connect with brains instead of brawn." The critic further observed, "One could make a fair argument for *Finding Forrester*—and *Good Will Hunting*—as steamy homoerotic fantasies detailing the pedagogic relationship between an older 'bear' and his dewy acolyte. Van Sant's previous forays in the buddy genre . . . would appear to justify the innuendo—even if his own upward mobility necessitates a tad more sublimation these days."

Playing—at one point—at 2,002 theaters in the United States, *Finding Forrester* grossed a respectable but not outstanding $51.768 million before it left domestic distribution. With too many reviewers (and some of the public) finding a déjà vu quality to *Finding Forrester*, the picture chalked up few awards. It did earn the Prize of the Guild of German Art House Cinemas for Gus at the Berlin International Film Festival in 2001 (he was also nominated there for a Golden Berlin Bear). Rob Brown won the Sierra Award—as Best Male Newcomer—from the Las Vegas Film Critics Society Awards. The teenage actor also earned recognition from the Young Artist Awards in the category of Best Performance in a Feature film—Leading Young Actor.

▼

BESIDES the already stated parallels between *Finding Forrester* and *Good Will Hunting*, the newer film expressed Van Sant's continuing fascination with unusual "family" units. Here there is Jamal Wallace's fatherless household with the older brother Terrell and the mother serving as "parents" to Jamal, while the latter is the intellectually far more mature of the trio. William Forrester, on the other hand, having lost his brother and parents in a short amount of time many years ago, has retreated from the world and become a voyeur of life (as had

Norman Bates to a far more drastic extent in *Psycho*). Now in the present Forrester becomes mentor/parent to the impressionable Jamal.

Also within *Finding Forrester*, the fragments shown of Claire's household reveal that the Spences' blue-blood pedigree and affluence have done nothing to establish a nurturing environment between the generations. And there is, of course, the "family" at Mailor-Callow, a mixture of teachers (as substitute parents) and the students as the offspring. Finally, *Finding Forrester* offers camaraderie among the street activities of the Bronx dwellers and, in particular, Jamal and his friends who find a way to express their group dynamics through pickup games of hoops or casual snacks at a burger joint.

In *Good Will Hunting* it had been the sport of brawling that received special cinematic attention from Gus in his slow-motion ballet of the schoolyard fight between Will and his friends versus their neighborhood enemies. In contrast, *Finding Forrester* focuses on basketball as an outlet for the young people's skills, competitive spirits, and aggression. Here again, Van Sant chooses to display fragments of the game played out in slow motion, which creates a special rhythm to the proceedings.

With so much of *Finding Forrester* set in the depressed Bronx, there is little opportunity for Van Sant to depict moments of visual beauty as he has done so elegantly in past movies. Yet, in isolated bits within *Finding Forrester*, there are images that far transcend the ordinary: the opening credits montage of Bronx neighborhood activity, the nighttime visit to Yankee Stadium by Forrester and Wallace, as well as the flow/rhythm of much of the basketball footage that gives an understated elegance to the sports activities.

The automobile again receives its due in a Gus film, this time in the arrivals of the publishing house assistant who is delivering supplies to the isolated Forrester. The yuppie visitor drives a prestigious BMW car, which prompts Jamal to put the snobbish assistant in his place with a rapid-fire outpouring of facts about the history of the German-based BMW corporation.

Just as in *Good Will Hunting*, where several scenes occur in the crammed confines of the therapist's office as Will does intellectual battle with Sean McGuire, so in *Finding Forrester* a goodly portion of the movie transpires in Forrester's dreary, antiquated apartment—his bastion against the outside world. Jammed with books, filing cabinets, television set, etc., it is brimming over with mementos of decades of claustrophobic living. In the several sequences tracing the progression of William and Jamal's growing friendship, the director constantly shifts angles and points of view to keep the footage from becoming visually stagnant.

Perhaps to compensate for structural weaknesses in the script's plot and characters there are more noticeable creative imbalances within *Finding Forrester* than in most of Van Sant's earlier film. Putting aside Connery's performance—which apparently owed a great deal to the star/producer's self-crafting—the rightness of Rob Brown's characterization is frequently undermined by the overplayed villainy of F. Murray Abraham's pernicious instructor. And having set up the two—teacher and student—as fierce competitors, the film goes weak and predictable when the resolution process between the two does occur. Equally, the screenplay lets down the reader in its failing to develop the complex relationship between African-American Jamal and Caucasian Claire. Their interfacing never leads to anything, and makes her presence in the movie a frustrating cipher. Their unresolved status lessens the impact of the entire film. (The sometimes abrupt editing within the Claire-Jamal interludes indicates that some of their story arc may have been deleted.)

Then, too, the presence of Matt Damon, who had risen to star status on the back of *Good Will Hunting*, also helps to throw *Finding Forrester* out of alignment. It may have been conceived as a cute nod to the past film and to the much-touted parallel between the two screen stories. Moreover, it probably was reasoned that Damon's much-discussed cameo would help the film at the box office. Yet this brief star turn pulls the viewer away from the Jamal Wallace story. It dilutes the scene's poignancy as we witness Wallace's learning of his mentor's passing. In short, it fumbles the already faltering plot progression to the tale's climax.

All in all, *Finding Forrester* is professionally slick and smart in most areas of execution, but it remains fairly unmemorable—even with repeated viewing. Despite Sean Connery's charisma or newcomer Rob Brown's sterling performance, there are no great scenes—again a product of the screenplay—to compare with the emotional highs of *Good Will Hunting*: Will's mind games/baiting of Sean McGuire, Skylar's teary confrontation with boyfriend Will, the pathos of Sean describing his deceased wife, Hunting's highly charged epiphany in McGuire's office, and the underrated sequence of Chuckie's morning stop-by at Will's place for what proves to be the final time. If *Finding Forrester* has any wonderful moments, they occur at Jamal's apartment as he, his mother, and his rap-singing brother banter tenderly with one another.

▼

AFTER the fact, Gus Van Sant acknowledged that *part of* what led him to make *Finding Forrester* was to earn money to keep afloat and to gain additional visibility from the establishment so he could more easily undertake his more personal film projects. As Van Sant reasoned to Stephen Garrett (*Time Out New York*) about Andy Warhol, to whom Gus has been often compared regarding their approach to life and creativity: "Warhol made his portraits to make money. He didn't do them because they were a good idea. It was a way to get cash flow into the Factory. So maybe it's the same thing [with me]."

When questioned whether *Finding Forrester* was another example of Gus selling out his maverick independent film status or, instead, a giant subversive act on his part, Van Sant told Garrett: "Maybe artistically, for my career, it's a subversive movie. I'm subverting my own stuff, but not the business." Was directing *Finding Forrester*, then, the *Time Out New York* reporter wanted to know, Gus's way of subverting the public's expectations of him? The filmmaker answered, "Yes. I'm always subverting that. But I think the truest form of subversion is changing the fabric of the system. *Psycho* was an attempt to completely subvert the business in a very wacky and bizarre and maybe not so positive way. It would have been quite subversive if it had worked, because it could have spawned endless amounts of frame-by-frame remakes of films."

While *Finding Forrester* was moving from being his current to a past screen project, Gus discussed its relationship to his other movies. As to whether the recurring mentoring themes in his pictures represents an obsession on his part, he perceived, "No. Friendship maybe, and family, but I'm not sure about mentorship. I think *Forrester* might also represent whoever your confidant is, not necessarily somebody older or a mentor. It also can be a girlfriend or boyfriend—just someone you talk to regularly, somebody who says, 'How was your day?' and you actually tell them instead of the formality." When asked if, in his movies, Gus is a Forrester or a student, Van Sant decided, "I think I'm more on the student side of things."

And proving that there is a flip side to the self-contained, often shy observer, Gus Van Sant gave this response when *USA Weekend*'s Michelle Hatty asked if Gus believed in happy endings. He said, "Sure. Yeah, I believe in sentimental endings."

THE ROAD TO NEW YORK AND BEYOND

I think a great story is the hardest thing for me to find as a filmmaker. That's what I'm always looking for.

Gus Van Sant, 1998

EVER SINCE GUS RELOCATED TO Portland in the early 1980s, it had been his adopted home and he was soon considered a "native" by the Oregon locals. But all that changed in 2000.

In March 2000, having decided that he now traveled so much for work and pleasure and was in Portland relatively infrequently, Van Sant sold his home at 1883 Southwest Vista Avenue for approximately $800,000—about $165,000 over what he had paid for the spacious residence in August 1990. For the time being, whenever he was in Portland he made the downtown Heathman Hotel his headquarters. Meanwhile, he purchased a co-op in lower Manhattan on West Canal Street, not too far from the Hudson River. It was in an old eight-story industrial building that had been converted into an upscale residency. Gus occupied the spacious two-floor penthouse, which boasted a beautiful panorama of New York City. Unlike his Portland mansion, which he had never had the time, funds, or inclination to effectively decorate, his new bachelor's pad was tastefully executed. Living on the floor beneath Gus's new home— each in his own apartment—were two of Van Sant's friends and coworkers, Joaquin Phoenix and Casey Affleck.

When Gus was asked why he had made the move, he said, "I have always wanted to live in New York, but I never could afford it. Now I can." As to being a New Yorker the filmmaker enthused, "It's great. I've noticed that there's so much input that your face starts to distort, and you start to become like a critic." As to whether he was homesick for Portland, he said, "Yeah, I already miss it. You know, [director] Todd Haynes moved there the same month I left. There's this other gay filmmaker in my place. It's very strange." On another occasion, Van Sant admitted that Portland had been his refuge—a "hideout"—from the Hollywood filmmaking establishment. He also commented of the City of Roses, "It's a small town and it can get very repetitive."

While *Finding Forrester* was in its editing phase in the second half of 2000, Gus found time for a bit of nostalgia. He linked up with childhood friends and classmates Jim Evans and John Howell in July 2000 to attend the thirty-year reunion of their Darien high school.

Also in this period, Gus contributed to *Genre,* a men's magazine. The September 2000 issue was devoted to photography and featured work by such artists as Gus, David LaChapelle, and Bruce Weber. Celebrity photographer Christopher Makos, guest editor for this installment of *Genre,* noted in his introduction to Van Sant's offering of "Digital Flowers": "These photographs by Gus Van Sant came out of left field. I imagined he would give me early shots of Keanu Reeves or River Phoenix taking a shower from his great movie *My Own Private Idaho*; but, no, these amazing flowers are part of a much deeper, more thoughtful artist than I knew. These are not photographs, but actual flowers pressed against a digital scanner. Van Sant brings originality and freshness to everything he does."

Gus had his reasons for providing Genre with his digital flowers: "All my stuff is in storage. I noticed that when you scan flowers you can really blow them up. Or you can go into the middle and scan just the middle part and make them huge. And you see stuff that you wouldn't normally see, like the stamen and the pistil and all that stuff. Otherwise, I had some casting photographs."

▼

ANOTHER reason for Van Sant's transfer to Manhattan became evident in September 2000 when it was announced that Gus had signed a pact with USA Films. It provided a two-year first-look deal with Van Sant's new production company named Meno Films. (Gus still maintained his Sawtooth Films for the loan-out of his personal services on film projects.) Longtime associate producer/executive Dany Wolf (*Ballad of the Skeletons, Psycho, Finding Forrester*) was Gus's production partner in the deal. Meno's office was located on Hudson Street in West Greenwich Village. Acting as office assistant for Meno was Jeremy Rizzi, a Westchester County native and graduate of New York University's film school. Jeremy had worked as assistant to Gus on *Finding Forrester* during its New York City shoot and from that sprang the offer for work at Meno.

▼

BEFORE making the big-budgeted *Finding Forrester* in the spring of 2000, Gus had directed *Easter*, one of the segments in the three-part film *Jokes*. It was a project promulgated by his young friend Harmony Korine. Korine, who wrote/directed *Julien Donkey-Boy* in 1997, had become a great advocate of Dogme 95, and this back-to-basics filmmaking approach appealed to Van Sant. (Dogme 95, created by four Danish directors, had several guidelines for making movies: the story must be contemporary, the film must be shot on location, the crew must use a handheld camera and employ natural light and direct sound, and the movie should avoid plot themes involving murder and weapons. Another of the Dogme 95 rules was that the film should not carry the director's credit.)

Easter was based on Korine's short story. It was shot in Paducah, Kentucky, and told of an albino couple residing in an all African-American community. The tale is pushed into gear when the husband concludes that he is gay and ends with the wife setting herself on fire on the front lawn of their house. It was shot at the home of the former chef of the local country club, one to which Gus Van Sant Sr. belonged when he and his wife had lived in the area in the 1990s. For Gus, making *Easter* allowed him an opportunity to return to his old stomping grounds, where he had spent childhood summers visiting relatives. *Easter* was shot on digital beta with Anthony Dod Mantle, who had lensed *Julien Donkey-Boy*, as the director of cinematography.

Relating how he came to do *Easter*, Gus said, "It all began when I saw the Dogme film by Thomas Vinterberg, *The Celebration*. I was really excited and inspired by the idea of going back to the basics of filmmaking. Then I saw a rough cut of *Julien Donkey-Boy*, and I thought that Harmony and Anthony Dod Mantle (director of photography for *The Celebration* and *Julien*) took the idea to another degree. *Easter* isn't a Dogme film per se, but in doing something smaller I got to see a little of what I've been trying to do since *Drugstore Cowboy*. I saw this documentary where Ingmar Bergman was shooting, and there were only five or six people on the set. I don't see why it's not possible to work like that more often."

As to the actual filming of *Easter*, Gus revealed, "When I was shooting, I started to pay less attention to the camera I was using, and more to the action, so I got out of focus and Anthony [Dod Mantle] got very, ah . . . brisk. My editor on *Finding Forrester*, Valdis Oskarsdóttir (also the editor on *Julien* and *Celebration*) doesn't like it when things are out of focus either. People from Copenhagen get really annoyed when things are out of focus."

Easter screened as a work-in-progress at the September 2000 Venice Film Festival. It was on the same lineup with Barbet Schroeder's *Our Lady of the Assassins*, a gay-themed film based on an autobiographical novel by Colombian Fernando Vallejo, as well as *O Fantasma*, by Portuguese filmmaker João Pedro Rodrigues, which featured explicit gay sex scenes.

Gus also contributed to the Eighteenth Annual Reel Music Festival sponsored by the Northwest Film Center in Portland. His cinematic piece was set to John Adams's pulsating "The Chairman Dances," an excerpt from Adams's 1987 opera *Nixon in China*. Gus used his Macintosh computer and its home movie program to intercut frames of smoke-belching factories with shots of an actor he had come across in Harmony Korine's *Julien Donkey-Boy*. (The man could do stunts with his mouth involving several lit cigarettes.) Other filmmakers who participated in the Reel Music Festival were Jim Blashfield, Joan C. Gratz, and Chel White.

The shorts were screened at the Arlene Schnitzer Concert Hall in Portland on Friday, January 12, 2001. The Oregon Symphony provided the musical accompaniment to the films. Reviewing Gus's *Smoking Man*, columnist Bill Smith (*Willamette Week*) described the entry as using "the thinnest of plots . . . to make an environmental statement about America's hedonistic wastefulness. It plays like a public service announcement-cum-Disney nature flick."

▼

NOW in his late forties, Gus had not slowed down. He assisted with an exhibit of his photos of William S. Burroughs Jr. held at the Portland Art Museum in late 2000/early 2001 and made an appearance at the Sundance Film Festival in January 2001. He also taught a two-hour filmmaking class in mid-January 2001 conducted at Portland's Guild Theater and sponsored by the Northwest Film Center. In addition, Gus made a cameo appearance—playing himself—in a gag sequence within Kevin Smith's feature film *Jay and Silent Bob Strike Back* (2001).

By now, Van Sant had found a new cinema property he wished to film. The offbeat vehicle was *Sarah* by JT LeRoy. *Sarah*, published in 2000 (it reached the #10 spot on the *Los Angeles Times*' best-seller list), chronicles the pilgrimage of an androgynous twelve-year-old whose mother, Sarah, is a "lot lizard" (i.e., truck stop prostitute). The lead character leaves the safety of his special world at the truck stopover to go on a mission. Wanting to become as well-known as his mother, he not only adopts her name and sex, but becomes embroiled in dangerous situations in the West Virginia wilds. In the midst of his fantastic adventures he is mistaken for a saint and must prove himself.

As unique as this book was, so was its author. JT LeRoy was born in 1980 in the South. He was raised for a time by his single mother, who gave birth to him when she was fourteen. At one point in his childhood when she moved away, it was ruled that he should live under foster care with his grandparents in West Virginia. Not wanting to participate in their deeply religious, strict environment, he took off. He later became a street person and all that that entailed. For a time he lived in San Francisco, as well as New York, Seattle, and Portland. After several years of therapy, LeRoy began writing short stories, doing interviews, etc. He has said, "I'd write and I'd be OK and then I'd stop writing and get really dangerous and do really bad things. As long as I was writing I was safe, I was OK. It became more important to me than drugs or alcohol. . . . Writing for me, is keeping me safe."

As JT continued his authoring, he also conducted interviews. His work began appearing in such forums as the *New York Press* and *Spin* magazine. For the December 2000 issue of *Paper* magazine, he interviewed Gus at the Leanie Hotel in San Francisco. In the course of their published conversation, JT mentioned that he had seen *My Own Private Idaho* when it played a return engagement at the Castro Theatre in San Francisco and how he had responded to the script's "devastatingly beautiful language and images of loss and longing."

LeRoy related in the piece that friends of his had given Gus a copy of *Sarah* to read. JT recalled, "When I got a message telling me to contact Gus Van Sant, I was scared. All I could do was play back the phone message again and again— for at least a week." He amplified further regarding Gus: "We've since become good friends, and are working on several projects together, including making *Sarah*, a story about magical transvestites, mother love and prostitution, into a movie. It often feels like some elaborate hallucination, surreal in the extreme."

What JT responded to in Van Sant, who is over twice his age, was that "[h]e's very real. . . . There are people that you have to prove you've done the whole deal to have any value. But Gus liked my work and took me seriously. . . . He's really taken me under his wing."

▼

IN May 2001, seemingly out of nowhere came news of Gus's actual next movie production. It was titled *Jerry*, and according to industry rumor it would deal with "two guys in the desert." The film, set to begin production in mid-2001, was to costar two *Good Will Hunting* players: Matt Damon and Casey Affleck. The $7 million feature, which would have strong improvisational elements to it, would utilize a small cast and crew, and have footage shot in Argentina, Utah, and Arizona's Death Valley. After several productions Van Sant was returning to his roots with this small film produced in the manner of his *Mala Noche*.

▼

BOLSTERED by his innate curiosity, Gus Van Sant continues to be drawn to the latest moviemaking styles—intrigued by their efforts to challenge established methodologies. For example, when he saw a print of *Satantango*, a black-and-white 1994 entry by Hungarian filmmaker Béla Tarr, Gus was ecstatic. "I'd never seen a seven-hour movie before, but now it seems viable. It's amazing to live with those characters for that length of time. . . . [Tarr] brings it all together." Van Sant saw Tarr's *Werckmeister harmóniák* at the Toronto International Film Festival and was so impressed that he sought to interest American distributors in releasing the picture. Gus said, "Here we are making these multimillion-dollar films, and Béla, who's one of the great living filmmakers, is about to have his film taken away by the bank. I feel like just sending him a check."

▼

AS to whether Gus will direct more gay-themed pictures, he says it depends on the current marketplace. "Fifty percent of the people working in show business are gay. . . . I think they'd like nothing better than to make gay films, but people are always analyzing what will make money. There's a new gay film on a contained budget coming out every month now, whereas that wouldn't happen, 10, 15 years ago. *Parting Glances* [1986] indicated that a modest gay story could be made. If it made the kind of money that action films make, they'd be making gay films."

Whether creating a movie with a homosexual story line or a feel-good mainstream drama, Van Sant's criterion still remains, "I want to make films that I'd like to go see." He amplifies, "I guess because I started outside the Hollywood system, the only way to write something for me was to write something original which Hollywood didn't make. So the way I look at things is still according to my own criteria or those around me, but certainly not according to how much money it will make at the box office."

When asked his advice for aspiring filmmakers, Van Sant says, "You need to do what you think you should and not listen to anyone else. . . . You need to do your work. Even though in the end it's always luck."

As to what he has discovered over the years to be the best filmmaking method, he says, "There's a lot of ways to make a movie. I like my own."

FILMOGRAPHY

Short Subjects

1967: *Fun with a Blood Root*. 1971: *The Happy Organ*. 1972: *Little Johnny*. 1973: *½ of a Telephone Conversation*. 1975: *Late Morning Start*. 1977: *The Discipline of DE*. 1982: *My Friend; Fly Flame*. 1983: *Where Did She Go?* 1984: *Nightmare Typhoon* (aka *Hello It's Me*); *Switzerland*. 1986: *Five Ways to Kill Yourself*. 1987: *Ken Death Gets Out of Jail; My New Friend; Junior*. c. 1988: *Five Naked Boys and a Gun*. 1991: *Thanksgiving Prayer*. 1996: *Ballad of the Skeletons; Color of a Brisk and Leaping Day*. 2000: *Easter*. 2001: *Smoking Man*.

Music Videos

1990: "Tarbelly and Featherfoot" (Victoria Williams); "Fame '90" (David Bowie). 1991: "I'm Seventeen" (Tommy Conwell); "Under the Bridge" (Red Hot Chili Peppers). 1992: "Bang, Bang, Bang" (Tracy Chapman); "The Last Song" (Elton John). 1993: "Just Keep Me Moving" (k. d. lang); "Runaway" (Deee-Lite); "Solitary Man" (Chris Isaak). 1997: "Understanding" (Candlebox). 1997: "Miss Misery" (Elliott Smith). 1998: "Weird" (Hanson).

Feature Films

As Executive Producer Only

Kids (Miramax, 1995); *Speedway Junky* (Regent Entertainment, 2001).

As Director

Alice in Hollywood (Round Productions, 1979) color, 29 minutes [unreleased].

EXECUTIVE PRODUCER: Marion Marzynski. Producer: Gus Van Sant. Associate producers: Peter Scranton, Sherri Lubov, and Melanie Traveler. Director/Screenplay: Van Sant. Sound: Tom Yore. Camera, Jean Desegonzac. Editor: Van Sant.

CAST: Anita Skinner (Alice), Mark Pixler (Roy Brown), John Berwick (policeman), Frank Birney (director's assistant), Nigel Bullard (Herb Gold), Donna Bruce (tourist), Theo Cleaver (motel manager), Jon Collins (man in elevator), Sam Diego (Vietnam veteran), Harry Lewelyn (director), Rae Maguire (mom), Tom Maguire (dad), Robert Martin (the major), Tom O'hara (cop), Dan Patterson (John Dramma), Elaine Parker and Alexa Power (autograph hounds), Wiley Pender (Stanley Dubrick), Alexa Power and Rae Maguire (bag ladies), Peter Scranton (chauffeur), Tom Sherohman (tourist), T. J. Skimmer (Big Jim Jones), Nancy Smith (naked lady), Melanie Traveler (talent agent), David Worden (Timmy), David Bynum, Beth Aroyo, Verina Berostent, Joan Leizman, Brian Ann Zoccola, Cici Holman, Debby Dugan, Steve Ecclesine, Dianne McKinstry, Greg Conser, Herb Winsted, and Michael Fleck (bits).

Mala Noche (Northern Film Co., 1985) black and white/color, 78 minutes. Not rated.
PRODUCER: Gus Van Sant. Production associates: Jack Yost and Chris Monlux. Director: Van Sant. Based on the story by Walt Curtis. Screenplay: Van Sant. Music: Creighton Lindsay. Sound: Pat Baum. Camera: John Campbell. Additional camera: Eric Alan Edwards. Editor: Van Sant.
CAST: Tim Streeter (Walt), Doug Cooeyate (Johnny), Ray Monge (Roberto Pepper), Nyla McCarthy (Sarah—Walt's Friend), Sam Downey (hotel clerk), Robert Lee Pitchlynn (drunk man), Eric Pedersen (policeman), Marty Christiansen (bar friend), Bad George Connor (wino), Don Chambers (himself), Walt Curtis (George), Kenny Presler (street hustler), Conde Benavides (arcade amigo), Cirsto Stoyos (Greek singer), Matt Cooeyate (boxcar amigo), Maruya Muñoz (lady with knife), Arturu Torres (voice of Johnny), Marselus Allen, Anne Buffen, Dieter Reshhe, Frank Euward, John Benneth, Pat Switzler, Steve Young, Fred Portra, G. H. Mackie, Judy Anne Leach, Katherine Serlo, Pablo Telles, Chris Monlux, Steve Foster, Havier Valle, Steven Hulse, and Denny Chericone (bits), Gus Van Sant (building tenant).

Drugstore Cowboy (Avenue Entertainment, 1989) color, 100 minutes. R-rated.
EXECUTIVE PRODUCER: Cary Brokaw. Producers: Nick Wechsler and Karen Murphy. Director: Gus Van Sant. Based on the novel by James Fogle. Screenplay: Van Sant and Daniel Yost. Production designer: David Brisbin. Art director: Eve Cauley. Set decorator: Margaret Goldsmith. Set dresser: Missy Stewart. Costume designer: Beatrix Aruna Pasztor. Music: Elliott Goldenthal. Music editor: Bill Bernstein. Sound: Ron Judkins, Mark "Frito" Long, Joel Iwataki. Supervising sound editor: Dane A. Davis. Camera: Robert Yeoman. Second unit camera: Eric Alan Edwards. Editors: Curtiss Clayton and Mary Bauer. Additional Editing: Caroline Ross.
CAST: Matt Dillon (Bob Hughes), Kelly Lynch (Dianne Hughes), James LeGros (Rick), Heather Graham (Nadine), Beah Richards

(drug counselor), Grace Zabriskie (Bob's mother), Max Perlich (David), William S. Burroughs Jr. (Tom the Priest), Eric Hull (druggist), James Remar (Gentry), John Kelly (cop), George Catalano (Trousinski), Janet Baumhover (neighbor lady), Ted D'Arms (neighbor man), Neal Thomas (Halamer), Stephen Rutledge (motel manager), Robert Lee Pitchlynn (hotel clerk), Roger Hancock (machinist), Mike Parker (crying boy), Roy Monge (accomplice), Doug Cooeyate (David's friend), Tom Peterson (TV commercial spokesperson), Woody (Panda the dog).

My Own Private Idaho (Fine Line Features, 1991) color, 104 minutes. R-rated.

EXECUTIVE PRODUCER: Gus Van Sant. Coexecutive producer: Allan Mindel. Producer, Laurie Parker. Line producer: Tony Brand. Director/Screenplay: Van Sant. Production designer: David Brisbin. Art director: Ken Hardy. Set decorator: Melissa Stewart. Costume designer: Beatrix Aruna Pasztor. Music: Bill Stafford. Sound: Reinhard Stergar, Roger Marts, Jan Cyr, and Jon Huck. Supervising sound editor: Kelley Baker. Camera: Eric Alan Edwards and John Campbell. Special camera: Bruce Weber. Editor: Curtiss Clayton. Assistant editor: Amy E. Duddleston.

CAST: River Phoenix (Mike Waters), Keanu Reeves (Scott Favor), James Russo (Richard Waters), William Richert (Bob Pigeon), Rodney Harvey (Gary), Chiara Caselli (Carmella), Michael Parker (Digger), Jessie Thomas (Denise), Flea (Budd), Grace Zabriskie (Alena), Tom Troupe (Jack Favor), Udo Kier (Hans), Sally Curtice (Jane Lightwork), Robert Lee Pitchlynn (Walt), Mickey Cottrell (Daddy Carroll), Wade Evans (Wade), Matt Ebert, Scott Patrick Green, and Tom Cramer (porno magazine cover boys), Vana O'Brien (Sharon Waters), Scott Patrick Green, Shaun Jordan, and Shawn Jones (café kids), George Comer (Bad George), Oliver Kirk (Native-American cop), Stanley Hainesworth (Dirtman), Joshua Halladay (Baby Mike), Douglas Tollenen (Little Richard), Stephen Clark Pachosa (Family Tree Hotel manager), Lannie Swerdlow (disco manager), Wally Gaarsland, Bryan Wilson, Mark Weaver, Conrad "Bud" Montgomery (rock promoters), Pat Patterson, Steve Vernelson, and Mike Cascadden (cops), Eric Hull (mayor's aide), James A. Arling (minister), James Caviezel (airline clerk), Ana Cavinato (stewardess), Melanie Mosely (lounge hostess), Greg Murphy (Carl), David Reppinhagen (yuppie at Jake's), Tiger Warren (himself), Massimo De Cataldo, Pao Pei Andreoli, Robert Egon, Paolo Baiocco (Italian street boys), Mario Stracciarolo (Mike's Italian client), Gus Van Sant (Family Tree Hotel bellboy).

Even Cowgirls Get the Blues (Fine Line Features, 1994) color, 95 minutes. R-rated.

PRODUCER: Laurie Parker. Line producer: Eric McLeod. Associate producer: Mary Ann Marino. Director: Gus Van Sant. Based on the novel by Tom Robbins. Screenplay: Van Sant. Production designer: Missy Stewart. Art director: Dan Self. Set decorator: Nina Bradford. Costume designer: Beatrix Aruna Pasztor. Title designer: Michael Hinton. Music: k. d. lang and Ben Mink. Choreographers: Ruby Burns and Jane Dryer. Stunt coordinator: Jake Crawford. Sound/Supervising sound editor: Kelley Baker. Sound: Jon Huck. Camera: John Campbell and Eric Alan Edwards. Special visual effects supervisor: Chel White. Editor: Curtiss Clayton. Associate editor: Amy E. Duddleston.

CAST: Uma Thurman (Sissy Hankshaw), John Hurt (the countess), Rain Phoenix (Bonanza Jellybean), Noriyuki "Pat" Morita (the Chink), Keanu Reeves (Julian Gitche), Lorraine Bracco (Delores Del Ruby), Angie Dickinson (Miss Adriana), Sean Young (Marie Barth), Crispin Gover (Howard Barth), Ed Begley Jr. (Rupert), Carol Kane (Cowgirl Carla), Victoria Williams (Cowgirl Debbie), Dee Fowler (Cowgirl Kym), Arlene Wewa (Cowgirl Big Red), Judy Robinson (Cowgirl Gloria), Heather Graham (Cowgirl Heather), Betsy Roth (Cowgirl Mary), Heather Hershey (Cowgirl Donna), Roseanne Arnold (Madame Zoe), Buck Henry (Dr. Dreyfus), Alan Arnold (Lionel), Ken Kesey (Sissy's daddy), Ken Babbs (Sissy's uncle), Grace Zabriskie (Mrs. Hankshaw), Michael Parker (pilgrim driver), Suzanne Solgot and Scott Patrick Green (pilgrims), Udo Kier (TV commercial director), Tom Peterson (crewman), Wade Evans (cameraman), Oliver Kirk (sheriff), Greg McMickle (FBI agent), Treya Jeffrey (young Sissy), Alexa (Rubber Rose bird expert), Eric Hull (White House undersecretary), Joe Ivy (FBI director), Lin Shaye (Rubber Rose maid), Chel White (brain surgeon), Molly Little (salsa singer), Sherry Alps, Eliza Butterfly, Bee Connolly, Stacey Ryder, and Tina Knaggs (cowgirls) William S. Burroughs (himself), Edward James Olmas (band member), Tom Robbins (narrator).

To Die For (Columbia, 1995) color, 107 minutes. R-rated.

EXECUTIVE PRODUCERS: Jonathan Taplin and Joseph M. Caracciolo. Producer: Laura Ziskin. Coproducers: Sandy Isaac and Leslie Morgan. Director: Gus Van Sant. Based on the novel by Joyce Maynard. Screenplay: Buck Henry. Production designer: Missy Stewart. Art director: Vlasta Svoboda. Set decorator: Carol A. Lavoie. Costume designer: Beatrix Aruna Pasztor. Music: Danny Elfman. Music editor: Ellen Segal. Supervising sound editor:

Kelley Baker. Sound: Robert Fernandez and Bill Jackson. Camera: Eric Alan Edwards. Editor: Curtiss Clayton. Associate editors: Amy E. Duddleston and Craig Hayes.

CAST: Nicole Kidman (Suzanne Stone), Matt Dillon (Larry Maretto), Joaquin Phoenix (Jimmy Emmett), Casey Affleck (Russell Hines), Illeana Douglas (Janice Maretto), Alison Folland (Lydia Mertz), George Segal (Hal Brady), Dan Hedaya (Joe Maretto), Wayne Knight (Ed Grant), Kurtwood Smith (Earl Stone), Holland Taylor (Carol Stone), Susan Traylor (Faye Stone), Maria Tucci (Angela Maretto), Tim Hopper (Mike Warden), Michael Rispoli (Ben DeLuca), Buck Henry (Mr. Finlaysson), Gerry Quigley (George), Tom Forrester and Alan Edward Lewis (fishermen), Nadine MacKinnon (sexy woman), Conrad Coates (weaselly guy), Ron Gabriel (Sal), Ian Health, Graeme Millington, and Sean Ryan (students), Nicholas Pasco (detective), Joyce Maynard (Suzanne's lawyer), David Collins, Eve Crawford, and Janet Lo (reporters), David Cronenberg (man at lake), Tom Quinn (skating promoter), Peter Glenn (priest), Amber-Lee Campbell (Suzanne at age five), Colleen William (Valerie Mertz), Simon Richards (Chester), Philip William (Babe Hines), Susan Backs (June Hines), Kyra Harper (Mary Emmett), Adam Roth and Andrew Scott (band members), Tamara Gorski, Katie Griffin, and Carla Renee (girls at bar), Misha (Walter the dog), Gus Van Sant (off-camera interviewer), Tom Peterson (TV commercial spokesperson).

Good Will Hunting (Miramax, 1997) color, 126 minutes. R-rated.

EXECUTIVE PRODUCERS: Su Armstrong, Bob Weinstein, Harvey Weinstein, and Jonathan Gordon. Coexecutive producers: Kevin Smith and Scott Mosier. Producer: Lawrence Bender. Coproducer: Chris Moore. Director: Gus Van Sant. Screenplay: Matt Damon and Ben Affleck. Production designer: Melissa Stewart. Art directors: James McAteer and Kenneth A. Hardy. Set decorators: Jaro Dick and Kathleen Rosen. Costume designer: Beatrix Aruna Pasztor. Music: Danny Elfman. Music supervisor: Jeffrey Kimball. Music editor: Kenneth Karman. Supervising sound editor: Kelley Baker. Sound: Steve Kohler. Special effects: Stephen Ricci, Edward Ricci, and William "Billyjack" Jakielaszek. Camera: Jean-Yves Escoffier. Editor: Pietro Scalia.

CAST: Robin Williams (Sean McGuire), Matt Damon (Will Hunting), Ben Affleck (Chuckie), Stellan Skarsgård (Prof. Gerald Lambeau), Minnie Driver (Skylar), Casey Affleck (Morgan), Cole Hauser (Billy), John Mighton (Tom), Rachel Majorowski (Krystyn), Colleen McCauley (Cathy), Matt Mercier, Ralph St. George, Rob Lynds, and Dan Washington (barbershop quartet), Alison Folland,

Derrick Bridgeman, and Vic Sahay (M.I.T. students), Shannon
Egleson (girl on street), Rob Lyons (Carmine Scarpaglia), Steven
Kozlowski (Carmine friend #1), Jennifer Deathe (Lydia), Scott
Williams Winters (Clark), Philip Williams (head custodian),
Patrick O'Donnell (assistant custodian), Kevin Rushton (courtroom
guard), Jimmy Flynn (Judge Malone), Joe Cannons (prosecutor),
Ann Matacunas (court officer), George Plimpton (psychologist),
Francesco Clemente (hypnotist), Jessica Morton and Barna Moricz
(Bunker Hill College students), Libby Geller (toy store cashier),
Chas Lawther (M.I.T. professor), Richard Fitzpatrick (Timmy),
Patrick O'Donnell (Marty), Frank Nakashima, Chris Britton, and
David Eisner (executives), Bruce Hunter and Robert Talvano (NSA
agents), Harmony Korine (jail inmate).

Psycho (Universal, 1998) color, 103 minutes. R-rated.
EXECUTIVE PRODUCER: Dany Wolf. Associate producer: James
Whitaker. Director: Gus Van Sant. Based on the novel by Robert
Bloch. Screenplay: Joseph Stefano. Production designer: Tom
Foden. Art director: Carlos Barbosa. Set designers: Tim Beach,
Kristen Davis, Nicole Koenigsberger, and G. Victoria Ruskin. Set
decorator: Rosemary Brandenburg. Costume designer: Beatrix
Aruna Pasztor. Mrs. Bates design: Rick Baker, Matt Rose, and
Chad Waters. Original title designer: Saul Bass. Title design adap-
tor: Pablo Ferro. Original music: Bernard Herrmann. Music pro-
ducer/adaptor: Danny Elfman. Supervising music editor: Kenneth
Karman. Technical advisers: Hilton A. Green and Marshall
Schlom. Stunt coordinator: Mickey Giacomazzi. Supervising sound
editor: Kelley Baker. Sound: Shawn Murphy. Camera: Chris Doyle.
Editor: Amy E. Duddleston.
CAST: Vince Vaughn (Norman Bates), Julianne Moore (Lila Crane),
Viggo Mortensen (Sam Loomis), William H. Macy (Milton
Arbogast), Anne Heche (Marion Crane), Robert Foster (Dr.
Simon), Philip Baker Hall (Sheriff Chambers), Anne Haney (Mrs.
Chambers), Chad Everett (Tom Cassidy), Rance Howard (Mr.
Lowery), Rita Wilson (Caroline), James Remar (patrolman), James
LeGros (used car dealer), Steven Clark Pachosa (police guard), O.
B. Babbs (mechanic), Flea (Bob Summerfield), Marjorie Lowett
(woman customer) Ryan Cutrona (chief of police), Ken Jenkins
(district attorney).

Finding Forrester (Columbia, 2000) color, 136 minutes. PG-13 rated.
EXECUTIVE PRODUCERS: Dany Wolf and Jonathan King. Producers:
Laurence Mark, Sean Connery, and Rhonda Tollefson. Director:
Gus Van Sant. Screenplay: Mike Rich. Production designer: Jane

Musky. Art directors: Darrell K. Keister and Arvinder Grewal. Set decorators; Susan Tyson and Cal Loucks. Costume designer: Ann Roth. Music: Bill Frisell. Music editor: Lisa Jaime. Supervising sound editor: Kelley Baker. Sound: Frank Rinella. Camera: Harris Savides. Editor: Valdis Oskarsdóttir.

CAST: Sean Connery (William Forrester), F. Murray Abraham (Prof. Robert Crawford), Anna Paquin (Claire Spence), Rob Brown (Jamal Wallace), Busta Rhymes (Terrell), April Grace (Ms. Joyce), Michael Pitt (Coleridge), Michael Nouri (Dr. Spence), Richard Easton (Matthews), Glenn Fitzgerald (Massie), Zane R. Copeland Jr. (Damon), Stephanie Berry (Janice), James Williams III (Fly), Damany Mathis (Kenzo), Damien Lee (Clay), Tom Kearns (Coach Garrick), Matthew Noah Word (Hartwell), Charles Bernstein (Dr. Simon), Matt Malloy (Bradley), Jimmy Bobbitt (rapper), Capital Jay (opposing player), James T. Williams II (student), Cassandra Kubrinski (Claire's friend), Sophia Wu (librarian), Gerry Rosenthal (student speaker), Tim Hall (student manager), Tom Mullica (old money man), David Madison (kid in the hall), Joey Buttafuoco (night man), James McCabe and William Modeste (referees), Daniel Rodriguez (hallway boy), Samuel Tyson (Creston player), Vincent Giordano (big band leader), Gregory Singer (violinist), Dean Pratt and Kerry MacKillop (trumpet players), Harvey Tibbs (trombone player), Jack Stuckey, Mark Lopeman, Mark Phaneuf, and Larry Wade (sax players), Conal Fowkes (piano player), Matt Munisteri (guitarist), John Meyers (drummer), Ron Morgan (Mailor-Callow priest), Alison Folland (*Jeopardy* TV show contestant), Alex Trebek (*Jeopardy* TV show host).

BIBLIOGRAPHY

interviews

James Alderman
Simon Babbs
Frank Birney
Jim Evans
Bill Foster
John Howell
Irv Letofsky
Paige Powell
Jeremy Rizzi
Tom Sherohman
Anita Skinner
T. J. Skinner
Steve Taravella
Gus Van Sant Sr.
Daniel Yost
Brian Ann Zoccola

books

Bocheris, Victor. *With William Burroughs: A Report from the Bunker*. New York: St. Martin's, 1996.

Brooks, Tim, and Earle Marsh. *The Complete Directory to Prime Time Network and Cable TV Shows: 1946–Present*. (7th ed.). New York: Ballantine, 1999.

Burroughs, William S. *The Adding Machine*. New York: Arcade, 1986.

———. *My Education: A Book of Dreams*. New York: Penguin, 1995.

Busch, Kristen. *The Matt Damon Story*. New York: Ballantine, 1998.

Caveney, Graham. *Gentleman Junkie: The Life and Legacy of William S. Burroughs*. Boston: Little, Brown, 1998.

Christensen, Loren W. *Skid Row Beat: A Street Cop's Walk on the Wild Side*. Boulder, Colo.: Paladin, 1999.

Cowie, Peter, ed. *Variety International Guide: 1999*. Los Angeles: Silman-James, 1998.

Curtis, Walt, with introduction by Gus Van Sant. *Male Noche & Other "Illegal" Adventures*. Portland, Oreg.: Bridge City Books, 1997.

Damon, Matt, and Ben Affleck, with introduction by Gus Van Sant. *Good Will Hunting*. New York: Miramax/Hyperion, 1997.

Diamond, Maxine, with Harriet Hemmings. *Matt Damon*. New York: Pocket Books, 1998.

Fuller, Graham. [introductory interview with Gus Van Sant]. *Even Cowgirls Get the Blues & My Own Private Idaho*. Boston: Faber & Faber, 1993.

Givens, Ron. *Robin Williams*. New York: Time Books, 1999.

Glatt, John: *Lost in Hollywood: The Fast Times and Short Life of River Phoenix*. New York: Primus/Donald I. Fine, 1995.

Grauerholz, James, ed. *Last Words: The Final Journals of William S. Burroughs*. New York: Grove Press, 2000.

Gray, Susan, ed. *Writers on Directors*. New York: Watson-Guptill, 1999.

Halperin, Ian, and Max Wallace. *Who Killed Kurt Cobain?: The Mysterious Death of an Icon*. Secaucus, N.J.: Birch Lane Press, 1998.

Harris, Richard, and Susan Farewell. *Hidden New England*. 6th ed. Berkeley, Calif.: Ulysses, 2000.

Hibbard, Allen, ed. *Conversations with William S. Burroughs*. Jackson, Miss.: University Press of Mississippi, 1999.

Humphries, Patrick. *The Films of Alfred Hitchcock*. New York: Portland House/Crown, 1986.

Johnston, Sheila. [essay on Gus Van Sant]. *Variety International Guide: 1999*. Los Angeles: Silman-James, 1998.

Kagan, Jeremy, ed. *Directors Close Up*. Woburn, Mass.: Focal Press, 2000.

Klein, Fred, and Ronald Dean Nolan, eds. *Ephraim Katz's The Film Encyclopedia*. 4th ed. New York: HarperResource/HarperCollins, 2001.

Laschever, Barnett D., and Andi Marie Fusco. *Connecticut: An Explorer's Guide*. Woodstock, Vt.: Countryman, 1999.

Lehr, Dick, and Gerard O'Neill. *Black Mass: The Irish Mob, The FBI and a Devil's Deal*. New York: PublicAffairs/Perseus Books, 2000.

LeRoy, JT. *Sarah*. New York: Bloomsbury, 2000.

Lyons, Donald. *Independent Visions*. New York: Ballantine, 1994.

MacDonald, Michael Patrick. *All Souls: A Family Story from Southie*. New York: Ballantine, 1999.

Matthews, Jill. *Hanson: MMMBop to the Top. An Unauthorized Biography*. New York: Archway/Pocket Books, 1997.

McNeil, Alex. *Total Television*. 4th ed. New York: Penguin, 1996.

Méras, Phyllis, and Tom Gannon. *Rhode Island: An Explorer's Guide*. Woodstock, Vt.: Countryman, 2000.

Merritt, Greg. *Celluloid Mavericks*. New York: Thunder's Mouth Press, 2000.

Morgan, Ted. *Literary Outlaw: The Life and Times of William S. Burroughs*. New York: Henry Holt, 1988.

Nickson, Chris. *Matt Damon: An Unauthorized Biography*. Los Angeles: Renaissance, 1999.
Odier, Daniel. *The Job: Interviews with William S. Burroughs*. New York: Penguin, 1989.
O'Neil, Tom. *Movie Awards: The Ultimate, Unofficial Guide to the Oscars, Golden Globes, Critics, Guild & Indie Honors*. New York: Perigee/Berkley, 2001.
Proulx, Annie. *Close Range: Wyoming Stories*. New York: Scribner, 1999.
Rechy, John. *City of Night*. New York: Grove, 1964.
Robb, Brian J. *Keanu Reeves: An Excellent Adventure*. London: Plexus, 1997.
———. *River Phoenix: A Short Life*. London: Plexus, 1995.
Robbins, Tom. *Even Cowgirls Get the Blues*. New York: Houghton Mifflin, 1976.
Rumler, John, and Dave Johnson. *The Insiders' Guide to Portland*. Helena, Mont.: Falcon, 1999.
Scott, Kieran. *Matt Damon*. New York: Aladdin/Simon & Schuster, 1998.
Skerl, Jennie. *William S. Burroughs*. Boston: Twayne Publishers, 1985.
Spoto, Donald. *The Art of Alfred Hitchcock*. New York: Anchor/Doubleday, 1992.
Stempel, Penny. *River Phoenix: They Died Too Young*. Philadelphia: Chelsea House, 2000.
Sullivan, Monica. *VideoHound's Independent Film Guide*. Farmington Hills, Mich.: Visible Ink, 1999.
Taylor, John Russell. *Hitch: The Life & Times of Alfred Hitchcock*. New York: Berkley, 1978.
Van Sant, Gus. *Even Cowgirls Get the Blues & My Own Private Idaho*. Boston: Faber & Faber, 1993.
———. *108 Portraits*. Santa Fe, N.Mex.: Twin Palms, 1992.
———. *Pink*. New York: Anchor/Doubleday, 1997.
Wellman, Sam. *Ben Affleck*. Philadelphia: Chelsea House, 2000.

magazines, periodicals, and other publications
Addiego, Walter, *Psycho* Film Review. *San Francisco Examiner*, 5 December 1998.
Anderson, John. *Even Cowgirls Get the Blues* Film Review. *Newsday*, 20 May 1994.
Andrews, Paul. "Director Gus Van Sant Gives Us Movies that Feel Like a Reality Check." *Seattle Times*, 9 September 1990.
Angeli, Michael. "River Phoenix." *Movieline*, September 1991.
Ansen, David. *Drugstore Cowboy* Film Review. *Newsweek*, 23 October 1988.
———. "Prince Hal in Portland." *Newsweek*, 15 April 1991.
———. "*Psycho* Analysis." *Newsweek*, 7 December 1998.
———. *To Die For* Film Review. *Newsweek*, 2 October 1995.

Appelo, Tim. "Searching for Truth in Van Sant's *Pink. Los Angeles Times*, 2 January 1998.

Arnold, Gary. *"Kids." Washington Times*, 25 September 1995.

Arrington, Carl Wayne. "Mighty Matt." *Rolling Stone*, 30 November 1989.

Ascher-Walsh, Rebecca. "Gus Van Sant." *Entertainment Weekly: Collectors Issue*, March 1998.

Atkinson, Michael. "Going Straight." *Gear*, February 2001.

Bagley, Christopher. "Gus Van Sant." *W* magazine, February 1998.

Baker, Jeff. *Pink* Book Review. *Oregonian*, 12 October 1997.

Barnes, Harper. "Into the Mainstream." *St. Louis Post-Dispatch*, 6 October 1995.

Baumgarten, Marjorie. *Even Cowgirls Get the Blues* Film Review. *Austin Chronicle*, 20 May 1994.

———. *My Own Private Idaho* Film Review. *Austin Chronicle*, 18 October 1991.

Beck, Marilyn, and Stacy Jenel Smith. Celebrities Column. *Los Angeles Daily News*, 29 June, 1994.

———. "Celebrities: What a Relief! Breathed Van Sant." *Los Angeles Daily News*, 28 December 2000.

Beggs, Charles E. "Oregon Ballot Issue Sparks Battle Over Gay Rights. Similar Measures Received Mixed Support Locally." *Seattle Times*, 26 September 1992.

Benson, Sheila. *Drugstore Cowboy* Film Review. *Los Angeles Times*, 11 October 1989.

Bernard, Jami. *Drugstore Cowboy* Film Review. *New York Post*, 6 October 1989.

Blair, Iain. "Gus Van Sant." *Film & Video*, January 1998.

Block, Adam. "Perchance to Dream." *Filmmaker*, fall 1993.

———. "Sex & Drugs." *Mother Jones*, September/October 1991.

"Bookworld" Column. *Washington Post*, 2 November 1997.

Boss, Kit. "The Real Drugstore Cowboy." *Seattle Times*, 22 October 1989.

Brodie, John. "Boston Uncommon." *Premiere*, January 1998.

Brooks, Caryn. "Spin" Column. *Willamette Week*, 21 October 1993.

Brown, Joe. *Even Cowgirls Get the Blues* Film Review. *Washington Post*, 20 May 1994.

Burlingame, Jon. "Herrmann's Ghost." *Daily Variety*, 21 October 1998.

Byrne, Bridget. "Sean Connery." *Weekly Variety*, 15 January 2001.

Cameron, Ann. *Even Cowgirls Get the Blues* Book Review. *The Nation*, 28 August 1976.

Campbell, Virginia. "The Times of Gus Van Sant." *Movieline*, October 1993.

Canby, Vincent. *Mala Noche* Film Review. *New York Times*, 1 May 1988.

———. *My Own Private Idaho* Film Review. *New York Times*, 27 September 1991.

"Chain's Founder, 3 Children Killed." *Seattle Times*, 29 November 1999.

Chanko, Kenneth M. "His Own Private Montana." *Boston Sunday Globe*, 15 May 1994.

Cinefle Column. *Screen International*, 24 February 1990.

Clark, Mike. *Psycho* Film Review. *USA Today*, 7 December 1998.

Corliss, Richard. "An Actress to Die For." *Time*, 9 October 1995.

Cowan, Ron. "Maverick Director Follows Risky Trail." *Statesman Journal*, 3 November 1989.

Cox, Dan. "Arquette Signs $1 Mil Deal for *Rangoon* Role." *Daily Variety*, 9 November 1993.

Crotty, James, and Michael Lane. "Gus Comes Clean." *Monk*, 1995.

Dawtrey, Adam. "Van Sant Hunting *Jerry*. *Daily Variety*, 16 May 2001.

Denby, David. *Drugstore Cowboy* Film Review. *New York*, 9 October 1989.

———. *Finding Forrester* Film Review. *The New Yorker*, 8 January 2001.

———. *Good Will Hunting* Film Review. *New York*, 8 December 1997.

———. *To Die For* Film Review. *New York*, 2 October 1995.

Diamond, Jamie. "When Visiting the Mainstream Is an Experiment." *New York Times*, 9 November 1997.

Dish Column. *Daily Variety*, 30 May 1996.

Djelal, Aixe. "News Things" Column. *Willamette Week*, 15 December 1993.

Doph, Dennis. "Inside Gus." *New York Native*, 12 February 1990.

Dretzka, Gary. "This Screenwriter Finds a Miracle." *Los Angeles Times*, 21 December 2000.

Dunn, Katherine. "The Slice" Column. *Willamette Week*, 10 September 1984.

Duran, Paul. "Van Sant Mulls his Oregon trail." *Daily Variety*, 15 May 1996.

Ebert, Roger. *Drugstore Cowboy* Film Review. *Chicago Sun-Times*, 27 October 1989.

———. *Even Cowgirls Get the Blues* Film Review. *Chicago Sun-Times*, 20 May 1994.

———. *Good Will Hunting* Film Review. *Chicago Sun-Times*, 25 December 1997.

———. *My Own Private Idaho* Film Review. *Chicago Sun-Times*, 18 October 1991.

———. *Psycho* Film Review. *Chicago Sun-Times*, 5 December 1998.

Egan, Timothy. "Northwest Noir: An Art of the Seriously Goofy." *New York Times*, 14 July 1991.

Ehrenstein, David. "Van Sant's Seeds of Success." *Los Angeles Times*, 7 July 1999.

Ehrman, Mark. "Getting Off to a Smart Start." *Los Angeles Times*, 4 December 1997.

Eimer, David. "Good Talent—Hunting." *Sunday Independent* (London), 1 March 1998.

Elder, Sean. "Young Actors Go Wild with Gus Van Sant." *Elle*, October 1991.

Even Cowgirls Get the Blues Book Review. *Publishers Weekly*, 23 February 1976.

Even Cowgirls Get the Blues Book Review. *The Booklist,* 15 May 1976.

Faust, Michael. "Gus Van Sant." *Buffalo News*, 21 October 1991.

Ferber, Lawrence. "Crossover Cowboy." *Frontiers*, 19 January 2001.

Finch, Mark. *Mala Noche* Film Review. *Monthly Film Bulletin* (London), August 1987.

Finding Forrester Presskit (2000).

Fleming, Charles. "Van Sant, Bartel Plan Warhol Pic." *Daily Variety,* 25 April 1990.

Fleming, Michael. "Hit Movie Makes Van Sant a Director *To Die For.*" *Weekly Variety*, 6 May 1996.

———. "Travolta Croons Again." *Daily Variety*, 14 January 1999.

Francke, Lizzie. *My Own Private Idaho* Film Review. *Sight and Sound* (London), April 1992.

Frook, John Evan. "Indie Van Sant Cuts Deal, Will *Die* for Colpix." *Daily Variety*, 27 August 1993.

Gallagher, Lawrence. "Life After *Drugstore.*" *Esquire*, October 1991.

Garey, Lisa. "Good Will Gus." *Swing*, vol. 4 no. 2, 1997.

Garner, Jack. "Director Van Sant Has Learned How Far He Can Go." Gannett News Service, 5 October 1995.

———. "*Finding Forrester*'s Director Found Good Will in Similar Movie." Gannett News Service, 21 December 2000.

Garrett, Stephen. "The Big Payback." *Time Out New York*, 14 December 2000.

Germain, David. "Finding His Way." Associated Press, undated.

Gleiberman, Owen. *Psycho* Film Review. *Entertainment Weekly,* 4 December 1998.

Gold, Richard. "Van Sant's *Drugstore Cowboy* Observes Abusive Lifestyle, and Therein Lies Hard Sell." *Weekly Variety*, 11 October 1989.

Goldstein, Patrick. "Feeling Nostalgic, Mother?" *Los Angeles Times*, 25 October 1998.

———. "They've Remade Hitchcock's Classic? What Are They? *Psycho.*" *Newsday*, 22 November 1998.

Gollogly, Naomi. "What Price Fame?" *Willamette Week*, 27 September 1995.

"Good Will Hunter." *Venice*, December 1997.

Good Will Hunting Presskit (1997).

Goodridge, Mike. "Close Up On: Gus Van Sant." *Screen International*, 12 January 2001.

Green, Oriana. "His Own Private Portland." *Just Out*, 15 December 2000.

Grimes, William. "How to Fix a Film at the Very Last Minute (or Even Later)." *New York Times*, 15 May 1994.

"Growing Pains" Column. *Premiere*, September 2000.

"Gus Van Sant." *Hollywood Reporter*, 11 February 1998.

Guthmann, Edward. "Private Dancer." *San Francisco Chronicle Magazine*. 17 December 2000.

Handelman, David. "Auteurs Turned Authors." *Harper's Bazaar*, October 1997.

———. "Northwest Passage." *Rolling Stone*, 31 October 1991.

Hardy, Ernest. "His Own Private Hollywood." *LA Village View,* 18 October 1991.

Harkness, Alistair. *Drugstore Cowboy* Film Review. *Edinburgh University Film Society Notes,* 1997–98.

Harris, Dana. "Thomas Takes Driver's Seat in *Speedway.*" *Hollywood Reporter,* 6 August 1998.

Hartl, John. "Gus Van Sant—Exploring New Territory—for the Satire *To Die For,* the Oregon Director Finds a New location and Pushes a Few Boundaries." *Seattle Times,* 5 October 1995.

———. "His *Private* Triumph—'Saint Gus' Has Become a Quirky, Moody Poet of Urban Alienation." *Seattle Times,* 13 October 1991.

———. "Portland Director Shines with Street Drama." *Seattle Times,* 29 May 1986.

———. "Two U.S. Hits at Cannes Also Part of Seattle Festival." *Seattle Times,* 6 September 1995.

Hatty, Michelle. "Gus Van Sant Shines a Light on the Unknown." *USA Weekend,* 17 December 2000.

Hinson, Hal. *Drugstore Cowboy* Film Review. *Washington Post,* 27 October 1989.

———. *Mala Noche* Film Review. *Washington Post,* 15 June 1990.

Hoberman, J. *Drugstore Cowboy* Film Review. *Village Voice,* 10 October 1989.

Hobson, Louis B. "*Psycho* Copycat Killer." *London Free Press,* 2 December 1998.

Hochman, David. "Gus Van Sant: Q & A." *US,* November 1995.

Hofler, Robert. "Good Will." *Advocate,* 31 March 1998.

Holden, Stephen. *Drugstore Cowboy* Film Review. *New York Times,* 6 October 1989.

———. *Finding Forrester* Film Review. *New York Times,* 19 December 2000.

Holm, D. K. "All About Gus." *Willamette Week,* 10 November 1991.

———. "American Dreamer: An Interview with Mike Rich." *Creative Screenwriting,* November/December 2000.

———. *Drugstore Cowboy* Film Review. *Willamette* Week, 26 October 1989.

———. "Great Gusto." *Willamette Week,* 19 November 1987.

Horowitz, M. G. "Camera Duo Dances Two-Step on *Even Cowgirls Get the Blues.*" *American Cinematographer,* November 1993.

———. "Cosmic Partners." *Pacific Northwest,* July 1993.

In the Know Column: "Marketing *Psycho*: Like a Nightmare." *Los Angeles Times,* 30 November 1998.

Indiana, Gary. "Saint Gus." *Village Voice,* 1 October 1991.

James, Caryn. *Even Cowgirls Get the Blues* Film Review. *New York Times,* 20 May 1994.

Johnson, Hillary. "To Die For." *In Style,* 1 October 1995.

Karbo, Karen. "Gus Stop." *Oregonian,* 20 October 1991.

Karger, Dave. "*Psycho* Babble." *Entertainment Weekly,* 9 October 1998.

————. "Star Pupil." *Entertainment Weekly*, 5 January 2001.

Kelleher, Terry. *Drugstore Cowboy* Film Review. *Newsday,* 6 October 1989.

Kemp, Stuart, and Chris Gardner. "New Van Sant Project Sports Damon, Affleck." *Hollywood Reporter*, 16 May 2001.

Keough, Peter. "Independents' Daze." *Boston Phoenix*, 1 January 1998.

Klady, Leonard. "Jenkes Set for *Heatstroke*." *Daily Variety*, 21 May 1999.

Kroll, Jack. *Even Cowgirls Get the Blues* Film Review. *Newsweek,* 30 May 1994.

Kronke, David. "Friends: The Movie." *Los Angeles Times*, 30 November 1997.

Kuntzman, Gersh. "Back in Business." *New York Post*, 25 September 1995.

Kutzera, Dale. "*Drugstore Cowboy* Set Against Bleak Landscape." *American Cinematographer,* June 1989.

Lacher, Irene. "Kelly Lynch, Ex-Model, Plays Drugstore's Spunky Junkie." *People*, 6 November 1989.

LaSalle, Mick. *To Die For* Film Review. *San Francisco Chronicle*, 6 October 1995.

LeClair, Thomas. *Even Cowgirls Get the Blues* Book Review. *New York Times*, 23 May 1976.

Leibowitz, Ed. "Filming Against the Tide—Renegade Director Gus Van Sant Made His Name with Gritty Movies and Incongruous Casting—Now Everyone's Doing It." *Daily Telegraph: Telegraph Magazine* (London), 15 November 1997.

LeRoy, J. Sarah. New York: Bloomsbury, 2000.

————. "The Psycho Analyst." *Paper*, December 2000

Levy, Emanuel. *Finding Forrester* Film Review. *Daily Variety*, 15 December 2000.

Levy, Shawn. "*Good Will* Goes a Long Way to Raise Funds with Premiere." *Oregonian*, 9 December 1997.

————. "Mr. Rich's Screen Test." *Sunday Oregonian*, 17 December 2000.

————. *Psycho* Film Review. *Sunday Oregonian*, 6 December 1998.

————. "Quiet on the Set." *Sunday Oregonian*, 24 December 2000.

"Lights, Camera, Oscars!" *Newsweek*, 16 January 1998.

Lippy, Tod. "Adapting *To Die For*." *Scenario,* summer 1996.

Lonsdorf, Amy. "Talking with *Even Cowgirls Get the Blues* Director Gus Van Sant." *Angelika Filmbill*, May/June 1994.

Loud, Lance. "Shakespeare in Black Leather." *American Film*, September/October 1991.

Lowenstein, Lael. "Rob Brown." *New York Daily News*, 18 December 2000.

Mahar, Ted. "Van Sant's Move a Bold One." *Oregonian*, 9 December 1990.

Maslin, Janet. *Good Will Hunting* Film Review. *New York Times*, 3 December 1997.

————. *Psycho* Film Review. *New York Times*, 5 December 1998.

————. *To Die For* Film Review. *New York Times*, 27 September 1995.

Matthews, Jack. *Good Will Hunting* Film Review. *Newsday*, 5 December 1997.

————. *My Own Private Idaho* Film Review. *Newsday*, 27 September 1991.

————. *To Die For* Film Review. *Newsday*, 27 September 1995.

Matthews, Peter. *Finding Forrester* Film Review. *Sight and Sound* (London), March 2001.

McCarthy, Todd. *Kids* Film Review. *Weekly Variety*, 29 May 1995.

———. *My Own Private Idaho* Film Review. *Daily Variety*, 9 September 1991.

———. *To Die For* Film Review. *Weekly Variety*, 29 May 1995.

McKenna, Kristine. "Another Risky Road." *Los Angeles Times*, 13 October 1991.

———. "Will Hollywood Rope the Director of *Drugstore Cowboy?*" *Los Angeles Times*, 26 December 1989.

Medved, Michael. *Even Cowgirls Get the Blues* Film Review. *New York Post*, 20 May 1994.

Mermelstein, David. "Miles Smiles on *Forrester*." *Daily Variety*, 19 January 2001.

Meyer, Thomas J. "Dropping In on the Down and Out." *New York Times*, 15 October 1991.

Millea, Holly. "Shooting Star." *Premiere*, December 1998.

Modderno, Craig. "Entertainment Marquee." Toronto International Film Festival, 1995.

"Morning Report" Column. *Los Angeles Times*, 12 January 1998.

"Morning Report" Column. *Los Angeles Times*. 30 June 1999.

Morris, Wesley. *Finding Forrester* Film Review. *San Francisco Chronicle*, 25 December 2000.

Mottram, James. "His Own Private Idealism." *The Independent*, 27 February 1998.

Muller, Bill. "Director Gus Van Sant Prefers to Do More with Less." *The Arizona Republic*, 24 December 2000.

Musetto, V. A. *Mala Noche* Film Review. *New York Post*, 4 May 1988.

Musto, Michael. "La Dolce Musto" Column. *Village Voice*, 16 June 1998.

My Own Private Idaho Presskit (1991).

Natale, Richard. "Master Class Is in Session." *Los Angeles Times*, 17 December 2000.

"New York Teen Makes Film Debut in *Finding Forrester*." *Jet*, 26 February 2001.

"News Things" Column. *Willamette Week*, 22 October 1998.

Nicholas, Jonathan. "Now Who Writes Songs That Make the Whole World Sing?" *Oregonian*, 5 September 1997.

Olson, Ray. *Pink* Book Review. *Booklist*, August 1997.

Osborne, Robert. "Rambling Reporter" Column. *Hollywood Reporter*, 30 October 1990.

"Patron Sant." *Time Out* (London), 25 March 1992.

Peach, Kindra. "Holiday Movie Confidential: *Psycho*." *Premiere*, November 1998.

Pearlman, Cindy. "Flashes" Column. *Entertainment Weekly*, 15 October 1993.

"People" Column. *Time*, 11 September 1995.

Peretz, Eugenia. "Horrors! A Remake." *Vanity Fair*, December 1998.

Petrikin, Chris. "Radio Daze in H'w'd." *Daily Variety*, 29 October 1998.

Pincus, Elizabeth. *To Die For* Film Review. *Harper's Bazaar*, 1 October 1995.

Pink Book Review. *Kirkus Reviews*, 15 August 1997.

Platt, Adam. "Just Reshoot Me." *Elle*, December 1998.

"Pop Eye" Column. *Los Angeles Times*, 19 August 1990.

Potter, Alicia. "Finding the Right Formula." *Boston Herald*, 2 January 2001.

Powell, Paige. "Gus Van Sant." *Interview*, December 1998.

Powers, John. "Sleeping Beauties: Gus Van Sant Hits the Road." *LA Weekly*, 18 October 1991.

Psycho Presskit (1998).

Rafferty, Terrence. *My Own Private Idaho* Film Review. *The New Yorker*, 7 October 1991.

Rainer, Peter. *Mala Noche* Film Review. *Los Angeles Times*, 1 December 1989.

Rebello, Stephen. "Return to Bates Motel." *Movieline*, December 1998/January 1999.

Redden, Jim. "Walk on the Wild Side." *Willamette Week*, 26 January 1989.

Ressner, Jeffrey. "His Own Private *Psycho*: Same Script, Different Shower." *Los Angeles*, 8 September 1998.

Reynolds, Dale. "A Gay Filmmaker *To Die for*." *Au Courant*, 17 October 1995.

———. "Gus Van Sant Gives Good Film." *Gay & Lesbian Times*, 8 August 1996.

Roberts, Jerry. "Gus Van Sant: Test of Independence." *Daily Breeze/News-Pilot/Rave!*, 29 September 1995.

———. "Van Sant Retains Stamp of the Indie." *Daily Variety*, 25 July 1995.

Roman, Shari. "Gus Van Sant." *Flaunt*, 12 January 2001.

Rosenthal, Stuart. "Drugstore Cowboy Rides Through a Bleak Terrain." *New York Times*, 20 November 1988.

Ross, Lillian. "The Pictures Named and Truthful in the Bronx." *New York*, 12 June 2000.

Rossi, Melissa, and D. K. Holm. "Gus Van Who?" *Pacific Northwest*, August 1989.

Rothman, Cliff. "A Chat with the Film Industry's Big 5." *Los Angeles Times*, 9 March 1998.

Rugoff, Ralph. "Walking on the Wild Side." *Premiere*, October 1991.

"Sant or Sinner." *Time Out* (London), 4 January 1995.

Sarris, Andrew. *Good Will Hunting* Film Review. *New York Observer*, 8 December 1997.

Scardapane, Dario. "On the Set: Lost Boys." *US*, November 1991.

Schackleton, Liz. "*2 die 4* Starts Rank-Trans Pacific Deal." *Screen International*, 20 May 1994.

Schickel, Richard. *Finding Forrester* Film Review. *Time*, 25 December 2000.

Schruers, Fred. "At the Multiplex" Column. *Rolling Stone*, 10 December 1998.

Schwager, Jeff. "Back in the Saddle." *Boxoffice*, February 1994.

"Short Takes" Column. *Daily Variety*, 28 September 1992.

Shulgasser, Barbara. *To Die For* Film Review. *San Francisco Examiner*, 6 October 1995.

Silverman, Jason. "Entering Normal." *Telluride Times Journal: Film Examiner*, 1995.

Simon, Brent. *Finding Forrester* Film Review. *Entertainment Today*, 15 December 2000.

"*Singles* Secrets: Northwestern Exposure." *Entertainment Weekly*, 5 March 1993.

Sischy, Ingrid. "Best Buddies: Matt Damon and Ben Affleck." *Interview*, December 1997.

Smith, Bill. "Performance" Column. *Willamette Week*, 10 January 2001.

Smith, Liz. Syndicated Column. *Los Angeles Times*, 2 April 1998.

Smith, R. J. "Has Gus Van Sant Gone *Psycho?*" *New York Times Magazine*, 29 November 1998.

Smith, Russell. "Van Sant's Vision." *Dallas Morning News*, 27 October 1991.

Snead, Elizabeth. "Gus Van Sant." *USA Today*, 27 September 1995.

"Stander Claims Slander in Suit." *Daily Variety*, 6 March 1991.

Stein, Elliott. "Gassing with Gus." *Village Voice*, 23 August 1988.

———. "Love in Vain." *Village Voice*, 4 January 1986.

Strat. *Mala Noche* Film Review. *Weekly Variety*, 5 March 1986.

Strauss, Bob. "Finding His Way." *Los Angeles Daily News*, 19 December 2000.

"Success Begets More (Or Does It?) With Ken Shapiro's Biog in Point." *Weekly Variety*, 1 July 1981.

Svetkey, Benjamin. "Red." *Entertainment Weekly*, 9 June 1995.

———. "Shower Power." *Entertainment Weekly*, 4 December 1998.

"Talking Stonewall." *Interview*, June 1994.

Taubin, Amy. *Good Will Hunting* Film Review. *Village Voice*, 9 December 1997.

———. "Gus Van Sant's Conventional Wisdom." *Village Voice*, 19 December 2000.

———. "Objects of Desire." *Sight and Sound* (London), January 1992.

———. *To Die For* Film Review. *Village Voice*, 3 October 1995.

———. "Trials and Tribulations." *Village Voice*, 24 May 1994.

Taylor, Ella. *Psycho* Film Review. *LA Weekly*, 11 December 1998.

Thomas, Kevin. "Screening Room: *Speedway Racer.*" *Los Angeles Times*, 15 April 1999.

"THR E-mail" Column. *Hollywood Reporter*, 3 October 1996.

"THR E-mail" Column. *Hollywood Reporter*, 13 May 1999.

Timpone, Anthony. Editorial Column. *Fangoria*, November 1998.

To Die For Presskit (1995).

Toushin, Abbi. "Sony's Logs *Forrester.*" *Daily Variety*, 5 December 2000.

Turan, Kenneth. *Even Cowgirls Get the Blues* Film Review. *Los Angeles Times*, 20 May 1994.

———. *Finding Forrester* Film Review. *Los Angeles Times*, 19 December 2000.

———. "Low-Life Serenade." *GQ*, July 1989.

———. *My Own Private Idaho* Film Review. *Los Angeles Times*, 18 October 1991.

————. *Psycho* Film Review. *Los Angeles Times*, 7 December 1998.

————. *To Die For* Film Review. *Los Angeles Times*, 27 September 1995.

Turnquist, Kristi. "A Creative Slant: John Callahan." *Oregonian*, 14 September 1999.

————. "Gus Van Sant." *Willamette Week*, 21 May 1984.

Van Sant, Gus. *Drugstore Cowboy* Interview/Transcript. Toronto Film Festival, September 1989.

————. "Gus Van Sant: Digital Flowers." *Genre*, 20 September 2001.

Villanueva, Annabelle. "Gus Van Sant." *Cinescape*, January/February 1999.

Vineberg, Steve. *Drugstore Cowboy* Film Review. *Film Quarterly*, spring 1989.

Walker, Alexander. *Good Will Hunting* Film Review. *This Is London,* 5 March 1998.

Wallace, Amy. "So, Just What Is in Store for the *Psycho* Remake?" *Los Angeles Times*, 22 July 1998.

Warren, Steve. "The Catcher in the Bronx." *Dallas Voice*, 22 December 2000.

Weinraub, Bernard. "An Ouster After Films Flounder." *New York Times*, 1 December 1998.

————. "At the Movies" Column. *New York Times*, 27 November 1998.

————. "How *To Die For* Managed to Open at Simpson Finale." *New York Times*, 10 October 1995.

Werner, Laurie. "Portrait of an Iron Lady." *Los Angeles Times*, 1 October 1995.

Whipp, Glenn. *Finding Forrester* Film Review. *Los Angeles Daily News*, 19 December 2000.

White, Maggi. "Van Sant Directs Matt Dillon Set of *Drugstore Cowboy*." *Downtowner*, 30 October 1989.

Wigginton, Mark. "Callahan Puts a Lot of Himself in New Animated Series Callahan." *Oregonian*, 22 October 2000.

William, Lena. "*To Die For* Opening." *New York Times*, 26 September 1995.

Williamson, Kim. "A Happy Woman." *Venice*, April 1993.

Young, Deborah. *Even Cowgirls Get the Blues* Film Review. *Weekly Variety*, 20 September 1993.

internet web sites

allmusic.com

Barnes. "There's Much More to 20-year-old Novelist J.T. Leroy Than Meets the Eye." Available at jtleroy.com/reviews/frontierweb.html.

Behar, Henry. "Gus Van Sant." Available at filmscouts.com/scripts/interview.

Clarke, Roger. "Gus Van Sant." Available at thislondon.com.

Datalounge.com.

Donadoni, Serena. "Renaissance Director." Available at Metrotimes.com (26 December 2000).

imdb.com.

Joyce, Cynthia. "*Pink* book review/interview." Available at salon.com (24 October 1997).

LaBruce, Bruce. "Gus Van Sant." Available at www.geocities.com/Hollywood
    Boulevard/3809/exclaim-int.html.
Miller, Laura. *Finding Forrester Film Review.*" Available at salon.com.
"On the set of Gus Van Sant's *Easter.*" Available at: www.angelfire.com/ab/
    harmonykorine/bruce.html.
PlanetOut.com.
Pride, Ray. "*Good Will Hunting* Film Review." Available at www.
    newcitychicago.com (22 December 1997).

dvd commentaries:
Drugstore Cowboy. Artisan, 1999.
Finding Forrester. Columbia, 2001.
Good Will Hunting. Buena Vista, 1998.
Psycho—1960. Universal, 1998.
Psycho—1998. Universal, 1999.
To Die For. Columbia Tristar, 1998.

INDEX

Y

Yeoman, Robert D., 94–95
Yost, Daniel, 58, 82–84
Young, Sean, 178, 188

Z

Zabriskie, Grace, 92, 95, 138, 142, 158, 178
Ziskin, Laura, 196, 207
Zoccola, Brian Ann, 37–39, 41

JAMES ROBERT PARISH, a former entertainment reporter, publicist, and book series editor, is the author of over ninety-eight published major biographies and reference books of the entertainment industry including *The Hollywood Book of Death, The Multicultural Encyclopedia of Twentieth-Century Hollywood, Jason Biggs, Whoopi Goldberg, Rosie O'Donnell's Story, The Unofficial "Murder, She Wrote" Casebook, Let's Talk—America's Favorite TV Talk Show Hosts, Gays and Lesbians in Mainstream Cinema, The Great Cop Pictures, Ghosts and Angels in Hollywood Films, Prison Pictures from Hollywood, Hollywood's Great Love Teams,* and *The RKO Gals.* Mr. Parish is a frequent on-camera interviewee on cable and network TV for documentaries on the performing arts. Mr. Parish resides in Studio City, California.